Advancing the Global Agenda for Human Rights, Vulnerable Populations, and Environmental Sustainability

Adult Education as Strategic Partner

A Volume in Adult Learning in Professional,
Organizational, and Community Settings

Series Editor

Carrie J. Boden
Texas State University

Adult Learning in Professional, Organizational, and Community Settings

Carrie J. Boden, Series Editor

Advancing the Global Agenda for Human Rights, Vulnerable Populations, and Environmental Sustainability: Adult Education as Strategic Partner (2021)
edited by Mary V. Alfred, Petra A. Robinson, and Elizabeth A. Roumell

Teaching and Learning for Adult Skill Acquisition: Applying the Dreyfus and Dreyfus Model in Different Fields (2021)
edited by Elaine M. Silva Mangiante and Kathy Peno

Unfinished Business: Compelling Stories of Adult Student Persistence (2019)
by Matt Bergman and Joann S. Olson

Transformative Learning in Healthcare and Helping Professions Education: Building Resilient Professional Identities (2019)
edited by Teresa J. Carter, Carrie J. Boden, and Kathy Peno

Leaps of Faith: Stories from Working-Class Scholars (2018)
edited by Anne C. Benoit, Joann S. Olson, and Carrie Johnson

A Guide to College Success for Post-traditional Students, 2nd Edition (2018)
edited by Henry S. Merrill

A Guide to College Success for Post-traditional Students (2017)
edited by Henry S. Merril

Mentoring in Formal and Informal Contexts (2016)
edited by Kathy Peno, Elaine M. Silva Mangiante, and Rita A. Kenahan

Building Sustainable Futures for Adult Learners (2014)
edited by Jennifer K. Holtz, Stephen B. Springer, and Carrie J. Boden

Advancing the Global Agenda for Human Rights, Vulnerable Populations, and Environmental Sustainability

Adult Education as Strategic Partner

Edited by

Mary V. Alfred
Texas A&M University, United States

Petra A. Robinson
Louisiana State University, United States

Elizabeth A. Roumell
Texas A&M University, United States

INFORMATION AGE PUBLISHING, INC.
Charlotte, NC • www.infoagepub.com

Library of Congress Cataloging-in-Publication Data

CIP record for this book is available from the Library of Congress
http://www.loc.gov

ISBNs: 978-1-64802-695-9 (Paperback)

976-1-64802-696-6 (Hardcover)

978-1-64802-697-3 (ebook)

Printed in the United States of America

CONTENTS

Foreword
Marcie Boucouvalas .... *ix*

Preface
Elizabeth Roumell, Mary V. Alfred, and Petra A. Robinson................ *xiii*

Introduction—Human Rights, Sustainable Development, and Adult
    Education: History, Foundation, and Context
Mary V. Alfred .... *xix*

SECTION I: HUMAN RIGHTS

1. The Critical Literacies Advancement Model (CLAM) as a Tool
    for Curriculum Development: Advancing Human Rights in
    Adult Education
    Petra A. Robinson and Maja Stojanović *3*

2. Integral Global Leadership Education for Human Rights,
    Transformation, and Sustainability
    Wanda Krause... *19*

3. Promoting Antibullyism to Advance Human Rights and
    Social Justice for Sexual Minorities Through Adult and
    Higher Education: An Antibullyist Approach
    Mitsunori Misawa *35*

4. Migration and Human Dignity: Rhetoric and Practice
    Chad Hoggan and Tetyana Kloubert *49*

v

5. Nexus of Vulnerability of Internally Displaced Persons (IDPs) in Africa, and Socioeconomic Development of the Black Nations
Debora A. Egunyomi and Kofo A. Aderogba 67

6. Community-Based Adult Education to Promote Human Rights and Health Equity in a Stigmatized Community in Canada
Roula Kteily-Hawa and Joseph Roy Gillis 83

7. Adults With Disabilities Need More and Better Learning Opportunities Around the World
Ashley Stepanek Lockhart, Ricardo Sabates, Nidhi Singal, and Thilanka Wijesinghe 99

8. North Koreans' Human Rights and the Situation of Foreign Popular Culture: An Adult Education Perspective
Jinhee Choi 117

SECTION II: ECONOMIC EMPOWERMENT: LABORING TO LEARN, LABORING TO EARN

9. A Human Capabilities Development Perspective in Adult Education
Elizabeth A. Roumell and Bora Jin 139

10. Unrealized Potential: Marginalized Youth Around the Globe, With a Focus on Turkey
Aydın Yücesan Durgunoğlu and Fatoş Dayıoğlu 157

11. Adult Students in Community Colleges and Economic Justice
Kyung-Hwa K. Yang 173

12. Looking for Educational Needs in the Community: Adult Educators' Roles Matter
Isaac Kofi Biney 189

13. Leveraging Continuing Medical Education in Addressing Health Disparities: Case Studies From the Republic of Ghana
Linda D. Caples and Christopher M. Dodgion 207

14. Strategies of Engagement and Support: Addressing the Holistic Needs of Veterans Pursuing Higher Education
Yvonne Hunter-Johnson, Sharlene Smith, Geleana Alston, and Aynur Charkasova 223

15. Life Status and Prospects of Community Education Workers
    Lixin Sun, Shuo Li, and Yuxin Song.. 243

SECTION III: ENVIRONMENTAL SUSTAINABILITY AND ADULT EDUCATION

16. Learning to Recreate the World: Adult Education for
    Environmental Sustainability
    Wendy Griswold 259

17. Citizen Science: Adult Education for Environmental
    Sustainability and Conservation
    Jill Zarestky and Lauren Vilen 277

18. Millennium Fellows as Catalysts for Global Climate Change
    Hilary Landorf, Yenisleidy Simon Mengana,
    and Birgitta Rausch-Montoto 291

19. (Mis)perceptions of Aboriginal Fishing: Why Adult Education
    Must Confront the "Environmental Indian" Stereotype
    Stanford T. Goto.. 307

20. Man-Environment Interaction in the Rainforests and
    Sustainable Development: Practical Implications for Adult
    Education
    Kofo A. Aderogba... 323

Conclusion—Adult Education for Human Rights and Sustainable
    Development: The Path Forward
    Petra A. Robinson, Mary V. Alfred, and Elizabeth Roumell.................339

About the Authors... *343*

FOREWORD

Marcie Boucouvalas
Virginia Tech University, United States

As this book goes to press, a tumultuous 2020 draws to a close and humanity is perched on the precipice of 2021, replete with the hope that a New Year might bring. What a timely moment in history for this publication to arrive! Humanity is still in the grips of a global pandemic (Coronavirus: COVID-19) that has created a voracious maelstrom affecting many fundamental structures and systems of society: education, business and industry, family, the economic system, governmental structures, and others. For many, work at home and learn at home have become the norm, at least for those who are still employed and those who have the needed infrastructure as well as the health to learn. Social distancing, lockdowns, restricted travels, and gatherings, and—for many—psychological stress and economic collapse abound, with resounding effects and impact on a wide swath of vulnerable populations this book addresses. Many now risk becoming further marginalized. We must not forget, as well, the sandwiched middle class, many of whom may be struggling but not eligible for public assistance. Might they also qualify as a vulnerable population?

In addition to these stressors, however, this pandemic has clearly offered a more profound understanding of our interconnectedness as a human species; at least the potential is there. Think about it. An invisible microbial force has offered humanity a commonly shared experience, extending in

Advancing the Global Agenda for Human Rights, Vulnerable Populations, and Environmental Sustainability: Adult Education as Strategic Partner, pp. ix–xii
Copyright © 2021 by Information Age Publishing

some instances even into indigenous populations purportedly safely sealed from the mass populace. Surely, there must be a better way of engaging or insulating such communities as they certainly qualify as a vulnerable population.

What kind of opportunities might this scenario present? "We're all in this together" has become a repeatedly resounding catch phrase that one might hear even over grocery store loudspeakers. Will this popularized refrain further awaken humanity to heed the call for action that the editors and authors of this book urge, especially, I might add, as we at some point progress into a post-COVID reality?

Citizens are living with uncertainty; society is tense. Simultaneously, social justice matters, social unrest, and racial issues, along with environmental issues, just to name a few, have erupted. Even those issues of concern originating in the United States have reverberated around the world. One tragic example is the heart-wrenching shooting deaths of members of the Black community by some members of the police force that in turn prompted worldwide demonstrations. Some citizens were also quick to emphasize, however, that we need to take time to express gratitude to members of the police force who do their utmost to guard against such situations whenever possible.

If there ever was a time to offer a publication of hope to society that focuses on both individual and societal healing, 2021 seems like a most receptive year, and this book provides a sorely needed guide. Attention to conceptual, historical, theoretical, and scholarly matters, balanced with practical implications, awaits the reader. Moreover, many chapters provide meaningful recommendations that have the power and potential to translate the material into action plans adapted to the reader's own context, country, or culture.

Set within the framework of the United Nations Sustainable Development Goals and mindful of the UN Universal Declaration of Human Rights, established in 1948 and currently one of the most translated documents in the world, this effort emerges from within the field of adult education and focuses on the role that adult educators, broadly defined, might contribute. Attention is also given to specific ongoing efforts of adult educators in various regions of the world as they attempt to address human rights issues and sustainability of people and planet.

What does the world need from adult education as a field of both study and practice, at this time and going forward? The editors and authors provide some compelling food for thought. Here is a book that casts a wide net in understanding global issues from both historical as well as contemporary perspectives and the role of adult education, broadly defined, in addressing such challenges. I wish I had access to a book of this nature when developing my first International Adult Education graduate course and syllabus in the mid-1980s, as it has the promise to be a welcome addition to a university curriculum.

Moreover, on a larger scale, the book has far-reaching potential and should prove useful for those from an array of other disciplines, sectors, and action groups as well: economists, psychologists, sociologists, environmentalists, cultural anthropologists, policy-makers, and many others, especially for engaging in the global partnership dialogues that the editors and authors advocate. Framed by and following the United Nations Sustainable Development Goals, as noted above, the authors call for addressing the quest for "partnerships and action" from a global context in tackling key issues facing humanity on planet earth. I can also see it being useful to raise the awareness of and act as a resource to the cadre of professionals worldwide engaged in the Learning Cities movement, where learning forms a core of the region's or city's development plan (i.e., economic development, social development, etc.). Fundamental is the development of partnerships among various sectors such as governmental, non-governmental professionals, civil society agents, corporate and private agents, policy makers, community development professionals, and others in trying to create Learning Cities.

The editors (Drs. Mary Alfred, Petra A. Robinson, and Elizabeth Roumell) all have compelling interest in international adult education and are eminently qualified, experienced, and passionately interested in increasing awareness and shedding light on this important topic. Moreover, all have sustained leadership roles in the field, particularly in a key professional association: the American Association of Adult and Continuing Education (Alfred as president, Robinson as 2020 and 2021 conference chair, and Roumell as a coeditor of the *Adult Education Quarterly*). Likewise, the chapter authors—many of whom hail from a variety of countries—lend an equally authentic voice with a spectrum of experiences in the study and practice of adult education.

The book issues a clarion call for a return to a human rights focus, along with continuing and increased need for social justice, as a key aim of adult education efforts. Equally stressed is a plea for more concentrated attention to the age-old need of an educated and active citizenry for democracy to flourish. A clear understanding of "we're all in this together" is evidenced especially with the call for a kind of leadership in which one partners and collaborates with other countries and cultures in addressing the increasingly complex issues facing our planet. Resonance with the United Nations Sustainable Development Goals "plan of action for people, planet, and prosperity" is abundantly clear.

You are about to enter a journey with these authors. Hear their voices, reach out to them, find your own creative ways in which to use the material, and share the adventure and any new insights gleaned as we pursue dialogue within professional and personal relations, groups, organizations, communities, countries, and cultures, effecting policy and public discourse in pursuing human rights and social justice in local and global arenas.

Arriving at a timely moment, their efforts shed light on how professionals and others can rise to the challenges with which humanity is beset. This book has the power and potential to lead the way forward.

PREFACE

Elizabeth Roumell, Mary V. Alfred, and Petra A. Robinson

This edited volume aims to provide the field of adult education a frame of reference for international issues, some guiding concepts, and germane examples of ways adult educators can partner toward advancing human rights globally, protecting and supporting vulnerable populations, and promoting adult learning in support of environmental and economic sustainability. The premise is that adult education, understood in a very broad sense, has had, and continues to play an important role in each of these arenas.

We have subdivided the book into three sections, and the volume's chapters are organized under the following subheadings: Human Rights, Work and Education, and Environmental Sustainability. To help navigate each section, the chapter titles identify the key concepts covered and, where relevant, the geographical region discussed. In each of the sections, the issues and topics discussed draw on broad conceptual ideas that can be applied across a wide range of contexts, even though various positions and arguments are developed and supported by drawing on specific cases and countries. Our contributing authors consider the implications for social justice and equity in the field of adult education and, more broadly, issues related to learning and earning, as well as partnering in support of environmental sustainability.

As a foundational introduction, Mary Alfred establishes the tenor of the volume by situating the global agenda for development within an historical context. Over the decades, the United Nations' agenda has been to promote human rights, world peace, and economic justice; elevate vulnerable populations socially and economically; and protect the environment upon which we all survive. Since the turn of the century, the UN has also created space for education as part of a collaborative platform for launching and pursuing a globally transformative agenda, among the latest of which are the 2009 Millennium Development Goals, followed by the 2015 Sustainable Development Goals. Historically, adult education has also created space to advance these social agendas through its teaching, research, and service engagements. This volume illustrates how adult education plays a partnership role in advancing the UN's 2015 agenda for sustainable development and beyond.

Section I on Human Rights considers the history of human rights beyond national boarders such as within international organizations, various sectors, or specific locations and contexts. Petra A. Robinson and Maja Stojanović (Chapter 1) present the idea that adult learners need to develop "multiliteracies" necessary for navigating and thriving in a turbulent and rapidly changing economy and world. They define human rights literacy and present the "Critical Literacies Advancement Model" as a framework to support education for social justice. The authors emphasize the importance of human rights literacy in elevating our consciousness of the wide range of systemic inequities that permeate our lifeworlds (including, but not limited to racial, economic, and cultural injustices). Wanda Krause (Chapter 2) explores the development of education leadership in a globalizing society confronted with many complex and "wicked" social, economic, and environmental dilemmas. Krause presents the "All Quadrants All Levels" model as a guiding framework for developing global curriculum in higher education and cultivating sustainable, socially conscious leadership.

Mitsunori Misawa (Chapter 3) defines human rights, social justice, and sustainability, explaining how these are mutually interdependent and reinforcing. Through the application of a human rights lens, Misawa illustrates the importance of counteracting bullyism, which is a pernicious threat to human rights and social sustainability. Chad Hoggan and Tetyana Kloubert (Chapter 4) present findings emerging from their research on migrants in Germany. Contextualized within the heated and polarized political rhetoric regarding international migration, they examine the role and purpose of adult education through the lens of Adorno's vision of antiauthoritarian education, and they discuss adult educators' social and democratic responsibilities in supporting refugees and migrants and upholding human rights. Debora Egunyomi, Kofo Aderogba, and Tai Solarin (Chapter 5) look at "internally displaced persons" across Africa, shedding light on vulnerable, displaced populations within national borders. Despite progress in African countries over the last 30 years, multifaceted economic and social challenges remain, especially for vulnerable women and children who are exposed to violence, abuse, and exploitation. Citizenship education can give people the knowledge and skills to understand, challenge, and engage with democratic society including politics, the media, civil society, the economy, and public law.

Roula Kteily-Hawa and Joseph Roy Gillis (Chapter 6) employ community-based participatory research and a critical theory approach in Canada to illustrate a working example of the powerful impact of uniting and integrating health and adult education through community mobilization in support of people with HIV, especially using community-based, participatory, and peer-led research. Authors Ashley Stepanek, Ricardo Sabates, Nidhi Singal, and Thilanka Wijesinghe (Chapter 7) turn to quality adult learning and education (ALE) as a powerful mechanism for creating more diversity, inclusion, equity, and social mobility for adults with disabilities. They highlight challenges and opportunities for learning for youth and adults with disabilities and offer insights from Botswana and Ireland to illustrate the potential of ALE for these vulnerable populations. And to wrap up the first section of the volume (Chapter 8), Jinhee Choi explores the role popular culture can play in expanding people's social consciousness within the North Korean context. Via informal learning and daily engagement with foreign popular culture, Choi offers a vision for how informal learning can serve as a medium for engaging in human rights learning and advocacy.

Section II of the volume covers the topic learning and earning toward economic empowerment. The chapters reveal how adult learning can play a pivotal role in establishing a foundation for human rights, greater human capabilities, more equitable learning and earning, as well as highlight the role adult education can play in developing more just and sustainable economies. Elizabeth Roumell and Bora Jin (Chapter 9) present a *human capabilities* approach to adult education and development. They assert that when individual flourishing is the focus of development, emphasizing the importance of both economic mobility and social equity, this, in itself, can help remove barriers, reduce inequalities, and promote individual and global well-being. Aydın Yücesan Durgunoğlu and Fatoş Dayıoğlu (Chapter 10) establish the importance of integrating young adults into the economy by way of discussing the challenges young Turkish adults face in acquiring an occupation, associated risks of not being integrated into the economy, and the importance of equitable learning opportunities, especially for disenfranchised populations. Next, Kyung-Hwa Yang (Chapter 11) discusses the role of education and learning in the community college context in the United States, focusing on the needs of nontraditional and adult learners. Yang emphasizes the critical role community colleges play in making learning opportunities available for marginalized populations, increasing their probability of success and social mobility, and working toward financial empowerment and economic justice.

Adult educators also play a critical role in partnering with communities for better educational, development, and health outcomes. Isaac Kofi Biney (Chapter 12) makes the case that adult educators can play an important and interactive role within communities and help identify barriers to learning and development. Biney takes Ghana as a context to illustrate the importance of adult education in community development, describes how adult educators can partner with communities to identify community needs and potential opportunities, and mobilize resources to find solutions to meet those community needs. Linda Caples and Christopher Dodgion (Chapter 13) present a case of continuing medical education (CME) in Ghana. They offer theoretical, cultural, and contextual considerations in the development and delivery of continuing medical education interventions. Adult educators can assist in investigating culture and context within pluralistic medical environments to help design and develop CME interventions that are perceived both as meaningful (culturally congruent) and clinically applicable (context relevant). Through intentional interaction with healthcare professionals, their patients, and the communities they serve, adult educators can assist in the process of knowledge translation to construct new community-specific interventions and training. Yvonne Hunter-Johnson, Sharlene Smith, Geleana Alston, and Aynur Charkasova (Chapter 14) present a picture of the varied challenges military veterans face in the United States when they choose to utilize their educational benefits and pursue higher education. Regarding this vulnerable population, they provide an overview of support services, best practices, and strategies that can be utilized as tools for success and discuss adult education theories and practices as strategies for making higher education institutions veteran-friendly.

Lastly, Sun Lixun, Shuo Li and Yuxin Song (Chapter 15) describe the status and professional prospects of community educators in China. Based on the findings from interviews with local workers, they provide a discussion of the challenges Chinese community educators face in terms of low social status, unsatisfactory remuneration, inadequate resources and working conditions, limited prospects for career advancement, and their need for more relevant professional development. The authors argue that community education should be more highly valued by regional and national leaders in China and that a more coherent and strategic framework for a system of lifelong learning is needed.

Section III of the book explores the role adult education and lifelong learning can play in supporting environmental sustainability. Wendy Griswold (Chapter 16), offers an encompassing vision of how adult educators can serve in helping people learn to re-create our world into one that values its natural and human resources. Griswold outlines the role of *education for sustainability* (EfS), "which is an education that prepares people to be far-seeing enough, flexible enough, and wise enough to contribute to the regenerative capacity of the physical and social systems upon which they depend." Her chapter highlights the insights, wisdom, and truths from EfS learners, including possible avenues for broadening adult education practice to support EfS. Jill Zarestky and Lauren Vilen (Chapter 17) deliberate the importance of *citizen science* and its critical role in helping the general public understand scientific assessments, discussing the impacts of our behaviors on the environment, and engaging the public toward greater ecological sustainability. Through citizen science learning, adults are exposed to and interact with nature, science, and scientists, ideally building interest, understanding, and practices around issues of conservation and sustainability. Hilary Landorf, Yenisleidy Simon Mengana, and Birgitta Rausch-Montoto (Chapter 18) illustrate a university Millennium Fellowship program that aims to develop leaders capable of engaging in changemaking processes to address some of the world's most complex challenges. They explore the question, "How can adult learners become catalysts for global climate change, particularly in the context of interdisciplinary and multi-faceted partnerships?" In Chapter 19, Stanford Goto writes, "As we face an ever-growing list of environmental challenges across North America, our society must find ways to engage productively with all stakeholders, including Aboriginal groups." Colonialism across North America has led us to mythologize, lionize, demonize, and fetishize Indigenous peoples' relationship with the environment. Goto explores the cultural challenges related to indigenous populations and environmental concerns in the state of Washington (in the United States), and asks the questions: How can we, as a society, alter our relationship with Native peoples and the environment?, How can we engage in critical self-reflection with the aim of decolonizing our preconceptions?, and What role might adult educators play in facilitating such transformative learning? Kofo A. Aderogba and Tai Solarin conclude Section III (Chapter 20) by looking at practical implications for adult education related to man-environment interactions within the context of the rainforests of southwestern Nigeria. They provide a context to help understand why it is vital to integrate environmental education (EE) into adult education, occupational and job training, enrichment learning, and community and public education. Such EE integrated education can teach communities how to live more sustainably and help the public better understand their role in mindfully managing and protecting the world's ecosystems.

This volume offers perspectives on how adult learning might contribute to per capita income, visions for democratic civic culture, means toward correcting social injustices, and ways for promoting sustainable human growth and well-being. Human rights, economic empowerment through education, and sustainable development are inextricably intertwined and necessary for creating a more stable, peaceful, prosperous, and socially just world. This book was inspired by the call for partnerships noted in Goal 17 of the Sustainable Development Goals. We believe that adult education plays an important role in building partnerships to join forces to face these global challenges together and can contribute to better societies with improved and ongoing human development, so that more people can live dignified, healthy, sustainable, and fulfilling lives.

INTRODUCTION

HUMAN RIGHTS, SUSTAINABLE DEVELOPMENT, AND ADULT EDUCATION

History, Foundation, and Context

Mary V. Alfred
Texas A&M University, United States

For more than seven decades, the United Nations (UN) has worked to advance human conditions globally through its historic agenda for a more peaceful, prosperous, and just world. Through the work of the General Assembly and programs like the world conferences on adult education, the organization has taken a leading role in bringing world leaders together to dialogue on global issues and set agendas for advancing social, economic, and environmental justice among and within the regions of the world. The underlying themes of the United Nations' agenda over the years have been human rights, world peace, economic justice, vulnerable populations, and protecting the environment. This introduction serves as a foundation for this book, placing the global agenda for development in an historical context as we set out to broaden the discourse on human rights, vulnerable populations, and sustainable development within the field of adult and continuing education.

Advancing the Global Agenda for Human Rights, Vulnerable Populations, and Environmental Sustainability: Adult Education as Strategic Partner, pp. xix–xxxv
Copyright © 2021 by Information Age Publishing
All rights of reproduction in any form reserved.

HISTORY AND MISSION OF THE UNITED NATIONS

The UN is an international organization founded in 1945 after World War II. At the time it was founded, 51 countries made up the UN and leaders pledged "to maintaining international peace and security, developing friendly relations among nations and promoting social progress, better living standards and human rights" (United Nations, 2015a, para. 1). Today, 193 countries comprise the United Nations. Through the General Assembly, the Security Council, the Economic and Social Council, and other strategic committees, representatives of member nations work to advance the global mission of the organization. The principles and structure of the United Nations Charter were ratified by its founding members and comprised the following goals:

a. maintain world peace,
b. improve international relations,
c. reduce poverty, hunger, disease, illiteracy, and promote individual rights and freedom
d. encourage and monitor actions and progress among nations to achieve the goals (United Nations, 2015a).
e. The main purposes clearly demonstrate world leaders' concern over the decimation of people and nations from the war and viewed national collaboration as a strategy for rebuilding. Today the UN works on a wide range of fundamental issues, all aimed at promoting human rights, protecting vulnerable populations, and sustaining the environment. Taken together, human rights and sustainable development frame the UN agenda.

UNESCO—A SPECIALIZED AGENCY OF THE UN SYSTEM

An important organization within the UN system is the United Nations Educational, Scientific and Cultural Organization (UNESCO). This organization was formed in 1945 and entered into formal agreement with the UN in 1946 where it was recognized as a specialized agency within the system. As noted in the agreement,

> Article 57 of the Charter of the United Nations provides that specialized agencies, established by intergovernmental agreement and having wide international responsibilities as defined as their basic instruments in economic, social, cultural, educational, health and related fields shall be brought into relationship with the United Nations. (UNESCO, 1946, p. 175)

Therefore, UNESCO was charged with "the function of advising the United Nations on the educational, scientific, and cultural aspects of matters of concern to the latter" (p. 175). To fulfill its mission, UNESCO was also charged with initiating studies and reports with respect to the areas of responsibilities noted above and to make recommendations regarding these matters to specialized UN agencies. Importantly, it would make recommendations for policies and activities to aid these agencies in fulfilling their mission towards the broad global agenda for human rights and sustainable development. Overall, the main objective of UNESCO is to contribute to peace and security in the world by promoting collaboration among nations through education, science, culture, and communication. According to Nesbit and Welton (2013), to promote these goals, "UNESCO has organized world assemblies and conventions, adopted several international treaties, and developed universal declarations on a wide variety of issues" (p. 1).

Adult education has been one of UNESCO's primary agenda since inception, directed first by the UNESCO Institute for Education (UIE) which was later renamed the UNESCO Institute for Lifelong Learning (UIL). Three major programs constitute UIL's mission: (a) lifelong learning policies, initiatives, and strategies; (b) adult learning and education; and (c) literacy and basic skills. Indeed, UNESCO has popularized and advanced declarations, concepts, and policies governing adult education, lifelong learning, and human rights.

Before moving to discussions of human rights, it is important to note despite the United States' founding of the UN and its long history of involvement in both UN and UNESCO, the Trump administration withdrew the United States from membership in UNESCO in October 2017 and from the United Nations Human Rights Council in June 2018. As such, as of 2020, the United States does not honor the goals or commitments established by the UNESCO and the Human Rights Council. However, there is the general agreement among world leaders that promoting human rights is central to sustainable development within and among nation states, and disregard for human rights thwarts national advancements on all fronts.

UN DECLARATION OF HUMAN RIGHTS

Soon after the founding of the UN in 1945, President Roosevelt in 1946, authorized the Commission of Human Rights, which was headed by the First Lady, Eleanor Roosevelt. The committee comprised of representatives of various countries to include the United States, Lebanon, China, Australia, Chile, France, Soviet Union, United Kingdom, among others (United Nations, 2015b). This multinational representation was important to provide opportunities for diverse political, religious, and cultural traditions to be factored into the discourse on universal human rights. The Universal Declaration of Human Rights (UDHR) adopted by the United Nations Assembly on December 10, 1948, is referred to as a milestone document that aimed to provide equal treatments to people across the globe despite country of origin and other identity dimensions or race, class, and gender (Gerber, 2011; Moka-Mubelo, 2019; Pocar, 2015). The Declaration represents a common standard of achievements and fundamental human rights for all nations and citizens. As Moka-Mubelo (2019) explained,

> The concept of human rights constitutes the standard from which we analyze, evaluate, and judge the action of our governments, the measure of understanding the morality of our living together as reasonable and rational beings, and the yardstick of international solidarity. (p. 40)

To that end, UN member nations must sign on to promote and abide by the provisions established in the proclamation. As a result, application for membership from other countries must be approved by existing members.

The Human Rights proclamation consists of 30 articles or conditions of freedom summarized as follows: the right to asylum; the right to freedom from torture, the right to free speech and the right to education; civil and political rights to include the right to life, liberty, free speech, and privacy (United Nations, 2015b). Included in the declaration are economic, social, and cultural rights, like the right to social security, health, and education. Specific to this volume is Article 26 stating that everyone has a right to education; that goal has permeated all agendas and declarations on the United Nations. Overall, the Human Rights Declaration emphasized equality, nondiscrimination, mutual respect for individuals and a vision of solidarity among nations. As Ferstman et al. (2018) explained, "The Declaration epitomized the aspirations of the immediate postwar period and seized upon the collective desire to chart a new path based on universal respect, common values, and recognition of the inherent dignity of the individual" (p. 1). The proclamation declaration represents a document of hope during a period under colonial rule when there was little mutual respect for diversity of political systems and wide disparities among cultures ideologies, languages, and religion (Ferstman et al., 2018; Gerber, 2011). Even then, the concept of human rights was interpreted and understood in terms of civil and political rights at the expense of cultural and social rights (Moka-Mubelo, 2019). Most recently the discourse is broadened to include those neglected social and cultural rights, thus highlighting gaps and inequities in various spheres across the world.

While there have been important advances since the Declaration was enacted over seven decades ago, major challenges remain with its implementation. For example, freedom, dignity, and rights of all individuals, as espoused in Articles 2 and 3 today depend on privilege as defined by race, color, class, gender, wealth, and nationality, among others (Gerber, 2011; Pocar, 2015). Moreover, the right to literacy and education, healthcare, freedom from poverty, violence, environmental degradation continues to dominate the work of the UN and other multinational organizations in their quest to realize the conditions set forth in this iconic Declaration of Human Rights. The consistent efforts of the United Nations to promote human rights through the sustainability of people and planet and the challenges of implementation are important foundational elements in the discourse of international adult education.

HUMAN RIGHTS AND SUSTAINABLE DEVELOPMENT

According to Mensah (2019), sustainable development has become a buzz-word in developmental discourse. As a foundational question, and one that is fundamental to this book, we ask, what is sustainable development and how is it conceptualized and theorized? Several development theories have been advanced to explain this international phenomenon that has become the bedrock of the United Nations Agenda. Drawing from Cerin (2006), sustainable development is the process of meeting human development goals while simultaneously preserving the natural systems and resources upon which the economy and society depends. Similarly, Zhai and Chang (2019) view *sustainable development* as an approach to development, using available resources in a way that allows them to continue to exist for others. A sustainable development agenda, therefore, aims at achieving social progress, environmental equilibrium, and economic growth (Enders & Remig, 2015; Mensah, 2019; Zhai & Chang, 2019). It means that we move away from detrimental socioeconomic activities and, instead, engage in activities that will result in positive environmental, economic, and social impact for current and future generations.

While theorists have traditionally regarded the pillars of sustainability to be production, distribution, and consumption (Enders & Remig, 2015; Mensah, 2019), this conceptualization ignores the social dimension of the phenomenon. *Social sustainability* encompasses many issues such as human rights, gender equality, public participation, and rule of law, all of which promote peace and social stability for sustainability development (Cerin, 2006). Cerin (2006) furthers the argument that the goal of sustainable development must result in meeting human development goals while at the same time sustaining the natural resources and ecosystem services upon which the economy and society depend. It must be the nexus between social conditions such as poverty and environmental destruction. In the case of global poverty, for example, sustainable development should aim to alleviate poverty within the existing environmental and economic resource of the society (Daly, 1992). According to the UN General Assembly, poverty reduction should be at the core of any sustainable development agenda (United Nations, 2020).

Human rights and sustainable development make up a symbiotic phenomenon, meaning that one cannot be achieved at the expense of the other. As Deputy Secretary-General Amina Mohammed asserted, "Human rights are core to a sustainable agenda and sustainable development is a powerful vehicle for the realization of all human rights" (UN News, 2019). Improving the sustainability of people and planet calls for all to partner, collaborate, and contribute to the UN agenda established by leaders of world nations—efforts that remain fraught with challenges. To that end, I draw from Enders and Remig (2015) who remind us,

> Many current trends around the globe are unsustainable. We are losing biodiversity and fertile soil; we are contributing to climate change on larger and larger scales; inequalities within and among generations are rising; poverty remains yet to be overcome. These challenges are interconnected and require a joint effort to give rise to sustainable and durable development patterns. (p. 1)

The joint effort that Enders and Remig (2015) speak of goes beyond collaborations and partnerships among nation states but expand the concept to include engagements among communities and citizens as well as private and public organizations. This idea of partnerships and collaboration is a motivation for this book that focuses on the contributions of adult and continuing education scholars and practitioners to the global agenda for human rights, advancing the life conditions of vulnerable populations, and protecting the environment for the present and future generations. However, before we examine adult education within the context of collaborations and partnerships for global change, it is important we present the efforts of the United Nations and the agendas that frame the work presented in the chapters to follow. While there are over 70 years of United Nations reports of summits, declarations, and agendas on these issues, I specifically concentrated on the last two resolutions adopted, namely the Millennium Development Goals (2000) and the Sustainable Development Goals (LeBlanc, 2015) as the backdrop for this book.

The Millennium Development Goals

In September 2000, the United Nations General Assembly, consisting of 191 member states, adopted the United Nations Millennium Declaration to reaffirm and rededicate its commitment to "a peaceful, prosperous and just world" (United Nations, 2000, p. 1). These goals drew from preexisting goals and targets dating back from aspirations espoused by the UN Assembly at its inception. The Declaration was just one of the outputs of the 2000 summit and comprised of the goals depicted in Table 1. The Millennium Development Goals (MDGs) emanated from several international conferences, assemblies, and meetings during the 1990s, which were themselves drawn from pre-existing goals and targets, some dating back to the beginning of UNESCO in 1945. The 2000 MDGs marked an historical global mobilization to achieve a set of important social priorities worldwide (Cerin, 2006) and emerged from the section of the Declaration addressing development and poverty eradication (McGillivray, 2008). These goals represent a response by the leaders of the UN community to the deplorable life conditions among many of the world's population. While a goal for the advancement of human rights is not visible in the declaration, it is embedded in each of the action items noted above. Clearly, the first seven goals address health and human conditions in lower-income countries, demonstrating interdependence among them, with each exacerbating the others.

As previously noted, poverty is at the core of the MDGs. Members of the Assembly demonstrated concern for the widening economic gaps and living standards between the richest and poorest countries of the world (Awortwi, 2016; Cerin, 2006; McGillivray, 2008; United Nations, 2000). As a result, they pledged to work to eradicate extreme poverty at its core, identifying targets or measures to be met by a given time frame, generally by 2015. As an example, the two targets for Goal 1—*Eradicating Extreme Poverty* were (a) decrease by 50% the proportion of people living on less than

Table 1

UN's Millennium Development Goals (2000)

1.	Eradicate extreme poverty and hunger
2.	Achieve universal primary education
3.	Promote gender equality and empower women
4.	Reduce child mortality
5.	Improve maternal health
6.	Combat HIV/AIDS, malaria, and other diseases
7.	Ensure environmental sustainability
8.	Develop a global partnership for development

Note. United Nations Millennium Declaration: Resolution adopted by the General Assembly (United Nations, 2000).

$1 a day by 2015, and (b) decrease by the same proportion and time frame the proportion of people who suffer from extreme hunger. As another example, the target for Goal 3—*Promote Gender Equality and Empower Women* was to eliminate gender disparity in primary and secondary education preferably by 2005 and in all levels of education by 2015 (McGillivray, 2008; United Nations, 2000). While the eight broad goals were qualitatively written, the targets provided quantifiable measures by which progress could be assessed within each nation state. To that end, responsibility for implementation rests with respective governments; however, there was mutual agreement of partnerships and collaborations among nation states in the war against poverty and the advancement of human conditions around the world. Targets within Goal 8—*Global Partnerships and Development* provide specific descriptors of how collaborations among developed and developing nations could address the MDGs. According to Awortwi (2016), the MDGs have influenced international budgets and affected the flow of international aid.

Despite the unprecedented support from around the world and the relative effectiveness of the MDGs, not all the targets of the eight goals were achieved. Results varied across regions, ranging from much success in more developed countries to less noticeable success in some less developed countries. However, it is important to recognize the global impact of this Declaration. As Jolly et al. (2009) noted, despite the commentaries, the goals have turned out to be one of the most recognizable ideas that changed the world. Similarly, according to Awortwi (2016),

> Without the MDGs, it is likely that the Millennium Declaration would have been shelved soon after its adoption. By articulating the complex challenges of the world into 8 goals, the MDGs have had unprecedented success in drawing international and national attention to the common enemy of our time: poverty and its various dimensions. (p. 1)

While the United Nations, through its General Assembly and the Millennium Declaration, was successful in bringing attention to world poverty, it did not eradicate extreme poverty in all its manifestations. Therefore, as with previous declarations, the United Nations reassembled the leaders of nation states to continue its work on humanizing the world, resulting in the 2015 Sustainable Development declaration.

The Sustainable Development Goals

The target date for the MDGs ended in 2015 and immediately the UN reconvened the Seventieth Session of the United States General Assembly to assess progress in the implementation of these goals within and among regions. While reports indicated success in many areas, remaining challenges were acknowledged, thus calling for more strategic action and resources. Among the chronic challenges were the eradication of poverty, gender inequality, and environmental sustainability (United Nations, 2015c). Therefore, the members of the Assembly, once again, engaged in setting an agenda "for people, planet, and prosperity" (United Nations, 2015c, p.1). The Resolution, *Transforming our World: The 2030 Agenda for Sustainable Development*, was adopted with 17 Sustainable Development Goals (SDGs) and 169 targets or measurable objectives that would build on and expand the Millennium Development Goals. These goals "seek to realize the human rights of all and to achieve gender equality and the empowerment of all women and girls. They are integrated and indivisible and balance the three dimensions of sustainable development: the economic, social and environmental" (United Nations, 2015c, p. 1). World leaders recognized that ending poverty would require integrating strategies that build economic growth and address a range of social needs to include education, health, social protection, and job opportunities and, at the same time, focusing on climate change and environmental protection. The goals and targets are projected over a 15-year period (2015–2030), during which countries would implement and seek to achieve desired results. The SDGs are listed in Table 2. The 2030 Agenda for Sustainable Development marks a paradigm shift towards a more balanced model of sustainable development with the ultimate goal that everyone is free from fear and want so they can reach their full potential as human beings (United Nations, 2015c). According to United Nations (2015c),

> The 17 Sustainable Development Goals … seek to build on the Millennium Development Goals and complete what they did not achieve. They seek to realize the human rights of all and to achieve gender equality and the improvement of all women and girls. They are integrated and indivisible and balance the three dimensions of sustainable development: the economic, the social, and environmental. (p. 3)

While adult education was not identified as a core development goal in the MDGs, it was clearly given significance in the Sustainable Development declaration. UNESCO's Institute for Lifelong Learning (2009) emphasized education and lifelong learning are central to the SDGs and fundamental to their achievement. Therefore, recognizing that adult education has a structural and pivotal role in promoting and implementing a global agenda for development, it was given a central role in the SDGs as identified by Goal 4—*Ensure inclusive and equitable quality education and promote lifelong learning opportunities for all* and its corresponding targets, SDG 4.3–4.7. These targets emphasize equal access to education for men and women,

Table 2

UN's Sustainable Development Goals (2015)

1.	End poverty in all forms everywhere.
2.	End hunger, achieve food security and improved nutrition, and promote sustainable agriculture.
3.	Ensure healthy lives and promote well-being for all at all ages.
4.	Ensure inclusive and equitable quality education and promote lifelong learning opportunities for all.
5.	Achieve gender equality and empower all women and girls.
6.	Ensure availability and sustainability management of water and sanitation for all.
7.	Ensure access to affordable, reliable, sustainable, and modern energy for all.
8.	Promote sustained, inclusive, and sustainable economic growth, full and productive employment, and decent work for all.
9.	Build resilient infrastructure, promote inclusive and sustainable industrialization, and foster innovation.
10.	Reduce inequality within and among countries.
11.	Make cities and human settlements inclusive, safe, resilient, and sustainable.
12.	Ensure sustainable consumption and production patterns.
13.	Take urgent action to combat climate change and its impacts.
14.	Conserve and sustainably use the oceans, seas, and marine resource for sustainable development.
15.	Protect, restore, and promote sustainable use of terrestrial ecosystems, sustainably manage forests, combat desertification, and halt, and reverse land degradation and halt biodiversity loss.
16.	Promote peaceful and inclusive societies and form sustainable development, provide access to justice for all, and build effective, accountable, and inclusive institutions at all levels.
17.	Strengthen the means of implementation and revitalize the Global Partnership for Sustainable Development.

relevant employment skills, gender equality, education access to vulnerable populations, literacy and numeracy development, and overall acquisition of knowledge and skills for global citizenship and sustainability of equality, equity, and human rights (United Nations, 2015c).

The SDGs have been referred to as the five Ps, representing areas critical to sustainable development. These key areas of focus include people, planet, prosperity, peace, and partnership. The *People* dimension of the agenda emphasized the commitment to end poverty and ensure that conditions are conducive for individuals to achieve their full potential with dignity and respect. The *Planet* dimension calls for environmental protection through sustainable consumption and production, management of natural resources, and guard against climate change. The *Prosperity* dimension requires that opportunities be made available for all citizens to benefit and enjoy economic, social, and technological advancements while living in harmony with nature. *Peace* is exemplified by promoting peaceful and inclusive societies devoid of war and violence. Finally, it is proposed that this agenda will be made possible through global *Partnerships*, with attention paid to the needs of the poorest and most vulnerable.

Taken together, the five Ps are intended to address the root causes of poverty, address such areas of hunger, health, education, gender equality, water and sanitation, energy, economic growth, industry, innovation and infrastructure, inequalities, sustainable cities and communities, consumption and production, climate change, natural resources, and peace and justice (Mensah, 2019). A key feature of the SDGs is that they are interconnected with positives and negatives of one goal similarly impacting one of more of the other goals. For example, investing in education has potential to positively impact health, poverty, inequalities, environment, and gender equality, to name a few. Similarly, LeBlanc (2015) pointed out that addressing issues of climate change could have complementary benefits for energy security, health, biodiversity, and water resources. Therefore, a major characteristic of the SDGs is that they are integrated and inseparable. Addressing one or more goals has benefits for the implementation of other goals. Hence, this systems approach frames the core of the SDGs.

One of the major criticisms of the SDGs was that human rights was not made a visible goal in the agenda for development. As Wilbur and Blaiklock (2015) noted, "Human rights could have provided an integrating framework to the SDGs. Instead, there is no cohesive approach, let alone a consistent rights-based approach, to the goals and targets" (p. 1). Although the SDGs are not framed explicitly in the language of human rights, most targets clearly reflect the content of human rights standards. As a point of emphasis, The UN Deputy Secretary General, Amina Mohammed, in her address to the 40th session of the Human Rights Council noted, "Human rights are core to the 2030 agenda, and sustainable development is a powerful vehicle for the realization of all human rights (UN News, March 7, 2020). Therefore, there is the general acceptance that human rights principles serve as core to the successful implementation of the SDGs.

The members of the Assembly recognized that ending poverty, one of the major drivers of the SDGs, must involve strategies for economic growth and address social needs to include education, health, social protection, work opportunities, while paying attention to environmental protection. Therefore, many question how the UN can hold countries accountable for implementing these ambitious goals when there are so many variabilities among them. As Mensah (2019) explained, the UN considers different national realities, capabilities, and levels of development. Moreover, it respects national policies, while making sure they are focused on the SDGs. In addition, the 169 targets serve as assessment indicators for monitoring progress. From all indications, there is a spirit of partnership among governments, private sectors, research endeavors, academia, and civil society organizations in support of this development agenda. Recognizing it takes all stakeholders in collaboration to realize this ambitious agenda, members of the assembly promoted global partnership as a strategic goal, noting,

> We are determined to mobilize the means required to implement this
> agenda through a revitalized Goal Partnership for Sustainable Develop-
> ment, based on a spirit of strengthened solidarity, focused on the needs of
> the poorest and most vulnerable and with the participation of all countries,
> all stakeholders and all people. (United Nations, 2015c, p. 2)

To that end, the United Nations advanced a massive media campaign, asking everyone to get involved in large and small ways to work toward improving the life conditions of people while protecting the environment for future generations. The call for partnership goes beyond collaboration among member nations and nongovernment organizations. It calls for educational institutions and academic programs, public and private corporations, communities, groups, and individuals to get involved in the implementation of this global agenda. Adult education, with its philosophy and foundation of social justice and human rights, has historically contributed to the global agenda for human and societal development since its inception. In this book, we make visible some of our contributions through the discourses of adult, community, and environmental education and offer recommendations of how the field can be more purposeful in its efforts at becoming a more strategic partner in promoting the global agenda for sustainable development.

ADULT EDUCATION AS AN HISTORIC PARTNER IN HUMAN RIGHTS AND SUSTAINABLE DEVELOPMENT

The field of adult and continuing education has historically played a pivotal role in advocating for social justice and bringing attention to social disparities across world nations, starting with the 1919 establishment of the World Association of Adult Education (WAAE). According to Boucouvalas (2002), the WAAE was founded to mobilize adult education as a platform that would make visible and address the intolerable life conditions that confronted individuals, communities, and nations worldwide. More specifically, the vision for the organization was the promotion of cultural awareness, international cooperation, and the wellbeing of adults through policy, research, and practice (Knoll, 2002). Therefore, even prior to the founding of UNESCO, adult education took on a pivotal role in international cooperation and development.

In 1929, the WAAE organized the first world conference on adult education in setting the precedent for international adult education partnerships to address problems facing human development across the globe (Alfred & Guo, 2020). As Alfred and Guo noted, while the WAAE was not sustainable beyond World War II, it paved the way for global partnerships that would set agendas for sustainable development through adult education. Following the WAAE, the United Nations Educational, Scientific, and Cultural Organization (UNESCO) and the International Council of Adult Education (ICAE) are two international bodies that made significant contributions to global adult education.

Like the concept of the WAAE, partnerships formed the foundation of these organizations and consisted of cooperation among government and nongovernment organizations (NGOs), educators, and other leaders to advance adult education as a platform to address global issues of social justice. Included in the agenda are the longstanding issues of education disparities, gender inequalities, poverty, health conditions, vulnerable population, peace, and the environment (Ireland & Spezia, 2014; Knoll, 2014). While there are distinct features of these two organizations—UNESCO, a government organization, and ICAE, drawing membership from NGOs—they hold a similar mission (Boucouvalas, 2011/2012; Ireland & Spezia, 2014).

While the WAAE was the start of global cooperation on adult education, consistent efforts at implementing an international agenda can be traced to the UNESCO's World Conference on Adult Education, the first of which was held at Elsinore, Denmark in 1949 (Alfred & Guo, 2020). Following the first conference, five other International Conferences on Adult Education (CONFINTEA) were held in various world regions to include, in succeeding order, Montreal, Canada (1960), Tokyo, Japan (1972), Paris, France (1985), Hamburg, Germany (1997) and Belem, Brazil (2009). These conferences are held approximately every 12 years with the seventh world conference (CONFINTEA VII) scheduled to be held in Morocco in 2022. With each assembly, world leaders, NGOs, and other regional representatives gather to discuss the status of lifelong learning and education for adults and to develop strategies and make recommendations for future development across world nations. The UNESCO's world regions include the African Continent, the Arab States, Asia and the Pacific Region, Europe and North America, and Latin America and the Caribbean.

Of notable mention is the fifth world conference on adult education (CONFINTEA V) held in Hamburg Germany in 1997. While the other previous conferences gave some mention to adult education, CONFINTEA V strongly emphasized the role of adult learning and nonformal education to lifelong learning, a concept UNESCO embraced in the 1970s to encompass the global and integrated dimension of learning in adulthood. Most importantly, CONFINTEA V also marked a turning point in the global recognition and commitment to adult learning and nonformal education (Alfred & Nafukho, 2010). Two significant landmark documents emerged from the conference that aimed to guide the direction of adult education globally. These were the *Hamburg Declaration on Adult Learning* and the *Agenda for the Future* (UNESCO, 1997). The Hamburg Declaration identified 27 commitments or position statements necessary to promote democracy, equity, and global citizenship through adult education. From the Declaration, an action plan, namely the *Agenda for the Future*, "was drawn up to serve as a framework for the planning and development of adult education and lifelong learning across the globe (Alfred & Nafukho, 2010, p. 96). Partnership was also key to implementation as the plan called for adult education to partner with governmental agencies and nongovernment organizations, employers and trade unions, universities and research centers, civil and community-based organizations, adult educators, and learners themselves (UNESCO, 1997). According to Nesbit and Welton (2013), CONFINTEA V was a defining moment for adult and continuing education as it positioned adult educators to address the challenges of democracy, peace and human rights, respect for diversity, economic and environmental sustainability, and workforce development. Adult education was, therefore, recognized as a viable platform for advancing the agenda for sustainable development.

With a mission parallel to that of UNESCO's, the ICAE was founded in 1972 during the UNESCO's third world Conference on Adult Education in Tokyo, Japan. ICAE draws its membership from NGOs and works in concert with UNESCO "to strengthen the structures of adult education and the role of adult education in the face of critical global issues" (ICAE, n.d., para. 7). With the emergence of social movements in the 1980s, for example, the women's movement, the peace movement, trade union movements, and movement of Indigenous peoples (ICAE, n.d.), the organization promoted international adult education as a platform whereby organizations for social change could launch and advance their transformative agenda—one that is aligned with the philosophy of the field. With the rise of new social movements around the world, adult education provides space to advance these social agendas through its teaching, research, and service engagements. Contemporary social movements, to include Black Lives Matter, Chicano Rights, Civil Rights, Disability Rights, Environmental

Justice, Immigration, LGBTQ, and the MeToo Movement, among others, aim to bring attention to social injustices and work to promote human rights among populations whose rights and human dignity continue to be compromised. It is, therefore, no surprise that throughout the global reports on adult education there is the recurring thesis that education and lifelong learning are central to the SDGs and fundamental to their achievement. According to UNESCO Institute for Lifelong Learning (2018), adult learning and education (ALE) "has [a] structural, enabling and pivotal role in promoting the implementation of the entire 2030 Sustainable Development Agenda" (p. 5). Similarly, Tarabini (2010) contended that the global agenda to improve people's lives and protect the environment begins with education. While education alone is not a panacea for the human and environmental problems of the world, with the required resources, it can play a significant role in helping to ameliorate some of these problems and improve life conditions globally. Therefore, this book is motivated by the call for partnerships and action and draws a group of contributors from various countries who together present a global view of adult educators at work to advance the global agenda for human rights and sustainability.

REFERENCES

Alfred, M. V., & Guo, S. (2020). Internationalization of adult and continuing education. In T. S. Rocco, M. C. Smith, R. C. Mizzi, L. R. Meriweather, & J. D. Hawley (Eds.), *Handbook of adult and continuing education* (pp. 61–70). Stylus.

Alfred, M. V., & Nafukho, F. (2010). International and comparative adult and continuing education. In C. E. Kasworm, A. D. Rose, & J. Ross-Gordon (Eds.), *Handbook of adult and continuing education* (pp. 93–102). SAGE.

Awortwi, N. (2016). Introduction: Tracking progress and challenges in the implementation of the MDGs in Africa. In N. Awortwi, & H. Musahara, H. (Eds.), *Implementation of the millennium development goals: Progresses and challenges in some African countries* (pp. 1–10). Addis Ababa, Ethiopia: OSSREA. http://www.jstor.org/stable/j.ctvh8qz53

Boucouvalas, M. (2002). International adult education: Past, present, and into the future. *Adult Learning, 13*(4), 23–26.

Boucouvalas, M. (2011/2012). Our global reach: UNESCO and ICAE as catalysts. *Adult Learning, 22*(4), 4–8.

Cerin, P. (2006). Bringing economic opportunity into line with environmental influence: A discussion on the Coase theorem and the Porter and Van de Linde hypothesis. *Ecological Economics, 56*(2), 209–225.

Daly, H. E. (1992). UN conference on environment and development: Retrospect on Stockholm and prospects for Rio. *Ecological Economics, 5*(1), 9–14.

Enders, J. C., & Remig, M. (2015). Theories of sustainable development: An introduction. In J. C. Enders & M. Enders (Eds.), *Theories of sustainable development* (pp. 1–5). Routledge.

Ferstman, C., Goldberg, A., Gray, T., Ison, L., Nathan, R., & Newman, M. (2018). *Contemporary human rights challenges: The universal declaration of human rights and its continuing challenges*. Routledge.

Gerber, P. (2011). Education about human rights: Strengths and weaknesses of the UN Declaration on Human Rights education and training. *Alternative Law Journal, 36*(4), 245–249.

International Council for Adult Education (ICAE). (n.d.). *History of ICAE*. http://icae.global/en/about/history-of-icae/

Ireland, T. D., & Spezia, C. J. (2014). *Adult education in retrospective—60 years of CONFINTEA*. UNESCO.

Jolly, R., Emmerij, L., & Weiss, T. G. (2009). *UN ideas that changed the world*. Indiana University Press.

Knoll, J. H. (2002). Adult and continuing education in international and supranational organizations. *Journal of Adult Education and Development, 59*. https://www.dvv-international.de/en/adult-education-and-development/editions/aed-592002/cultural-dialogue-and-adult-education/adult-and-continuing-education-in-international-and-supranational-organizations

Knoll, J. H. (2014). The history of the UNESCO international conferences on adult education—from Helsingor (1949) to Hamburg (1997): International education policy through people and programmes. In T. D. Ireland & C. J. Spezia (Eds.), *Adult education in retrospective—60 years of CONFINTEA* (pp. 13–28). UNESCO.

LeBlanc, D. (2015). *Towards integration at last? The sustainable development goals as a network of targets*. DESA Working Paper No. 141. https://www.un.org/esa/desa/papers/2015/wp141_2015.pdf

McGillivray, M. (2008). The millennium development goals: Overview, progress, and prospects. In M. McGillivray (Ed.), *Achieving the millennium development goals: Studies in developmental economics and policy* (pp. 1–19). Palgrave McMillan.

Mensah, J. (2019). Sustainable development: Meaning, history, principles, pillars, and implications for human action: Literature review. *Cogent Social Sciences, 5*(1), 1–21. https://www.cogentoa.com/article/10.1080/23311886.2019.1653531

Moka-Mubelo, W. (2019). Towards a contextual understanding of human rights. *Ethics and Global Politics, 12*, 40–52.

Nesbit, T., & Welton, M. (2013). Editors notes. In T. Nesbit & M. Welton (Eds.), Adult education and learning in a precarious age: The *Hamburg Declaration* Revisited. *New Directions for Adult and Continuing Education, 138*, 1–7.

Pocar, F. (2015). Some thoughts of the universal declaration of human rights and the "generations" of human rights, *Intercultural Human Rights Law Review, 10*, 43–53.

Tarabini, A. (2010). Education and poverty in the global development agenda: Emergence, evolution and consolidation. *International Journal of Educational Development, 30*, 204–212.

United Nations Millennium Development Goals. (2000). *The Millennium Development Goals*. https://www.ndi.org/sites/default/files/Handout%207%20-%20Millennium%20Development%20Goals.pdf

Wilbur, C., & Blaiklock, A. (September 29, 2015). SDG Series: With SDGs now adopted, human rights must inform implementation and accountability. *Health and Human Rights Journal.* https://www.hhrjournal.org/2015/09/sdg-series-with-sdgs-now-adopted-human-rights-must-inform-implementation-and-accountability/

UN News (March 7, 2019). Human rights 'core to sustainable development': Deputy UN chief. https://news.un.org/en/story/2019/03/1034261

UNESCO. (1946). *Agreement between the United Nations and the United Nations Educational, Scientific and Cultural Organization.* http://portal.unesco.org/en/ev.php-URL_ID=48886&URL_DO=DO_TOPIC&URL_SECTION=201.html

UNESCO. (1997). *CONFINTEA adult education: The Hamburg declaration and the agenda for the future.* https://unesdoc.unesco.org/ark:/48223/pf0000116114

UNESCO Institute for Lifelong Learning. (2009). *Global report on adult learning and education.* Hamburg, Germany. https://unesdoc.unesco.org/ark:/48223/pf0000186431

United Nations. (2015a). *History of the UN: 70th Anniversary.* https://www.un.org/un70/en/content/history/index.html

United Nations. (2015b). *Universal declaration of human rights.* https://www.un.org/en/udhrbook/pdf/udhr_booklet_en_web.pdf

United Nations. (2015c). *Transforming our world: The 2030 agenda for sustainable development.* https://sustainabledevelopment.un.org/content/documents/21252030%20Agenda%20for%20Sustainable%20Development%20web.pdf

United Nations. (2000). *United Nations Millennium Declaration: Resolution adopted by the General Assembly.* https://www.un.org/en/development/desa/population/migration/generalassembly/docs/globalcompact/A_RES_55_2.pdf

United Nations. (2020). *Progress towards the sustainable development goals: Report of the Secretary-General.* https://sustainabledevelopment.un.org/content/documents/26158Final_SG_SDG_Progress_Report_14052020.pdf

Zhai, T. T., & Chang Y. C. (2019). From general principles of civil law to general provisions of civil law: A historical leap in contemporary Chinese civil law. *Social Sciences in China, 2,* 85–91.

SECTION I

HUMAN RIGHTS

CHAPTER 1

THE CRITICAL LITERACIES ADVANCEMENT MODEL (CLAM) AS A TOOL FOR CURRICULUM DEVELOPMENT

Advancing Human Rights Literacy in Adult Education

Petra A. Robinson and Maja Stojanović
Louisiana State University, United States

In our rapidly changing society, various factors (mores, values, economics, technology, politics, terrorism, globalization) frame the context of our educational structures and systems, including adult education. As Manley (1974) pointed out, "every educational system in history has reflected the interpretation placed by each society upon its own needs" (p. 140). These contextual and influential factors also affect how, when, why, and where adults learn because "the nature of society at any particular point in time determines the relative emphasis placed on adult learning" (Merriam et al., 2007, p. 5). Therefore, sociocultural factors inform the curriculum content and influence the setting within which education and learning will occur; these factors also drive the motivations for learning.

Advancing the Global Agenda for Human Rights, Vulnerable Populations, and Environmental Sustainability: Adult Education as Strategic Partner, pp. 3–18

Arguably, the most influential, constant, and modern inventions influencing adult learning in general are the internet and the personal computer, which sparked the ensuing information technology revolution. Globalization, advanced by the information technology revolution, has forced adults to experience various new paradigms: information exchange, economic development, cultural migration, among others, in all sectors ranging from financial to medical and to the educational environment. The resulting impact on these transformations in society and the world in general gives way to "dramatic changes in the way we live and work—and even maybe think" (Forester, 1987, p. 1). These changes compel us to embrace new concepts and new, critical "literacies" in order to adapt and function effectively in society. We argue herein that today's literacy requirements continue to evolve over time and in ways that far exceed those of 15, 10, or even 5 years ago.

While the COVID-19 global pandemic emphasized the relevance and crucial nature of information literacy—which Sturges and Gastinger (2010) argue is a human right—as well as computer literacy and other forms of digital literacy, it also unearthed various issues related to access and systemic inequity in these and other areas. Additionally, the circumstances of the pandemic also underscored the importance of other literacies necessary for navigating and thriving—and in some instances simply surviving—in today's globalized society. These other kinds of socially constructed literacies, similarly described as multiliteracies (New London Group, 1996) and in New Literacy Studies (Bruce, 1998), are especially important to the field of adult education, in part because "adult learning does not occur in a vacuum. What one wants to learn, what opportunities are available, the manner in which one learns—all are to a large extent determined by the society in which one lives" (Merriam et al., 2007, p. 25), which we argue can be seen more clearly as countries such as the United States and other nations grapple with the global pandemic. Moreover, learning and living during a global health pandemic must be viewed within the context of the persistent historic racial prejudice and social injustice confronting many of the world's nations, with specific attention to the United States.

For purposes of this chapter, we seek to describe and emphasize the importance of human rights literacy within the context of recent social events and unrest and how these current events have elevated our consciousness on the wide range of systemic inequities (including, but not limited to racial, economic, and cultural injustices) that permeate our lifeworld. The field of adult education, fundamentally known for critical, radical, emancipatory theories and practical applications to teaching and learning, has been and should remain concerned with matters of equity and social justice. Therefore, key stakeholders such as policy makers, funders, curriculum designers, and other practitioners should respond by offering adult learners the necessary tools to battle these inequities. This should be done by "fostering the spirit of critical reflection" as stipulated in the principles of critical practice in adult education (Brookfield, 1985, p. 48) by providing structured opportunities for adult learners to examine and critique widely accepted values and beliefs, particularly those that infringe upon basic human rights.

The central focus of this chapter is on the importance of human rights literacy as a necessary critical tool for navigating our contemporary, media-saturated, globalized society and for challenging social inequities. By means of this human rights lens, we also explore the role adult educators play in promoting equity and social justice within the practice of teaching and learning.

In the first section of the chapter, we present key definitions and con-ceptualizations, while drawing attention to how these definitions compare to traditional definitions of literacy. Then, we describe human rights lit-eracy as a means of challenging systemic inequities. In the third section, we discuss human rights literacy using the critical literacies advancement model (CLAM; Robinson, 2020) as a framework to underscore how adult educators can conceptualize their thinking about it and how to best support its acquisition, advance other critical nontraditional literacies, and in turn promote equity and social justice. To conclude, we further make the case for the inclusion of human rights literacy in the adult education curriculum. In support, we list available resources, such as activities, websites, and books that adult educators may find useful.

Defining Human Rights Literacy and Human Rights Education

An archaic, but most widely accepted view of the concept of literacy limits the definition to refer to one's ability to read and write. However, even earlier definitions of literacy exist to refer to the ability of a "learned person," and for example, in the Middle Ages, literacy was limited only to the ability to read Latin (Venezky, 1990, p. 3). Venezky (1990) suggested that the term has actually evolved with the evolution of spoken languages. Christopherson (1997) pointed out that, in traditional terms, literacy con-sists of three basic components, reading, writing, and arithmetic, indicating there is a need for a more encompassing meaning to the word literacy. While Christopherson also listed "computer literacy, media literacy, eco-logical literacy, [and] financial literacy" (p. 169) as other kinds of literacies that we need to attain, there are additional nontraditional literacies the author does not list, some later described in this chapter (see Robinson, 2020 for a more comprehensive list).

Scholars have yet to agree on a more current and inclusive definition of literacy, especially as the demands for various kinds of literacies increase.

The definition of the term literacy we found most encompassing and appropriate for the purposes of this chapter is offered by UNESCO (n.d.): "a means of identification, understanding, interpretation, creation, and communication in an increasingly digital, text-mediated, information-rich and fast-changing world" (para. 3). The pluralistic nature of UNESCO's definition allows for its application in multiple contexts and across various conceptualizations, including that of critical, nontraditional literacies necessary in a global society, such as human rights, equity, and social justice literacies.

It is not only the term literacy that seems challenging to define. In discussing the developments in human rights education, Roux (2019) wrote about "the complexity of human diversities (global diversities) and understandings of human rights" (p. 7) that make human rights literacy a broad concept. One example Roux highlighted is related to issues of race and the colonial other, which are often analyzed as geographically related concepts, instead of globally relevant issues. The problem with such analyses is that they fail to address these pressing issues on a global level, thus failing to examine all of them in their entirety. We argue that introducing human rights literacy into educational curricula would be the first step to overcoming these and similar issues in the global society.

Human rights education (HRE) was conceptualized with the idea of addressing the issues of inequity and injustice while promoting "awareness about the rights accorded by the Universal Declaration of Human Rights (UHDR) and related human rights conventions, and the procedures that exist for the redress of violations of these rights" (Tibbitts & Fernekes, 2011, p. 87). In broader terms, HRE is defined as including knowledge and skills; values, attitudes, and behavior; and action aimed at defending and promoting human rights (United Nations Human Rights Office of the High Commissioner, 2010). As an extension of this concept, human rights literacy education development programs should aim not only to promote awareness of the UDHR but also to equip individuals with skills necessary to critique oppressive practices and work "towards transformation with the difference of a bottom-up approach with the subjects of rights of the human rights as starting point" (Roux, 2019, p. 22). This makes human rights literacy education vital for challenging exploitation and inequities and promoting equity and social justice.

Human Rights Literacy: A Strategy for Challenging Systemic Inequities

The Universal Declaration of Human Rights of 1948 is described as a "milestone document" (United Nations, n.d.) that outlines fundamental rights inherent to all people, regardless of race, sex, nationality, ethnicity, language, or any other status. Accordingly, human rights literacy is connected to these fundamental rights as described by the United Nations (UN); it refers to speaking the "common language of humanity" (United Nations, 1998), and more pointedly, as Becker and associates (2015) suggested, to the "understandings of dignity, equality, and freedom that demand transformative action toward an open and democratic society" (p. 9). Furthermore, human rights literacy, developed through human rights education, is expected to examine the world in a way that acknowledges violations to these rights and offer critique and practical support for what Baxi (1994) described as,

> the consciousness of peoples of the world who have waged the most persistent struggles for decolonization and self-determination, against racial discrimination, gender-based aggression and discrimination, denial of access to basic minimum needs, environmental degradation and destruction, systematic 'benign neglect' of the disarticulated, disadvantaged and dispossessed (including the indigenous peoples of the Earth). (p. 1)

The need for human rights literacy education is also supported by the UDHR, as Article 26.2 posits that "education shall be directed to the full development of the human personality and to the strengthening of respect for human rights and fundamental freedoms" (United Nations, 1948). This suggests human rights literacy education (also referred to as human rights education) is itself a fundamental right and, therefore, ultimately a responsibility.

For at least a decade, human rights education has been a part of international education policy planning (Ramirez et al., 2007) and a part of its own field of scholarship and practice (Mihr & Schmitz, 2007). Additionally, the United Nations Educational, Scientific and Cultural Organization (UNESCO) (2009) signaled the importance and significance of literacy, describing it as a fundamental human right and the foundation for lifelong learning. From their standpoint, literacy is considered essential to social and human development in its ability to transform lives, because it is a key tool to empower and improve one's status, health, income, and even one's relationship with the world.

Notwithstanding, as evidenced throughout contemporary society, these fundamental rights are not always equally guaranteed. With increasing demographic and other societal shifts, the need for more effective education systems is even more apparent (Robinson et al., 2013). Cases from recent history offer evidence to suggest the need for a more systematic educational change that would allow—and encourage—the development of multiple, critical, nontraditional literacies. One such issue is exemplified in the "educational deficit" contextualized as "a shortfall between the educational reality that children experience around the world and what governments have promised and committed to through human rights treaties" (The Education Deficit, 2016, para. 5). This signals the failure of governments to honor the fundamental human right to education, which is necessary for equity and social justice. Similarly, according to the Associated Press (2018), a federal judge in the United States, in hearing a case based on the poor reading skills of students at several Detroit schools on the right to a quality education, dismissed the lawsuit, suggesting that students have no right to literacy. The decision is paradoxical in nature as the judge posited that individual illiteracy has a detrimental impact on the society.

Central to the case was the argument that the schools were in "slum-like conditions" and "functionally incapable of delivering access to literacy" (Associated Press, 2018, para. 4), which suggests a violation of the right to equitable education for all, stipulated by the UDHR. This decision is flawed, not only because of its obvious disregard for basic educational rights, but also because of the implications it has for the society. This action is also in direct contradiction to the 2030 Agenda for Sustainable Development and specifically to Sustainable Development Goal 4 that aims to "ensure inclusive and equitable quality education and promote lifelong learning opportunities for all" (United Nations, 2020, para. 2). Dismissing the right to basic, high quality literacy education results in further educational and societal inequities. It means barring individuals from developing the skills needed for success and the development of other critical literacies necessary for making informed decisions and promoting equity and social justice in the global society (Robinson, 2020). As such, development of human rights literacy is essential as being mutually interdependent and reinforcing of other literacies. In other words, human rights literacy can lead to other literacies, including foundational. It follows that critically literate individuals would be more equipped to recognize societal inequity and to be in a better position to address it.

Theoretical Framework

As highlighted throughout this book, adult education is characterized by an ethical valence in that it is concerned with promoting human rights, equity, and social justice. In turn, we use the critical literacies advancement model (Robinson, 2020) to foreground our discussion and underscore the function and interconnectedness of multiple critical literacies (see Figure 1.1). We also use the model to position human rights literacy as a critical mechanism that can play an integral role in promoting positive social change in today's world. This framework is a useful lens for guiding the conceptualization and arguments of this chapter. It centers equity as a societal ideal for which we must strive, suggesting that by developing intertwined, multiple critical literacies we can effectively work toward promoting positive social change. This change has implications for increasing justice whether it be distributive, procedural, retributive, or restorative, as evidenced in racial, cultural, economic, political, or other forms of justice in today's society.

Figure 1.1

Critical Literacies Advancement Model

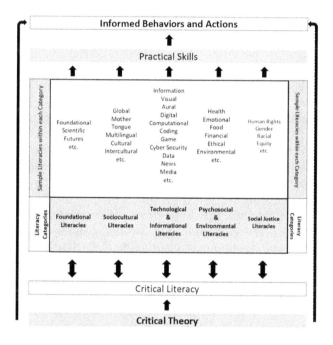

Source: Robinson (2020).

Grounded on a foundation of critical theory and specifically with critical literacy as a building block, this model argues for a deeper understanding of socially constructed concepts and themes related to power, inequality, marginalization, oppression, and other forms of injustice in society. The framework also demands an expanded understanding of literacy and illustrates how a critical analysis of the various groups of literacies act in tandem with one another. The model highlights the importance of critical thinking and developing multiple literacy skills, such as human rights, equity, and global literacies, in order to actively help advance or promote informed decision-making, which, Robinson (2020) argued, has potential implications for leading to positive social change, especially in terms of equity and social justice.

The model effectively organizes or categorizes different contemporary literacies into one of five main topical areas—foundational literacies, socio-cultural literacies, technological and informational literacies, psychosocial and environmental literacies, and social justice literacies. For purposes of this chapter, we focus on the social justice literacies category, which Robinson (2020) explained, includes literacies such as human rights literacy (our central focus), gender literacy, racial literacy, and equity literacy. Broadly encompassing a wide range of critical justice-oriented literacies, the social justice category, like the others, includes various examples, but the lists are not exhaustive. These are displayed with bidirectional arrows to reflect the dynamic nature of the model as well as the fluid nature of how these literacies interact and are perceived in society.

In terms of human rights literacy, there is an obvious connection to equity and social justice as human rights reflect a broad value system that is not confined or related to any kind of group membership including common social groupings or classifications (e.g., those based on race, gender, or citizenship of a particular country or region). In fact, these rights apply to everyone, and as such, they are not (to be) encumbered by political or other influential contextual ideologies but are to be explored through education that is open-ended, exploratory, and directed toward problem solving. This problem-solving nature is inherent in the critical literacies advancement model as it highlights how the development of critical literacy skills (such as human rights literacy) is useful for advancing other critical literacies that can lead to the development of practical skills that lead to informed behaviors and actions that can ultimately lead to positive social change.

This model is then a strong basis for demonstrating the connection of human rights literacy to the development of other literacies such as social justice literacy, equity literacy, racial literacy and so on. Furthermore, it provides a framework to show how it can help systematize ways to support the adult education goal of eliminating injustice in education and society overall.

The Argument for Human Rights Literacy Education

The critical nature of human rights literacy places it as an essential component of an adult education curriculum. In support of this, the Vienna Declaration and Programme of Action (1993) made the argument that,

> States should strive to eradicate illiteracy and should direct education towards the full development of the human personality and to the strengthening of respect for human rights and fundamental freedoms. The World

Conference on Human Rights calls on all States and institutions to include human rights, humanitarian law, democracy and rule of law as subjects in the curricula of all learning institutions in formal and non-formal settings. (§ D, art. LXXIX)

Further, as adults learn within the context of a society interconnected with power configurations related to economic, social, and political structures, there must be an understanding of these systems and their impact upon learning and knowledge, as well as the impact of learning and knowledge upon them. As Wilson and Cervero (2001) posited, "adult education has a significant role in the distribution of not only knowledge but also of social, economic, and political power" (p. xv). We argue that critical education and human rights literacy education hold this responsibility to reveal these power systems to learners, to illustrate various positionalities, systems, oppressions, and structures that contribute to hegemony.

Freire's (1970/1972) emancipatory adult education work supports this kind of revelation with the juxtaposition of *banking education* with *problem-posing education*: "Whereas banking education anesthetizes and inhibits creative power, problem-posing education involves a constant unveiling of reality. The former attempts to maintain the submersion of consciousness; the latter strives for the emergence of consciousness and critical intervention in reality" (Freire, 1970/1972, p. 137). It supports the concept of transformational learning and education as it encourages a critical reflection of the status quo. Brookfield (1997) articulated the importance of critical reflection to "the democratic project" and posited that this critical thinking and reflection is "a uniquely adult education process" (p. 17). This confirms the importance of incorporating human rights literacy in the adult education curriculum, not only for awareness but also for reflection in which the ultimate goal is social transformation.

Situated in a public educational context that is rife with instances of inequitable treatment, in a mixed-method study, Brown (2006) sought to explore the effects of an alternative, transformative andragogy designed to be responsive to the challenges of preparing education leaders committed to social justice and equity. The findings of the study point to how participation in transformative learning processes and strategies can increase students' perceived growth in awareness, acknowledgement, and action toward social justice. This is a follow up on an earlier call to challenge educators (in this instance professors in higher education) to "retool their teaching and courses to address issues of power and privilege—to weave social justice into the fabric of educational leadership curriculum, pedagogy, programs, and policies" (Brown, 2004, p. 78). Likewise, since instructional design can provide opportunities for social transformation among communities of color (Robinson & Lewis, 2011), we also support including a human rights literacy focus on adult education curriculum toward an agenda of creating social action. This action, we propose, will engender greater understanding and realization of human rights for all, garnered through the support of human rights education or literacy in a systematic way, built into the adult education curriculum whether in formal, nonformal, or informal settings.

Given the direct connection human rights literacy has with critical literacy and critical thinking more specifically, as illustrated in the critical literacies advancement model (Robinson, 2020), we see its inclusion in adult education curriculum in direct support of Target 4.4 of Sustainable Goal 4, which speaks to skill acquisition beyond work-specific skills, extending to high-level cognitive and noncognitive/transferable skills such as problems solving and critical thinking, among others. Human rights education teaches many skills that can help with conflict identification and peaceful resolution, negotiation, mediation, and consensus building. Additionally, as indicated in Target 4.7 of Sustainable Goal 4, it is vitally important to "[strengthen] education's contribution to the fulfilment of human rights" (United Nations, 2020). As advocates for human rights, we operate under the premise that it is equally important not only to understand these human rights, but also to engender active protection and securing of these basic rights to which we are all entitled, through sustainable and practical means that can lead to permanence of a more equitable and just society.

Resources and Implications for Practice

United Nations Sustainable Education Goal (United Nations, 2020) is focused on promoting lifelong learning opportunities, inclusive of childhood and adult education. There are considerable research findings and resources for childhood education and literacy development (e.g., UNESCO's 101 good practices in Human Rights Education, 2009; HRE USA Curriculum Integration Guide, 2021). Because of a variety of available educational resources for young learners, as adult educators frame human rights literacy curricula, it may be useful for them to examine topics included in the young learners' curricula and adapt their instructional plans according to their adult learners' needs.

To address the gap in adult human rights education, we list best practices and offer strategies for inclusion in adult education curricula. We also provide a summary of available resources for adult human rights literacy development (Table 1.1), offering specific suggestions for adapting those originally designed for younger learners.

Although we have not offered an extensive list of educational resources for developing human rights literacy in this section, we tried to select a

Table 1.1

Adult HRE Resources

Source	Materials	Advantages
Office of the United Nations High Commissioner for Human Rights https://www.ohchr.org/	• The Universal Declaration of Human Rights (available in over 500 languages) • A "simplified" version of the Declaration available at https://www.ohchr.org/Documents/Publications/ABCannexesen.pdf • Collection of educational resources, including multimedia and other virtual resources, collected between 1995 and 2004	• Accessible to speakers of different languages • The simplified version suitable for learners with different needs • Digital resources
Human Rights Education USA https://hreusa.org/	• HRE Curriculum Integration Guide Lesson Plans (readings and discussion activities; designed for younger learners but applicable in adult education settings) • Human Rights Education Library (selection of online webinars and virtual conferences)	• Users can browse the HRE Library by topic
University of Minnesota's Human Rights Library http://hrlibrary.umn.edu/ Note: links need update	• One of the largest collections (more than 65,000) of documents related to human rights • Links to other relevant websites and resources	• Online repository • Target audience includes human rights educators, activists, scholars, and students • Documents available in Arabic, Chinese, English, French, Japanese, Korean, Russian, Spanish, and Swedish

(Table conintued on next page)

Table 1.1 (Continued)

Adult HRE Resources

Source	Materials	Advantages
University of Minnesota's Human Rights Resource Center http://www.hrusa.org/ Note: links need update	• Training for human rights educators • Human rights education resources • Activities and curricula • Reading and annotated bibliographies (e.g. *The Bells of Freedom* (Action Professionals Association for the People, 1996); compilation of 24 exercises aimed at developing human rights literacy and has printed versions in English and French) • Developmental and Conceptual Framework for HRE (Flowers, n.d.)—lists educational goals, key concepts, and practices	• Digital resources
Center for Human Rights Documentation & Research of Columbia University in New York https://library.columbia.edu/libraries/chrdr.html	• Human Rights Web Archive	• Free resources • Online content • Available in 60 languages
The Advocates for Human Rights https://www.theadvocatesforhumanrights.org/	• Lesson plans and toolkits for teaching young learners (possible adaptation for adult education) • Resources for adult educators (e.g., 24 human rights topics which can be used to plan human rights literacy syllabi and curricula)	• Digital resources
Amnesty International https://www.amnesty.org/en/	• Course on human rights defenders in four languages • Human rights writing education toolkit in three languages • Human rights education blogs	• Free • Digital resources • Resources in multiple languages
Centre for Human Rights and Citizenship Education of the Dublin City University https://www.dcu.ie/chrce/index.shtml	• Scholarly articles, books, and book chapters • Resources for teachers	• Categorized by age and topic

diverse range of resources including digital libraries, educational syllabi and curricula, activities, exercises, and multimedia which adult educators can use as they incorporate human resource literacy courses in their curricula.

Discussion and Conclusion

As we write this chapter and wrestle with the (now-recent) unwarranted murders of George Floyd, Breonna Taylor among (too many) other Black people at the hands of police we take special note of the many "No Justice, No Peace" picket signs among the "Black Lives Matter" signs at the large protests happening all over the United States and the world. This gives us pause to reflect on some of the words of Emperor Haile Selassie's speech addressing racial discrimination to the United Nations General Assembly in New York in 1963, some of which were memorialized in Bob Marley's (1976) song titled *War*,

> Until the philosophy which holds one race superior and another inferior is finally and permanently discredited and abandoned:
> That until there are no longer first-class and second-class citizens of any nation:
> That until the color of a man's skin is of no more significance than the color of his eyes:
> That until the basic human rights are equally guaranteed to all without regard to race:
> That until that day, the dream of lasting peace and world citizenship and the rule of international morality will remain but a fleeting illusion, to be pursued but never attained.... We Africans will fight, if necessary and we know that we shall win, as we are confident in the victory of good over evil.

We take this critical moment to direct our attention to the words of a less widely known, but equally meaningful song by Peter Tosh (1977), titled *Equal Rights* in which Tosh pleads for equal rights and justice, singing,

> Everyone is crying out for peace,
> None is crying out for justice
> I don't want no peace
> I need equal rights and justice

The theses of both of songs clearly lay out a call for a fight. This fight, we propose, is an important one that sits squarely in the realm of adult education and demands that adult educators do the work necessary to address oppression and inequity in society, through this fight for equal rights and for justice. One tactical strategy in this fight is to include human rights literacy education in adult education curricula.

We have illustrated, through the frame of the critical literacies advancement model, the interconnectedness of nontraditional literacies and underscored the importance of human rights literacy and propose its inclusion as an integral component of adult education curriculum as a means of taking socially responsible action. This action contributes to the larger discourse on inequities and has the potential to create a shared vocabulary of how equity and social justice are understood or interpreted in society and to support the development of a cadre of skills to help confront inequity and deconstruct seemingly benign social structures that contribute to power relations that threaten social justice. Additionally, human rights literacy has the potential to empower adults, especially those who have been forced to the margins of society, to recover and reclaim political, economic, and social power.

To further support this effort and adult educators more specifically, and because there is no central repository for human rights literacy, we have included links to a variety of applicable resources that may be helpful in getting the process started. It is clear that including human rights education for the development of human rights literacy as a mainstay or building block of adult education curricula is one way to build a future in which there is hope for a just and humane society.

REFERENCES

Action Professionals Association for the People (APAP). (1996). *The bells of freedom.* http://hrlibrary.umn.edu/

Associated Press. (2018, July 3). *Judge tosses Detroit school's case, says no right to literacy.* https://apnews.com/

Baxi, U. (1994, December 9). *Human rights education: The promise of the third millennium?* [Paper presentation]. The Conference of the United Nations Member States and Non-Governmental Organizations, New York, NY, United States.

Becker, A., De Wet, A., & Van Vollenhoven, W. (2015). Human rights literacy: Moving towards rights-based education and transformative action through understandings of dignity, equality and freedom. *South African Journal of Education, 35*(2), 1–12. https://doi.org/10.15700/saje.v35n2a1044

Brookfield, S. D. (1997). Assessing critical thinking. *New Directions for Adult and Continuing Education, 1997*(75), 17–29.

Brown, K. M. (2004). Leadership for social justice and equity: Weaving a transformative framework and pedagogy. *Educational Administration Quarterly, 40*(1), 77–108. https://doi.org/10.1177/0013161X03259147

Brown, K. M. (2006). Leadership for social justice and equity: Evaluating a transformative framework and Andragogy. *Educational Administration Quarterly, 42*(5), 700–745. https://doi.org/10.1177/0013161X06290650

Bruce, B. (1998). New literacies (Technology). *Journal of Adolescent & Adult Literacy, 42*(1), 46–49. https://www.learntechlib.org/

Christopherson, J. (1997). *The growing need for visual literacy at the university.* Selected Readings from the Annual Conference of the International Visual Literacy Association, Cheyenne, WY, United States.

Cole, A. (1976). *War* [Recorded by B. Marley]. On Rastaman Vibration.

Flowers, N. (n.d.). *Human rights here and now: Celebrating the universal declaration of human rights.* http://hrlibrary.umn.edu/

Forester, T. (1987). *High-tech society: The story of the information technology revolution.* The MIT Press.

Freire, P. (1972). *Pedagogy of the oppressed* (M. Bergman Ramos, Trans.). Harmondsworth Penguin. (Original work published 1970)

HRE USA. (2021). *HRE Curriculum Integration Guide.* https://hreusa.org/hre-guide/

Manley, M. (1974). *The politics of change: A Jamaican testament.* Andre Deutsch Limited.

Merriam, S., Caffarella, R., & Baumgartner, L. (2007). *Learning in adulthood: A comprehensive guide* (3rd ed.). John Wiley & Sons.

Mihr, A., & Schmitz, H. P. (2007). Human rights education (HRE) and transnational activism. *Human Rights Quarterly, 29*(4) 973–993. https://www.jstor.org/stable/20072833

New London Group. (1996). A pedagogy of multiliteracies: Designing social futures. *Harvard Educational Review, 66*(1), 60–93. https://english.utk.edu/

Ramirez, F. O., Suárez, D., & Meyer, J. W. (2007). The worldwide rise of human rights education. In A. Benavot, C. Braslavsky, and N. Truong (Eds.), *School knowledge in comparative and historical perspective* (pp. 35–52). Springer.

Robinson, P. A. (2020). *The critical literacies advancement model (CLAM): A framework for promoting positive social change.* https://digitalcommons.lsu.edu/

Robinson, P. A., & Lewis, C. W. (2011). The troubling context of urban education: Instructional design as a source of transformation for students of color. *Journal of Curriculum and Pedagogy 2*(8), 109–112. https://doi.org/10.1080/15505170.2011.624889

Robinson, P. A., Rice, D., Stoddart, D., & Alfred, M. V. (2013). Lifelong learning in Jamaica: Coherent pathways to higher education. *International Journal of Scholarly Academic Diversity, 1*(15), 1–11. http://www.nationalforum.com/

Roux, C. (2019). The 'literacy turn' in human rights and human rights education. In C. Roux & A. Becker (Eds.), *Human rights literacies: Future directions* (pp. 3–30). Springer.

Sturges, P., & Gastinger, A. (2010). Information literacy as a human right. *Libri, 60*(3), 195–202.

The Education Deficit. (2016, June). *Failures to protect and fulfill the right to education through global development agendas.* https://www.hrw.org/

Tibbitts, F., & Fernekes, W. R. (2011). *Human rights education.* In S. Totten & J. E. Pedersen (Eds.), *Teaching and studying social issues: Major programs and approaches* (pp. 87–117). Information Age Publishing.

Tosh, P. (1977). *Equal rights* [Recorded by P. Tosh]. On Equal Rights. Columbia Records.

United Nations. (1948). *Universal declaration of human rights.* https://www.un.org/

United Nations. (1998, January 30). *Human rights common language of humanity, secretary-general says in message launching season of non-violence.* https://www.un.org/

United Nations. (2020). *Sustainable development goal 4.* https://sdg4education2030.org/

United Nations. (n.d.). *Human rights.* https://www.un.org/

United Nations Human Rights Office of the High Commissioner (OHCHR). (2010, July 27). *Plan of action for the second phase (2010–2014) of the World Programme for Human Rights Education.* https://www.ohchr.org/

UNESCO. (2009). *101 good practices in human rights education.* http://www.unesco.org/

UNESCO. (n.d.). *Literacy.* https://en.unesco.org/

Venezky, R. L. (1990). Definitions of literacy. In R. L. Venezky, D. A. Wagner, & B. S. Ciliberti (Eds.), *Toward defining literacy* (pp. 2–16). International Reading Association.

Vienna Declaration and Programme of Action. (1993). https://www.ohchr.org/

Wilson, A. L. & Cervero, R. M. (2001). Adult education and the struggle for knowledge and power: Practical action in a critical tradition, *Adult Education Research Conference.* https://newprairiepress.org/

CHAPTER 2

INTEGRAL GLOBAL LEADERSHIP EDUCATION FOR HUMAN RIGHTS, TRANSFORMATION, AND SUSTAINABILITY

Wanda Krause
Royal Roads University, Canada

The COVID-19 crisis brought increasing recognition of the numerous, shared, global challenges that face humanity. It is critical we cultivate the requisite human capabilities required to lead change around the world. In this chapter, because we share these complex, interconnected global challenges, I argue that higher education institutions have an increasing responsibility and role to play in influencing positive change through the promotion of leadership-oriented educational programs. I suggest higher education's role lies in developing the leadership capabilities that are essential for transformational and "integral" change. Thus, this chapter centers on the question: How can we better prepare global leadership who can advance an *integral* agenda?

Leadership programs focused on *integral thinking* can equip and prepare students to navigate turbulent times and become more adaptable, nimble,

Advancing the Global Agenda for Human Rights, Vulnerable Populations, and Environmental Sustainability: Adult Education as Strategic Partner, pp. 19–33
Copyright © 2021 by Information Age Publishing
19

and resilient. Such leadership capabilities also align with the pursuit of the United Nations' 17 Sustainable Development Goals (SDGs). These 17 SDGs aim to address complex global challenges and intractable social problems. This agenda is focused on ensuring the flourishing of individuals, families, societies, and a healthy planet. The SDG change framework also recognizes the significance of individual behavior and actions in seeking solutions to the world's most pressing issues.

My overall goal in this chapter is to present a framework and approach that can help us prepare new leadership who can advance an agenda for positive change in the world. First, I will touch on some of the global challenges relevant to the field of adult education. Then, I introduce an *integral framework*, referenced as the *all quadrants all levels* (AQAL) model, that can serve as a guide for educators in developing curriculum and educational practices that promote global development toward mutual benefit, planetary leadership in solution-seeking, and adaptive change. Next, I present an overview of key principles of an *integral leadership mindset* and methodology. Finally, I close with a discussion focused on "integral" and "global" perspectives, and how we might realize a vision of integral leadership in education.

GLOBAL PERSPECTIVES IN ADULT EDUCATION

A global perspective is one that sees beyond issues as isolated phenomena within local contexts. Hence, it is also one in which the logic used to make sense of the world is inclusive and integrates many different perspectives, ways of seeing, doing, and being. Our current times call for the teaching, learning, and dissemination of knowledge, skills, and capabilities that transcend linear thinking and narrowly defined disciplinary knowledge. Such an education requires a conceptual framework and dynamic approach situated within a rigorous learning context.

There are no quick fixes to the issues we face globally, such as human rights abuses, disease contagion, economic disparity, climate change, mobility and refugee crises, homelessness, human trafficking, or war and unrest, to name only a few. Our world presents us many "wicked problems." The concept of *wicked problems* originated in organizational planning literature (Rittel & Webber, 1973), but has also been used to describe emerging societal and policy problems that do not neatly fit with the conventional models of policy analysis (Peters, 2017). These emerging problems were defined as "complex" because they involve "multiple possible causes and internal dynamics that could not be assumed to be linear, and have very negative consequences for society if not addressed properly" (Peters, 2017, p. 385). *Wicked problems* are characterized as being difficult to pinpoint and define, and the leading cause of such problems (usually humans) is also expected to be a part of finding tenable solutions (Thatcher et al., 2020). In order to learn how to solve these problems, we need to study the complex relationships that contribute to such matters; the involvement and influence of powerful actors and forces; and how they impact individuals, communities, and societies around the world.

Most disciplines adhere to a dominant paradigm of thought characterized by either/or thinking and false binaries; the separation of humans from nature; conceptual fragmentation that categorizes material, social, and spiritual worlds as set apart from each other; and the isolation of the individual from their community context (Berzonsky & Moser, 2017). The result of such false dichotomies has been a human capital paradigm that over-focuses on the individual and economic growth at the expense of collective life, well-being and health, social inclusion and civic participation, and environmental sustainability. In addition to material and economic matters (Krause, 2012, 2018), cultural sensitivity is paramount, and the social and political aspects of the environment must also be taken into consideration (Earley & Ang, 2003; Eisen, 2015; Krause, 2012; Masakowski, 2018; Terlizzi, 2014). Sensitivity to the cultural, sociopolitical, and economic aspects within the global context must help inform an understanding of, and take into consideration, the multifaceted and diverse nature of the collective struggle in addressing, navigating, refusing, and transforming these interdependent relationships. Cultural sensitivity and awareness of these complexities are key in developing effective and socially conscientious leadership (Earley & Ang, 2003; Masakowski, 2018; Van Dyne et al., 2012). Peters (2017) further argued that while many scholars and leaders acknowledge the emergence of complex challenges and wicked problems, seeking to define them, a substantial gap persists in reference to developing and operationalizing possible solutions. This chapter attempts to touch on this gap by introducing an educational framework that promotes the development of key leadership capabilities necessary for addressing the world's wicked problems. The imperative is to bring a global and multifaceted worldview into the educational environment.

AN INTEGRAL AND GLOBAL FRAMEWORK

The purpose of articulating an integral, global conceptual framework is multifaceted. Addressing economic, social, and ecological issues that often appear intractable requires an approach that respects the world's complexities and interdependent nature. Wilber (2007) argued that in order to find solutions to the world's most vexing problems, humankind needs to rely on the integration and application of many different forms of knowledge.

A more encompassing conceptualization of the world must acknowledge that many of our intransigent problems are transnational, meaning neither do they respect the arbitrary borders between countries nor the differences in humankind's understanding of them. An integral, global interpretation of the world would aim to integrate multiple forms of knowledge into a more transdisciplinary and holistic lens serving as a guide to addressing the multidimensional problems of increasing threat.

Wilber (2007) presented a comprehensive, chronological map of the evolution of the individual, society, and the biosphere since the beginning of history that brings together multiple worldviews, forming what he refers to as "global and integral" visions. In his conceptual map of the world, which he described as encompassing "all quadrants, all levels, all states, and all lines," Wilber integrated world views from religion, psychology, sociology, Eastern and Western philosophy, and science to present an alternative representation of basically "everything we know" (Hardman, 2009 ; Wilber, 2007). Such an "integral" framework situates human history and progressive educational concepts within a larger transdisciplinary web of ideas (Murray 2009).

Akin to Bronfenbrenner's (1979) systems view, which argued the importance of comprehending individual development in relationship to their context and environment, an integral approach also works to explore the evolving interactions between interrelated systems. Bonfrenbrenner defined development as "a lasting change in the way a person perceives and deals with his environment" (p. 3). This imperative of considering the individual in relation to others and their environment helps in mapping these reciprocal influences. The notion of one's *lifeworld* (German: *Lebenswelt;* Treitel, 2000) also described the way in which individuals experience (German: *erleben;* Treitel, 2000), interact with, and make sense of their surrounding contexts and world, and emphasized that individual development occurs in relationship to others and to their social and material environments. Together, these concepts offer an integrated and interdependent ecological perspective of human development.

A focus on human situatedness is important because it is often neglected in wider efforts to support human development. An integral worldview offers a way for individuals to map the self in relationship to these wider systems and to strategize how facilitating learning at the individual level can work toward more effective problem-solving and personal and societal transformation. To recognize the individual within the broader systems and the context from which they emerge, and understanding how individuals might also influence these systems, is a critical, first step toward addressing such problems.

Autonomous agency and subjectivity broadly refer to the ability of an individual or entity to act upon another entity with conscious intentionality

(Allen, 2002). Foucault and colleagues (1988) argued that individuals can effect change on their own "bodies and souls, thoughts, conduct and way of being, to transform themselves in order to attain a certain state of happiness, purity, wisdom, perfection" (p. 18). It is this individual agency and ability to learn how to effectively function within one's lifeworld that is of importance, as a primary mechanism toward catalyzing change. Kraus (2015) noted, however, that one's subjectivity is, in fact, strongly influenced by the world or environment in which one operates, and by the social and material conditions of their reality.

One significant advantage of Wilber's (2007) integral perspective is that it offers a conceptual framework to help individuals think about issues related to one's own personal health and well-being within the wider systems of planetary health. At this particular juncture in human history, lifelong learning and higher education programs may be able to play pivotal role in cultivating an integral, solution-seeking mindset where people can learn to lead change, not only through effectiveness, efficiency, performance, and impact, but also, more significantly, as human development and growth focused on mutuality and interdependence. Knowing how best to support individual and collective well-being, and how to collaboratively create change, requires identifying the key factors for enhancing global perspectives in adult education. The conceptual framework I am putting forward as a foundation for leadership education follows from integral global theory's quadrant model and stages of development.

INTEGRAL MODELS FOR DEVELOPMENT

Bronfenbrenner (1979) suggested that "within each culture and subculture there exist[s] a blueprint for the organization for every type of setting" (p. 4), or discernable patterns that help in understanding how different aspects of the world interrelate. In a similar vein of thinking, an "integral approach" essentially provides a map for understanding the world. As a result of this map's applicability across, within, and between disciplinary boundaries, integral global theory (hereafter referred to as IGT) has been widely embraced by individuals associated with a variety of fields. These include art, business, ecology medicine, consciousness studies, religion, criminology, psychology, healthcare, nursing, politics, and sustainability among others (Esbjörn-Hargens, 2011).

IGT's signature phrase "all-quadrants, all-levels," often referred to as the *AQAL model*, is shorthand for the multiple interrelating aspects of reality taken into consideration within an integral approach (Wilber, 1995, 2003). *Integral* means comprehensive, balanced, and inclusive (Wilber et al., 2008). The AQAL model helps reveal four key dimensions of the world:

(1) the internal spheres of the individual psychology, spirituality, mental models, and worldview, (2) the physicality of individuals and their outward behaviours and actions, (3) the collective or cultural domain of a society, and (4) the sociostructural systems, institutions, and environmental drivers (see Table 2.1).

Table 2.1

Integral AQAL Model of the Individual and Collective

The interior of the individual (I)	*The exterior of the individual (IT)*
• Understanding • How we organize reality, make meaning of the world, reason (action logics) • Values • Subjective process of inquiry • States of being INDIVIDUAL VALUES	• Actions • Skills • Techniques • Roles • Background • Performance COMPETENCY/BEHAVIOR
The interior of the collective (WE)	*Systems & structures (ITS)*
1. Shared worldviews 1. Values we hold (i.e., belonging, trust, reciprocity, tolerance, collaboration) 1. Process of participation and inclusion CULTURE	• Rules • Policies • Laws • Economic, social, political structures • Paradigms ENVIRONMENT/SYSTEMS

In this chapter, I primarily focus on the quadrants and levels of development. The four quadrants include individual, interior or "self-change" (upper left, UL, quadrant); collective interior or "cultural change" (lower left, LL); individual exterior or "behavioral change" (upper right, UR); and collective exterior or "systems change" (lower right, LR). Internal change and growth can occur on the individual level (see Table 2.1, UL); or on a collective, group, organizational, or nation-wide level (LL). Meadows (1999) asserted that the internal, individual level can be a key leverage point for engendering change, as it is where individual well-being and happiness reside. Internalized change, however, not only constitutes individual, subjective experience, but is also embedded within the cultural norms (LL) and patterned interactions of their external environments (LR).

The two quadrants on the left (UL, LL) that focus on internal meaning-making help us think about how a person perceives from their personal, subjective experience, and how cultures inform human understanding and interaction. Unfortunately, the upper-left quadrant, which focuses on internal, individual experience and meaning-making, is largely absent in organizational strategic planning, operation of social institutions, and larger global initiatives. Inclusive educational curricula that incorporate both UL and LL perspectives can help individuals learn more about themselves, their contextualized experiences, and their cultural situatedness. Such curricula also support the exploration of the connections between these levels of understanding, and growth in in people's awareness of their interconnectedness within their local contexts and the world.

Such educational curricula must be able to articulate how it will help students develop awareness and cognitive tools to peel back layers of individual bias, and cultural assumptions about the self, others, and the world. This "peeling back" facilitates the development of the capability to see from multiple perspectives, essentially enhancing their ability for greater growth. It is equally important to explore the shared ideas and collective minds of a society (Meadows, 1999), represented in AQAL's lower left quadrant (see Table 2.1, LL). As viewed through the social collective, we can also map how growth occurs through the interaction of individuals with one another and within their social and cultural environments.

Curricula situated in the LL quadrant would promote interdependent learning focused on generating a shared understanding of the pivotal social roles in advancing health and well-being for all, serving as a key building block for planetary health. One key challenge in this quadrant is centered around building tolerance and acceptance. Within the LL quadrant, individuals can begin to shift their thinking away from "us versus them" orientation, and begin to identify and build commonalities between peoples. Intercultural capabilities can be enhanced through educational curricula that focus on accepting that individuals and groups may have different ways of knowing, being, and doing, and acknowledging how these all add to the tapestry of humanity. Intercultural capabilities must progress beyond mere tolerance toward the acceptance and appreciation of the different facets of humanity. Educators can, for example, strive to move away from fear-based thinking toward mutual understanding, acceptance, and curiosity, and ultimately to the appreciation and synthesis of the different ways of being, doing, and seeing. Such capabilities are particularly important when addressing the wicked problems that we face locally and on a planetary level.

INTEGRAL GLOBAL LEADERSHIP PROGRAMMING

Wheatley (2005) defined the current state of reality as "the era of many messes. We have created some of these (although not intentionally) because we act on assumptions that can never engender healthy, sustainable societies and organizations" (p. 2). In a turbulent or chaotic context, the relationships between cause and effect are difficult to determine, shifting constantly, making it difficult to identify solutions. Masakowski (2018) argued that leaders are often presented with crises for which there are no blueprints or sets of rules for managing them. Be that as it may, climate change, infectious diseases and pandemics, and escalating racism all offer opportunities for meaningful growth into leadership. In order to cultivate leadership with the necessary capabilities to advance a socially conscious agenda within our increasingly complex world, I further elaborate some key elements of IGT leadership education.

Education is central to teaching leaders how to succeed (Masakowski 2018). The collective political will to intervene through a curriculum that embraces an integral mindset, however, is nearly impossible as long as the deepest underlying values and paradigms of thought remain beyond societal inspection (Berzonsky & Mozer, 2017). Educational curricula must seek to identify and engender awareness of basic human rights—a fundamental condition for respect and reverence for planetary health, transformation, and sustainability—and map how these are fundamentally interrelated. IGT leadership curricula are meant to support transformational change through conscientization, whereby the individual, at the microlevel, cannot be disconnected from planetary health, at the macrolevel. To bridge the individual microlevel with the macroplanetary level, the IGT perspective highlights the role of subjectivity in shaping the individual who can promote both individual and planetary thriving through one's own daily practice. Based on the AQAL model, I elucidate the learning dispositions of *conscientization* and *planetary health*.

Conscientization

The AQAL framework undergirds learning practices for cultivating dispositions toward greater global consciousness and planetary health. In adult education, we often refer to the notion of conscientization as part and parcel of individual and social transformation. *Conscientization* comes from the Portuguese word *conscientizacio´n*, which means to perceive the dialectic unity between the self and the object (Freire, 1970). It also conveys the idea of developing, strengthening, and changing one's consciousness. It is a "mobilization of consciousness aiming to produce critical historical knowledge about oneself, and about the groups to which one belongs, thereby producing a new understanding and giving sense to one's temporal and spatial place in society, from one's specific lifeworld" (Montero, 2009, pp. 72–73). Cultivating conscientization establishes the link between the self and systems. Adult learning can serve as a context where conscienti-zation is exercised as a way of cultivating leadership as a disposition of leading-the-self before leading others, one's community, or initiatives to address indomitable problems on the macrolevel.

This IGT dispositional learning approach offers "a powerful content-free framework that is suitable to virtually any context, can be used at any scale [and it] allows the practitioner to select the most relevant and important tools, techniques, and insights" (Esbjörn-Hargens, 2010, p. 33). Instead of the conventional delivery of content-driven curricula, the IGT approach seeks to promote integral ways of thinking in relationship to vari-ous subjects, but also ways to think about one's everyday lived experience. Conscientization can also contribute to a broader, macrolevel ethic-of-care (Noddings, 2013) that extends the understanding of the self within systems, mapping how socially conscious leadership can influence the promotion of global human rights and the empowerment of marginalized populations.

Planetary Health

The aspiration of planetary health requires a broader, macrolevel ethic-of-care and supports the state of the natural systems on which our civilization depends. Cultivating this leadership disposition works toward safeguarding planetary health and all whose well-being depends on it. *Planetary health* is defined as:

> The achievement of the highest attainable standard of health, wellbeing, and equity worldwide through judicious attention to the human systems— political, economic, and social—that shape the future of humanity and the Earth's natural systems that define the safe environmental limits within which humanity can flourish. (Horton & Lo, 2015, p. 1921)

A planetary health orientation sees all parts as supporting the whole, moving from "seeing parts to seeing wholes, from seeing people as help-less reactors to seeing them as active participants in shaping their reality" (Senge, 2006, p. 69).

Horton and Lo (2015) asserted that we grossly underestimate the intricate interplay of environmental, political, and sociocultural resil-ience. "The threats that our species faces are not abstract physical risks.... The risks we face lie within ourselves and the societies we have created" (p. 2021). They echoed Butzer's (2012) ardent call to focus on influenc-ing "leaders, elites, and ideology" as a way of fostering planetary health. A recent report from the Rockefeller Foundation-Lancet Commission on Planetary Health also amplified the need for leadership to work toward the UN's SDGs for improved planetary health. Addressing such wicked problems and pursuing the SDGs, however, requires a multidimensional perspective and multidisciplinary leadership.

Leadership Education

The cultivation of conscientious, self-aware leadership within broader systems squarely fits within the purview of educational institutions: adult, lifelong, and higher learning present valuable opportunities to promote such leadership. IGT leadership education can help individuals transform their worldview and better understand how to support long-term and sustainable change. An IGT approach means considering all the pieces that build a whole and healthy individual; fostering a positive culture that places equality, diversity, and inclusion at the heart of education; and influencing policies, structures, governance systems, and economic conditions to support human rights and empowerment. IGT leadership development must be conceived in terms of dispositions that promote concrete actions across each level of lived reality, and encompassing all four AQAL quadrants.

By categorizing these spheres of growth into quadrants, we can map, plan, and better grasp what tools to use to support individual well-being and empowerment. For example, the two quadrants on the left side of the AQAL model allow educators to map and plan learning that advances an appreciation and celebration of human diversity by breaking down the various biases we hold individually (UL), and jointly pursuing equity and inclusion as part of our collective existence (LL). It is in these two quadrants where inclusion can be cultivated by addressing the phenomenon of unconscious (or implicit) bias. Unconscious bias occurs when people rely on assumptions about other people and situations, and make rapid and automatic judgments without conscious awareness. These assumptions and judgments are informed by people's upbringing and the educational, social, political, and economic environments that shaped their formative years; their past and current cultural environments; and their individual experiences and internal states. IGT leadership education informed by the UL quadrant of the AQAL model supports learning empathy, peeling back the layers of our own biases for greater self-awareness, building conscientiousness, and taking greater steps toward practicing an ethic-of-care in our judgment and actions.

The detection and development of wide-ranging leadership capabilities can only occur if we use a theoretical model that also renders these behaviors into visible action (Bronfenbrenner, 1979). In order to promote the leadership capabilities that contribute to transformation, human flourishing, and sustainability (LR), we must also be able to systematically map the desirable, individual actions and behaviors (UR). People's resulting individual actions and behaviors (UR) then contribute to and impact their communities and cultures (LL). Adults learning how to become IGT leaders (UL) can work to influence and create the social conditions, contexts, and drivers (LL) that promote healthier, more conscientious actions (UR), which ultimately work toward collective, global well-being and planetary health (LR).

Educators endeavouring to support positive change in the world want their students to grow into leaders operating from mature developmental stages or "action logics" (UL) (see Torbert et al., 2004). Kegan (1982) argued that human development is not merely about learning new things, but rather entails periods of significant worldview transformation (UL). People can develop more inclusive worldviews with which they can think, see, and act as individuals, but also to inform their interactions with others, their communities, and for greater social impact (UR) (Mezirow). Kohlberg (1981) also suggested there are stages of adult moral development (UL), and that advanced moral reasoning is a precursor to ethical behaviour (UR). These human development theories suggest that individual subjectivity and internal development (UL) form the basis for people's observable behaviors (UR). Therefore, these human development stages can assist educators in locating and understanding people's current worldviews, and guide the design of relevant learning and working experiences (Kegan, 1982).

As several IGT theorists contend, certain stages of personal growth are imperative for sustainability in leadership (Brown, 2011; Robinson, 2018; Torbert et al., 2004). Individuals occupying more mature stages (Brown, 2011; Leonard, 2004; Robinson, 2018) who have developed more inclusive mindsets (UL), are also more likely to possess the necessary capabilities to make contributions to sustainability initiatives (UR). Even so, such personal growth occurs continuously over time. Educational institutions that offer a framework for learning that emphasizes how individuals, organizations, and systems progress through stages of development are better positioned to generate leaders who will think in terms of complexity (Brown, 2011; Robinson, 2018). Murray (2009) explained:

> "Integral" can be seen as pointing to four things: a (meta-) model or framework (a system of concepts for interpreting the world), a methodology (a set of injunctions or principles for inquiring about the world), a community (the embodied group or groups of people using integral models and methods), and/or a set of skills or capacities (a developmental stage that points past modern and post-modern cultural perspectives, and past formal operational modes of thinking). (p. 2)

IGT leadership education supports development within all quadrants to foster well-being and health of the individual, collective, and system at all levels.

Unfortunately, many educational programs and curricula fail to address all four AQAL quadrants; to emphasize how they are necessarily interrelated; and to explain why it is essential to understand these connections for IGT leadership. Most disciplines tend to focus thinking and action within one of the four quadrants and neglect the others. For example, education tends to focus on individual, internal meaning-making, or the UL quadrant, although it should be clear that all quadrants are directly implicated in human learning and development. Similarly, disciplines tend to focus on one of the levels, neglecting the rest (e.g., psychology vs. sociology). The field of education tends to focus on the individual as the unit-of-analysis of interest, often overlooking the cultural, organizational, and macrostructural levels. Disciplines often fail to consider the other levels and quadrants, and how these interrelate when it comes to adult learning and leadership development. An IGT framework is needed to integrate the siloed disciplines into multidisciplinary problem-solving. The goal is to support transformation in a world of perceived chaos.

An IGT perspective can help advance leadership within education, the workplace, and communities. Intentionally learning and working from an IGT perspective helps cultivate increased awareness of our shared challenges globally, though we may choose to seek solutions locally. It contributes to a conscientious disposition and intentionality of action which are key means for creating a healthier, more secure, civil, and peaceful world. IGT leadership development also works to expand the concept and study of change and transformations beyond the local context toward global consciousness and systems' interconnections. To identify and create the opportunities necessary in cultivating individual, collective, and planetary well-being, IGT leadership education and its conception of human rights, societal transformation, and ecological sustainability has become a categorical learning imperative.

CONCLUSION

In recent decades, on the one hand, we have witnessed notable developments in the direction of greater equality for marginalized and racialized groups and improved awareness of the impact we have on the planet. On the other, the year 2020 revealed the growing disparities in social, economic, and health equity; the ever-present reality of the oppression of marginalized and racialized groups; and the continuing devastation of the planet. The literature emerging from the COVID-19 pandemic illustrated the differential impacts on health and economy for women, and the rampant systematized racism inherent in societies that threatens our collective well-being. The Black Lives Matter movement, once again, highlighted the glaring and pervasive human rights abuses against Blacks in the United States and globally. The AQAL model can help us seek more nuanced, complex understandings of how human thought and behaviors in all quadrants and across all levels contribute to the systemic oppression of Black, Indigenous, and Peoples of Color.

Such efforts necessarily require and must involve changes in our values and ways of thinking about the world (Berzonsky & Moser, 2017). Based on the AQAL model, the proposed IGT approach offered in this chapter works toward cultivating more sustainable leadership development through adult and higher education. Through IGT leadership, we will be better equipped to contribute to positive change in the world, address the lack of human rights globally, and provide a roadmap for greater ecological sustainability. Change within one area will be difficult to sustain if it is not complimented with changes in the other areas. Learning how to do this must also happen in the workplace and within our communities, and a place to grow the necessary and associated capabilities for sustainable leadership can be well served through adult learning and higher education.

REFERENCES

Allen, A. (2002). Power, subjectivity, and agency: Between Arendt and Foucault. *International Journal of Philosophical Studies, 10*(2), 131–49.

Berzonsky, C. L., & Moser, S. C. (2017). Becoming homo sapiens sapiens: Mapping the psycho-cultural transformation in the anthropocene. *Anthropocene, 20,* 15–23.

Bronfenbrenner, U. (1979). *The ecology of human development: Experiments by nature and design.* Harvard University Press.

Brown, B. C. (2011). *Conscious leadership for sustainability: How leaders with late-stage action logics design and implement sustainability initiatives* [Doctoral dissertation]. Fielding Graduate University.

Butzer, K.W. (2012, March). Collapse, environment, and society. *Proceedings of the National Academy of Sciences, 109*(10), 3632–3639.

Earley, P. C., & Ang, S. (2003). *Cultural intelligence: Individual interactions across cultures.* Stanford University Press.

Eisen, S. (2015). Raumschach negotiations. In M. McFate & J. H. Laurence (Eds.), *Social sciences goes to war* (pp. 331–354). Oxford University Press.

Esbjörn-Hargens, S. (2010). *Integral theory in action: Applied, theoretical, and constructive perspectives on the AQAL model.* State University of New York Press.

Esbjörn-Hargens, S. (2011, April). Integral teacher, integral students, integral classroom: Applying integral theory to education. *Next Step Integral,* 1–42.

Foucault, M., Martin, L. H., Gutman, H., & Hutton, P. H. (1988). *Technologies of the self: A seminar with Michel Foucault*. University of Massachusetts Press.

Freire, P. (1970). *Pedagogy of the oppressed*. Herder & Herder.

Hardman, G. J. (2009). Regenerative leadership: An integral theory for transforming. *Future, 31*(3), 15–22.

Horton, R., & Lo, S. (2015). Planetary health: A new science for exceptional action. *Lancet, 386*(10007), 1921–1922.

Kegan, R. (1982). *The evolving self.* Harvard University Press.

Kohlberg, L. (1981). *Essays on moral development, Vol. I: The philosophy of moral development*. Harper & Row.

Krause, W. (2012). *Civil society and women activists in the Middle East*. I. B. Tauris.

Kraus, B. (2015). The life we live and the life we experience: Introducing the epistemological difference between "lifeworld" (lebenswelt) and "life conditions" (lebenslage). *Social Work and Society. International Online Journal, 13*(2). http://www.socwork.net/sws/article/view/438

Krause, W. (2018). Leadership lessons from women in high-risk environments. In S. Steffen, S. Rappaport, & S. Trevenna (Eds.), *Evolving leadership for a sustainable future: A path to collective wellbeing* (pp. 83–98). Emerald.

Leonard, A. (2004). *Integral communication* [Doctoral dissertation]. University of Florida. http://www.integral-life-practice.com/wpcontent/uploads/2011/06/integral-communication_by_adam_b_leonard.pdf

Masakowski, Y. (2018). Inclusive leadership and the dynamics of multinational military operations. In J. L. Chin, J. E. Trimble, & J. E. Garcia (Eds.), *Global and culturally diverse leaders and leadership: New dimensions and challenges for business, education and society* (pp. 233–252). Emerald.

Meadows, D. (1999). *Leverage points: Places to intervene in a system*. The Sustainability Institute. http://donellameadows.org/wp-content/userfiles/ Leverage_Points.pdf

Montero, M. (2009). Methods for liberation: Critical consciousness in action. In M. Montero & C. Sonn (Eds.), *Psychology of liberation* (pp. 73–92). Springer.

Murray, T. (2009, June). What is the integral in integral education, *Integral Review, 5*(1), 96–134.

Noddings, N. (2013). *Caring: A relational to ethics and moral education*. University of California Press.

Peters, G. B. (2017). What is so wicked about wicked problems? A conceptual analysis and a research program. *Policy and Society, 36*(3), 385–396.

Rittel, H. W. J., & Webber, M. M. (1973). Dilemmas in the general theory of planning. *Policy Sciences, 4,* 155–169.

Robinson, J. (2018). *Reimagining sustainability leadership for this historical moment* [Master's thesis]. Royal Roads University.

Senge, P. (2006). *The fifth discipline: The art & practice of the learning organization*. Crown Business.

Terlizzi, A. (2014). Cross-cultural competence and civil-military operations. In R. G. Sands & A. Greene-Sands (Eds.), *Cross-cultural competence for a twenty-first-century military* (pp. 131–139). Lexington Books.

Thatcher, A., Lang-Morales, K., Garcia-Acosta, G. (2020). A future ethical stance for HFE toward sustainability. In A. Thatcher, K. Zink, & K. Fischer, K. (Eds.), *Human factors for sustainability* (pp. 51–74). CRC Press, Taylor & Francis Group.

Torbert, B., Cook-Greuter, S., Fisher, D., Foldy, E., Gauthier, A., Keeley, J., Ross, S., Royce, C., Rudolph, J., Taylor, S., & Tran, M. (2004). *Action inquiry: The secret of timely and transforming leadership*. Berrett-Koehler.

Treitel, C. (2000). The culture of knowledge in the metropolis of science, spiritualism and liberalism in fin-de-siècle Berlin. In C. Goschler (Ed.), *Wissenschaft und* Öffentlichkeit *in Berlin*, 1870–1930 (pp. 127–155). Franz Steiner.

Van Dyne, L., Ang, S., Ng, K.-Y., Rockstuhl, T., Tan, M.L., & Koh, C. (2012). Sub-dimension of the four-factor model of cultural intelligence: Expanding the conceptualization and measurement of cultural intelligence. *Social and Personal Psychology Compass, 6*(4), 295–313.

Wheatley, M. J. (2005). *Finding our way: Leadership for an uncertain time*. Berrett-Koehler.

Wilber, K. (1995). An informal overview of transpersonal studies. *The Journal of Transpersonal Psychology, 27*(2), 107.

Wilber, K. (2003). *Excerpt D from the Kosmos Trilogy, Vol. 2: The look of a feeling: the importance of post/structuralism.* http://wilber.shambhala.com/html/books/kosmos/excerptD.

Wilber, K. (2007). *A theory of everything: An integral vision for business, politics, science, and spirituality* (2nd ed.). Shambhala.

Wilber, K., Patten, T., Leonard, A. & Morelli, M. (2008). *Integral life practice: A 21st century blueprint for physical healthy, emotional balance, mental clarity, and spiritual awakening.* Integral Books.

CHAPTER 3

PROMOTING ANTIBULLYISM TO ADVANCE HUMAN RIGHTS AND SOCIAL JUSTICE FOR SEXUAL MINORITIES THROUGH ADULT AND HIGHER EDUCATION

An Antibullyist Approach

Mitsunori Misawa
The University of Tennessee, United States

The United Nations Educational, Scientific and Cultural Organization (UNESCO), one of the most influential organizations focusing on human rights and globalization under the United Nation (UN) for over 70 years, has at its foundation that human rights are fundamental rights for all people on Earth to be able to live as full human beings. Integral to that belief has been the development of frameworks for advocating and practicing human rights so that every human being is able to live in and contribute to society without any malicious penalties because of where they were born

Advancing the Global Agenda for Human Rights, Vulnerable Populations, and Environmental Sustainability: Adult Education as Strategic Partner, pp. 35–47
Copyright © 2021 by Information Age Publishing
All rights of reproduction in any form reserved.

and who they are. These ideas are based on humanistic and progressive thought that considers all people to be essentially good. Human rights ensure everyone is fully able to participate in society to make it better for all (Kruger et al., 2015), to contribute to society to make it better (Armstrong et al., 2010), and to advance social justice in society. This fundamental notion of human rights is important because it gives us a mutual understanding that we as global citizens have the potential to contribute to the global society with harmony and peace.

However, human rights are often ignored or discarded when conflicts and fights among individuals (the micro), communities (the mezzo), and nations (the macro) take place (Austin et al., 2005; Singer & Sage, 2015). One contemporary sociocultural problem that runs contrary to the human rights agenda is bullying. Bullying is endemic and widespread across the world (Namie & Namie, 2009) and has become a critical social problem in contemporary society including adult and higher education (Misawa & Rowland, 2015; Washington, 2015). It impacts not only individuals who are the targets or victims of bullying, but also organizations and society at large. Researchers and scholars have identified and agreed that bullying damages individuals and groups both physically and psychologically (Misawa, 2017; Randall, 2001). Although the term *bullying* is often associated with developmental issues of children, it also appears in adulthood and carries into adult and higher education where adolescents and adults come to learn, teach, and work (Keashly & Neuman, 2010). However, the term is often used to capture bullying generically, which means it is treated as one size-fits-all category and does not capture specific types of bullying such as gendered bullying (Gilbert et al., 2013; Johnson-Bailey, 2015; Misawa et al., 2019), racial bullying (Fox & Stallworth, 2005), homophobic bullying (Misawa, 2017; Rivers, 2011), or the intersectionality of those types (Misawa, 2015, 2017).

When addressing homophobic bullying or bullying based one's sexual orientation, it is important to consider sociocultural contexts where sexual orientations and sexualities are addressed. Sexual minorities who are lesbian, gay, bisexual, and queer (LGBQ) populations, have historically been discriminated against and marginalized in societies, with only a few countries having legalized same-sex marriage or civil unions or decriminalized same-sex relationships (Englander, 2011). Even in countries that have legalized same-sex marriage, sexual minorities still experience discrimination and homophobic bullying. If contemporary adult and higher education should focus on equity, diversity, inclusion, and social justice, then scholars and practitioners should focus on how they can reduce and eliminate homophobia, heterosexism, and homophobic bullying (Hill & Grace, 2009; Rivers, 2011). The purpose of this book chapter is to examine the type of bullying related to sexual orientation and dig into antibullyist practices that can promote and advance human rights and social justice for sexual minorities within adult and higher education. The term *sexual minorities* will be used throughout this chapter to refer to LGBQ populations. The author of this chapter understands that there have been lively discourses among scholars in social sciences, gender studies, and LGBT studies about usages of the term *sexual minorities* and *LGBQ*. However, because the section of the book is about human rights for minorities, this chapter will specifically focus on sexual minorities such as lesbians, gays, bisexuals, and queers, their human rights and antibullyism. This chapter will first address relevant literature on human rights and sustainability for sexual minorities. Then, it will focus on bullying and homophobic bullying and how bullying influences sexual minorities. Last, this chapter will address implications for adult and higher education practitioners regarding homophobic bullying in their research and practice that can help them reduce and minimize homophobic bullying.

RELEVANT LITERATURE

While bullying has been an important topic and has become more popular to discuss in social sciences, like education including adult and higher education, it still needs some background within the scope of human rights, particularly homophobic bullying. This section will explore some aspects of human rights from a global perspective including the definition by UNESCO, sustainability, multiculturalism, and diversity and will address bullying in general and homophobic bullying.

Human Rights in UNESCO

Human rights are fundamental rights to everyone everywhere. UNESCO was the first agency of the United Nations to adopt "the Universal Declaration of Human Rights on 10 December 1948, that has clear implications in every field of the organization's activities, education, natural and social and human sciences, culture, and communications and information" (UNESCO, 2020a, para. 6). UNESCO deals with five specific human rights within the UN system: the right to education, the right to take part in cultural life, the right to enjoy the benefits of scientific progress, the right to freedom of opinion and expression, and the right to water and sanitation. In particular, UNESCO promotes cultural and social aspects of human rights as "many very important cultural rights, which should be given equal attention, such as the right to participate in cultural life, enjoy one's culture, etc." (UNESCO, 2020b, para. 3). Based on UNESCO's notion of human rights, human rights are for and to all people with an understanding of our various positionalities and sociocultural identities in society. Human rights intrinsically value and appreciate differences and are important social and cultural rights that allow everyone to participate in various cultures as global citizens. According to the UNESCO, human rights are fundamental rights that are:

> inherent to all human beings, regardless of race, sex, nationality, ethnicity, language, religion, or any other status. Human rights include the right to life and liberty, freedom from slavery and torture, freedom of opinion and expression, the right to work and education, and many more. Everyone is entitled to these rights, without discrimination. (United Nations, n.d.)

Although this definition of human rights provided by UNESCO sounds appropriate and seems to be inclusive for sustaining a harmony among diverse societies and nations with diverse cultures globally, these "everyone's rights" have often not been provided or protected in our history. Human rights for minorities were often violated by majorities with horrible historical outcomes in terms of how people treated others. People's sociocultural identities and positionalities have determined how they were treated in different social contexts and locations. For example, during World War II, Jews were murdered by Nazi Germany just for being Jews and gays, lesbians, and queers (or homosexuals) were marked as criminals and taken prisoner (Hill & Grace, 2009). In the U.S. context, although People of Color, mostly Black Americans, gained civil rights through the Civil Rights Movements, they are still often not treated equitably to their White counterparts and lack the more basic human rights. Racist incidents continue to occur that target Black Americans, including recent murders where police officers have murdered Black men and women under the guise of law enforcement. These murders have developed into a larger social movement where people act together towards antiracism to become a more democratic society. These incidents reveal that racism continues to impact the lives of People of Color and is deeply ingrained in U.S. society.

Similarly, the LGBTQ populations or sexual minorities have fought law enforcement and society for a long time. Some counties still have laws that explicitly ban same-sex relationships and unions, although most developed countries have been become more inclusive. Sexual minorities continue as well to experience hate crimes done to them for nothing more than being who they are as LGBTQ people (Misawa, 2009). In some nations, though, sexual minorities are gradually obtaining the rights to be treated as full human beings. However, identity-based hate crimes continue to happen very frequently to sexual minorities as they have historically for a long time. For instance, the top three identity-based hate crimes were related to race/

ethnicity, religion, and sexual orientation in 2018. According to the 2018 hate crimes data from the FBI's Uniform Crime Report Program, over 7,000 hate crime incidents involving about 8,500 offenses were reported as hate crimes, and of those, about 17% were hate crimes related to sexual orientation while hate crimes related to race/ethnicity and religion were 59.6% and 18.7% respectively (Federal Bureau of Investigation, 2019). So, minorities with any type of socioeconomic or sociocultural identity continue to be second- or third-class citizens even in these awakening contemporary societies. Despite the vision of the foundation of human rights set by UNESCO, people continue to have to work to gain "everyone's rights" and do so in a way that keeps peace among various sociocultural perspectives in diverse populations.

The concept of human rights is that they are for everyone under the assumption that people should be able to live freely and democratically under a safe and protected condition where mutual understanding of respect and civility exist. Human rights are also meant to meet fundamental needs of people and promote a harmonious relationship among them (Freeman, 2017). Education including adult and higher education is one of the fundamental human rights for all. However, when taking into account human rights from diverse sociocultural perspectives, not all are treated equally.

Human Rights and Sustainability

Armstrong et al. (2010) factor human rights into social sustainability where ethics and civilities are practiced including respect and acceptance of diversity and inclusion. Human rights from this perspective depend on social sustainability, meaning the degree of harmony and equity among people, how they treat one another in a context, and how positionality is practiced among them.

To make a connection between human rights and sustainability, it is important to understand how sustainability works in a social and global setting. One of the important areas in sustainability is to consider how people treat resources including the processes of planning, implementation, and evaluation that contain deliberative practices to sustain resources for future generations (Hansmann et al., 2012; Purvis et al., 2019). This futuristic way of practice has a notion that there is a limited amount of resources for us to use and that we will need to be considerate for the needs of the present without compromising the ability of future generations to meet their needs (Basiago, 1995). Portney (2015) espoused that "sustainability is a concept that focuses on the condition of Earth's biophysical environment" (p. 4) and its related sustainable elements that consist of natural and human resources. Springer et al. (2015) also stated that when focusing on higher education and adult learners, educators and practitioners need to be able to consider the elements of sustainability. There are several ways to present what sustainability looks like, but, in general, scholars and practitioners in sustainability agree that there are three areas or pillars in order to be sustainable: economic, environmental, and social (Purvis et al., 2019). Figure 3.1 shows those three pillars and the intersected area in the middle is an optimal area where a balanced sustainability exists in terms of economy, environment, and society, and it represents a summary of the work of Hansmann et al. (2012), Purvis et al. (2019), and Springer et al. (2015).

Figure 3.1

Three Pillars of Sustainability

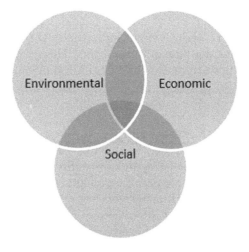

Note. There is a fair understanding of sustainability using three or more pillars and domains in the literature. This figure is based on work by Hansmann et al. (2012), Purvis et al. (2019), and Springer et al. (2015). The alternate content presented is drawn from and represents a summary of their work.

The first pillar of sustainability is economic that focuses on developing and maintaining a healthy economic system in society. In a capitalist society, having strong economic power and sustaining such power are considered a way to sustain the condition of society. The economic pillar, including economic development and sustainable economy, has long been seen as a process to achieve an ideal condition of economy (Portney, 2015). In order to gain more economic power in a capitalist society, it is important to maximize profit from available resources.

The second pillar of sustainability focuses on environmental sustainability, which proposes how we currently use natural resources and how we deal with environmental issues that will influence future generations. The assumption of this pillar of sustainability is that our resources are restricted, and environments have pivotal roles in our daily lives in society. To achieve environmental sustainability, we must understand and conserve our limited resources so that we can wisely use them. This type of sustainability urgently asks us to conserve and recycle current resources, which will reduce serious environmental issues in the future.

The third pillar of sustainability focuses on the social aspects of sustainability, which include protecting people from unethical practices and politics and promoting social justice and equity for all. This type of sustainability encompasses human behaviors as well as ethics and civility within society at large (Vallance et al., 2011). That includes human rights based on ethics and harmony that guarantee mutual protection and understanding of each other and how to act and behave in a social context to create an environment where people can live freely and democratically. Some groups of people, like sexual minorities, still strive to gain fundamental human rights, equality, and equity (Ladson-Billings, 1995; Misawa, 2007) although the essence of human rights is to sustain peace among people and nations on Earth. Under this pillar of sustainability, harmonious relationships among people and nations at large will develop and maintain civil society (Dempsey et al., 2011). In order for us to do that, it is important to understand how sustainability is situated within human rights because sustainability is a way to maintain balance and peace among different social systems.

The three different pillars of sustainability cannot exist independently. Springer et al. (2015) espoused how those three elements of sustainability could incorporate into educational sustainability in higher education and adult learning and stated:

> Elements of sustainable practices in education include creating a university environment that increases awareness of environmentally sustainable development, creates an institutional culture of sustainability, educates for environmentally responsible citizenship, fosters environmental literacy for all, practices institutional ecology, involves all stakeholders, collaborates for interdisciplinary approaches, ... and maintains the movement. (p. xviii)

Gibson (2006) also espoused and addressed how those three pillars are not in isolation but rather integrative and not mutually exclusive, as shown in Figure 3.1. Sustainability is an integrative element of the economic, environmental, and social pillars (Gibson, 2006). All of them are interrelated and reciprocal and contain some justice components. The social pillar intersects with not only the environmental pillar but also the economic pillar.

Social Sustainability Through Human Rights to Fight Against Homophobic Bullying

One can practice social equity to create a more inclusive and diverse social environment (Langhelle, 2000) that leads to social sustainability. The same can be said for antibullying practice for all including sexual minorities. Diversity, inclusion, and equity are important aspects when educating learners to be more multicultural and intercultural. When we focus on differences, we often look for obvious differences like physical appearances and presumed stereotypes that often have negative connotations. While we are becoming and after we have become global citizens in contemporary society, conflicts and negative influences can still make us behave uncivilly. When we value and appreciate differences, we should be able to respect each other, be empathic to each other, and understand each other without discriminating and marginalizing one another (Clohesy, 2013; Misawa, 2010; Washington, 2015). We actually have more similarities than differences in many ways (Collins & Bilge, 2020; Washington, 2015), but that does not cancel out the differences for everyone because there are multiple levels of power dynamics in various social contexts based on our positionality (Misawa, 2010), and such power dynamics determine who is more powerful or less in any given context.

Bullying deals with power dynamics and a power imbalance between a victim and a perpetrator, or perpetrators, and has been a critical social issue because it occurs at any time in anyplace as long as there are two or more people in the context. Bullying is prevalent in contemporary society including educational settings, workplaces, and community settings (Twale & De Luca, 2008). One of the conventional assumptions about bullying is that bullying is a childhood developmental issue that will disappear when people enter into adulthood because early research focused on childhood developmental behaviors like mobbing (Monks & Coyne, 2011; Olweus, 1993). Childhood psychologists and behavioral analysts frequently used the term *mobbing* to describe how several children would attack a child in a playground like a bird is mobbed by many birds (Olweus, 1993). Such types of mobbing are now seen as a cluster power dynamic between a victim and perpetrators (Misawa, 2015). Bullying similarly occurs within power dynamics but is more individual based although bullying often includes more than one victim or one perpetrator (Misawa, 2017; Monks & Coyne, 2011; Namie & Namie, 2009).

Homophobic bullying is a type of bullying that targets a sexual minority person because their sexual minority status is still not accepted in many of today's social contexts, which are based on heterosexism, where heterosexuals are privileged as the majority (Misawa, 2015, 2017; Rivers, 2011). Homophobic bullying has to deal with power dynamics between a sexual minority and a (heterosexual) perpetrator in a heterosexist society, and has characteristics of unethical and uncivil behaviors from the perpetrator to victim. Homophobic bullying is a bullying incident that involves a victim who is a sexual minority and "somehow less than the perpetrator physically, psychologically, or by their sociocultural position" (Misawa, 2015, p. 8) or a victim who fits the perpetrator's homophobic stereotype, and a perpetuated recurrent or singular incident (Misawa, 2017). Also, homophobic bullying is unwanted or unwarranted by the victim who is a sexual minority, and it is a type of intimidating, humiliating, offensive, threatening, or exclusionary conduct on part of the perpetrator that sustains the perpetrator's "position of power and destroys the victim's well-being, dignity, and safety or is significant enough to cause the victim physical and/or psychological harm" (Misawa, 2015, p. 8). Therefore, homophobic bullying substantively and negatively impacts sexual minorities and runs contrary to human rights based on social sustainability.

ANTIBULLYISM IN ADULT AND HIGHER EDUCATION

Homophobic bullying is a serious social issue because it violates dignity and safety of sexual minorities. In order to reduce and ultimately eliminate such ill behavior, the field of adult and higher education can utilize antibullyist practices. *Antibullyism* is an approach from the social sustainability sphere that one's human rights and dignity are protected as it promotes the idea that bullying is not acceptable. There are several practical strategies for an antibullyist approach. First, educators and practitioners in adult and higher education can set ground rules and expectations when interacting with each other in class or when having group and class discussions at the beginning of an educational activity. Some bullying behaviors occur during educational activities (Misawa et al., 2019; Washington, 2015). Therefore, an antibullyist practice requires a set of rules so that learners can civilly interact with each other with respect.

In addition to setting ground rules and expectations, antibullyism requires educators and practitioners in adult and higher education to be able to understand the diverse perspectives and experiences of their learners. As adult learners bring their own lifelong experiences with them to educational settings, educators and practitioners need to be able to learn how each learner utilizes his or her prior knowledge and experiences in the educational environment because life experiences shape how people think, act, and behave in a society (Merriam & Bierema, 2014). Their experiences are often negative with regard to others' positionality and have negativities towards certain groups of people like sexual minorities, and those negativities can develop conflicts among the learners and can create a hostile environment conducive to homophobic bullying as they shape presumptions and biases towards sexual minorities. So, as antibullyist educators and practitioners, it is important to take into account how positionality and sociocultural identities operate in an educational context.

Also, educators and practitioners in adult and higher education can create a safer space where caring and empathy are ingrained and integrated. Sexual minorities are most likely discriminated against and marginalized in the heterosexist society and communities including adult and higher education. Showing care and being able to be empathic are key to an antibullyist practice because victims of bullying are often perceived to be hypersensitive (Misawa et al., 2019) and not to be taken seriously. Victims often have no one to talk to or no place to go to cope with their experiences of being bullied (Misawa, 2015). They need to be heard with empathy and caring. In particular, sexual minorities are already marginalized and discriminated by heterosexuals and the heterosexual society, and they often do not have any ways to cope with their experiences with bullying. So, creating a caring space for sexual minority learners is an important aspect of practicing antibullyism in adult and higher education.

CONCLUDING THOUGHTS

This chapter has covered how human rights tie into social sustainability with a focus on sexual minorities and antibullyism practice in adult and higher education. In a society that values human rights, it is important for scholars and practitioners in adult and higher education to take into account the social element of sustainability, which focuses on human relations, equity, and social justice. The problem of homophobic bullying is one area of human rights that educators can take action on in the classroom and in interactions with students, other faculty, and staff. For an antibullyist practice, educators need to make sure that learners are behaving civilly and respectfully with each other. Educators and practitioners in adult and higher education have an important role in promoting antibullyism, and a direct role in creating a bully-free learning environment for all learners.

REFERENCES

Armstrong, A. C., Artmstrong, D., & Spandagou, I. (2010). *Inclusive education: International policy & practice.* SAGE.

Austin, M. J., Coombs, M., & Barr, B. (2005). Community-centered clinical practice: Is the integration of micro and macro social work practice possible? *Journal of Community Practice, 13*(4), 9–30.

Basiago, A. D. (1995). Methods of defining 'sustainability'. *Sustainable Development, 3*, 109–119.

Clohesy, A. M. (2013). *Politics of empathy: Ethics, solidarity, recognition.* Routledge.

Collins, P. H., & Bilge, S. (2020). *Intersectionality* (2nd ed.). Polity Press.

Dempsey, N., Bramley, G., Power, S., & Brown, C. (2011). The social dimension of sustainable development: Defining urban social sustainability. *Sustainable Development, 19*, 289–300. https://doi.org/10.1002/sd.417

Englander, D. (2011). Protecting the human rights of LGBT people in Uganda in the wake of Uganda's "Anti Homosexuality Bill, 2009." *Emory International Law Review, 25*,1263–1316.

Federal Bureau of Investigation. (2019). *Hate crime statistics, 2018.* https://ucr.fbi.gov/hate-crime/2018

Fox, S., & Stallworth, L. (2005). Racial/ethnic bullying: Exploring links between bullying and racism in the U.S. workplace. *Journal of Vocational Behavior, 66*, 438–456.

Freeman, M. (2017). *Human rights.* John Wiley & Sons.

Gibson, R. B. (2006). Beyond the pillars: Sustainability assessment as a framework for effective integration of social, economic and ecological considerations in significant decision-making. *Journal of Environmental Assessment Policy and Management, 8*(3), 259–280.

Gilbert, J. A., Raffo, D. M., & Sutarso, T. (2013). Gender, conflict, and workplace bullying: Is civility policy the silver bullet? *Journal of Managerial Issues, 25*(1), 79–98.

Hansmann, R., Mieg, H. A., & Frischknecht, P. (2012). Principal sustainability components: Empirical analysis of synergies between the three pillars of sustainability. *International Journal of Sustainable Development & World Ecology, 19*(5), 451–549.

Hill, R. J., Grace, A. P., & Associates. (Eds.). (2009). *Adult and higher education in queer contexts: Power, politics, and pedagogy.* Discovery Association Publishing House.

Johnson-Bailey, J. (2015). Academic incivility and bullying as a gendered and racialized phenomena. *Adult Learning, 26*(1), 42–47.

Keashly, K., & Neuman, J. (2010). Faculty experience with bullying in higher education. *Administrative Theory and Praxis, 32*(1), 48–70. https://doi.org/10.1177/0091415015591108

Kruger, T. M., Savage, C. E., & Newsham, P. (2015). Intergenerational efforts to develop a healthy environment for everyone: Sustainability as a human rights issue. *The International journal of Aging and Human Development, 80*(1), 27–40.

Ladson-Billings, G. (1995). But that's just good teaching! The case for culturally relevant pedagogy. *Theory into Practice, 34*(3), 159–165.

Langhelle, O. (2000). Sustainable development and social justice: Expanding the Rawlsian framework of global justice. *Environmental Value, 9*, 295–323.

Merriam, S. B., & Bierema, L. L. (2014). *Adult learning: Linking theory and practice.* Jossey-Bass.

Misawa, M. (2007). Political aspects of the intersection of sexual orientation and race in higher education in the United States: A queer scholar of color's perspective. *Journal of Curriculum and Pedagogy, 4*(2), 78–83.

Misawa, M. (2009). Where is out citizenship in academia? Experiences of gay men of color in higher education. In R. J. Hill & A. P. Grace (Eds.), *Adult and higher education in queer contexts: Power, politics, and pedagogy* (pp. 111–126). Discovery Association Publishing House.

Misawa, M. (2010). Musings on controversial intersections of positionality: A queer crit perspective in adult and continuing education. In V. Sheared, J. Johnson-Bailey, S. A. J. Colin, E. Peterson, & S. D. Brookfield (Eds.), *The handbook of race and adult education: A resource for dialogue on racism* (pp. 187–199). Jossey-Bass.

Misawa, M. (2015). Cuts and bruises caused by arrows, sticks, and stones in academia: Theorizing three types of racist and homophobic bullying in adult and higher education. *Adult Learning, 26*(1), 6–13.

Misawa, M. (2017). Investigating technology usage and perceptions on cyber-mob-bullying in higher education in the United States among college-age youth: A correlational study at a research institution. *Annali online della Didattica e della Formazione Docente, 9*(13), 279–299.

Misawa, M., Andrews, J. L., & Jenkins, K. M. (2019). Women's experiences of workplace bullying: A content analysis of peer-reviewed journal articles between 2000 and 2017. *New Horizons in Adult Education and Human Resource Development, 31*(4), 36–50.

Misawa, M., & Rowland, M. L. (2015). Academic bullying and incivility in adult, higher, continuing, and professional education. *Adult Learning, 26*(1), 3–5.

Monks, C. P., & Coyne, I. (Eds.). (2011). *Bullying in different contexts.* Cambridge University Press.

Namie, G., & Namie, R. (2009). *The bully at work: What you can do to stop the hurt and reclaim your dignity on the job* (2nd ed.). Sourcebooks.

Olweus, D. (1993). *Bullying at school: What we know and what we can do.* Blackwell.

Portney, K. E. (2015). *Sustainability.* The MIT Press.

Purvis, B., Mao, Y., & Robinson, D. (2019). Three pillars of sustainability: In search of conceptual origins. *Sustainability Science, 14,* 681–695. https://doi.org/10.1007/s11625-018-0627-5dsa

Singer, J. B., & Sage, M. (2015). Technology and social work practice: Micro, mezzo, and macro applications In K. Corcoran (Ed.), *Social workers' desk reference* (3rd ed., pp. 176–188). Oxford University Press.

Springer, S. B., Boden-McGill, C. J., & Holtz, J. K. (2015). Introduction. In J. K. Holtz, S. B. Springer, & C. J. Boden-McGill (Eds.), *Building sustainable futures for adult learners* (pp. xvii–xxi). Information Age Publishing.

Twale, D. J., De Luca, B. M. (2008). *Faculty incivility: The raise of the academic bully culture and what to do about it.* Jossey-Bass.

Rivers, I. (2011). *Homophobic bullying: Research and theoretical perspectives.* Oxford University Press.

Randall, P. (2001). *Bullying in adulthood: Assessing the bullies and their victims.* Taylor & Francis.

United Nations. (n.d.). *Peace, dignity and equality on a healthy planet.* https://www.un.org/en/global-issues/human-rights

United Nations Educational, Scientific and Cultural Organization. (2020a, March 11). *UNESCO and the universal declaration on human rights.* https://en.unesco. org/udhr#

United Nations Educational, Scientific and Cultural Organization. (2020b, March 11). *Culture for sustainable development.* http://www.unesco.org/new/en/culture

Vallance, S., Perkins, H. C., & Dixon, J. E. (2011). What is social sustainability? A clarification of concept. *Geoforum, 42,* 342–348.

Washington, E. T. (2015). An overview of cyberbullying in higher education. *Adult Learning, 26*(1), 21–27.

CHAPTER 4

MIGRATION AND HUMAN DIGNITY

Rhetoric and Practice

Chad Hoggan
North Carolina State University, United States

Tetyana Kloubert
The University of Augsburg, Germany

With more than 250 million people living outside their country of origin, migration is a ubiquitous worldwide phenomenon (United Nations Department of Economic and Social Affairs, 2017). The challenge of helping migrants successfully transition is especially important for those countries prosperous enough to attract a disproportionate share of migrants, such as the United States and Germany, who with 19% and 4.7% respectively of total migrants, are two of the top three migrant destinations (United Nations Department of Economic and Social Affairs, 2017). (Saudi Arabia is tied with Germany at 4.7%.) The way that countries help migrants integrate into society reveals much about their underlying premises and values concerning human life. This challenge poses important questions for the host country, not only about such issues as societal structure and

Advancing the Global Agenda for Human Rights, Vulnerable Populations, and Environmental Sustainability: Adult Education as Strategic Partner, pp. 49–65

role expectations, but perhaps most important, conceptions of what it means to be human, regardless of whether or not a person has a migration background.

Compared to the United States, Germany has a more comprehensive system for facilitating the transition of migrants to their new society, as well as a unique historical background that has influenced their rhetoric toward the treatment of migrants. This chapter presents a qualitative study of adult educators working with migrants in Germany. In it we report on a subset of the overall findings that relate specifically to the adult educators' perceptions of their work as it pertains to the human dignity of those whom they serve. This analysis of German rhetoric and practice can provide insights for other countries facing similar challenges.

BACKGROUND

In 2016, Danish writer and publicist, Janne Teller published an article in the leading German newspaper *Frankfurter Allgemeine Zeitung* provocatively entitled, "How the German Sense of Guilt Saves the European Reputation." Describing the European way of "dealing with" migration, and accentuating a special German *raison*, or rationale, of migration politics, Teller posits that Germany, with its experience of unprecedented barbarism and violation of human rights during World War II, learned from this history and developed an ethical basis for politics meant to prevent future occurrences of such atrocities.

> In choosing a response to the current refugee crisis, European countries should look to Germany. But not just to its current specific rhetoric and policies that—despite falling far short of the needs—still wager more humane than most of the rest of Europe's. Yet, much more so as to the reasons why: a profound understanding of the costs for future generations of nations acting inhumanely.... When last September [2015] at the height of the influx, Hungary put up barbed wire fences and sent in riot police, Angela Merkel [the chancellor of Germany] said *Welcome*. (Teller, 2016, para.1)

Teller argues that Germany's historical experiences of the last century influence its political culture and public discussion, increasing sensibility to the rights (and violation of the rights) of minorities, as she stated:

> The German lessons of Holocaust and World War II lie not just in a consti-
> tutionally safeguarded and staunchly defended democratic system, a myri-
> ad of laws protecting the rights of minorities, and in the oft repeated *Never
> again*. The perhaps most important lesson lies in the rare understanding of

the long-term damage that you do to yourself and your descendants, when at a moment while holding the power baton—even when led by a tyrant you'll later disown—your nation disregards the humanity of fellow human beings. What it does to yourself to define another human being as less worthy, as *the other*, to abuse *the other*, to humiliate, violate or kill 'the other' through active choice or simply through denying *the other* the basic tools and human rights of dignified survival. The lesson the Germans learned is: *You don't get over it. You never get over it.* (Teller, 2016, para.18, italics added)

Teller (2016) is referring here to the September 2015 decision by Angela Merkel to allow numerous refugees (mostly stuck in Hungary) to enter Germany in a streamlined, unbureaucratic way. When other member countries of the European Union were insisting on a numerical limit for how many migrants each would allow into its borders, Merkel countered that the human right of protection from political persecution cannot be limited to a certain number of people (Große, 2019). This bold decision made her simultaneously a savior and an object of hatred. Upon making this commitment, she turned to her country with what has become her most famous statement: "Wir schaffen das" ["We will manage this"], and many people answered her appeal for solidarity and humanity. Photos of volunteers receiving migrants at Munich Central Station in summer 2015 continue to shape the image of refugee-friendly Germany.

Other Germans reacted differently, however, and resentment toward and even hatred of refugees grew across the country. In 2016, the Federal Criminal Police Office registered 994 attacks on refugee shelters [compared to, for instance, 2014 when there were 199 attacks] (Bundeskriminalamt, 2016, p. 39). Ever since then, Germany has been divided; fringe racist groups and xenophobic attitudes exist concomitantly with far-reaching initiatives of solidarity and humanistic engagement. Merkel brought into the discussion about migration the ethical question of shared responsibility for humanity and each human being. She connected migration with respect for human dignity and emphasized the migrant as individual human beings rather than by their classification as part of a larger group (e.g., "migrants" or "Syrians"). "There are no crowds, but individual people come to us" (Frigelj, 2016). The public discourse in Germany around the ethical aspects of migration and integration politics became more and more polarized.

On the one hand, there is a deep commitment to and responsibility for the humanity and principles of human rights. On the other hand, migration is narrated as a "problem" for the society in terms of societal cohesion and overarching unity, connected with strong emotions, such as the existential fear of losing jobs, social security, and cultural norms. The so-called Leipzig Authoritarianism Study (Decker & Brähler, 2018) showed that 36% of Germans said that foreigners only come to the country to take advantage of the welfare state. More than a quarter would send foreigners back to their homeland if jobs in Germany became scarce. Around 36% considered the Federal Republic to be "alienated" to a dangerous degree by foreigners.

For those in the country whose views on migration stem from ethical and theoretical considerations, Germany's underlying approach to migration is based, in part, on their confrontation with the defining negative moment of their history: the horror of the Holocaust. Facing this history forced Germany (and other societies) to pose to themselves the question of how to prevent possible future atrocities and to critically reflect on the societal structures and narratives that might promote anti-humanistic attitudes. The role and purpose of education was examined through this lens as well. The dominant question was how had it become possible for (even well-educated) people to follow fascist ideologies and support murderous practices? Had education somehow been complicit in an entire generation's willingness to obey and to develop hostility against the Other and eventually follow a murderous regime?

THEORETICAL ORIENTATION

Education scholars have used a variety of theoretical foundations upon which they reach a similar conclusion, that people have the right to be protected from atrocities and to be regarded with dignity as an individual. Noddings (2013), for instance, suggested an ethics of care for any pedagogical situation. This ethic requires a commitment to responsiveness, relatedness, and a general concern for others as the fundamental attitudes of any educator (as a foundation for any ethical decision making). Nusbaum (2011) addressed the recognition of human dignity through her list of 10 basic human capabilities that need to be addressed and assured in a society. Besides the obvious demand to consider every individual's capability of living a life of adequate duration, Nussbaum cited the capability of living for and with others, the capability of formulating the concept of good and reasoning critically about one's life plans, and the capability of living one's own life rather than the life of someone else. Another key theorist is Adorno, whose essay "Education after Auschwitz" (1966/2003) requires an educational focus on individual human dignity as a necessary precondition to prevent antihuman behavior such as the Holocaust in the future.

Referring to the Holocaust, the postulate "never again" has since 1949 remained the *raison d'état* for the Federal Republic of Germany. The German constitution, the Basic Law, Article 1, defines "human dignity" as the criterion for all legislation and all state power. The roots for this decision lie in the heritage of German Enlightenment, especially in Kant's *Metaphysics of Morals* proclaiming that human beings should be treated as an end in themselves and not as a means to achieve somebody else's ends

(Kant, 1785]1903, p. 429). Adorno presented with his essay a new "peda-gogical categorical imperative" that continues to frame discussions around pedagogy in and beyond Germany (Heyl, 1997). According to Adorno (1966/2003), "The premier demand upon all education is that Auschwitz not happen again" (p. 19). "Education after Auschwitz" is meant by Adorno as "Education towards Autonomy": the autonomous citizen is characterized by the ability to critically reflect on social conditions and to make (political) judgments and ethical decisions on this basis and to co-shape her world and society through her actions (pp. 19–33).

Adult education literature often draws on Adorno and others from the critical theoretical tradition to provide a foundation for emancipatory edu-cational practice (Mayo, 2009; Welton, 1995), critical thinking (Brookfield, 2004), critical discourse (Murphy & Fleming, 2010), and communicative, as opposed to instrumental, action (Mezirow, 1981). Using Adorno's thought in reflecting on adult education practice provides direction for learning from the past for the future, for exercising humanistic principles of adult education, and for focusing on its role in shaping the society in which we want to live—keeping in mind the constant danger of a regression to barbarism.

Brookfield (2004) emphasized the importance of Adorno's thought for adult education, as it draws attention to the danger of instrumentalized reasoning, subservient to practical utilitarian ends. When we focus exclu-sively on resolving "short term practical problems" (p. 69), we disconnect our thinking "from pondering universal questions such as how we should live and treat each other" (p. 69) and can easily fall prey to the dominant ideology of capitalism, where people "calculate their sense of self-worse in purely economic terms" (p. 70). Similarly, Fox (2020) argued that Adorno's "Education after Auschwitz" provides a "critical compass ... that can not only inform a pedagogy, but also practice: one that can support practi-tioners' artwork, and their 'gut reactions' and resistances to poor policies and practices" (p. 118). He emphasized how Adorno's work highlighted such ethical principles as compassionate thinking, openness to alternative, criticality, reflexivity, attentiveness to the person.

THE RESEARCH STUDY

This ethical framework that undergirds the "Welcome" migration policy of Merkel exists side-by-side with an opposing ethic that cares only for the supposed interests of current citizens and devalues the humanity of migrants. Merkel's espoused ethics would therefore be mere empty rhet-oric if not actually applied to the structures and practices dealing with immigrants. The study reported here sought to understand the ways in which current practices in Germany manifest and/or contradict the ethical framing of migration and education based on the principle of human dignity described above. It presupposes that migration prompts many transitional challenges, in aspects essential for human well-being, such as identity and sense of belonging, and that insight into these difficulties would illuminate potential answers to important questions about conceptions of migrants, of human dignity, and of humanity in general.

The study explored the perceptions of educators who teach or advise migrants, as they are in a unique position to see the challenges that migrants face that are not addressed, or perhaps even exacerbated, by current conceptions of migration and the resulting structures and practices of Germany. They also are in a unique position of having worked personally with hundreds of migrants each; therefore, they have a perspective born of experiences with many people during processes of transition to life in a new country.

Qualitative, problem-centered interviews (Witzel & Reiter, 2012), approximately 60–90 minutes in length, were conducted with ten educators/counselors between December 2019–January 2020. Questions revolved around their perceptions, based on professional experiences, of their students' learning needs that are not encompassed or addressed adequately by existing structures and processes; the adaptive challenges presenting the greatest difficulties for the migrants with whom they work; and the ways in which these practitioners adapt their practice in response to their perceived needs of their learners. All participants were given the option of conducting their interview in German or English; all chose to speak in English. The interviews were audio-recorded and transcribed. Data were then analyzed thematically. The first round of coding focused specifically on the interviewees' perceptions of the learning needs and desires, as well as the most acute learning challenges, of migrants. In the process of this analysis, we saw an unexpected trend throughout the data and, therefore, conducted a second round of coding focusing on the ethical foundations and aspirations of the adult educators. We summarized these categories into themes and used the MAXQDA software program to obtain an overview of the categories and their relationships with the themes and subthemes. The concepts of autonomy, human dignity, responsibility, and humanity emerged primarily from the second round of coding. The theoretical perspective of "Education after Auschwitz" was then used to better comprehend the data. We considered Adorno's categorical imperative ("The premier demand upon all education is that Auschwitz not happen again" (Adorno 1966/2003, p. 19) as an ideal that might be insightful in the contemporary moment, a voice that helps us in the migration debate to reflect upon questions of educational ethics as counterpart to the practical and pragmatic questions of migration and integration. The findings present the subjective perspective of the interviewees and give insights into the strategies they use in their educational practice, but also insight into their meta-reflection on the guiding principles that underlie their practice.

PRESENTATION OF THE FINDINGS

Two related findings of the study are presented here to illustrate the ethical foundations and aspirations of the adult educators who participated in our study. They are: (1) orientation on the individual as a person, and (2) supporting autonomy. These findings demonstrate the challenges of migration in the specific context of Germany and provide a backdrop against which to discuss the relationship between these challenges and the underlying conceptions of migrants and human dignity embedded in the policies and practices of Germany.

Orientation on the Individual as a Person

Migrants have many immediate needs, especially during the first year in their new country. They need to abide by and, therefore, first learn about the bureaucratic system of their new country and its requirements in order to retain legal residency and access available support systems. They need to find employment and, therefore, learn the requirements to demonstrate their qualifications to continue working in their respective professions, the process of finding and applying for a job according to the norms of their professions in the new country, and/or the opportunities to receive additional training in order to qualify for a job. The systems in place to facilitate these pragmatic needs reflect and communicate important messages about how migrants are perceived by their new society, whether as things to be used or as humans deserving respect.

For example, a common practice in Germany is for the Arbeitsamt (government job center) to compile a list of needed jobs in the local area. Then, when migrants make an appointment with this office to inquire about jobs, they are advised to apply (and, if necessary, prepare) for jobs on that list. This practice is not without a logic: The migrant wants a job, and the local area has a need for specific labor. Participants in our study, however, provide a cautionary perspective on this practice.

One interviewee explained that this practice, if implemented without considering the long-term needs of the individual migrants, conveys an underlying perspective that migrants are viewed primarily for their usefulness as a source of labor. Besides the fact that this approach ignores the individual skills, desires, biographies, and inspirations of the individual, Wilhem explained, it is also not in the long-term best interests of the country.

> You are doing a job because right now there is a lot of need for this job, but not everybody is a good nurse. Of course, what other opportunities are on the German labor market right now is one aspect, but not the only aspect when I am choosing my future professional career…. There are many different pieces we have to fit together.

Wilhelm emphasized the need to reflect on one's own principled framework of educational counselling, taking into account limitations such as time, costs, and other considerations, but still trying to remain loyal to one's own principles. He formulated his own guideline emphasizing, "follow the needs of the persons who come to you and not the other way around. Don't make them fit."

Alexander, who teaches a required course for migrants, spoke similarly of the need to think differently about the students in his classes, to consider the uniqueness of individuals who just happen to be in the condition of migration rather than thinking of them as (the myth of) homogenous migrants—or, moreover, thinking of them only in their condition and role of being migrants. An example provided was the design of the curriculum that exclusively focuses on teaching German history and does not allow for the recognition of, and integration of, the migrants' histories that prompted them to migrate. As Alexander noted,

> One must see that these people have a history. And in the school, we can follow only a curriculum. But we must consider their history, the difference, the difference of the people. And this history is very important for them and for their learning. If you have some people from Douma in Syria, there was in the news about a bombing in Douma, then you can do nothing. That must be seen that they have their history. They have their psychological needs…. That should be considered and respected in a way…. And we in the course often overwhelm them with our experiences.

Participants reported in various ways their perceptions that migration is connected with feelings of loss and as a challenge to one's identity. Learning in this situation necessarily includes the need to find a balance between stability and rapid change, which often involves un-learning patterns of thinking and living that are no longer useful. As the following quotation from Alexander's interview illustrates: "Some of them are 40–50 years old and they developed habits of living in a certain way, and they have their own way of life. And it worked in their home country, but it doesn't work in Germany." This learning of new patterns of thinking and living in a new culture necessarily involves simultaneous inducements to cling to both the old and the new cultures.

> To learn ... how much of their culture they can hold on to and how much they're willing to get into a new culture. There needs to be a balance. They don't have to give up their culture, you know. But when they come from especially Iran and Afghanistan, then it's a brand new culture and it's different, and they don't initially like it because they don't know how to relate (to) people. (David)

David argued that the host society needs to acknowledge diversity as an integral characteristic so that the people can integrate into their new society without feeling pressured to abandon their uniqueness, identity, and culture.

> Now, they're not able to totally integrate. They realize that because they look different and they act different. You know, it's okay; they don't have to, totally. But they have to at least fit in, to be willing to learn enough to fit in.... Not to try becoming something you're not, but integrated enough to function.

This idea of integration that does not require complete assimilation is only possible if society is committed to the conception of migrants first and foremost as humans, deserving of acknowledgement and respect for their individual needs, desires, histories, and cultures.

Supporting Autonomy

Whereas the first finding highlights the defining value of adult education as respect for people as individuals (rather than as a means to anyone else's ends or purposes), the second finding emphasizes the logical extension of that premise to migrant education. Namely, people have the right to be self-determining, and the role of adult education is to help learners develop in the ways important to them and to foster their ability to think and act autonomously. Whether or not someone has migrated to another country has no bearing on this premise. Therefore, the task of adult education is to help learners develop their own path rather than advise them onto a path dictated solely by the needs of their new society. Returning to the example of immediate labor market needs, Wilhelm explained:

> And even if they don't know their specific goals, I try to figure out what could be the options, and step by step we are making them more concrete. In the end it has to be always very concrete. You have to give these people

a ... like a lead-map. A time lead-map. What will be the next steps, where do I have to address in order to make it more transparent and in order to empower them?

An important distinction made by the adult educators in this study was the difference between developing this type of life path *with* people rather than for people. Migrants often have immediate learnings needs, and developing and strengthening their own autonomy may not be among their primary goals. While pursuing the above-mentioned strategy, Wilhelm steers his efforts toward supporting the long-term ability of his learners to think and act for themselves in the new society. At the same time, he is not oblivious of the pragmatic sides of migrants' lives, especially when they are confronted with immediate, urgent needs and the frustrations of being in an unknown system.

> People coming to Germany need clear perspectives and clear decisions. They feel disoriented and lost in an unknown context. They request instruction, a clear decision made for them by someone more knowledgeable.... Many expect something I couldn't offer them. "You make the decision what is good for me. Tell me what would be a good future professional career in Germany." ... That's the first thing I say, "No that's not my decision. It's *your* decision. I try to support you. I create some kind of transparency of the German educational system, of the labor market. We work out together some alternatives, some potential professional pathways." And at the end they often accept: "I [the migrant] make the decision."

Participants emphasized that education and counseling services for migrants need to be sensitive not to impose or reinforce feelings of helplessness and powerlessness. Migrants are often already susceptible to these feelings simply by virtue of their experiences and situation of being a migrant, whether through painful experiences of leaving (sometimes fleeing) their home countries, legal restrictions, various social discriminations, and so forth. A common theme in the data is that the role of adult education is not to simply give instructions and "hold hands," but to support the development of a sense of autonomy, including agency and self-efficacy.

Adam described the ideal role of the educator/counselor as a kind of "perinatologist" (obstetrician specializing in high-risk pregnancies) for helping the migrant develop the skills, confidence, and habit of making their own decisions in their new country. This includes providing necessary information, but also being transparent about seemingly obscure structures and systems, explaining the strategies, developing and suggesting alternatives from which to choose, helping design concrete steps for the short- and long-term goals, and codesigning a metaphorical road map. The underlying principle of this pedagogical attitude is to see the person in her wholeness, the entire individual: According to Adam, "You really take the person with his [*sic*] circumstances, with his backgrounds, private background, etc. And say, okay, these other factors are relevant, and we speak about all these factors and see how we can fix it."

This perspective on developing autonomy, according to some participants, is supported by their experience with migrants. As Martin noted,

> Refugees do not want to ask for help, especially for more help even when it is needed. They want to feel themselves capable to act and to give and not only to receive....
>
> It's not for everyone, but for lots of them [it is] hard to ask: "Please help me. Please help me more. I need more help." And they want always to give something back, and they realize sometimes they can't and it's a problem ... because they want to help but they cannot give something back. And so, they don't ask for the help.

Wilhelm explained the balance between providing what his clients request and trying to help them perceive options and possibilities that might work well for them, but of which they are unaware. As he shared,

> From my point of view, it starts with a good counseling, which is very essential.... So that you can create transparency for these people and to give them a solid base for their own decisions. Because when you always say, 'Well, it's your decision," .... Of course, they need a solid information base and clear perspective to decide what to do.... They tell me a perspective, and I can't really figure it out. For me it doesn't really fit. Then I ask and quite often you see that the decisions or the goals here in Germany are highly based on their knowledge from what works in their home countries.

Participants described how migrants are often confronted with discouraging experiences, and then when they have goals, plans, and projects they want to pursue, they often give up because they do not see the paths that can lead them to their goals. These challenges arise because there exist different implicit systems in the way each society operates. Teaching, therefore, is about building bridges between different systems and opening doors. As Wilhelm explained, "In order to make things work here for them, they need to do things in a certain way. And if it is done differently in a row until somebody bridges that for them and says: 'Oh wait, this is a difference.'" Procedural knowledge and strategic planning, therefore, are especially important as Wilhelm further explained, "They need so much, but how can we break it down to little parts? What do I need today, you know, and be able to achieve short term goals?"

These data illustrate how these participants, in the planning and enacting of their educational offerings, exercise short-, mid-, and long-term perspectives. They strive to help their learners address immediate learning needs while also maintaining a view on their long-term ability to build and conduct an autonomous life in their new society.

DISCUSSION

Adorno (1966/2003) linked the responsibility for preventing future catastrophes against humanity ("relapse into barbarism") to the question of how a society thinks about and shapes learning and education of individuals. Adorno's core requirement was to "turn to the subject," to reflect about personal attitudes and dispositions about people (p. 20). He conceptualized his thought with the term "education after Auschwitz" that necessarily would include "education for autonomy." Autonomy presupposes for him the capacity to think and to act for oneself while also developing a humanistic ethic toward every other human being. He warned against and criticized the reification of consciousness, a common concept among critical theory scholars, describing through this term "the calculation of purposefulness/ utility of human interaction, through following the instrumental logic of perceiving other people as objects to reach one's own goals" (p. 27). This attitude indicates the tendency to perceive another human being as mere object without feeling any connection or "warmth" toward this person. The resulting "coldness" manifests in the absence of affective sympathy toward others, that is, placing oneself in the perspective of another person, experiencing openness, connection, and devotedness (Gruschka et al., 1994). This coldness was, for Adorno ([1966]/2003), a key factor in allowing atrocities such as the Holocaust to happen: "If people were not profoundly indifferent toward whatever happens to everyone else except for a few to whom they are closely bound and, if possible, by tangible interests, then Auschwitz would not have been possible, people would not have accepted it" (p. 30).

Adorno's educational and societal philosophy emphasized that our conception of ourselves and the world has a deep effect on the society in which we live. He advocated for a "general enlightenment that provides an intellectual, cultural, and social climate in which a recurrence would no longer be possible, a climate, therefore, in which the motives that led to the horror would become relatively conscious" (Adorno, 1966/2003, p. 22). He warned against utilitarian perceptions of learning because this leads to assimilation, adaptation, and reified consciousness, rather than to autonomy and maturity. It is dangerous because it produces objects who only follow orders rather than thinking subjects. Furthermore, he called for an education on Auschwitz, which encourages us to raise our voices for humanity and for reason. Adorno criticized the supposed necessity of organizing the educational process toward specific, externally defined goals. Therefore, nobody has the right to decide what people should be educated for, as this would contradict Kant's (1785/1903) postulation that humans should be considered an end in themselves rather than an object for others' use. For Adorno (1966/2003), education, therefore, means neither an effort of "human formation" nor "mere transfer of knowledge," but rather the creation of a setting that fosters the autonomy and agency of a person. "The single genuine power standing against the principle of Auschwitz is autonomy ... : the power of reflection, of self-determination, of not cooperating" (i.e., blindly submitting to those who are in power; p. 23).

An essential element of Adorno's education for autonomy was a focus on empathy, raising awareness against all forms of discrimination of a vulnerable group. "Tomorrow a group other than the Jews may come along, say the elderly, who indeed were still spared in the Third Reich, or the intellectuals, or simply deviant groups" (Adorno, 1966/2003, p. 32). Adorno's (1966/2003) thoughts revolved around the idea of education, and explicitly adult education, as a catalyst for possible social change through appropriate educational settings (Kloubert, 2014, pp. 37–38).

How does the demand on education expressed and conceptualized by Adorno (1966/2003) relate to the process of migration and especially to the educational offers for migrants? We see in the data that the German adult educators in this study authentically reflected on the values inherent in the ethical conception of migrants as humans (as described in the beginning of this chapter). They see in some formal structures (e.g., Arbeitsamt job-advising processes) the possibility to either be consistent or inconsistent with those ethics, depending on how they are implemented. From the data in this study, we see the crucial role those adult educators play in implementing formal programs for migrants in a way that respects the human dignity of the migrants with whom they work.

To transform Adorno's (1966/2003) scenario into educational practice requires a shift from the logic of pragmatism of integrational efforts to the idealism of helping people grow and develop their humanistic nature. We recognize that this admonition holds the potential to be accused of utopian thinking, and we counter that possible critique with the argument that, as per Adorno, the development of individual humanistic nature is necessary in order to prevent barbarism. We see in the philosophy of Adorno and the perspectives of the participants in this study a basis for the argument that learning processes fostering autonomy, criticality, and empathy are necessary in order to build a humanistic democratic society.

Practically speaking, such an education would include strategies described by the adult educators in this study, such as: (a) recognizing and incorporating migrants' histories into the curriculum rather than solely conveying the history of the host country, (b) helping migrants develop self-efficacy in their new society rather than simply telling them what to do, and (c) accepting diversity and encouraging uniqueness rather than coercing migrants to assimilate into a supposedly homogeneous society. Existing practices, therefore, need to be constantly evaluated in terms of the extent to which they foster and support the ethical pedagogical goals of putting each individual at the center of any societal practices, advancing an ethical relationship to alterity/otherness, and avoiding the treatment of learners as mere objects serving the needs of others, including the needs of their new country.

If we consider migrants first and foremost as humans, as an end in themselves rather than as objects for the use of others, and as being in a temporary state of vulnerability due to their status as migrants, then we should be concerned with each individual's experience, biography, expectations, life choices, narratives, learning needs, and so forth. Learning is thus primarily about increasing individual agency, especially in terms of migrants' capacity to act, to co-shape their relationship with different systems/structures, to judge and to act in their new contexts, and to make sense of their experiences and influence their own lifeworlds. As discussed previously, urgent life challenges will likely prompt migrants to focus solely on short-term solutions to those challenges, and there may also exist cultural differences that make the development of autonomy and agency seem like a foreign concept to migrants. Nevertheless, education with short-, mid-, and long-term perspectives necessarily must address both the immediate challenges as well as the mid- and long-term needs of learning how to build a life for oneself and participate effectively in the coshaping of society.

We argue that fundamental principles such as respect for human dignity, with its acknowledgment of human agency and autonomy, are fundamental pillars that must be used as the basis for the design of societal structures, including those designed to serve migrants. An obvious implication is the difference between treating migrants as if they have "deficiencies" and need to be "taught" how to act in the new society and treating them as humans in a hopefully temporary vulnerable situation of migration, who have the right to maintain their uniqueness, but who also need to learn how to function in their new society. This difference is perhaps subtle, but nevertheless essential. It implies the core assumption that any educational efforts fully acknowledge the dignity of a (learning) individuum and are directed toward fostering his or her agency, autonomy, and ability to act in their new social contexts. Admittedly, developing and fostering agency is a long-term process. Aligning education and consulting structures for migrants does not automatically mean that the result of this process will be a humanistic democratic society. Nevertheless, this is an essential step toward such an idealistic vision.

We are aware that Adorno's (1966/2003) requirements cannot be limited to just adult educators, but they must be extended to anyone living in the democratic society. The prevention of barbarism begins with preventing the pre-conditions to barbarism. It is not only about state politics of letting migrants in, but also about creating societal structures that enable these ethical principles to be realized in different situations. Migration, integration, and social transformation thus become a project of the society.

The rhetoric around migration revolves around questions of political and ethical obligations of the host country, as well as expectations toward newcomers. Strong are the voices who demand a societal normative and cultural guideline to which migrants must adapt. The ethical requirements of society, be it German or another, are by necessity premised on the *dignity of a person as the highest ethical priority*, which then requires the development of a culture of growth and openness (for society as well as for migrants), where the premier demand is not just to prevent any future barbarism (as Adorno described), but to cocreate an environment where diversity and pluralism are celebrated and supported.

Lessons learned from German history provide a lens to think about politics, structure, and educational issues in ethical terms. The ideal underlying assumption is not the feeling of guilt, as described above by Teller (2016), but rather a feeling of responsibility, as exemplified in a famous speech by German president Richard von Weizsäcker: "In our country, a new generation has grown up to assume political responsibility. Our young people are not responsible for what happened over forty years ago. But they are responsible for the historical consequences" (Weizsäcker, 1985, p. 11). Weizsäcker (1985) pointed out the lesson learned from history is a "guideline for our behavior now and in tackling the unresolved problems that lie ahead" and gave a concrete example:

> If we remember how people persecuted on grounds of race, religion and politics and threatened with certain death often stood before the closed borders with other countries, we shall not close the door today on those who are genuinely persecuted and seek protection with us. (p. 9)

A critical examination of the past with the goal to learn from it for the future might give hope for a better social climate, and this task is in any country far from complete (Kloubert, 2014); Germany is not the only country that has committed atrocities against humanity. The United States, just as other countries, might reflect on its lessons (un)learnt from historical barbarisms committed and consider the nuanced forms that the logic that led to Auschwitz can lead to barbarism in innumerable other forms. A country's perspective toward, and resulting treatment of, migrants is one indication of its underlying logic toward people as either things or as humans, and these perspectives will either promote or prevent barbarisms in the future.

REFERENCES

Adorno, T. (1966/2003). *Can one live after Auschwitz?: A philosophical reader*. Stanford University Press.

Brookfield, S. D. (2004). *The power of critical theory: Liberating adult learning and teaching*. Jossey-Bass

Bundeskriminalamt (BKA). (2016). *Kriminalität im Kontext von Zuwanderung* [Criminality in the context of immigration]. https://www.bka.de/SharedDocs/Downloads/DE/Publikationen/JahresberichteUndLagebilder/KriminalitaetImKontextVonZuwanderung/KriminalitaetImKontextVonZuwanderung_2016.html;jsessionid=52817906B9A08601063A020A8CBF098A.live0601?nn=62336

Decker, O., & Brähler, E. (2018). *Flucht ins Autoritäre. Rechtsextreme Dynamiken in der Mitte der Gesellschaft* [Flight into the Authoritative: Extreme right dynamics in the middle of the society]. Psychosozial-Verlag.

Fox, J. (2020). Theodor Adorno 'Education after Auschwitz': Contributions toward a critical social work pedagogy. In C. Morley, P. Ablett, C. Noble, & S. Cowden (Eds.), *The Routledge handbook of critical "pedagogies for social work* (pp. 108–119). Routledge.

Frigelj, K. (2016). *Merkels Spagat zwischen, "null Toleranz" und „offenen Armen"* [Merkel's split between zero tolerance and open arms]. Die Welt. https://www.welt.de/politik/deutschland/article147400364/Merkels-Spagat-zwischen-null-Toleranz-und-offenen-Armen.html

Große, P. (2019). *Deutschland und die Flüchtlinge: Wie 2015 das Land veränderte* [Germany and the refugees: How 2015 changed the country]. Deutsche Welle. Deutschland und die Flüchtlinge: Wie 2015 das Land veränderte | DW | 11.02.2019

Gruschka, A., Pollmanns, M., & Leser, C. (Eds.). (1994). *Bürgerliche Kälte und Pädagogik: Moral in Erziehung und Gesellschaft* [Citizens' Cold and Pedagogy: Morality in Education and Society]. Buchse der Pandora.

Heyl, M. (1997). *Erziehung nach Auschwitz. Eine Bestandsaufnahme* [Education after Auschwitz: An Overview]. Krämer-Verlag, Hamburg.

Kant, I. ([1785]/1903). Grundlegung zur Metaphysik der Sitten. In I. Kant (Ed.), *Gesammelte Schriften* (Vol. IV, pp. 387–463). Prussian Academy of Sciences.

Kloubert, T. (2014). *Aufarbeitung der Vergangenheit als Dimension der Erwachsenenbildung* [Coming to terms with the past as a dimension of adult education]. Peter Lang.

Mayo, P. (2009). *Flying below the radar? Critical approaches to adult education*. In M. W. Apple, W. Au, & L. A. Gandin (Eds.), *The Routledge international handbook of critical education* (pp. 269–280). Routledge.

Mezirow, J. (1981). A critical theory of adult learning and education. *Adult Education, 32*(1), 3–24.

Murphy, M., & Fleming, T. (Eds.). (2010). *Habermas, critical theory and education*. Routledge.

Noddings, N. (2013). *Caring: A relational approach to ethics and moral education* (2nd ed.). University of California Press.

Nussbaum, M. C. (2011). *Creating capabilities: The human development approach*. The Belknap Press of Harvard University Press.

Teller, J. (2016). *Wie das Deutsche Schuldgefühl die Europäische Ehre rettet* [How the German sense of guilt saved the European honor]. Frankfurter Allgemeine Zeitung. https://www.faz.net/aktuell/feuilleton/debatten/janne-teller-zur-last-der-deutschen-geschichte-14221785.html

United Nations Department of Economic and Social Affairs. (2017). *International migration report*. United Nations.

Weizsäcker, R. (1985). *Speech by president Richard von Weizsäcker during the ceremony commemorating the 40th anniversary of the End of War in Europe and of National-Socialist Tyranny*. https://www.bundespraesident.de/SharedDocs/Downloads/DE/Reden/2015/02/150202-RvW-Rede-8-Mai-1985-englisch.pdf?__blob=publicationFile

Welton, M. R. (1995). *In defense of the Lifeworld: Critical perspectives on adult learning*. State University of New York Press.

Witzel, A., & Reiter, H. (2012). *The problem-centred interview*. SAGE

CHAPTER 5

NEXUS OF VULNERABILITY OF INTERNALLY DISPLACED PERSONS (IDPS) IN AFRICA AND SOCIOECONOMIC DEVELOPMENT OF THE BLACK NATIONS

Debora A. Egunyomi
University of Ibadan, Nigeria

Kofo A. Aderogba
Tai Solarin University of Education, Nigeria

According to the Office of the United Nations High Commissioner for Refugees [UNHCR] (2016), the largest population of the internally displaced persons [IDPs] can be found in Syria, Colombia, the Democratic Republic of Congo, Iraq, Sudan, and Azerbaijan, each with an IDP population of over one million. The number in the Middle East and North Africa [MENA] has continued to rise sharply, reaching at least 9.1 million by the end of 2013. This represents an increase of at least 53% on 2012 figure, more than twice the number in 2011 and five times more than the figure 10 years before then. Again, displacement has increased exponentially since

Advancing the Global Agenda for Human Rights, Vulnerable Populations, and Environmental Sustainability: Adult Education as Strategic Partner, pp. 67–82
Copyright © 2021 by Information Age Publishing

the start of the Syrian conflict in 2011, and the country has surpassed Iraq in having the largest displacement crisis of the MENA. Indeed, 71% of all IDPs in the region were in Syria (UNHCR, 2016).

As reported by the Office of the UNHCR (2016), insecurity and armed conflict in Syria, Libya and Yemen have hampered humanitarian access and made it difficult to profile those affected. Official statistics based on IDPs' registration is unreliable (International Organization for Migration's [IOM] Displacement Tracking Matrix [DTM] Team, 2015; Internal Displacement Monitoring Center [IDMC], 2016). In countries such as Syria, where the authorities are parties to the conflicts, IDPs were often wary of registering. In addition, the criteria for registration of the IDPs varied across the region and did not always reflect the definition of an IDP as set out in the Guiding Principles on Internal Displacement. In Iraq, registrations varied from one government to another, and de-registration was based on the acceptance of financial incentives rather than the achievement of a durable solution. Any lack of monitoring means little is known about the extent to which IDPs have been able to return, integrate locally or settle elsewhere in the country (IDMC, 2015).

Adverse weather conditions complicated the situation of some IDPs displaced by conflict in 2013: Severe rain in Yemen destroyed about half of the tents in three displacement camps in Hajjah governorate in August, affecting about 12,000 people. Within the same period, winter storm of Alexandra in mid-December prompted the international community to increase humanitarian aid in Syria. IDMC (2016) records show that by the end of 2014, a record-breaking 38 million people had become displaced within their ancestral homes (and places of abode) due to violence. Eleven million of them were newly uprooted in 2014, that is, equal to 30,000 people a day, according to the Norwegian Refugee Council's Geneva-based IDMC (IDMC, 2015).

The UNHCR cared for about 26 million of the world's IDP population in 2014 alone. The IDMC's Global Overview (IDMC, 2016) reports that most of the increase in new displacement during that year was the result of protracted crises in the Democratic Republic of Congo, Iraq, Nigeria, South Sudan, and Syria. In total, the five countries accounted for 60% of new displacement worldwide (UNHCR, 2016).

Iraqi civilians suffered the worse displacement, with at least 2.2 million displaced in 2014, while at least 40% of Syria's population, or 7.6 million people, have been displaced, that is, the highest number in the world. Europe, for the first time in more than a decade, also suffered massive, imposed displacement. This was caused by war in eastern Ukraine, where more than 640,000 people fled their homes (UNHCR, 2015). At the end of 2014, it was estimated that 38.2 million IDPs worldwide, the highest level since 1989, and the first year for which global statistics on IDPs were available.

In Africa, new displacement associated with conflicts and violence was 2.4 million; and 1.1 million was due to disasters. Some states experience conflicts and violence as well as disasters. These are Niger Republic, Nigeria, Democratic Republic of Congo, Ethiopia, and Somalia. Conflicts and violence characterize Chad Republic, Cameroon, Central African Republic, Burundi, South Sudan, Sudan, Libya, and Egypt. States such as Guinea, Mozambique, Madagascar, Malawi, and Kenya experienced displacement due to disasters (Aderogba et al., 2018; IDMC, 2016).

While we acknowledge displacement worldwide, this chapter describes IDP situations in Africa with practical implications for Adult Education. Emphasis is on displacements caused by conflicts and violence drawing from data and information available through 2015.

THE AFRICAN NATIONS

Africa, the world's second largest and second-most-populous continent, is about 30.31 million km^2 including its adjacent islands. Its total land surface area is about 20.40% of the world. With 1.1 billion people as of 2013, (and it is fast growing in population), it accounts for about 15% of the world's population. The continent includes Madagascar and various archipelagos. It is diverse in various respects and hosts a diversity of ethnicities and languages. Physical environments, economy, historical ties, and government systems are also diverse.

In the late 19th century, European countries colonized most parts of the continent. Thus, most of the present states originate from a process of decolonization in the 20th century. They held about 97% of the African territories (Brown, 2014; Mamdani, 1996). The Berlin Conference of 1884–85 was an important event in the political history of African ethnic groups. The independence movement gained momentum following World War II, which left major European powers weakened. In 1951, a former Italian colony, Libya, gained independence. In 1956, Tunisia and Morocco won their independence from France. Ghana followed suit the next year, becoming the first of the sub-Saharan colonies to be granted independence. Most of the rest of the continent including Nigeria (1960) became independent over the next decade.

Today, Africa contains 55 sovereign countries, most of which have borders that were drawn during the era of European colonialism. Since colonialism, the African states have frequently been hampered by instability, corruption, violence, and authoritarianism. Many of the states are republics that operate under some form of presidential system of government. However, few of them have been able to sustain democratic governments, and many have instead cycled through a series of coups, producing military dictatorships (Gordon & Donald, 1996).

As stated by Gordon and Donald (1996), great instability was mainly the result of marginalization of ethnic groups and unwarranted attacks under their political leaders. Between early 1960s and late 1980s, the continent had more than 70 coups and 13 presidential assassinations. Border and territorial disputes were also common, with the European-imposed borders of many nations being widely contested through armed conflicts.

However, in the 21st century, the number of armed conflicts steadily declined, and government are more stable. Many countries are abandoning communist-style command economies and opening for market reforms, leading to increase in foreign investment mainly, from China. This has spurred quick economic growth in many countries, seemingly ending decades of stagnation and decline (Khazan, 2013; Sandbrook, 1985). Politically, there are clear signs of increased networking among the African organizations and states.

The political associations such as the African Union [AU] offers hope for greater cooperation and peace between the states of the continent. But extensive human rights abuse still occurs in several parts of the continent, repeatedly even under the oversight of the states (Khazan, 2013). Often and recently, Coted'Ivoire, Democratic Republic of Congo, Sierra Leone, Nigeria, Liberia, Zimbabwe, and Sudan are countries where major human rights violations have been repeatedly reported (African Union, 2013; International Committee of the Red Cross [ICRC], 2014, 2016; Harry, 2013).

Despite her abundant resources, Africa remains the world's poorest and most underdeveloped continent (Asante, 2007; Gordon & Donald, 1996; Khazan, 2013). The World Bank (2008), like Sandbrook (1985), posits that this situation stems from corrupt governments, human rights violations, failed central planning, high levels of illiteracy, lack of access to foreign capital, and frequent tribal and military conflict, among others. Also, according to the United Nations (2003), the world's bottom 24 ranked nations (151st to 175th) were all Africans. The report goes on to say that poverty, illiteracy, malnutrition and inadequate water supply and sanitation, as well as poor health, affect a large proportion of the people who reside in the continent. The population has rapidly increased over the last 40 years. In some states, more than half of the population is under 25 years of age (United Nations, 2013). The total number of people increased from 229 million in 1950 to 630 million in 1990, and as of 2014, the population of Africa was estimated at 1.2 billion (UNICEF, 2014). It is projected that Africa's rapid population growth will soon overtake the only two nations currently larger than its population, India and China's 1.4 billion people each (United Nations, 2013).

Therefore, it could be inferred that the contrasting nature of the continent and diversity of its people and their cultures, resources, economy and the poverty level, and low level of illiteracy constitute the causes of the challenges of the African nations. With the attendant global warming and climate change, there are probably multiplicity of challenges that severally led to insurgence, civil unrest, economic crisis, communal clashes, natural disasters, unsustainable government policies and programs, to name a few, that have also led to severe displacement of people from their ancestral homes.

CAUSES AND NEXUS OF THE INTERNAL DISPLACEMENTS

Causes and sources of internal displacement, vulnerability and challenges are multifaceted with women and children being most impacted in many regions. The following expatiates.

Major Causes, Sources, and Statistics of Internal Displacement: IDMC (2016) observed that there were 12.5 million IDPs in the 21 sub-Saharan countries that it monitored as of the end of 2013 accounting for more than a third of the global total. Nigeria, the Democratic Republic of the Congo [DRC] and Sudan had the largest populations and were closely followed by Somalia and the Central African Republic [CAR]. The number of up to 3.3 million IDPs from Nigeria contributed to a rise in the overall figure for the region, from 10.4 million at the end of 2012. This made Nigeria the country with the largest IDP population on the continent of Africa.

Struggles for political power, extremist violence, disputes over natural resources, and inter-communal violence that were often linked to land were some other causes. In many cases, however, conflict and violence were the outcome of some complex mix of causes (UNHCR, 2016). In South Sudan, a struggle for political power had ethnic overtones from the outset but transformed into widespread interethnic violence, while in the Central African Republic, a coup led by a Muslim-dominated armed coalition, led to widespread retaliation between Muslim and Christian groups and indiscriminate attacks on people based on their religious affiliation.

Central Africa was the subregion worst affected by displacement in 2013, with the largest population movement taking place in the DRC, CAR, Sudan, and South Sudan. The crisis in CAR, which began towards the end of 2012, got escalated and intensified dramatically. By the end of the year, almost a million people fled their homes, more than half of them in the capital Bangui. This was a seven-fold rise on the figure of 130,000 at the end of 2012. Political violence also flared up in South Sudan in December, displacing almost as many people in a month as in the rest of the year put together, and bringing the number of new IDPs in the country to 383,000 (IDMC, 2016). According to the IDMC, two most intractable conflicts of the region also caused new large-scale displacements. In the DRC, up to a million people fled their homes in the east of the country, increasing the number of IDPs in the region. In Sudan, at least 470,000 people were displaced in the Darfur region and in South Kordofan, North Kordofan and Blue Nile States.

In Nigeria, the radical Islamist armed group, *Boko Haram*, stepped up the campaign it had been waging since the 1990s for an independent state and the objective is to abolish Western education. In 2014, its brutal attacks triggered the displacement of more than 300,000 people in the north-eastern states—Borno, Adamawa, and Yobe, according to the National Emergency Management Agency (NEMA) (2015). The figure however, rose to over 2 million in 2015 (Olawale, 2016). It is brutal, but avoidable. Certainly, many of the instances led to massive displacement of individuals, families, and communities.

Vulnerability and Challenges: The IDPs trapped in both their regions' unfolding emergencies and their long-running conflicts are in dire need of protection and assistance. Hundreds of thousands of people in the CAR, the DRC, Somalia, South Sudan, and Sudan faced significant threats to their physical security, including armed attacks and clashes, forced recruitment, arbitrary killings, sexual violence, and abductions. For example, in Uganda, the return of those who had fled the conflict between the government and the Lord's Resistance Army [LRA] was marred by land disputes, some of which have led to violence, the destruction of property, marginalization and secondary dislocation. The returnees to northern Mali found their homes occupied or destroyed and their land littered with remnants of explosives. Ethnic tensions were heightened, in some cases, causing further displacement of communities accused of association with one party to the conflict or another. In Nigeria, access to livelihood opportunities was a significant factor in determining IDPs' settlement choices. Right of entry to land, restitution and tenure security were among the many challenges they faced in making a sustainable living (Aderogba et al., 2018; Olawale, 2016). In Burundi, most of the IDPs would prefer to integrate locally, but others thought they would have a better chance of reestablishing their livelihoods if they returned to their places of origin. In Côte d'Ivoire, in contrast, returnees found their land occupied or sold illegally, leaving them unable to rebuild their lives. State supports were not always available or effective beyond the end of the crises and were not always in line with the IDPs' choices. In Mali, the government's clear preference once the Islamist insurgency had been defeated was for the IDPs to return to their homes, but after nearly two years in displacement, an increasing number preferred to stay in their places of refuge.

Most IDPs do not live in camps. This situation makes the achievement of durable solutions to their problems important not only to themselves, but also to their host families and communities. Relative improvements in security in some areas of Somalia contributed to about 63,000 people returning, either assisted or under their own arrangements. In many countries, including some of those with large, displaced populations such as South Sudan and Sudan, return movements were not sufficiently monitored or tracked, thus any information available is sparse and not quite reliable (IDMC, 2016).

All over the conflict-ridden countries, few steps were taken to implement the UN Framework on "Ending Displacement in the Aftermath of Conflicts," but the appointment of a durable solutions coordinator in Côte d'Ivoire signaled an important opportunity to design plans and programs that bridged the gap between humanitarian and development actions (Hugo, 1993). In all, women and children were the most vulnerable.

Vulnerability of Women and Children: Over 80% of the IDPs were women and children, and gender-based violence [GBV] was widespread in the CAR, DRC, Somalia, South Sudan, and Nigeria. Displaced women and girls were reportedly exposed to sexual violence while getting firewood or fetching water, or when using latrines that were often shared with men (Human Rights Watch, 2016; Olawale, 2016). Makeshift shelters in camps and settlements, poor lighting, and the ease with which armed men enter the camps only added to the risks. Some IDPs resorted to harmful traditional practices such as forced and early marriages were found to be more common during displacement. Domestic violence was also a major problem, made worse by stress, loss of livelihoods and shifts in gender roles as a result of displacement (Hugo, 1993; Human Rights Watch, 2016; IDMC, 2016).

Internally displaced children were particularly exposed to all forms of violence, abuse, and exploitation. Armed groups frequently recruited those as young as nine years old to serve as combatants. Female suicide bombers were becoming significant in states like Nigeria. Separation from their families leaves displaced children more vulnerable as they must fend for themselves, in some cases, as heads of households. It has been estimated that the number of unaccompanied children among CAR's IDPs was more than 60,000 (IDMC, 2016).

According to the IDMC (2016) reports, the complexity of displacement patterns in Africa made the achievement of durable solutions in 2013 uneven at best, and called for nuanced and tailored responses including humanitarian, development, human rights, and peace building initiatives. In the DRC and Somalia, for example, at least two-thirds of the IDPs in some areas of the countries were thought to have suffered multiple displacements, either repeatedly from their places of origin or onwards from their places of "refuge." The governments were not doing enough to protect the displaced women and girls and ensure they have access to basic rights and services. Moreover, the government failed to sanction those who abused the IDPs among whom were camp leaders, vigilante groups, policemen, and soldiers.

Human Rights Watch (2016) writes about sexual abuse, including rape and exploitation, of 43 women and girls living in seven internally displaced persons' camps in Maiduguri, the Borno State capital in Nigeria. The victims had been displaced from several Borno towns and villages, including Abadam, Bama, Baga, Damasak, Dikwa, Gamboru Ngala, Gwoza, Kukawa, and Walassa. In some cases, the victims had arrived in the under-served Maiduguri camps, where their movement was severely restricted after spending months in military screening camps. The report, in part, states:

> These women and girls are not getting much-needed support for the horrific trauma they suffered at the hands of *Boko Haram*, ... people who should protect these women and girls are attacking and abusing them; victims were drugged and raped, while 37 were coerced into sex through false marriage promises and materials; and abandoned when they became pregnant. They suffered discrimination, abuse, and stigmatization. (Human Rights Watch, 2016)

The situations were not much different in Darfur, Somalia, Uganda, Sudan, South Sudan, Democratic Republic of Congo and Cote d'Ivoire (Das et al., 2016; Dauda, 2010; UNHCR, 2007, 2010, 2015; Vincent, 2000). The women and girls' movement were often restricted, and they became victims of rape and or sexual exploitation even when they accepted offers of friendship or marriage from men in positions of authority. But the causative factors have not been seriously addressed in many of the countries.

PREDICAMENTS VIS-À-VIS PROTECTION AND NEEDED ASSISTANCE

The responsibility for protecting and assisting IDPs was shared among the UN agencies, namely UNHCR, UNICEF, WFP, UNDP, Office of the High Commissioner for Human Rights, the intergovernmental organizations, the ICRC and other international NGOs. The international set-up is referred to as the collaborative approach. But there have been series of vilification against the collaborative approach by some social critics and governments. Roberta (2006 pp. 105–106) in his "Strengthening Protection of IDPs: The UN Roles" observed as follows:

Nearly every UN and independent evaluation has found the collaborative approach deficient ... there is no real focus of responsibility in the field for assisting and protecting the IDPs.... There is also no predictability of action, as the different agencies are free to pick and choose the situations in which they wish to become involved based on their respective mandates, resources, and interests. In every new emergency, no one knows for sure which agency or combination thereof will become involved.

Likewise, there have been: (a) sectoral responsibilities to different humanitarian agencies, most notably with the UNHCR taking on the responsibility for the protection and management of camps and emergency shelters; (b) the cluster approach conceived amid concerns about coordination and capacity that arose from the weak operational response to the crisis in Darfur in 2004 and 2005; and (c) the critical findings of the Humanitarian Response Review [HRR] commissioned by the then Emergency Relief Coordinator [ERC] (originally rolled out and evaluated in four countries: DRC, Liberia, Somalia and Uganda). The clusters were originally concentrated in nine areas: Logistics (WFP); Emergency Telecommunications Cluster (WFP); Camp coordination and management (UNHCR for conflict-generated IDPs and IOM for natural disaster-generated IDPs); Shelter (IFRC for natural disasters; UNHCR for conflict situations); Health (WHO), Nutrition (UNICEF); Water, sanitation, and hygiene promotion (UNICEF); Early recovery (UNDP); Protection for conflict-generated IDPs (UNHCR and UNICEF); and OHCHR for natural disaster generated IDPs. These were later expanded to include agriculture and education. But there was no international treaty which applies specifically to IDPs. Some have advocated a redefinitions and protections for refugees to apply to generic IDPs.

One outcome of the reviews is the document, *Guiding Principles on Internal Displacement* (United Nations, 2004, pp. 2–15), which lays out the responsibilities of states before displacement (that is, to prevent displacement) as well as during and after displacement. The principles were endorsed by the UN General Assembly, the African Commission on Human and People's Rights [ACHPR] and by the signatories to the 2006 Pact on Security, Stability and Development in the Great Lakes Region, including Sudan, DRC, and Uganda. Unfortunately, the Guiding Principles were found to be non-binding (UNHCR, 2016).

By and large, the IDPs caught up in the African region's unfolding emergencies and its long-running conflicts remain in dire need of protection and assistance in various forms: They faced significant threats to their physical security, including armed attacks and clashes, forced recruitment, arbitrary killings, sexual violence, and abductions, that is, apart from emotional and psychological threats.

The internally displaced children and women were particularly exposed to all forms of violence, abuse, and exploitation. The international community has at various times also intervened to help. But again, many country-participants were also driven by political considerations, which further undermine their effectiveness. For instance, a Libyan prime minister once created a bureau for IDPs within his office. However, the strategy, legislation and the response that were to follow did not materialize, nor was the government able to reestablish its authority over the country, or to rein in its many armed groups. Undoubtedly, that was sometimes embarrassing to the governments and nationals of the countries concerned. A case in point is Yemen, where the cabinet approved a national policy on internal displacement, but there is lack of influence in many of the affected regions.

SOCIOECONOMIC REPERCUSSIONS FOR AFRICA

The implications are unwarrantedly sore for Africa. In the source communities, social and economic activities were disrupted: animals and economic plants were lost; residences and infrastructures destroyed, and new ways of life ought to be found. The communities, therefore, need peace and stability more than help, particularly because the alternative, if prolonged, would mean that the African region would further start lagging in terms of infrastructure, education, and other development indices. Conversely, economic activities in communities and regions where there were conflicts were dwindling due to the massive migrations and death of people, mostly able-bodied men, and women. Food processing and production were reduced and there were virtually no more contributions to the GDP of the nations concerned, and of Africa as a whole.

At each of the IDP destinations, the IDPs compound the social problems of infrastructure, namely, water, food, electricity and power, medical care, education, among others. In the process of displacement, lives lost means changes in the socioeconomic status of individuals and families. Local, state, and national governments are overburdened and so also is the international community. As a result, the abused children and women are no longer empowered nor educated for their immediate and distant future.

Though the IDPs have begun to advocate their rights through IDP organizations, they are characterized by lower levels of political participation in comparison to members of the host communities, who have better established political networks. The IDPs' access to the formal labor market is quite limited. They typically only have occasional and temporary access to miniature jobs in construction or domestic services, and these have never been sustainable anywhere (ICRC, 2014; IDMC, 2015, 2016).

Rape, sexual violence, and kidnapping form part of strategies adopted as weapons of war to punish, intimidate, destabilize and to drive people away from their lands. This is the case in the northeast of Nigeria, Cote d'Ivoire, Uganda, Sudan, and Central African Republic. These evil acts dehumanized the women and made them flee conflict areas. They were strategies of aggression which instilled fear in the women and dissuaded them from moving around.

Generally, with the endemic IDPs' circumstances, Africa is facing series of interconnected economic and humanitarian crises which, if not attended to with urgency, will utterly disrupt basic life-support systems, contribute to the worsening of already fragmented security structures, and perpetuate the underdevelopment and indebtedness of African nations.

Practical Implications for Adult Education: Promoting Citizenship Education

The foregoing has sufficiently demonstrated that certain emotional states and conducts for sustainable cohabitation and civilizations are imperative but deficient in the African nations and regions. To secure the future of communities, all citizens who must also train, nurture and bring up younger generations in citizenship engagement and participation must be educated in the Citizenship Education [CE], an aspect of Adult Education, therefore. This is "educating individual, from early childhood, to become clear-thinking and enlightened citizens who participate in decisions concerning society. 'Society' is here understood in the special sense of a nation with a circumscribed territory which is recognized as a state" (Meyer, 1995). The United Nations Educational, Scientific and Cultural Organization (UNESCO, 2014, 2017) also acknowledge the avowal. Knowledge of institutions, and an awareness that the rule of law applies to social and human relationships of a nation form part of the citizenship education. According to UNESCO (2017), taken in that sense, the Citizenship Education is based on the distinction between:

- the individual as a subject of ethics and law, entitled to all the rights inherent in the human condition (human rights); and
- the citizen—entitled to the civil and political rights recognized by the national constitution of the country concerned.

All human beings are both individuals and citizens of a society to which they belong. Therefore, human rights and citizen rights are interdependent.

One of the roles that will be played by the Citizenship Education will be training of "good citizens, in other words, it trains citizens to know and to be aware of the human and political issues that are at stake in their individual community or the nation at large" (United Nations Educational, Scientific and Cultural Organization [UNESCO] & The United Nations

Office on Drugs and Crime [UNODC], 2019, p. 1). Thus, there must be combined efforts to provide a comprehensive program for teaching the Africans, particularly those on the African continent, to engage in a civilized societal manner through the CE. Certainly, whoever wants to live in a community, including immigrants who hope to become legal citizens must learn about the culture, policies, history, and governmental structure of the country and region.

CE should begin at a very young age and continue into adulthood as a process of lifelong learning. Single-issue politics, and democracy and learner rights are known and common in literature (Thaxton, 2018; Young Citizen, 2019). These are taught as academic subjects like politics or sociology. Undoubtedly, these are required of every citizen who will make the society governable and well managed (Olawale, 2019; UNESCO & UNODC, 2019).

According to Olawale (2019), democracies need active, informed and responsible citizens, citizens who are willing and able to take responsibility for themselves and their communities, and contribute to the political processes. It will give people the knowledge and skills to understand, challenge, and engage with democratic society including politics, the media, civil society, the economy, and the law. It will help to develop self-confidence and a sense of agency, and successfully deal with life changes and challenges such as bullying and discrimination. It will give them a voice in the life of their schools, their communities, and the society at large.

Regardless of the level it is taught, to be good citizens, people should study and learn a few key concepts: They should understand why citizenship is important in making democracies work. They need to understand the goals of citizenship and the importance of meeting those goals through hard work and dedication. Moreover, by knowing and applying these goals, citizens, and their communities benefit (Greenberg, 1992; Thaxton, 2018; Young Citizens, 2019).

Citizenship education can help link citizens to their political communities in social and legal ways. Good citizens have the right and responsibility to recognize and overcome contradictions of ideals that concern equality of rights for all. Overall, it will train the citizens to be good and motivate them to exhibit ethical and moral characteristics. It is important that Africans are properly educated so they can make judgments and have convictions about citizens' rights and responsibilities to serve their communities and participate in the social and political world. Young Citizens (2019) observed and writes that:

> accustomed to discussing their differences in a rational way in the primary years, they are more likely to accept it as normal in their adolescence ...
> helps to equip young people to deal with situations of conflict and contro-

versy knowledgeably and tolerantly. It helps to equip them to understand the consequences of their actions, and those of the adults around them … learn how to recognize bias, evaluate argument, weigh evidence, look for alternative interpretations, viewpoints and sources of evidence—to give good reasons for the things they say and do, and to expect good reasons to be given by others. (Young Citizens, 2019)

It is therefore imperative and a must to teach elements of CE in all classes and venues where adults meet and learn to be able to become adept in learning and teaching how to distinguish prejudice, appraise argument, study evidence, look for alternative interpretations, viewpoints, and sources of evidence (Young Citizen, 2019).

CONCLUSION

The diverse resources of Africa as a continent have not been reasonably positively harnessed to the advantages of the states, regions, and the entire continent. The development of the socioeconomic resources has been placed in comatose state but requiring peace and harmony to rejuvenate and thrive. Religious, political, and civil unrests that flourish in different geographical and ethnic groups have been responsible for the lethargic social and economic conditions. Whereas the UNHCR was mandated by General Assembly Resolution 428 (V) of 14th December 1950 to lead and coordinate international action for the worldwide protection of refugees and the resolution of refugee problems, there is no international humanitarian institution which has the overall responsibility of protecting and assisting the refugees as well as the internally displaced. The IDPs suffer deprivations, lack of shelter, medical care, sexual harassment, and humiliation; lack of protection, restriction of movement; and inadequate sanitation, food, education, and all essentials of life. Though several organizations have stepped in to meet the challenges, quite a lot still needs to be done.

Towards achieving viable and sustainable African communities and states, there should be a paradigm shift, drastic departure from the past through concerted collaboration of the African Union [AU], regional economic communities, states, and religious bodies. Particularly for sustainability in the camps and after the camps, each IDP should be equipped with life skills for economic survival. This could range from carpentry and joinery, block making, tailoring, tie and dying, soap making, dress making, fashion designing, laundry and dry-cleaning, farming, to printing and bindery, computer data processing, film making, computer and electronic repairs, among others. They must be sufficiently empowered.

Africa should no longer be referred to nor perceived as a dark continent. All adult learning and engagements should not fail at addressing aspects of the aberrations. The IDPs are humans, Africans, that should be free and catered for like other Africans in their own land. The widespread issues of warfare, drought, diseases, hunger, political corruption, illiteracy, poor healthcare delivery systems, AIDS, poverty, and others must be addressed head-on to allow for sustainable development in Africa.

REFERENCES

Aderogba, K. A., Majaro-Majesty, H. O., & Adeniyi, A. A. (2018). Challenges of Internally Displaced Persons (IDPs) and sustainable community development in Nigeria. In A. Oredehin, A. Robin, & T. Ola (Eds.) *Education and international relations for national development: A book of reading in honour of Professor Owoeye, A.* (pp. 50–67). Lead City University.

Asante, M. (2007). *The history of Africa,* Routledge.

Brown, S. T. (2014). Planning Kampala: Histories of sanity intervention and informal space. *Critical African Studies, 6* (1), 71–90.

Das, T. K.., Haldar, S. K.., Gupta, I., & Kundu, S. (2016). *Deprivation of internally displaced persons: Case studies in India (*1st ed.). Power.

Gordon, A. A., & Donald, L. G. (1996). *Understanding contemporary Africa.* Lynne Rienner.

Greenberg, D. (1992). *Education in America—A view from Sudbury Valley, democracy must be experienced to be earned.* https://hvsudburyschool.com/education-in-america-excerpts/

Harry, N. U. (2013). African youth, innovations and the changing society. *Huffington Post.* https://www.huffpost.com/entry/african-youth-innovation-_b_3904408

Hugo, G. (1993). Migrant women in developing countries in Department of Economic and Social Information and Policy Analysis. *Internal Migration of Women in Developing Countries: Proceedings of the United Nations Expert Meeting on the Feminization of Internal Migration.* United Nations.

Human Rights Watch. (2016). *Insurgency: Women and children vulnerability.* Human Rights Watch. https://www.hrw.org/news/2016/10/31/nigeria-officials-abusing-displaced-women-girls

International Committee of the Red Cross.(2014). *ICRC position on internally displaced persons.*

International Committee of the Red Cross. (2016). *Kampala convention: What it means for the ICRC and the displaced in Africa.*

International Displacement Monitoring Centre. (2015). *2014 African report on internal displacement.*

Internal Displacement Monitoring Center. (2016). *Internal displacement global displacement global overview of the trends and development in 2006.* Internal Displacement Monitoring Centre, Norwegian Refugee Council.

International Organization for Migration's Displacement Tracking Matrix Team. (2015). *207 Local government areas covering 13 states of northern Nigeria show the concentration of IDPs.*

Khazan, O. (2013, July 4). The three reasons why the United States is so interested in Africa right now. *Quartz.*

Mamdani, M. (1996). Citizenship and subject: Contemporary Africa and the legacy of late colonialism. *Kampala Foundation*, p. 16.

Meyer, B. P. (1995). Introduction—A culture of democracy: A challenge for schools. *Social Sciences, 38*(2), 197–204.

National Emergency Management Agency. (2015, May 17). Nigerian training abductors of Chibok Girls while Borno youth remain jobless. *Champion Newspapers:* Online News: For a Better Nigerian. https://newsrescue.com/buhari-is-training-abductors-of-chibok-girls-while-borno-youth-remain-jobless/

Office of the United Nations High Commissioner for Refugees. (2016, July). United Nations High Commissioner for Refugees Worldwide population overview. *UNHC Review.*

Olawale, R. (2016, May 9). Strategies for rehabilitating IDPs in Nigeria, Champion Newspapers: Online News: For a better Nigerian. https://opinion.premiumtimesng.com/2016/09/04/nigeria-displacement-crisis-overcoming-challenges-spurring-actions-olawale-rotimi-opeyemi/

Roberta, C. (2006), Strengthening protection of IDPs: The UN roles. *Georgetown Journal of International Affairs,* (Winter-Spring), 105–106.

Sandbrook, R. (1985). *The politics of Africa's economic stagnation.* Cambridge University Press.

Thaxton, C. (2018). *Citizenship education: Goals and importance.* U.S. Politics & Civics Lesson Plans/Social Science Courses.

United Nations. (2003). *Human development report 2003. Millenium Development Goals: A compact among nations to end human poverty.* http://hdr.undp.org/sites/default/files/reports/264/hdr_2003_en_complete.pdf

United Nations. (2004). *Guiding principles on internal displacement.*

United Nations. (2013). *Past and Future Population of Africa.* Department of Economic and Social Affairs, Population Division.

United Nations Educational, Scientific and Cultural Organization (UNESCO). (2014). *Global citizenship education. Preparing learners for the challenges of the 21st century,.*

United Nations Educational, Scientific and Cultural Organization. (2017). *Schools in action, global citizens for sustainable development: a guide for students.*

United Nations Educational, Scientific and Cultural Organization & United Nations Office on Drugs and Crime (UNESCO & UNODC). (2019). *Strengthening the rule of law through education: A guide for policymakers.*

United Nations High Commissioner for Refugees. (2007). *The protection of internally displaced persons and the role of United Nations High Commissioner for refugees (UNHCR).* EXCOM Informal Consultative, United Nations.

United Nations High Commissioner for Refugees. (2015, June). *UNHCR–Global Trends-Forced Displacement in 2014.*

United Nations High Commissioner for Refugees. (2010, June). *Handbook for the protection of internally displaced persons, global protection cluster*.

United Nations International Children Emergency Fund. (2014, August 13). *UNICEF Report: Africa's population could hit 4 billion by 2100*. National Public Radio.

United Nations Office for the Coordination of Humanitarian Affairs [UNOCHA]. (2018). *Global Report 2018: World Humanitarian and Country Report Icon. 2018*. https://reliefweb.int/report/world/unhcr-global-report-2018

Vincent, M. (2000). IDPs: rights and status, *Forced Migration Review*, *30*(8), 16–24.

World Bank. (2008). *The developing world is poorer than we thought, but no less successful in the fight against poverty*.

Young Citizens. (2019). *The importance of Citizenship Education*. Citizenship Foundation. https://www.youngcitizens.org/FAQs/7-the-importance-of-citizenship-education.

CHAPTER 6

COMMUNITY-BASED ADULT EDUCATION TO PROMOTE HUMAN RIGHTS AND HEALTH EQUITY IN A STIGMATIZED COMMUNITY IN CANADA

Roula Kteily-Hawa
Brescia University College at Western University, Canada

Joseph Roy Gillis
University of Toronto, Canada

This chapter evokes community-based participatory research and a critical theoretical approach to examine how individual, organizational, social, institutional, political, economic, and environmental factors and underlying assumptions influence health, health equity, human rights, and the well-being of a diverse vulnerable group: racialized women living with human immunodeficiency viruses (HIV). Herein is a historical analysis of the community-driven response to the HIV epidemic, with a focus on a stigmatized community in Ontario, Canada: racialized women living with HIV particularly from the South Asian community.

This chapter describes historical community-based education initiatives from the 1980s onward as documented in a variety of sources especially

Advancing the Global Agenda for Human Rights, Vulnerable Populations, and Environmental Sustainability: Adult Education as Strategic Partner, pp. 83–97

materials and communications from community-based organizations and academic sources covering the spread and community-based response to the HIV epidemic. The extent and impact of these education efforts will be analyzed within a social determinants of health lens and an intersectional analysis within an adult education framework. The impact of both (a) external and internal HIV stigma and (b) racism and homophobia will also be considered as factors influencing community response. Finally, government funding initiatives and the changing political and social climate in Ontario will be considered while honoring the integral role of adult educators in (a) working with the community (formally and informally) and (b) shaping policies and practices.

This chapter traces the evolution of several related movements (e.g., health promotion, violence against women, women's health, gay rights, and the AIDS movement) in conjunction with changes to Canadian health-related policies. A case is made for this evolution leading to the right time for the community-based, participatory action and research movement. The chapter culminates in a working example of the powerful impact of integrating health and adult education through community mobilization especially using community-based participatory research and peer-led research.

ADULT EDUCATION AND HEALTH: POLICY AND PRACTICE

Health care providers have always been involved in improving individuals' health. The introduction of the *Medical Care Act* 50 years ago gave Canadians universal access to publicly funded health services (Health Canada, 1966). This enabled people to be more actively involved in their own health resulting in a gradual transformation in the relationship between health care providers, health professionals, and adult educators.

Another contributing factor to this transformation was the growing importance of health promotion as a movement in Canada and globally. This movement recognizes the active role individuals and communities have in taking control over their health. In 1986, the first international conference on health promotion was held in Ottawa, Canada wherein a new charter of health promotion principles was developed. Referred to as the *Ottawa Charter* (World Health Organization [WHO], 1986), it continues to inform health promotion strategies around the world.

The *Ottawa Charter* had a significant impact on changing the health service delivery model. It moved health beyond just the health care sector and put it on the agenda for policy makers at all sectors and levels (WHO, 1986). For effective health promotion initiatives, the *Ottawa Charter* recommended actions to build healthy public policy, create supportive environments, strengthen communities, develop personal skills, and reorient health services to support individuals and communities while respecting their cultural needs. The *Ottawa Charter* recognized health as a human right and identified fundamental conditions for achieving good health: social, political, economic, and physical environmental factors (WHO, 1986). Later, these conditions and factors, which are requisites for health promotion, became part of the social determinants of health (SDOH) approach.

In conjunction with an increased recognition for initiatives that focus on health promotion and engage and empower individuals and communities, a *population health* approach emerged. It is largely a criticism of healthcare as a determinant of health (Evans & Stoddart, 1990). *Population health* encompassed research that examined the additional health effects of poverty, income inequality, racism, and socioeconomic status (Evans et al., 1994).

After a decade of research using a population health model in Canada, the framework came under extreme scrutiny due to its reliance on large quantitative data sets, its failure to question the causes of health inequity and its disregard for the role of human agency in health promotion (Labonte et al., 2005). As well, the relationship among capitalism, social inequalities, and health disparities was deemed lacking (Coburn et al., 2003), and the political context in which health and intersectoral policies affect social inequalities was missing (Friedman & Starfield, 2003). The need for both the promotion of human agency and the development of an explicit theory that would critically examine the causes of poverty (Labonte et al., 2005) resulted in a shift towards *critical* population health research.

EMPOWERING COMMUNITIES THROUGH ADULT HEALTH EDUCATION: A CRITICAL THEORY LENS

As a critical lens for conducting health research gained significance, "the necessity of locating health in social and historical contexts shaped by power [was established]" (Labonte et al., 2005, p. 11). One of the main goals of critical health research was to gain a "deeper understanding [that] seeks the reconstruction of social, economic and political relations along emancipatory lines [to] improve the health and well-being of all people" (Labonte et al., 2005, p. 10). Community engagement was deemed necessary to achieve this goal.

Building on the importance of having a critical lens for conducting health research, Leona English (2012) proposed a "critical theory of adult health learning," whereby "adult health learning brings a teaching and learning perspective [that] stresses the need to focus on adults as participants, critical thinkers, and agents of change" (p. 13). This Marxian-informed perspective is focused on challenging ideology, unmasking power, challenging social and economic systems that are based on privilege, and "incorporating an understanding of gender and race on adult learning and the health of communities" (p. 21).

Over time, via a critical lens on health research, the relationship between health professionals and adult educators solidified, whereby health providers recognized the necessity for having adult educators as partners to meet individuals and communities' unique needs. Adult educators took on an informal role of improving the health of diverse communities particularly marginalized communities. These educators relied on adult learning principles to create innovative ways to promote health. The integration of health and adult education through community mobilization was seen through the use of community-based participatory research practices, storytelling, and peer education models.

AIDS ACTIVISM IN CANADA THROUGH CRITICAL CONSCIOUSNESS AND SOCIOPOLITICAL ACTION

The 1960s, 1970s, and 1980s witnessed the resurgence of the women's movement in Canada and globally, including a movement focused on women's health and reproductive rights (Boscoe et al., 2004; Miles, 1989). With the women's health movement taking a central role in health promotion, there were increased demands on improving access to health services and the health of all (Epp, 1986). For social movements to be successful, there must be a transition from insights to action. Consciousness-raising principles and critical consciousness, both central to adult education (Freire, 1970; Watts & Hipolito-Delgado, 2015), can challenge existing structural barriers such as gender, race, ethnicity, sexual orientation, and socioeconomic status. Consciousness also gives voice to marginalized and stigmatized populations through sociopolitical action (Boscoe et al., 2004; Miles, 1989; Watts & Hipolito-Delgado, 2015).

The violence against women movement is one example of a movement that was fairly successful in reaching its goals in the past half century. Starting with critical consciousness and transitioning to sociopolitical action, this movement relied on *everyday organizing*, which recognized activism within shifting sociopolitical climates (McAdam, 1982; Rupp & Taylor, 1999; Watts & Hipolito-Delgado, 2015). This movement relied mostly on both activism that developed over time and institutional responses to violence against women in Canada.

In more detail, feminist activists and organizations engaged in campaigns to promote their conceptualizations of violence against women. These conceptualizations ranged from recognizing that men's enactment of physical, sexual, and other forms of violence against women constituted a social problem to responding to survivors of violence with dedicated feminist services (McCarthy & Zald, 1977). At the grassroots level, women's shelters and rape crisis centers carried out dual functions They offered services for women and advocated for social change. Concurrently, provincial and national organizations planned and maneuvered more open social change agendas (Rupp & Taylor, 1999).

Inordinately affected by HIV, the gay population in Canada was one of the vulnerable groups that learned from the experiences of the women's health movement in community activism (Vickers, 1988). As the acquired immunodeficiency syndrome (AIDS) epidemic first appeared in the early 1980s among gay men and people infected through blood transfusions, the epidemic was soon known as *the gay disease*. Feeling a threat to their identities, and due to a slow response from Canada's health systems, the gay community organized small groups of volunteers and demanded better access to services and safe blood supplies to address this threat.

Also, increased vulnerability resulting from homophobia pushed gay right activists to mobilize communities through education and community-based initiatives, programs and activities all characterized by innovation and social action. Just like feminist activists, gay community activists operated through everyday organizing and political action, which relied heavily on consciousness raising to elicit institutional responses to address the AIDS epidemic. Starting with grass roots movement, the AIDS movement in Canada quickly gained importance and pressured the government for policy changes (Adam, 1987; Rayside & Lindquis, 1992).

Steps such as "fostering awareness of sociopolitical circumstances, encouraging critical questioning, and fostering collective identity" (Watts & Hipolito-Delgado, 2015, p. 847) are often necessary to bridge the gap between critical consciousness and political action. Attendant sociopolitical actions in the AIDS movement resulted in the Empowerment Of People Living with HIV/AIDS. The *Denver Principles*, a pseudo Bill of Rights and Declaration of Independence, was formalized in 1983 while a group of activists, along with men living with AIDS, met as part of a gay and lesbian conference in Denver, United States. This declaration condemned any attempts to be labelled as *victims* and asserted their rights as *the people of AIDS* (Adam, 1987; Rayside & Lindquis, 1992).

NATIONAL RESPONSE TO HIV AND COMMUNITY-BASED PARTICIPATORY RESEARCH

The role of community became central in the AIDS movement. The first Canadian national AIDS conference took place in Montreal, Canada in 1985. This event gave birth to the *Canadian AIDS Society*, the first national body representing AIDS community groups across the country (Adam, 1987; Rayside & Lindquis, 1992). Capitalizing on critical consciousness and external allies gave voice to marginalized communities and put pressure on the federal government to make policy changes related to AIDS and sexual health (Adam, 1987; Rayside & Lindquis, 1992).

By 1987, the province of Ontario had introduced a reasonably progressive AIDS curriculum in all schools. In 1988, AIDS activism was at its peak, culminating in the formation of a new *National Coalition of People Living with HIV*. Similar to the *National Action Committee on the Status of Women*, the National HIV Coalition very quickly became the official voice for people living with AIDS and an umbrella for many grass roots and community-based organizations demanding change. Feeling extreme pressure, the Federal government was forced to change its policies to address the AIDS epidemic (Rayside & Lindquis, 1992).

With the spread of HIV across Canada, all sectors of the government, nongovernment organizations, health care providers, researchers and community activists got involved, and a Pan-Canadian response was deemed necessary in order to address this new threat. Responding to public protests of Canadian HIV/AIDS activists, a three-year *National AIDS Strategy* with dedicated annual funding was launched by the Federal government in 1990 (Rayside & Lindquis, 1992).

By 1991, most of the country's school children were being taught about AIDS. In the city of Toronto, Ontario, public health authorities made condoms accessible to high school students, and anonymous testing for HIV became available. The *Ontario Human Rights Commission* added sexual orientation as part of its human rights code, and discrimination against people living with HIV became illegal (Rayside & Lindquis, 1992).

In the mid-1990s, there was a marked shift in the response to the HIV epidemic as people living with HIV demanded more involvement and control over services and research that affected their lives (Roy & Cain, 2001; Travers et al., 2008). The 1994 *Paris AIDS Summit* was a significant moment in history in the AIDS movement. The summit culminated in international recognition of the importance of the *Greater Involvement of People Living with HIV/AIDS* (GIPA) principle (UNAIDS, 2004; Van Roey, 1999), which evolved over time to MIPA (Meaningful Involvement of People Living with HIV). The GIPA/MIPA principles later had a profound impact in how research in the area of HIV was to be conducted. It led to the birth of community-based participatory research, where participants are involved in meaningful ways in every step of the research (Israel et al., 1998).

The 1998 consultations led by the Canadian Federal government with various stakeholders at all levels (e.g., grass-roots, community-based AIDS service organizations, and people living with HIV) resulted in a *Canadian Strategy on HIV/AIDS* with dedicated ongoing funding reaching $42.2 million in 1998 (Public Health Agency of Canada [PHAC], 2012a). Having a national strategy facilitated collaborations across all sectors and established HIV as a human rights issue whereby local communities' needs must be addressed (PHAC, 2012a).

With community-based learning involving vulnerable populations gaining importance, groups learned together and worked toward achieving social justice. Peer education models, commonly used in adult education, were adopted in HIV prevention interventions as educational, motivational, and skills-building approaches to reduce the risk of HIV (Coates et al., 2008). AIDS service organizations and other community-based organizations serving vulnerable groups living with or at risk of HIV led initiatives for HIV and sexual health education, prevention and outreach and worked towards reducing and eliminating HIV-related stigma and discrimination (PHAC, 2012a). What started as a grass-roots movement in the early 1980s gave voice to vulnerable communities. Gradually, community-based research—by the community, for the community—gained importance and significance in the HIV field.

As both health and adult education disciplines concurrently became more integrated, the notion of community-engaged health research—that is, methods that allow for communities, researchers, and practitioners to learn together and from one another—materialized as an important tool for deepening an understanding of how underrepresented groups navigate adversity (Egan, 2012; Zieghan, 2012). With roots in adult education and social justice (Freire, 1970), community-based participatory research emerged as a new field, where participants gain equitable opportunities to actively engage in and collaborate through the research process. This enhanced involvement often leads to collective emancipation from adversity such as HIV and other sexual stigma and discrimination (Egan, 2012).

ADULT SEXUAL HEALTH EDUCATION AS AN HIV PREVENTION TOOL

In the context of community-based HIV prevention programs, adults are routinely presented with new and different dilemmas while engaging with their communities and other peers. These experiences require reflection skills, which can be developed through critical reflexive practices including journaling and reflective debriefing. Using these reflective practice strategies, HIV prevention and education programs have helped adults gain skills that can lead to transformative learning (Mezirow, 1981, 1991). Other theories aside from transformative learning can also inform sexual health education including social constructivism and experiential learning.

According to social constructivism (Vygotsky, 1978), learning is a collaborative process, and knowledge develops from individuals' interactions with their culture and society. For example, Vygotsky (1978) believed that community plays a central role in the process of making meaning (i.e., the process of interpreting or making sense of life events, relationships, and oneself). As such, HIV education and prevention initiatives in community-based settings provide adult participants and learners with repeated occasions to experience real-life events where they are able to assimilate and apply knowledge from their training and community-engaged learning opportunities thereby increasing their capacity as learners in sexual health (Campbell, 2004; Peterson et al., 2017).

Based on Kolb's (1984) experiential learning theory, "learning is the process whereby knowledge is created through the transformation of experience" (p. 38). New experiences provide the drive for the development of new concepts. As such, effective experiential learning is positioned in concrete experience, which provides opportunities for learners to observe and reflect. This reflection gives rise to a new idea or the modification of an existing concept, which learners can then apply to the world around them resulting in new experiences.

In this context, adult learners in HIV education and prevention programs not only apply the training they undergo but refine and enhance their critical reflexive praxis. For clarification, reflection involves giving serious thought and consideration to an action to gain personal insights. Reflexivity entails examining one's thoughts (via introspection) with a concern for how one's identity (e.g., the people of AIDS) influences and biases one's understanding of and outlook on the world (i.e., positionality) (Ryan, 2005). Through reflection, reflexivity and community-engaged research and initiatives, adult learners gain the opportunity to view themselves not only as learners but as leaders in sexual health with the capacity to disseminate relevant information (Campbell, 2004; Peterson et al., 2017).

HIV/AIDS STIGMA IN SOUTH ASIAN WOMEN COMMUNITIES IN ONTARIO

The AIDS movement that had started in the 1980s with gay activism continued and mobilized different groups including both women and Aboriginal peoples living with HIV. The late 1990s and early 2000s saw a shift in HIV research with a new focus on the lived experiences of people living with HIV. As the GIPA/MIPA principles continued to gain significance in HIV research, community-based participatory research became central, focusing on the involvement and inclusion of marginalized communities in all steps of the research process (Travers et al., 2008).

As part of a comprehensive response to HIV across Canada, women were identified as one of eight key populations at risk of or affected by HIV and experiencing HIV stigma (PHAC, 2012b). One Ontario community that has faced a particularly high degree of HIV stigma is the South Asian community, especially in the Greater Toronto Area (GTA). GTA South Asian women living with HIV are particularly stigmatized, silenced, and lacking discourse on sexual health (Hawa et al., 2017; Vlassoff & Ali, 2011). HIV/AIDS stigma is damaging because it impedes HIV prevention efforts, discourages condom-use related to denial and creates barriers to HIV testing and health care (Berkley-Patton et al., 2009). In addition, South Asian women experience racism and social exclusion, which form barriers to sexual health and HIV/AIDS resources (Kteily-Hawa & Chikermane, 2017; Wong et al., 2019).

South Asians represent one of the fastest growing populations in Canada. Census data from 2016 showed that over 1.96 million people self-reported their ethnic origin as South Asian, representing one-quarter (25.1%) of the visible minority population and 5.6% of the entire Canadian population (Statistics Canada, 2017a). The term *South Asian* refers to diverse communities of people whose self-reported ethnic or cultural origins are specific to countries in South Asia: Bangladesh, Bhutan, India, Maldives, Myanmar, Nepal, Pakistan, and Sri Lanka (Statistics Canada, 2017a). Immigrants usually maintain loyalty and ties to both home and host countries and as such, diaspora can play a role in the production of their identities (Ashutosh, 2012). This "dual-place" orientation influences their ways of knowing and how they negotiate agency as it pertains to their HIV status.

South Asian Canadian immigrant women living with HIV are an under-researched group despite being part of one of Canada's largest ethnic minority groups. Furthermore, HIV/AIDS prevention campaigns are often thwarted for several reasons: gender norms and expectations, South Asian community's silence on sex, challenges inherent in managing cultural value conflicts, intimate and sexual relationship power dynamics, lack of knowledge on prevention practices, and sexually transmitted infection (STI) stigma. Thwarted prevention makes South Asian women much more vulnerable to HIV infection (Kteily-Hawa & Chikermane, 2017; Kteily-Hawa & Underhill, 2018; Wong et al., 2019). This situation is exacerbated by the lack of South Asian-specific community-based HIV service organizations. Only one exists in Canada that provides HIV prevention and support services and culturally specific sexual health promotion—the Alliance for South Asian AIDS Prevention (ASAAP) in Toronto (Wong et al., 2019), to be discussed.

Moreover, there is a dearth of South Asian-specific HIV/STI surveillance data to ensure equitable access to sexual health services and programs and to inform policies. Canadian public health practice currently emphasizes communicable disease surveillance. Provincial and territorial efforts to collect data about race and ethnicity vary with some never submitting their data to the Public Health Agency of Canada (PHAC, 2014). Because insufficient data means South Asians are not considered an HIV-at-risk population, these communities receive minimal resources for HIV prevention and sexual health promotion. In fact, resources are almost non-existent for this community. This is an unfavorable situation, because the invisibility presents a false assurance of not being vulnerable and further perpetuates HIV-stigma denial and misconceptions (Wong et al., 2019).

PEER-BASED HIV PREVENTION AND HEALTH PROMOTION

In the early 2000s, adult educators working with organizations engaged with women living with HIV turned to peer-led and peer-based programming and research in HIV prevention and health promotion. The widespread use of this approach has been acknowledged, wherein "health messages may have greater credibility when they come from someone who is seen as similar to the 'receiver' of the message" (Kelly, 2010, p. 141). The process of peers educating peers has been shown to be quite effective especially regarding participatory research (Backett-Milburn, 2000). Peer-led research enriches community engagement efforts thereby contributing to community capacity building (Campbell, 2004; Peterson et al., 2017).

In particular, the aforementioned ASAAP emerged as a response to insufficient culturally inclusive HIV and sexual health resources for and research about South Asian women in the GTA. ASAAP is a community-based organization that developed Brownkiss, which is a peer-led program that promotes HIV risk awareness using storytelling (Ragulan & Chikermane, 2014). Through Brownkiss, women gain access to positive spaces to engage in dialogue about HIV discrimination and stigma.

In more detail, Brownkiss facilitates women peer leaders' use of blogging to tell their stories and lived experiences with HIV/AIDS. Through this process, they become more aware of how sexual decision-making among South Asian women in diaspora is shaped or constrained by the interaction of individual and structural factors. This strategy has proven effective. These within-culture stories have resonated with likeminded readers because community silence was broken and dialogue that challenges systemic marginalization and sexual taboos was promoted (Ragulan & Chikermane, 2014).

Acknowledging the absence of South Asian HIV-positive women's experiences in Canada's HIV/AIDS movement, an innovative storytelling initiative arose (Wong et al., 2019). In 2013, ASAAP arranged for 12 GTA South Asian women living with HIV to engage in collaborative writing to chronicle their struggles and resilience. The result was an anthology titled *More Than Fiction: POZ Women Share Their Stories* (Islam et al., 2014). POZ (sounds like oz) is from the first syllable of *positive* for HIV. Upon reading the collection, South Asian women, community stakeholders and researchers all affirmed the effectiveness and powerfulness of the peer-led storytelling strategy (Islam et al., 2015).

With an appreciation of how well storytelling seemed to work with the GTA South Asian women's community, a partnership was formed that used an adult education framework to explore how stories and peer-led adult programming could be further integrated into the South Asian's community health education. A combination of academic researchers, service providers, and knowledge users designed and executed an exploratory study that they called the *Storytelling for Sexual Health Study* (SSSH). They wanted to know how well GTA South Asian women responded to fact-based versus story-based self-directed HIV/STI prevention learning materials. They were especially interested in the potential of peer leadership models to promote dialogue about HIV stigma. South Asian women adult peer leaders were trained to help administer the SSSH. Results confirmed that study participants preferred story-based interventions over factsheets. The former augmented their knowledge of HIV/STIs and mitigated HIV-related stigma (Kteily-Hawa et al., 2020; Wong et al., 2019).

Importantly, the SSSH affirmed that narrative-based HIV/AIDS education is a culturally appropriate means of knowledge transfer within South Asian communities. The inherent parasocial (vicarious) contact with story characters (a) increased HIV knowledge, (b) decreased stigma and (c) reduced risk of re-stigmatization (Kteily-Hawa, Hari, et al., 2019). This form of adult education provided a viable way for marginalized voices to be heard, empathized with, and respected leading to behavior change (Wong et al., 2019).

CONCLUSION

This chapter traced an historical analysis of the community-driven response to the HIV epidemic ending with a focus on a stigmatized Canadian community: racialized women living with HIV in the GTA South Asian community. It traced the evolution of several related movements (e.g., health promotion, violence against women, women's health, gay rights, and the AIDS movement) in conjunction with changes to Canadian health-related policies leading to the right time for the community-based, participatory action and research movement. The chapter further illustrated the powerful impact of integrating health and adult education through community mobilization especially using community-based participatory research and peer-led research. Partnerships among researchers, South Asian women living with HIV/AIDS and HIV service organizations proved especially helpful for giving a voice to marginalized women living with HIV/AIDS in Canada.

REFERENCES

Adam, B. (1987). *The rise of a gay and lesbian movement*. Twayne.

Ashutosh, I. (2012). South Asians in Toronto: Geographies of transnationalism, diaspora, and the settling of differences in the city. *South Asian Diaspora*, *4*(1), 95–109. https://doi.org/10.1080/19438192.2012.634566

Backett-Milburn, K., & Wilson, S. (2000). Understanding peer education: Insights from a process evaluation. *Health Education Research*, *15*(1), 85–96. https://doi.org/10.1093/her/15.1.85

Berkley-Patton, J., Goggin, K., Liston, R., Bradley-Ewing, A., & Neville, S. (2009). Adapting effective narrative-based HIV-prevention interventions to increase minorities' engagement in HIV/AIDS services. *Health Communication*, *24*(3), 199–209. https://doi.org/10.1080/10410230902804091

Boscoe, M., Basen, G., Alleyne, G., Bourrier-Lacroix, B., & White, S. (2004). The women's health movement in Canada: Looking back and moving forward. *Canadian Woman Studies*, *24*(1), 7–13.

Campbell, C. (2004). Creating environments that support peer education: Experiences from HIV/AIDS prevention in South Africa. *Health Education*, *104*(4), 197–200. https://doi.org/10.1108/09654280410546682

Coates, T., Richter, L., & Caceres, C. (2008). Behavioural strategies to reduce HIV transmission: How to make them work better. *Lancet*, *372*(9639), 669–684. https://doi.org/doi:10.1016/S0140 6736(08)60886-7

Coburn, D., Denny, K., Myhkalovskiy, E., McDonough, P., Robertson, A., & Love, R. (2003). Population health in Canada: A brief critique. *American Journal of Public Health*, *93*, 392–396. https://doi.org/10.2105/ajph.93.3.392

Egan, J. P. (2012). Advocacy, care, promotion, and research: Adult educators working with the community for health. In L. M. English (Ed.), *Adult education and health* (pp. 64–75). University of Toronto Press.

English, L. M. (2012). A critical theory of adult health learning. In L. M. English (Ed.), *Adult education and health* (pp. 13–25). University of Toronto Press.

Epp, J. (1986). *Achieving health for All: A framework for health promotion*. Government of Canada. https://www.canada.ca/en/health-canada/services/health-care-system/reports-publications/health-care-system/achieving-health-framework-health-promotion.html

Evans, R., Barer, M., & Marmor, T. (Eds.). (1994). *Why are some people healthy and others not? The determinants of the health of populations*. Aldine de Gruyter.

Evans, R. D., & Stoddart, G. L. (1990). Producing health, consuming health care. *Social Science and Medicine*, *31*(12), 1347–1363. https://doi.org/10.1016/0277-9536(90)90074-3

Freire, P. (1970). *Pedagogy of the oppressed*. Continuum International.

Friedman, D., & Starfield, B. (2003). Models of population health: Their value for US public health practice, policy and research. *American Journal of Public Health*, *93*, 366–369. https://doi.org/10.2105/ajph.93.3.366

Hawa, R., Underhill, A., Logie, C., & Loutfy, M. (2017). Social contexts and HIV vulnerabilities among South Asian women in the Greater Toronto Area: Examining social norms. *Health Care for Women International*, *39*(2), 129–153. https://doi.org/10.1080/07399332.2017.1397157

Health Canada. (1966). *Canada Care Act*. http://publications.gc.ca/collections/collection_2017/lois-statutes/YX4-1966-64-eng.pdf

Islam S., Ragulan S., & Chikermane, V. (Eds.). (2014). *More than fiction: POZ women share their stories*. Alliance for South Asian AIDS Prevention. http://www.catie.ca/en/resources/morefiction-poz-women-share-their-stories

Islam, S., the More than Fiction Team, Chikermane, V., Chambers, L., & Sherpa, C. D. (2015). More than fiction: POZ women share their stories: ASAAP anthology project. *Canadian Journal of Infectious Diseases and Medical Microbiology*, *26*(Suppl. B), 43B.

Israel, B., Schulz, A., Parker, E., & Becker, A. (1998). Review of community-based research: Assessing partnership approaches to improve public health. *Annual Reviews Public Health*, *19*, 173–194. https://doi.org/10.1146/annurev.publhealth.19.1.173

Kelly, J. A. (2010). Popular opinion leaders and HIV prevention peer education: Resolving discrepant findings, and implications for the development of effective community programmes. *AIDS Care, 16*(2), 139–150. https://doi.org/10.1080/09540120410001640986

Kolb, D. A. (1984). *Experiential learning* (Vol.1). Prentice-Hall.

Kteily-Hawa, R., & Chikermane, V. (2017). Clearing space for multiple voices: HIV vulnerability amongst South Asian immigrant women in Toronto. *Atlantis*, *38*(1), 247–257.

Kteily-Hawa, R., Hari, S., Soor, J., Wong, J. P., Chikermane, V., Chambers, L. A., & Vahabi, M. (2020). Paradigm shifts in sexual health: Quantitative analysis of story and fact-based health education interventions. *Canadian Journal of Human Sexuality, 29*(1), 45–56. https://doi.org/10.3138/cjhs.2018-0037

Kteily-Hawa, R., Hari, S., Wong, J. P. H., Chikermane, V., & Chambers, L. (2019). Development and implementation of peer leader training for community-based participatory sexual health research. *Progress in Community Health Partnerships: Research, Education, and Action, 13*(3), 303–319. https://doi.org/10.1353/cpr.2019.0058

Kteily-Hawa, R., & Underhill, A. (2018). Examining gender relations among South Asian Immigrant women living with HIV in the Greater Toronto Area: Theoretical implications *Critical Studies in Gender, Culture, and Social Justice, 38.*2, 205–218. http://journals.msvu.ca/index.php/atlantis/article/view/3402/205-218%20PDF

Kteily-Hawa, R., Islam, S., & Loutfy, M. (2019). Immigration as a crisis tendency for HIV vulnerability among racialised women living with HIV in Ontario, Canada: An anti- oppressive lens. *Culture, Health and Sexuality, 21*(2), 121–133. https://doi.org/10.1080/13691058.2018.1453087

Labonte, R., Polanyi, M., Muhajarine, N., McIntosh, T., & Williams, A. (2005). Beyond the divides: Towards critical population health research. *Critical Public Health, 15*(1), 5–17. https://doi.org/10.1080/09581590500048192

McAdam, D. (1982). *Political process and the development of black insurgency, 1930-1970.* University of Chicago Press.

McCarthy, J., & Zald, M. N. (1977). Resource mobilization and social movements: A partial theory. *American Journal of Sociology, 82*(6), 1212–1241. https://www.jstor.org/stable/2777934

Mezirow, J. (1981). A critical theory of adult learning and education. *Adult Education, 32*(1), 3-24. https://doi.org/10.1177/074171368103200101

Mezirow, J. (1991). *Transformative dimensions of adult learning.* Jossey-Bass.

Miles, A. (1989). Women's challenge to adult education. *Canadian Journal for the Study of Adult Education, 3*(1), 1–18.

Peterson, P., Sackey, D., Kay, M., Correa-Velez, I., & Nicholson, C. (2017). Using a peer led researcher to connect with vulnerable communities around health. *International Journal of Integrated Care, 17*(3), 1–8. http://doi.org/10.5334/ijic.3177

Public Health Agency of Canada. (2012a). *Strengthening federal action in the Canadian response to HIV/AIDS.* http://www.phac-aspc.gc.ca/aids-sida/fi-if/fa-if/2-eng.php

Public Health Agency of Canada. (2012b). *Population-specific HIV/AIDS status report: Women.* https://www.canada.ca/en/public-health/services/hiv-aids/publications/population-specific-hiv-aids-status-reports/women.html

Public Health Agency of Canada. (2014). *Population-specific HIV/AIDS status reports.* https://www.canada.ca/en/public-health/services/hiv-aids/publications/population-specific-hiv-aids-status-reports.html

Ragulan, S., & Chikermanc, V. (2014). *Brownkiss: A storytelling model of engagement* [Poster presentation]. 20th International AIDS Conference, Melbourne, Australia. http://pag.aids2014.org/EPosterHandler.axd?aid.10110

Rayside, D. M., & Lindquis, E. A. (1992). AIDS activism and the state in Canada. *Studies in Political Economy, 39*(1), 37–76. https://doi.org/10.1080/19187033.1992.11675417

Roy, C. M., & Cain, R. (2001). The involvement of people living with HIV/AIDS in community-based organizations: Contributions and constraints. *AIDS Care, 13*(4), 421–432. https://doi.org/10.1080/09540120120057950

Rupp, L. J., & Taylor, V. (1999). Forging feminist identity in an international movement: A collective identity approach to twentieth-century feminism. *Signs, 24*(2), 363–386. https://www.jstor.org/stable/3175646

Ryan, T. (2005). When you reflect are you also being reflexive? *Ontario Action Researcher, 8*(1), Article #2. https://oar.nipissingu.ca/PDFS/V812E.pdf

Statistics Canada. (2017). *Data tables, 2016 census   Ethnic origin* (Catalogue No. 98-400-X2016187). https://www12.statcan.gc.ca/census-recensement/2016/dp-pd/dt-td/index-eng.cfm

Travers, R., Wilsona, M. G., Flickerc, S., Gutaa, A., Bereketa, T., McKaya, C., van der Meulena, A, Cleverlyg, S., Dickief, M., Globermana, J., & Rourke, S. B. (2008). The greater involvement of people living with AIDS principle: Theory versus practice in Ontario's HIV/AIDS community-based research sector. *AIDS Care, 20*(6), 615–624. https://doi.org/10.1080/09540120701661690

UNAIDS. (2004). *2004 Report on the global HIV/AIDS epidemic: 4th Global report.*

Van Roey, J. (1999). *From principle to practice: Greater involvement of people living with or affected by HIV/AIDS (GIPA).* UNAIDS. https://data.unaids.org/publications/irc-pub01/jc252-gipa-i_en.pdf

Vickers, J. (1988). Bending the iron law of oligarchy. In J. D. Wine & J. L. Ristock (Eds.), *Women and social change: Feminist activism in Canada* (pp. 75–95). James Lorimer and Company.

Vlassoff, C., & Ali, F. (2011). HIV related stigma among South Asians in Toronto. *Ethnicity and Health, 16*(1), 25–42. https://doi.org/10.1080/13557858.2010.523456

Vygotsky, L. S. (1978). *Mind in society.* Harvard University Press.

Watts, R. J., & Hipolito-Delgado, C. P. (2015). Thinking ourselves to liberation? Advancing sociopolitical action in critical consciousness. *Urban Review, 47*, 847–867. https://doi.org/10.1007/s11256-015-0341-x

Wong, J. P., Kteily-Hawa, R., Chambers, L. A., Hari, S., Chikermane, V., Ragulan, S., Islam, S., & Vahabi, M. (2019). Exploring the use of fact-based and story-based learning materials for HIV/STI prevention and sexual health promotion with South Asian women in Toronto, Canada. *Health Education Research, 34*(1), 27–37. https://doi.org/10.1093/her/cyy042

World Health Organization. (1986). *Ottawa Charter for Health Promotion.* https://www.who.int/healthpromotion/conferences/previous/ottawa/en/index1.html

Zieghan, L. (2012). Community-engaged health research: Communities, scientists, and practitioners learning together. In L. M. English (Ed.), *Adult education and health* (pp. 46–64). University of Toronto Press.

CHAPTER 7

ADULTS WITH DISABILITIES NEED MORE AND BETTER LEARNING OPPORTUNITIES AROUND THE WORLD

**Ashley Stepanek Lockhart, Ricardo Sabates,
Nidhi Singal, and Thilanka Wijesinghe**
University of Cambridge, United Kingdom

Disability affects more people than we think and with different outcomes (UNESCO, 2019). According to the World Health Organization (WHO), approximately 785–975 million people aged 15 years and older are living with a form of disability (2011), many in developing countries (WHO, 2015). Compounding matters is how "disability may increase the risk of poverty, and poverty may increase the risk of disability" along with "social exclusion and disempowerment, not just lack of material resources" (WHO, 2011, p. 10). Quality adult learning and education (ALE) is a powerful mechanism for breaking this cyclical relationship and creating more social inclusion, diversity, equity, and social mobility for this group. ALE has a strategic role given the large numbers of people with disabilities who miss out on school or have low learning levels due to previous education experiences.

Advancing the Global Agenda for Human Rights, Vulnerable Populations, and Environmental Sustainability: Adult Education as Strategic Partner, pp. 99–116
Copyright © 2021 by Information Age Publishing

Education exclusion of people with disabilities remains a concern despite global efforts since the Universal Declaration of Human Rights in 1948 and Convention on the Rights of Persons with Disabilities (CRPD) in 2006. Youth and adults with disabilities were also prioritized in the Belem Framework for Action (BFA), the global ALE policy agreed in 2009 (UIL). In it, UNESCO Member States committed to significant financing of quality and inclusive lifelong learning opportunities through responsive programs catering to the differentiated learning needs of youths and adults with disabilities. These commitments were reinforced by Sustainable Development Goal (SDG) 4 to "ensure inclusive and equitable quality education and promote lifelong learning opportunities for all" (United Nations, 2015). SDG 4 is operationalized into 10 targets that are globally monitored for country progress. Disability is highlighted in Target 4.5, which "ensure[s] equal access to all levels of education and vocational training for the vulnerable, including persons with disabilities" (United Nations, 2015). Adult education is the focus of Target 4.3, in terms of technical, vocational, and tertiary education, including university, and Target 4.4, based on skills development.

Despite the many global commitments outlined above, ALE for youth and adults with disabilities has been largely neglected in policies and programs in different countries, and within research and advocacy (Groce & Bakhshi, 2011). Less is known about participation, quality, and any financial mechanisms to support such programs nationally or regionally within countries. Moreover, we have little information on monitoring strategies to track progress of learning outcomes and broader impact, also to improve provision based on the right to education and contextual relevance. Few data sources exist that are specific to this group, and the academic literature is scarce on the subject of creating learning opportunities for adults with disabilities.

In this chapter, we focus on findings across the five global monitoring areas of the BFA (UNESCO Institute of Lifelong Learning, 2010): policies, governance, finance, participation, and quality provision. Explained more in the next section, we use global data collected in 2016 and 2019 by the UNESCO Institute of Lifelong Learning (UIL) to highlight challenges and opportunities for learning for youth and adults with disabilities across these five areas. To complement the analysis, we offer additional insights from two countries, Botswana and Ireland, to illustrate current ALE potential for this group. From the combined analysis, we then discuss the implication of three key points emerging from the review of evidence: (a) disaggregating disability data by type and degree, (b) diversifying learning outcomes, and (c) improving quality learning by building up the knowledge base. We note a central tension between meeting the diverse needs of this group while not disassociating them from general development trends.

GLOBAL MONITORING OF
ADULT LEARNING AND EDUCATION

Our review of data and case studies is framed around ALE global monitoring. During the Sixth International Conference on Adult Education (CONFINTEA VI) in 2009, UNESCO Member States committed to follow the recommendations in the BFA. This included changes in thematic areas of policy, governance, finance, participation, and quality provision to ensure that countries fulfilled the learning potential of youth and adults, emphasizing those with disabilities as a target group. Since 2009, UIL has gathered data at country level by using a global survey to monitor overall and disaggregated progress on ALE, which is analyzed and published in the Global Report on Adult Learning and Education (GRALE).

The first report in 2009, GRALE 1, made the case for prioritizing adult learning in global, regional, and national agendas. It focused on strengthening the policy environment and governance framework and fostering participation, particularly for disadvantaged groups. Adults with disabilities are only mentioned once in the report, indicating their lack of emphasis at the time (Groce & Bakhshi, 2011). The second global report, GRALE 2, in 2013 focused on literacy as the foundation for further learning opportunities for youth and adults. Participation rates were mainly reported by gender, whereas youth and adults with disabilities remained invisible from global monitoring.

The third global report, GRALE 3, in 2016 raised concerns about the invisibility of ALE for youth and adults with disabilities. A major issue was the need to target specific groups with policy to reduce inequalities in accessing ALE to support those most in need (UIL, 2016). This extended to our target group, as "adults with disabilities tend to be a vulnerable minority in many countries, but also a heterogeneous group with different learning needs depending on the type of disability" (UIL, 2016, p. 52). The fourth global report, GRALE 4, in 2019 (UIL) found this group had some of the lowest participation rates in ALE globally, at just 36% in the 135 countries that responded to the survey. With exception of some open-ended responses, little evidence was presented in this or previous global reports about any specific interventions that target and support youth and adults with disabilities. The next section presents key open-ended responses from GRALE 3 and 4 for this group.

EVIDENCE FROM GRALE 3
AND 4 FOR ADULTS WITH DISABILITIES

While the global reports did not directly analyze youth and adults with disabilities, we were granted access to data from GRALE 3 and 4 to examine in more detail open-ended responses to illustrate progress on the five thematic areas of the BFA. From these responses, we separated those describing any changes for youth and adults with disabilities and reorganized them across the five thematic areas (policy, governance, finance, participation, and quality provision) to obtain insights not previously known. This information is also combined with relevant quantitative data in GRALE 3 and 4.

The political commitment and implementation capacity of governments is crucial for the ALE sector to reach youth and adults with disabilities. In 2015 (GRALE 3), only 24 out of 139 participant countries (17%) reported them as a main target group (UIL, 2016). In both GRALE 3 and 4, some countries gave open-ended responses describing ALE political commitment, including legislation, for this group. These include prioritizing youth and adults with disabilities in law and policy guidelines and focusing on inclusive and special education in ALE to reduce exclusion patterns (see Table 7.1 for key examples). In terms of governance in both survey cycles, responses indicate broad consultation, interministerial coordination and cross-collaboration between local government and external stakeholders (Table 7.2).

In 2018 (GRALE 4), out of 148 countries, 28% (41 countries) reported not much prioritizing ALE funding for youth and adults with disabilities, while 25% (37 countries) said they did somewhat. Those that prioritized a lot of ALE funding for this group were 28% (41 countries), while 18% (27 countries) did not know if they did or not. In the same survey cycle,

Table 7.1

Key Examples of ALE Political Commitment for Youth and Adults With Disabilities

Country	Open-Ended Response	Dataset
Bangladesh	prioritizing "youth and men and women with special needs," exceptionally broken down by disability type	GRALE 3
Bolivia	focusing on "inclusive education ... prioritizing sectors ... in a situation of exclusion, marginalization or discrimination"	GRALE 3
Colombia	developed "General Guidelines and Orientations for the Formal Education of Young People and Adults in Colombia" (*Documento de Lineamientos generales y orientaciones para la educación formal de personas jóvenes y adultas en Colombia*) to promote the right to education through "implementation of affordability, accessibility and acceptability" of provision, "paying appropriate attention to adults with disabilities"	GRALE 4

Note. Open-ended responses extracted from the original primary datasets collected by UIL for GRALE 3 and 4, some of which were used in the global reports.

Table 7.2

Key Examples of ALE Governance for Youth and Adults With Disabilities

Country	Open-Ended Response	Dataset
Cyprus	its collaboration "between the Sports For All ... program and municipalities, communities, non-profit organisations to implement sport programs for adults, people with disabilities ... [to] improve the development of synergies among the several stakeholders and enhance the governance of the sector"	GRALE 4
Malaysia	Regarding its Eleventh Malaysian Plan 2016–2020 towards realizing Vision 2020, which maps the country's growth according to economic and social dimensions, "inter-ministries programs ... ensure ... the lifelong learning agenda benefits all targeted groups under RMKe-11, like ... the disabled"	GRALE 4
Paraguay	"between November 2009 and 2011, a broad process of collective participation was carried out ... [including] people with disabilities"	GRALE 3

Note. Open-ended responses extracted from the original primary datasets collected by UIL for GRALE 3 and 4, some of which were used in the global reports.

some countries provided more information about funding in open-ended responses, see Table 7.3 for key examples. Some call for financing project proposals and a funding directive targeting youth and adults with disabilities, also a mixed-sourced fund, vouchers, and a dedicated center. Most funding initiatives for adults with disabilities aim to increase work skills and employability.

There was progress in countries reporting ALE participation for youth and adults with disabilities over the last decade. First, the proportion of countries without any knowledge of participation by this group declined from 46% in 2015 to 30% in 2018. In addition, while 27 out of 100 countries (27%) reported an increase in participation for adults with disabilities between 2009 and 2015, 49 out of 144 countries (36%) reported an increase in their participation between 2015 and 2018—a significant improvement. Open-ended responses in GRALE 3 and 4 point to guidelines for more inclusion of youth and adults with disabilities and programs tailored to them, many focusing on job training (see Table 7.4 for key examples).

Yet, reaching adults with disabilities with national programs remains scarce in the global reports. In 2015, 60 out of 139 countries reported youth and adults with disabilities were among the hardest to reach for programs, and only 14 out of 139 reported that national programs were perceived as

Table 7.3

Key Examples of ALE Finance for Youth and Adults With Disabilities

Country	Open-Ended Response	Dataset
Estonia	a call for proposals in 2016 for financing projects, "including adults without basic or secondary education or vocational training, who are less active in lifelong learning; for example, people with special needs" to offer work skills and competence training	GRALE 4
Montenegro	a Fund for Professional Rehabilitation and Employment of Persons with Disabilities, an integral part of Employment Agency of Montenegro; it is financed through "special contribution paid by employers, budget of Montenegro, budget of local self-government unit on the territory of which [the] disabled person resides or from donations and support by domestic and foreign legal and natural persons"	GRALE 4
South Korea	vouchers for adults with disabilities from low-income households and who may have limited basic and secondary education—"they can earn degrees or take part in programs for self-development," an initiative that is exceptionally not linked to training and employability; the country also funds the National Center for Lifelong Education Promotion for the Disabled with KRW 1.3 billion, equivalent to approximately 1.1 million USD	GRALE 4

Note. Open-ended responses extracted from the original primary dataset collected by UIL for GRALE 4, some of which were used in the global report.

Table 7.4

Key Examples of ALE Participation for Youth and Adults With Disabilities

Country	Open-Ended Response	Dataset
Colombia	in reference to "a flexible educational model for literacy," there is now published "guidance for paying appropriate attention to adults with disabilities"	GRALE 4
Georgia	"since 2015 [the] Ministry of Health, Labour and Social Affairs in Cooperation with [the] Ministry of Education and Science ... started short-term training" with "priorities ... given to persons with special educational needs, persons with disabilities"	GRALE 4
Hungary	its "dual-VET" with "special attention ... to the most vulnerable, low-qualified, low-skilled adults who have no or limited access to adult learning facilities ... such as people living with changed working abilities"	GRALE 4

successful (GRALE 3). In 2018, 36% (52 countries) reported an increase to ALE provision for this group while 35% (50 countries) reported no change, 3% (4 countries) reported a decrease, and 26% (37 countries) did not know if there was a change (GRALE 4). In the same cycle, countries gave information about provision quality—such as specialized materials and textbooks, and different research and evaluation initiatives—to better understand how to improve access, quality, and progression for this group (Table 7.5).

COUNTRY CASE STUDIES: BOTSWANA AND IRELAND

Based on evidence in global reporting, two countries, Botswana and Ireland, were selected as examples that illustrate the potential of ALE for youth and adults with disabilities. These two countries take different approaches to offering ALE for this group in line with their respective national priorities,

Table 7.5

Key Examples of ALE Quality, Including Research, for Youth and Adults With Disabilities

Country	Open-Ended Response	Dataset
Malta	evaluating "inclusive practices in the provision of lifelong learning courses," such as "specific educational support needs and disabilities … [to] broadly highlight … challenges faced by center coordinators, educators, and learners in the identification, maintenance and effective support of an adult learner" from this group	GRALE 4
Mexico	"a national consultation to review the contents of the MEVyT modules," or the Education Model for Life and Work (*Modelo Educación para la Vida y el Trabajo*—MEVyT), focused on the Braille population	GRALE 4
South Korea	its National Center for Lifelong Education Promotion for the Disabled conducts research to develop programs "by disability type and characteristics," also specialized textbooks and learning materials; also linking Lifelong Learning Accounts—which "accumulates various learning experiences of individuals in online learning accounts for improved management, linking them with educational background and certification, or using them for employment"—with the Korea National Institute for Special Education for "the training history of special education teachers"	GRALE 4

Note. Open-ended responses extracted from the original primary dataset collected by UIL for GRALE 4, some of which were used in the global report.

infrastructural capacities, demographics, and other factors. We found the difference in approach beneficial for analysis, while acknowledging country size and language (English) were also main considerations. These examples cannot be said to be representative of the Global South or Global North and are not comparable, but they point to some common trends that are discussed in relation to GRALE in the next section.

Literature reviewed for the case studies resulted from Boolean searches—a method to narrow or broaden collection by combining words—in ERIC, BEI, APA PsycInfo, and eBook Collection (EBSCOhost) databases. We used broad phrases with different combinations of "adult learning and education" and "disability," and searches by disability type. The UNESCO digital library was also searched. Because of the large amount of literature in Ireland, collection went from year 2000 to the present. As a result, peer-reviewed articles, reports, policy papers, book chapters, conference proceedings, and a PhD dissertation were reviewed, totaling 17 documents for Botswana and 30 for Ireland. This literature was verified through online checks of public information for each country, especially for Botswana since some sources are quite dated, adding to the reference list. Summaries of each case on youth and adults with disabilities are to follow based on the five thematic areas of the BFA (UNESCO Institute of Lifelong Learning, 2010).

Case Study: Botswana

ALE plays a significant role in Botswana in developing literacy skills associated with economic development, impacting nearly all sectors and social life (Adekanmbi & Modise, 2000). However, there is no legislation in Botswana for people with disabilities, and the country has not signed the CRPD (cited in the chapter introduction). The constitution does not call for nondiscrimination on the grounds of disability, which makes progress in this area mostly dependent on political will (Mukhopadhyay & Moswela, 2016).

That said, there are country policies that address this target group, most visibly the National Policy on Care for People with Disabilities (NPCPD) put in place in 1996, which outlines a country response to coordinating service delivery across sectors. In it, ALE for youth and adults with disabilities aims to fully develop their abilities and responsibility for their well-being (Abosi, 2000). In 2013, the government designed an Inclusive Education Policy Plan to further address the learning needs of people with disabilities (Monyatsi & Phibion, 2015). The United Nations Development Programme (UNDP, 2019) is currently working with Botswana to develop a national disability strategy policy and law, including consulting people with disabilities in the country, laying the groundwork for acceding to the CRPD.

A few other country policies directly and indirectly support ALE for this group. The Long-Term Vision for Botswana (Republic of Botswana, 1997a) specifies that participation in society should be unrestricted, and it calls for providing centers for social and civic interaction for youth and adults with disabilities (Adekanmbi & Modise, 2000). The Industrial Development Policy for Botswana (Republic of Botswana, 1998) targets women and people with disabilities to increase participation in professional, scientific, technical, and managerial learning opportunities (Adekanmbi & Modise, 2000). The National Policy on Vocational Education and Training (Republic of Botswana Government, 1997b) focuses on skills development through formal and non-formal training for different sectors of the economy, including self-employment. And the National Youth Policy addresses unemployment by calling for special support for the disadvantaged (Republic of Botswana, 1996b).

While information is limited (and dated) about ALE governance for youth and adults with disabilities, a study was conducted in the 1970s on different disabilities prevalent in the country, which the Ministry of Health responded to with other sectors, including the Ministry of Education. The result was the Special Education Division (Government of Botswana, n.d.). Generally, in terms of vocational education and training, provision is offered from certificate to diploma levels through various institutions (Ookeditse, 2018), including seven technical colleges owned by the government. "Data published by Commonwealth Education Online (2015) indicates that tertiary education in Botswana is provided by approximately thirty vocational and technical training centres, four teacher-training colleges, two colleges of education and two universities" (Monyatsi & Phibion, 2015, p. 60). A distinctive feature is the brigade system, comprised of small, community-owned entities offering skills training, income-generating activities, and rural development projects (Raditloaneng, 2000), which is key since 75% of people in Botswana live in rural areas. The government gives financial and technical support (Ookeditse, 2018) and sits on the board of trustees (Raditloaneng, 2000).

The NPCPD highlights the ongoing inability of persons with disabilities to access quality education, citing infrastructure weakness, made worse by "a lack of resources, geographical distances, and physical and social barriers" (Republic of Botswana, 1996a, p. 3). Casey (1998) confirmed that access to vocational education and training was an issue for youth and adults with disabilities because of barriers to facilities, low quality learning, especially for those with severe disabilities, and inadequate funding. The net result is poorer life outcomes; for example, 74% remain unemployed (Abosi et al., 1999).

ALE participation in Botswana is supported from basic education to junior secondary, mainly for out-of-school youth and those without formal education. There are also extension programs in health, agriculture, and commerce; continuing education through part-time training for people with disabilities (Modise, 2015); and specialist training through public and private organizations (Republic of Botswana, 1997c). In addition to theater (Adekanmbi & Modise, 2000), other learning modalities include mass media for youth and adults through national radio, community development, and cooperative education (Youngman, 1998). ALE contexts include the armed forces, church organizations, and the adult education association.

The Centre for Continuing Education at the University of Botswana leads part-time and distance learning programs at tertiary level (Modise, 2015). The university supports youth and adults with disabilities based on non-discriminatory admission procedures, wider access, and support services. The Disability Support Services Unit (DSSU) enables this work with "diagnostic support and needs assessment, assistive devices, as well as psychosocial networks, and referrals" (Monyatsi & Phibion, 2015, p. 61). Along with improving access to physical infrastructure, the university hired staff to enhance discussions on the diverse learning needs of this group, but funding challenges and social perceptions limit progress.

In GRALE 4, Botswana reported providing learning materials for adults with special needs. However, we have no other evidence on the quality of learning for youth and adults with disabilities in the country. There is extensive critical analysis of the Botswana National Literacy Plan (BNLP), shedding light on ALE quality for this group since illiteracy inhibits their social development (Mukhopadhyay & Moswela, 2016). Issues are weak teaching, a lack of content development with learners, and no program review (Maruatona, 2002, 2004). It does not address development, such as poverty alleviation, limiting the acquisition of critical thinking, among other competencies for social transformation. Teachers themselves may be marginalized, with basic qualifications and not much training to empower the adult learner. Another issue is the language of instruction may not match with learners' preferred language.

In summary, ALE policies exist in Botswana for youth and adults with disabilities, though legislation does not—a problem addressed in the forthcoming national strategy policy and law to domesticate the CRPD (UNDP, 2019). The literature does not extensively describe governance or any funding for this group, indicating a few knowledge gaps. There is also a gap in monitoring, which limits evidence-based responses. We know little about how youth and adults with disabilities participate in ALE, or about learning quality disaggregated by disability types. Therefore, it is not known whether provisions match specific learning needs.

Case Study: Ireland

Ireland has a long ALE history linked to outreach programs (European Association for the Education of Adults [EAEA], 2011) for the disadvantaged (McGill & Morgan, 2001). The Department of Education and Skills mainly organizes ALE through a rights-based approach, also emphasizing "capacity for delivery, policy formulation, research and evaluation" (EAEA, 2011, p. 4) for system performance.

Joint work on ALE for youth and adults with disabilities is written into Ireland's legislation, which has strengthened in the last two decades. It includes the Disability Act 2005, National Disability Strategy 2004, and Education for Persons with Special Educational Needs (EPSEN) Act 2004, Employment Equality Acts 1998–2015, and Equal Status Acts 2000–2015. The independent Irish Human Rights and Equality Commission (IHREC) "prevent[s] discrimination and protect[s] human rights" (Banks et al., 2018, p. 2) for them. The country also ratified the CRPD (Government of Ireland, 2015), and policies align with the European Union in this area.

Several governance strategies focus on further and higher education for this group to enhance their independence and employability. The National Disability Strategy Implementation Plan 2013–2015 took this approach (SOLAS, 2014), carried forward by the National Disability Inclusion Strategy 2017–2021 through actions linking departments and councils. The Further Education and Training (FET) Strategy 2014–2019 aligned with these continued by the Comprehensive Employment Strategy for People with Disabilities 2015–2024 through three-year action plans with a monitoring framework (Government of Ireland, 2015). The independent National Disability Authority (NDA) guides implementation.

Ireland is currently in the Strategy's Phase Two Action Plan 2019–2021, which delegates to responsible bodies with clear deliverables, monitoring criteria, and milestones. Actions for youth and adults with disabilities include building awareness of training for early school leavers and providing specialist support to build capacity. Management of the "Ability Programme" is also prioritized, as is progression from pre-apprenticeship to full apprenticeship programs and learning pathways, and reviewing FET (Government of Ireland, 2019). The "Ability Programme" is a relatively new "pre-activation programme for young people with disabilities" linking those distant from the labor market to training, personal development, and work exposure (Department of Employment Affairs and Social Protection, 2018). As of June 2018, it was awarded €16 million for 27 projects over three years.

Further to funding for youth and adults with disabilities, the country's "Back to Education" initiative promotes flexible, part-time post compulsory formal education supported by financial schemes (EAEA, 2011). Most FET offered through the local Education and Training Boards (ETBs) are free. Annually, public FET costs approximately $800m+ (SOLAS, 2014), though it is not clear how much goes to our group, or by disability type and degree. This amount is necessary to maintain basic levels, acknowledging programming tends to cost more for people with disabilities. The Fund for Students with Disabilities (FSD) is a key source for "further and higher education institutions … [with] the necessary assistance and equipment to enable … access" (Higher Education Authority, n.d.).

According to public information online, it is possible to participate in part-time and full-time ALE courses, including literacy and vocational training through ETBs. Formal qualifications are not necessary, though some courses require completion of secondary school, and courses can lead to certificates, including the leaving certificate. Ireland has a national qualifications framework that integrates learning pathways, for example to move from community education to further and higher education. There is also work placement, training networks (e.g., Skillnet Ireland), and skills training with state agencies.

However, access to education for people with disabilities in Ireland has come under scrutiny. A 2018 report prepared for IHREC by the Economic and Social Research Institute (ESRI) shows students with disabilities are more likely to face barriers, including disliking school, resulting in poorer learning outcomes (Banks et al., 2018). Expectations are lower for this group, which can compromise progressing to further and higher education and employment. For those who do progress, transition planning and retention are issues. Studies show discrimination on entry to higher education varies by disability type.

We know from GRALE 4 that Ireland reported a 2016 SOLAS study to understand barriers to participation and quality for youth and adults with disability in FET. Findings were that legislation does not remove all barriers, including "negative peer experiences, low expectations of teachers, and a lack of disability specific accommodations" (Mooney & O'Rourke, 2017, p. 11). Confirming other findings, this can result in early school leaving. Full-time courses may overexert youth and adults with disabilities, requiring a shift to more flexible approaches (Mooney & O'Rourke, 2017). Curricula did not always match demand, and many instructors were not using universal design learning (UDL; Mooney & O'Rourke, 2017). Also, guidance on courses may not be clear, and progression to further and higher education is largely unmonitored. That said, the study did not disaggregate by disability type and ALE, focusing more broadly on the long-term unemployed and vulnerable groups.

In summary, evidence suggests that ALE legislation and policies in Ireland are in place for youth and adults with disabilities based on regional and international benchmarks. The literature describes governance along with funding for this group, yet not uniformly. There is a knowledge gap on the disaggregation of disability data and ALE (acknowledging some sub-groups are researched), suggesting progress for everyone in this group should be looked at through more targeted inquiry across all sub-groups to better inform responses.

DISCUSSION BASED ON GRALE AND CASE STUDIES

Three key points emerged from the combined analysis of global monitoring and the case studies of Botswana and Ireland for improving ALE for youth and adults with disabilities. These are (a) disaggregating disability data by type and degree, (b) diversifying learning outcomes, and (c) improving quality learning by building up the knowledge base.

On the first point, global monitoring in GRALE 3 says youth and adults with disabilities are often a vulnerable minority and have different learning needs depending on disability type (UIL, 2016). GRALE 4 tells us this group had some of the lowest global participation rates, but we have no data on which sub-groups participated (i.e., those with sensory, physical, psychological, or emotional, intellectual and learning disabilities, which could further disaggregate to specific conditions and severity). Understanding ALE provision for youth and adults with different types of disabilities is important not just for addressing the specific needs of this group, but also to ensure there is diversity and inclusion to foster better participation and learning for all—therefore not disassociating them from general development trends. For instance, disability data for ALE is not disaggregated in either of the case studies presented here, thus failing to give us any idea of meaningful access and quality.

Open-ended responses to GRALE 4 suggest some disaggregation, for example, Mexico's work on developing content in MEVyT modules for the Braille reading population. Another example is South Korea's National Center for Lifelong Education Promotion for the Disabled, which researches disability types to improve programming. Also, in GRALE 3, Bangladesh reported prioritizing "youth and men and women with special needs," exceptionally broken down by disability type. Unfortunately, these are isolated cases where some level of disaggregation is taking place rather than a normative practice. Considering young people and adults with disabilities as a homogenous group limits ALE's strategic role to deliver on the right to education, and the realization of other human rights, to improve inclusion, diversity, equity, and social mobility for this group. Therefore, more efforts are needed in ALE global monitoring to collect disaggregated data by disability type while remaining situated in the larger discussion about progress on global policy commitments.

On the second point, learning outcomes in global monitoring and the case studies for youth and adults with disabilities are largely oriented to skills formation for economic development, employability, and livelihoods. Therefore, most ALE programing and provisions tend to focus on literacy and enhancement of basic skills to this end, which are important to set the foundation for higher order competencies. Skills development in ALE for youth and adults with disabilities also focuses on vocational education and training to get this group into the labor market. This is very important, since the unemployment rate for this group tends to be very high. Participation of youth and adults with disabilities in the labor market can have further benefits in terms of health and wellbeing (UIL, 2016).

However, focusing exclusively on economic outcomes is unlikely to provide full inclusion, equity, and social mobility for youth and adults with disabilities. ALE can further prioritize subjects for social transformation, including the development of socioemotional skills, critical thinking, and active engagement in social and environmental issues. GRALE 3 and 4 acknowledge the social benefits of ALE, but global monitoring and the case studies generally ignore these subjects for youth and adults with disabilities. Education has a central role in promoting self-respect, increased confidence, and advocacy, as noted in Hammad and Singal (2015) and Singal et al. (2011). Thus, broadening learning outcomes in ALE can significantly promote the inclusion of persons with disabilities in larger development goals.

The final point is the quality of ALE for youth and adults with disabilities continues to be of concern, even if some actions are being taken to improve the learning process. In terms of access, GRALE 4 tells us 36% (52 countries) reported an increase to ALE provision for youth and adults with disabilities. However, having access does not mean ALE is tailored to disability type and degree, which is inextricably linked to assessments of quality and the effectiveness of ALE for this group. GRALE 4 indicates that some countries—including Ireland, Malta, Mexico, and South Korea—are doing research to improve inputs to learning for youth and adults with disabilities (e.g., on teaching, curricula, and learning materials), but it is not always disaggregated by disability type (e.g., the 2016 SOLAS study).

Knowledge of ALE quality for youth and adults with disabilities is limited in the current literature, global monitoring, and the case studies. This knowledge gap compromises our ability to establish social norms of best principles and practices to enhance teaching and learning for this group according to the right to education and other global policy aims and general development trends (e.g., reducing the high unemployment rate for this group in different countries, increasing active participation in civic and community issues to influence and shape society). It also limits establishing norms on quality teaching and learning to meet the differentiated needs of sub-groups to raise their specific learning outcomes and improve broader impacts for them. This gap echoes a bigger issue raised previously, which is the overall lack of a detailed evidence base on ALE for this group. This is a huge problem that the research community must address, in response to Groce and Bakhshi's (2011) call of action to make any real progress globally for youth and adults with disabilities.

CONCLUSION

Established in the introduction, quality education is a powerful mechanism for breaking the cyclical relationship of disability and poverty (WHO, 2011) and creating more social inclusion, diversity, equity, and social mobility. In particular, and according to global policy commitments such as the BFA (UNESCO Institute of Lifelong Learning, 2010) and SDG 4 (United Nations, 2015), quality ALE has a strategic role in this process given the large numbers of people with disabilities who miss out on formal education or have low levels of learning due to their previous education experiences. However, what this chapter has found through an examination of relevant findings across the five global monitoring areas of policies, governance, finance, participation, and quality provision, and in looking at the case studies of Botswana and Ireland, is that progress is hampered by a lack of disaggregated data on disability types, limited learning outcomes, and not enough information to improve provision. Advancing normative practice in this area, which is necessary to promote more and better learning opportunities for youth and adults with disabilities around the world, will not happen until the knowledge base is strengthened to more fully inform and influence decision-making for both policy and implementation.

REFERENCES

Abosi, O. C. (2000). Trends and issues in special education in Botswana. *The Journal of Special Education*, *34*(1), 48–53. https://doi.org/10.1177/002246690003400105

Abosi, O., Sison, W., & Nwaogu, P. (1999). *Situational analysis of some adults with disabilities in Botswana*. Council for the Disabled.

Adekanmbi, G., & Modise, O. (2000). The state of adult and continuing education in Botswana, In S. A. Indabawa, A. Oduaran, T. Afrik, & S. Walters (Eds.), *The State of Adult and Continuing Education in Africa* (pp. 72–85). German Adult Education Association, Institute for International Cooperation. https://eric.ed.gov/?id=ED453359

Banks, J., Grotti, R., Fahey, E., & Watson, D. (2018). *Disability and discrimination in Ireland: evidence from the QNHS Equality Modules 2004, 2010, 2014*. https://www.esri.ie/publications/disability-and-discrimination-in-ireland-evidence-from-the-qnhs-equality-modules-2004

Casey, E. (1998). *A study on access to vocational education and training for students with severe disabilities in Botswana*. Government Printers.

Department of Employment Affairs and Social Protection. (2018). *Annual report 2018.* https://www.gov.ie/en/publication/b32a83-annual-report-2018/

European Association for the Education of Adults. (2011). *Country report on adult education in Ireland.* https://eaea.org/wp-content/uploads/2018/01/ireland_country-report-on-adult-education-in-ireland.pdf

Government of Botswana (n.d.). *National Policy on Care of People with Disabilities.* http://168.167.134.123/en-gb/Citizens-Residents/Social%20Services/Pages/National-Policy-On-Care-of-People-with-Disabilities.aspx

Government of Ireland. (2015). *Comprehensive Employment Strategy for People with Disabilities.* http://www.justice.ie/en/JELR/Comprehensive%20Employment%20Strategy%20for%20People%20with%20Disabilities%20-%20FINAL.pdf/Files/Comprehensive%20Employment%20Strategy%20for%20People%20with%20Disabilities%20-%20FINAL.pdf

Government of Ireland. (2019). *Comprehensive Employment Strategy Phase Two Action Plan 2019–2021.* https://www.gov.ie/en/publication/59d403-comprehensive-employment-strategy-action-plan-2019-2021/

Groce, N., & Bakhshi, P. (2011). Illiteracy among adults with disabilities in the developing world: a review of the literature and a call to action. *International Journal of Inclusive Education, 15*(10), 1153–1168. https://www.tandfonline.com/doi/abs/10.1080/13603116.2011.555068

Hammad, T., & Singal, N. (2015). Education of women with disabilities in Pakistan: Enhanced agency, unfulfilled aspirations. *International Journal of Inclusive Education, 19*(12), 1244–1264. https://www.tandfonline.com/doi/abs/10.1080/13603116.2015.1043962?journalCode=tied20

Higher Education Authority (n.d.). *Fund for Students with Disabilities.* https://hea.ic/funding-governance performance/funding/student-finance/fund-for-students-with-disabilities/

Maruatona, T. (2002). A critical analysis of literacy practice in Botswana. *Adult Basic Education, 12*(2), 82–99. https://eric.ed.gov/?id=EJ656925

Maruatona, T. (2004). State hegemony and the planning and implementation of literacy education in Botswana. *International Journal of Educational Development, 24,* 53–65. https://www.sciencedirect.com/science/article/abs/pii/S0738059303001123

McGill, P., & Morgan, M. (2001). *A report for the Centre for Cross Border Studies: Ireland's learning poor—adult educational disadvantage and cross-border cooperation.* http://crossborder.ie/irelands-learning-poor/

Modise, O. M. (2015). Building the profession of adult education: the case of the University of Botswana's Department of Adult Education. *Creative Education, 6,* 2481–2492. https://m.scirp.org/papers/62436

Monyatsi, P. P., & Phibion, O. S. (2015). Facilitating access to higher education for students with disabilities: strategies and support services at the University of Botswana. In T. Halvorsen, H. Ibsen, & V. M'kumbuzi (Eds.), *Knowledge for a sustainable world: A Southern African-Nordic contribution* (pp. 55–70). African Minds. http://www.africanbookscollective.com/books/knowledge-for-a-sustainable-world

Mooney, R., & O'Rourke, C. (2017). *Training with particular reference to long term unemployed persons and other vulnerable individuals.* https://www.solas.ie/f/70398/x/432b2fa3ba/barriers-to-fet-final-june-2017.pdf

Mukhopadhyay, S., & Moswela, E. (2016). *Situation analysis of disability rights in the context of Botswana.* Open Society Initiative for Southern Africa. http://rodra.co.za/images/countries/botswana/research/Situation%20Analysis%20Report%20of%20Disability%20Rights%20in%20the%20Context%20of%20Botswana%20-%202016.pdf

Ookeditse, G. (2018). *Teachers' views about postsecondary planning and effective transition programs for students with disabilities* [Doctoral dissertation, Ball State University]. http://cardinalscholar.bsu.edu/handle/123456789/201113

Raditloaneng, W. N. (2000). Adult education as vocational training: The case of brigades in Botswana. In K. P. King & T. R. Ferro (Eds.), *Proceedings of the Second Eastern Regional Adult Education Research Conference* (pp. 189–194). University Park, Pennsylvania.

Republic of Botswana. (1996a). *National Policy on Care for People with Disabilities, Presidential Directive Cab: 5/96.* Ministry of Health.

Republic of Botswana. (1996b). *The National Youth Policy.* Government Printer.

Republic of Botswana. (1997a). *Long term vision for Botswana: Towards prosperity for all.* Publisher not indicated.

Republic of Botswana. (1997b). *National Policy on Vocational Education and Training.* Ministry of Labour and Home Affairs.

Republic of Botswana. (1997c). *National Development Plan 8, 1997/98-2002/03.* Government Printer.

Republic of Botswana. (1998). *Industrial Development Policy for Botswana. Ministry of Commerce and Industry.* Government Printer.

Singal, N., Jeffery, R., Jain, A., & Sood, N. (2011). The enabling role of education in the lives of young people with disabilities in India: Achieved and desired outcomes. *International Journal of Inclusive Education, 15*(10), 1205–1218. https://www.tandfonline.com/doi/abs/10.1080/13603116.2011.555076

SOLAS (Further Education and Training Authority). (2014). *Further Education and Training Strategy 2014–2019.* https://www.gov.ie/en/publication/1d219a-further-education-and-training-strategy-2014-2019/

United Nations Development Programme. (2019, November 25). *Botswana: rights of persons with disabilities.* https://www.bw.undp.org/content/botswana/en/home/operations/projects/democratic_governance/convention-on-the-rights-of-persons-with-disabilities.html

UNESCO. (2019). *Global education monitoring report, 2019: migration, displacement and education: building bridges, not walls.* https://unesdoc.unesco.org/ark:/48223/pf0000265866

UNESCO Institute of Lifelong Learning. (2010). *Belém Framework for Action: Harnessing the power and potential of adult learning and education for a viable future.* https://uil.unesco.org/adult-education/confintea/belem-framework-action

UNESCO Institute of Lifelong Learning. (2016). *3rd global report on adult learning and education: The impact of adult learning and education on health and well-being, employment and the labour market, and social, civic and community life.* https://unesdoc.unesco.org/ark:/48223/pf0000245913

UNESCO Institute of Lifelong Learning. (2019). *4th global report on adult learning and education: leave no one behind—participation, equity and inclusion.* https://unesdoc.unesco.org/ark:/48223/pf0000372274

United Nations (2015). *SDG 4, Target 4.7.* https://sustainabledevelopment.un.org/sdg4

World Health Organization. (2011). *World report on disability.* https://www.who.int/disabilities/world_report/2011/report/en/

World Health Organization. (2015). *WHO global disability action plan 2014–2021: Better health for all people with disability.* https://www.who.int/disabilities/actionplan/en/

Youngman, F. (1998). Botswana. In J. Draper (Ed.), *Africa: Adult Education, Chronologies in Commonwealth Countries* (pp. 26–32). Centre for Adult and Continuing Education in association with NIACE and SIDA. https://eric.ed.gov/?id=ED423433

CHAPTER 8

NORTH KOREANS' HUMAN RIGHTS AND THE SITUATION OF FOREIGN POPULAR CULTURE

An Adult Education Perspective

Jinhee Choi
Seoul National University, South Korea

Freedom is an achievement, not a gift. We do not acquire freedom—we grow into freedom…. The first step toward liberation is taken when an individual begins to understand what inhibits, frustrates, subjugates him. We learn to be free when we know what we desire freedom for and what stands in the way of freedom.

—Eduard C. Lindeman (1926, pp. 70–71)

Among world nations, North Korea is known to place low to last in civil and political rights rankings, the Workers' Party of Korea (WPK) government denying the people the human rights of freedom of thought and information. However, desiring culture in the poor and repressive country, many North Koreans use illegal mobile technology and consume banned foreign media. A number of scholars have examined the influence of foreign media on North Koreans' perceptions and actions, for instance,

Advancing the Global Agenda for Human Rights, Vulnerable Populations, and Environmental Sustainability: Adult Education as Strategic Partner, pp. 117–135
Copyright © 2021 by Information Age Publishing

defection. Social scientists have also studied the material conditions that have impacted the behavior of North Koreans in the first two decades of the twenty-first century: economic crisis, famine, decentralization, the rise of capitalist markets, the growth of a merchant/middle class, and special economic zones. Although useful and valid, the available research directs little attention to the situation of foreign popular culture in raising North Koreans' human rights awareness. This chapter addresses the neglected problem from the perspective of adult education, with special attention on foreign popular culture in the cultural and civil education of North Koreans.

In the classic statement by Lindeman, adult education is inclusive situation–approach learning—structured around the adult learners' needs and interests in work, recreation, family-life, and community-life situations—which takes experience as its textbook, sets the learning process in reality, rebuilds life values, and gives meaning to life. In an adult education point of view, popular culture is situationally within the needs and interests of recreation and community, and it can be used to learn about self, society, and life. A contending school of philosophical thought argues against popular culture as a profit-driven culture industry, which banally, destructively, and falsely prescribes formulas, conventions, and judgments for passage into a miserable monopolized life under capitalist domination (Adorno, 2001; Strinati, 2004). Nevertheless, the scholarly literature explains that popular culture is utilizable in adult learning and in semiotic resistance against dominant meanings (Storey, 2018; Tisdell & Thompson, 2006).

In order to demonstrate the constructive aspect of foreign popular culture on North Koreans' human rights awareness, the author divides the chapter into two parts. The first part describes the political context of universal human rights and North Korea, North Korean human rights violations, and the official *chuch'e* ideology and restriction of human rights. The second part documents the influence of foreign popular culture in North Korea and investigates informal learning through foreign popular culture. The discussion illustrates that the North Korean people are a pedagogically oppressed population—a significant portion of which is discontent with the limitations of life in the closed society—and are spontaneously striving to relate their personalities to a world of global entertainment that is more astonishing and less inhibited than the politically and ideologically exhortative mass culture of the party-state arts studios. With the experience of foreign popular culture, North Koreans receive ideas of freedom, thought, and choice that allow them to learn and create alternative modes of intellection, expression, and action.

PART I. NORTH KOREANS' HUMAN RIGHTS

Universal Human Rights and North Korea

Since the enormous humanitarian catastrophes of the Pacific War and the Second World War (1931–1945), protection of human rights has been a major world priority. In 1948, the United Nations General Assembly issued the Universal Declaration of Human Rights (UDHR), which was approved by 48 member countries. Consisting of a preamble and 30 articles, the historic document upholds "recognition of the inherent dignity and of the equal and inalienable rights of all members of the human family" as foundational to freedom, justice, and world peace, centering on the grand principle of "life, liberty and security of person" (General Assembly of the United Nations [UNGA], n.d.). In 1993, with the precedent of the UDHR, 171 countries advocated the universality of human rights at the World Conference on Human Rights in Vienna, Austria, and in the Vienna Declaration and Programme of Action (VDPA). Complementing the UDHR on universal human rights, Article 5 of the VDPA reads,

> All human rights are universal, indivisible and interdependent and inter-related. The international community must treat human rights globally in a fair and equal manner, on the same footing, and with the same emphasis. While the significance of national and regional particularities and various historical, cultural and religious backgrounds must be borne in mind, it is the duty of States, regardless of their political, economic and cultural systems, to promote and protect all human rights and fundamental freedoms. (World Council of Human Right [WCHR], 2020)

According to the VDPA, universal human rights form a unit, transcend the differences of nation-states, and are *erga omnes* obligations, universal obligations of all states. To actualize recognition of human rights, the UN General Assembly created the Office of the High Commissioner for Human Rights (OHCHR) to champion and defend all human rights. Among the duties of the OHCHR, the office identifies issues of concern, conducts evidence-based research, and develops human rights indicators to support the monitoring of international human rights violations and to implement action plans and remedies.

Although the fundamental principle of universal human rights in the VDPA was unanimously adopted, significant complications arise in its interpretation and implementation. Centrally, the global human rights mechanism lacks the power of enforcement. Case in point: Article 1 of the VDPA says it is "the solemn commitment of all States to fulfill their obligations to promote universal respect for, and observance of, all human rights and fundamental freedoms" (WCHR, 2020). However, many UN member states see human rights protection as interference in internal affairs, and many states prioritize economic growth over national human rights programs (Alizadeh, 2011). Not surprisingly, many UN member states have ratified international human rights instruments without instantiating them. North Korea counts among such states. Another difficulty arises from the liberal capitalist model of human rights advanced in the VDPA. Some scholars appraise the structural relations underlying the model as perpetuating global inequality and violations of human rights (Ho, 2007). Others have argued that the model is complicit in militarized global capitalism (Williams, 2010). A further apparent problem consists in "the limits of a discourse on human rights that will remain inadequate, sometimes hypocritical, and in any case formalistic and inconsistent with itself as long as the law of the market ... maintain[s] an effective inequality" (Derrida, 1994, as cited in Williams, 2010, p. xvi). Consequently, the structural and discursive contradictions bound up with such documents as the VDPA decisively impact North Korean human rights issues, enabling the regime with the well-known rationale of "imperialism" to deny universal human rights to all peoples in North Korea.

North Korean Human Rights Violations

As reported by the Commission of Inquiry on Human Rights in the Democratic People's Republic of Korea (CoIDPRK), an initiative of the United Nations Human Rights Council (UNHRC), North Korea has committed "systematic, widespread and grave violations of human rights" (UNHRC, 2014, para.1). The CoIDPRK defines North Korean human rights violations as "crimes against humanity" (para. 75–76). Moreover, the commission lists nine categories of violations:

1. Violations of the right to food
2. The full range of violations associated with prison camps
3. Torture and inhuman treatment
4. Arbitrary arrest and detention
5. Discrimination, in particular in the systemic denial and violation of basic human rights and fundamental freedoms
6. Violations of the freedom of expression
7. Violations of the right to life
8. Violations of the freedom of movement
9. Enforced disappearances, including abductions of nationals of other States (para. 3)

Despite the efforts of international organizations and civil societies to discourage North Korean human rights violations, little evidence has emerged from within the country of government policies to manifest human rights reform. Several international indicators reinforce suspicions about the monopoly the state-regime has on information control and prohibition of freedom of thought. For example, in the 2020 World Press Freedom Index, the annual ranking of 180 countries based on press freedom, North Korea places at the bottom (Reporters Without Borders [RSF], 2020b). Reporters Without Borders has pointed to the ranking and other factors as confirming state–regime efforts to block the North Korean citizenry from information access (RSF, 2020a). In addition, Freedom in the World 2020, a global report on political rights and civil liberties, gives North Korea a score of 0 out of 40 on political rights and 3 out of 60 on civil liberties (Freedom House, 2020). With the low freedom scores, the pro-democracy organization Freedom House characterizes present-day North Korea as a "one-party state led by a dynastic totalitarian dictatorship" (Freedom House, 2020). Using other assessment criteria, political scientists in the recent past have non-unanimously described North Korea as fading totalitarian, failing, or eroding totalitarian, and autocratic post-totalitarian (McEachern, 2010; Scobell, 2008; Silberstein, 2010).

Academic and humanitarian sources reveal two main reasons for the lack of improvement on North Korean human rights issues: an ineffective international human rights system and the uncooperativeness of the national government (Fahy, 2019; Human Rights Watch, 2020). The existing international human rights system is unable to negotiate real social-political change for the benefit of the North Korean citizenry because nation–states have different priorities and political interests. Notably, the People's Republic of China adheres to a 1998 bilateral repatriation agreement with North Korea rather than observing the UN 1951 Refugee Convention and its 1967 Protocol ("China's Repatriation," 2012). Also, the current government of South Korea has prioritized inter-Korean dialog and engagement and stopped cosponsoring the UN General Assembly resolution on North Korean human rights (Ministry of Foreign Affairs, 2019). In the case of the United States, its response to North Korea has been inconsistent, depending on the frequently alternating Democratic and Republican administrations—with each new administration, the policies change as a result of conflicting tactical interests. Most recently, Republican President Donald Trump met three times with North Korean leader Kim Chŏng-ŭn on June 12, 2018, in Singapore; February 27–28, 2019, in Vietnam; and June 30, 2019, at the Korean Demilitarized Zone (DMZ). However, the focus of the meetings was denuclearization, sanctions, and rapprochement, not human rights.

While the international situation works in the favor of the North Korean state–regime, it continues to view international human rights allegations as political threats from foreign powers, echoing what late leader Kim Chŏng-il declared 27 years ago in 1994:

> The imperialists now violently interfere in other countries' affairs and trample upon other nations' sovereignty [Note: The general reference is proximate in time to the United States-led Persian Gulf War in 1990 to 1991—JC]. They try to justify these acts under the excuse of "defense of human rights." Human rights cannot be conceived separately from the independence of countries and nations. Human rights can never be ensured for people who are dominated by foreign forces. Human rights are rights to independence which must be exercised by the people in the political, economic, ideological, cultural and all other spheres of social life. The "human rights" advertised by the imperialists are privileges of the rich, privileges to do anything on the strength of money. ... We will never tolerate any imperialist interference or arbitrariness aimed at infringing upon the sovereignty of our country and nation, which we will staunchly safeguard [Note: The word translated as "nation" is *minjok*, or "ethnic-race"—JC]. (Kim, n.d., pp. 26–27)

That is to say, in North Korea, human rights are coterminous with a nationally particularist *Staatsrecht* (right of the state). Therefore, the North Korean state-regime perceives international demands for disclosure of its domestic human rights situation as an endangerment to state and ethnic-racial sovereignty and as a pretext for hostile foreign regime-change.

Chuch'e Ideology and Restriction of Human Rights

Of the reported North Korean human rights violations, the most critical problem is the "absolute monopoly over information and total control of organized social life" (UNHRC, 2014, para. 26). The UN rapporteur observes, "Control over and surveillance of the population persists" (UNHRC, 2020, para. 14). Such controls are seen in the state media, which only releases politically approved content. In addition, the general use of telephones is bound to regional services that state agencies monitor. Under strenuously imposed controls over information and freedom of thought, North Koreans lack opportunities to develop basic notions of universal human rights. The lack of human rights awareness is also a consequence of the state ideology of *chuch'e* (subject). On the political meaning of the term, it first appeared in a 1955 speech by Kim Il-sŏng, the first leader of North Korea, signifying the "Korean revolution" (Kim, 1965, p. 315; cf. Hwang, 2010; Korean News, 2005). Afterward, in 1961–1964, during the

Sino-Soviet split, North Korean sources stopped translating the word and then, in 1965, publicized the definitions "independent stand" and "spirit of self-reliance" (David-West, 2011, p. 182n1; Kim, 1965, pp. 494n39). In grand principle, *chuch'e* ideology calls the North Korean people masters, but in political practice, the people are servants of the all-powerful great leader (*suryŏng*; chieftain). The late defected Hwang Chang-yŏp, system-izer and establisher of Kim's ideology, says North Korean absolutism is a highly degenerated form of Stalinism (Hwang, 2002a, 2002b, 2002d, 2010). He explains that there is no concept of individual human rights in the absolutist-Stalinist system in North Korea:

> North Korea is currently a society where respect for human rights has yet to exist. Human rights cannot co-exist with the absolutism of the Great Leader. Only the Great Leader has absolute human rights; all others are simply his vassals. An individual's fate and human rights belong not to the individual but to the Great Leader. How can the right to oppose the abso-lutism of the Great Leader exist in a society where the highest moral value is considered to dedicate one's body and soul to the Great Leader? No mat-ter how much the Great Leader and his agents infringe on people's human rights, it is considered acts of blameless morality. In an advanced country [such as the United States—JC], a president has to answer to the Congress for his sex scandals [i.e., the Clinton/Lewinsky affair], but in North Korea, no one can question the Great Leader's behavior or his agents' infringe-ment of human rights. (Hwang, 2002c)

What is more, the state-regime infringes on human rights through indirect and direct forms of violence:

> The root of the problem of human rights violations in North Korea lies in the absolutism of the Great Leader.... The basic force that is sustaining absolutism of the Great Leader is the Workers' Party of Korea and the mili-tary [i.e., Korean People's Army]. Party dictatorship and military dictator-ship both have the characteristic of being dependent on violence for their existence. The difference is that in party dictatorship, violence is preceded by organizational and ideological control, whereas military dictatorship ap-plies violence directly. (Hwang, 2002d)

Under an absolutist system of party and military violence, North Koreans are culturally and ideologically indoctrinated to believe that their social-political life is the bestowment of the great leader, whom the state-regime justifies in 1930s to 1950s Soviet-Stalinist idiom as the benevolent father of the people. (North Korea was liberated, modeled, and founded under the Soviet Army in 1945–1948, during the era of High Stalinism, and was a Soviet satellite until the Korean War in 1950–1953.) The North Korean citizenry being figurative children of the great leader, they are familialy obligated to be filial and loyal to him. Utilizing the politically religious and patricentric great leader ideology, North Korea has sustained a political culture of totalitarian familism, curtailing freedom of thought, conscience, and religion, as well as other basic human rights. Studies on North Korean defectors in South Korea have confirmed that the people are deficient in awareness and understanding of their human rights (Lee, 2020). Human rights researchers cite defectors who ascribe the problem to Kim family worship and forced ideological education (Lee & English, 2016).

The assertion of ideology in North Korea has a sociological basis. Confronted with economic and social pressures, the North Korean state-regime needs to protect itself by strengthening the monolithic *chuch'e* ideology and, in turn, increasing human rights violations. Since the loss of fraternal trading partners following the collapse of the Soviet Union and the Eastern Bloc in 1989–1991, North Korea has been unable to reliably distribute food and commodities to the people, with natural disasters, policy mismanagement, and economic sanctions exacerbating the crisis. A famine situation from the early 1990s to 1998 led to the spread of unofficial markets, for the people's food needs, throughout the country (Haggard & Noland, 2007). In 2002, the state-regime legalized an incipient form of authoritarian state-capitalism yet is contending with bottom-up social pressures, an influential capitalist merchant class, and illegal foreign media exposure among laypeople and officials (David-West, 2013).

Defensively reacting to the threatening social changes, the North Korean state–regime has responded by intensifying security policies and ideological indoctrination, enhancing propaganda through mobile technology, and reinforcing technological surveillance and suppression (S. Yoon, 2020). Tellingly, three years into his hereditary rule in 2014, Kim Chŏng-ŭn declared ideology to be "the most powerful weapon … the one and only weapon" of the ruling party, emphasizing, "'Exceptions' must never be permitted in ideological work," and "Ideological workers … must use the ideological 'scalpel' promptly to root out the causes of such misdemeanours," with the party ideological position "established in the form for attack" (n.d., pp. 1–2, 8, 17). Subsequently, in 2019, he mandated, "We will intensify the struggle against anti-socialist and non-socialist deeds and tighten moral discipline, and the working people's organizations will scrupulously carry out ideological education" (Korean News, 2020). Kim's position on ideology and ideological education is consistent with his grandfather Kim Il-sŏng's "Theses on Socialist Education" speech of 1977. As state ideological repression intensified, the number of human rights violations in North Korea has purportedly increased. The UN rapporteur surmised that the situation in 2020 would worsen because of low crop production, firmer border control, continued surveillance, and trade bans in face of the COVID-19 pandemic, and ongoing international sanctions (UNHRC, 2020).

THE SITUATION OF FOREIGN POPULAR CULTURE

Foreign Popular Culture in North Korea

Despite intensification of ideological control in North Korea under Kim Chŏng-ŭn, available information points to the influence of foreign popular culture on the North Korean people. The dissemination of popular culture occurs in several ways, including through informal markets situated along the North Korean border with P. R. China. The development is not new. Foreign culture and information started entering the country as a result of the great famine and loosened state controls in the mid-1990s (Zhang & Lee, 2019). With access to foreign popular culture, previously unavailable information is unofficially introduced, traded, and spread throughout North Korea. Chinese and North Korean brokers and smugglers illegally deal in miscellaneous commodities and media productions—films, news, soap operas—and distribute them by way of private transactions. Smugglers also sell 12-volt television sets, solar battery chargers, and battery-powered Notetels (EVD players) with attached screens (Kretchun et al., 2017). Availability of such commodities has enabled independent media consumption among North Koreans. The markets and the purchase-and-distribution system have turned the people of North Korea into active media consumers.

Foreign popular culture also enters North Korea via the initiatives of South Korea-based human rights activists and civil rights organizations (Baek, 2018; Kim Kil-sŏn's P'yŏngyang mansa, 2019). Individuals and groups organize and distribute commodities ranging from basic to customized, to electronic, to media commodities (Table 8.1). The goal of the activists and the organizations is to inform North Koreans about the outside world, in a manner similar to that of Cold War-era West Germany in relation to East Germany (Daily NK, 2007). Since the early 2000s, activists have exploited the geography of the North-South frontier region as well as forces of nature, such as tidal waves and wind currents, sending commodities in plastic bottles or large balloons to promote freedom of information and the press across the DMZ. To date, the success or failure of these activities has not been clearly verified. However, the public censure of the North Korean state-regime and its crackdowns on the inflow of unapproved foreign commodities indicate some degree of success (Ha, 2018). Defectors' testimonies about the ways in which they received and used the commodities also seem to signify the effectiveness of the products (Kim Kil-sŏn's P'yŏngyang mansa, 2019).

Table 8.1

Foreign Cultural and Industrial Commodities in North Korea

Commodity Types	Commodity Items
Basic	Apparel (clothes, socks, underwear), food (candies, rice, snacks), medicine (aspirin), money (U.S. dollar bills)
Customized	Defectors' books and pictures, leaflets (fact sheets)
Electronic	CDs, DVDs, MP4 players, radios, SD cards, USBs, VCDs, VHS
Media	Cartoons, films, news reports, soap operas, songs, television shows

Note. Compiled from *Voice of America* (Korean) news website and "Kim Kil-sŏn's Pyongyang mansa" *YouTube* vlog.

Apparently responding to the cascade of commodities, Kim Chŏng-ŭn said in 2014 that the "imperialists … are persisting in their attempts to infiltrate corrupt reactionary ideology and culture into our country with our service personnel and young people as the target" (n.d., pp. 15–16). And he ordered party ideological workers to "sweep up non-socialist practices and decadent ideology and culture by means of our revolutionary ideology and culture" and to "sweep away alien ideological trends and lifestyles" (pp. 16, 19). In 2020, the North Korean state media also denounced South Korean films and television dramas as anti-national, false, impure, and propagandistic fabrications that are made for profit and that lack standards and discretion (Kim, 2020). Likewise, the party–state media condemned freedom of expression as being indiscreet and unhealthy, creating "social evil" (*sahoe ak*), spreading fake news, and justifying military provocations (Cho, 2020). Armed with the official positions of Kim and the state media, overzealous North Korean authorities can punish those who disseminate or consume unapproved foreign or South Korean popular culture. If the authorities require a legalistic justification, they could cite Articles 193, 194, and 195 against "decadent culture" and "enemy propaganda" in the Criminal Law of the Democratic People's Republic of Korea (2009).

Contrarily, though, even with the threat of incarcerated work for possessing, distributing, or consuming decadent/enemy popular culture, an estimated 85% of North Koreans secretly watch Hollywood and South Korean productions (S. Yoon, 2020). Documented drivers of foreign media consumption are "entertainment, psychological comfort, distraction and a source of practical information" (Kretchun et al., 2017, p. 31). Precisely because North Koreans "lack various needs" in their home country, "such media contents offer North Koreans a functional alternative to fulfilling desires for escape, as well as for change, compensation, substitut[ion], and social interaction" (Chung, 2019, pp. 148, 152). Of the various illegal foreign products, many North Koreans reportedly enjoy South Korean popular culture, particularly Korean Wave (*hallyu*) films, because of the shared language and ethnicity, which allow for the indirect experience of another social reality (Chung, 2019). Younger generations of North Koreans, who have been strongly affected by the Korean Wave, even adopt South Korean fads, slang, speech, styles, and the standard dialect (Chung, 2019; Lerner, 2015; Thae, 2019). Needless to say, not every North Korean enthuses over Korean Wave productions. The film depictions of liberal capitalist values and material wealth contradict conservative and puritanical North Korean *chuch'e*-Stalinist values and challenge a spartan way of life many North Koreans accept as normal. For example, some North Koreans are known to be surprised and shocked at the open romantic expression of couples in Korean Wave music or soap operas, such expression being taboo in North Korean public spaces.

Broadly, North Korean media and film directly and indirectly focus on stories about the great leader's magnificence and the people's loyalty to the leader, the party, and the state, not on romance for its own sake. One case in point is the North Korean-made/Koryo Tours-funded comedy *Comrade Kim Goes Flying* (*Kim tongmu nŭn hanŭl ŭl nanda*, 2012). Besides divergent moral attitudes to romance, depictions of rich advanced-industrial South Korea in Korean Wave films do not square with recurring North Korean propaganda of South Korea as a total U.S. colony with a lopsided economy and a despairing population wracked with drug addiction, drug crime, and suicide. In actuality, drug crime is low in South Korea, and suicide— a worldwide mental health problem—stood at 0.0266 percent in 2018 (Country Security Report [OSAC], 2020; L. S. Kim, 2019; World Health Organization, 2020; J. S. Yoon, 2020). Importantly, drug crime and suicide also exist in North Korea (Demick, 2014; Hassig & Oh, 2015; Scalapino & Lee, 1972; Thae, 2019). Regarding the extent of Korean Wave influence, defectors have said the effect depends on audience age, region, and formal institutional experience, such as military service.

Informal Learning Through Foreign Popular Culture

Scholars, humanitarian activists, and defectors have pointed to the substantial impact of Korean Wave popular culture on North Koreans' perceptions and understandings of social reality, affecting their ideas of the state and human rights. T'ae Yŏng-ho, a defected North Korean diplomat turned member of the South Korean National Assembly, mentions that watching a Korean Wave film favorably informed and transformed his understanding of capitalist ideology and pluralistic society:

The Taebaek Mountains ([*Taebaek sanmaek,*] 1994) left a very strong impression on me. It is one of the first South Korean films I ever watched in my life, in 1997 when I was working as the secretary at the [North Korean] embassy in Denmark. ... The main message I got from the film is that Communism cannot overwhelm capitalism because the ideology, Communism, does not allow independence of human beings, as well as the differences between the ideologies and the existence of different groups of classes in the society. The film taught me that a diversity of ideologies and cultures within one society is always better than the monolithic system. The film gave me an alternative approach to the Communist ideology and changed my viewpoint towards the society and the happenings in the North Korean regime. (Thae, 2019, pp. 57–58)

In other words, the South Korean feature film functioned as a medium for informal learning, (re)educating T'ae in comparative ideology, political systems, and civil liberties. He adds that, in face of North Korean human rights violations, access to external information can educate and inspire the North Korean people to rise up and rebel against the Kim Chŏng-ŭn regime (Thae, 2019). T'ae's case is not exceptional with North Korean defectors whom the Korean Wave has affected. Within North Korea, the exposure to and influence of foreign popular culture creates disillusionment in the regime, builds horizontal connections among regular citizens, sows the seeds of democratic civil society, initiates revolutions in the mind, and challenges the repressive state ideology (Lerner, 2015).

Informal learning through foreign popular culture, in general, and South Korean popular culture, in particular, also links education in politics and civics to education in everyday life. Kim Kil-sŏn, a defected propaganda officer from an army think-tank in Pyongyang, elaborates on what is learnable from South Korean drama and how the audience assimilates the information:

The drama of North Korea is only a propaganda-agitation means to realize the ideology and leadership of the great leader and, highlighting devotion, drives the entire North Korean people to loyalty and filial piety.... The substance of Republic of Korea [South Korean] drama and North Korean drama is different; when the drama of the Republic of Korea enters North Korea, people learn how to put on makeup, how to dress, how to speak, have a house, and buy things—since everything in the human world is learned, how much will be learned? Now, [South Korean drama] gets into border regions exclusively, not entering more deeply, [but] in the time of the liberalization of North Korea, the role of [South Korean] drama can achieve more great things than a speech. Through drama, without being forced and without being instructed, consciousness is reconstructed, spoken to in an instant, and in Republic of Korea drama, the genre gives a general common-sense idea of how lawbreaking people live within the framework of constitutionalism! (Kim Kil-sŏn's P'yŏngyang mansa, 2019)

Kim makes five instructive points in the above passage: (1) leader-centered ideology and politics are overdetermined in North Korean drama; (2) human life is more fully represented in South Korean drama; (3) South Korean drama in North Korea is more fruitful than formal North Korean discourses; (4) the minds of the audience are more intuitively receptive to South Korean drama; and (5) rule of law in South Korean society is imparted through South Korean drama. In spite of generalization in Kim's statement, the living experience of North Korean defectors, including the earlier-cited T'ae Yŏng-ho, confirms the pedagogical utility of foreign popular culture in the social-life education of North Koreans. Even if there is a monopolized life in South Korea, the market economic system is what the defectors objectively find themselves in when they arrive in the country. As an integral part of that system, South Korean popular culture can serve the *function* to acculturate North Koreans and acclimate their needs to the positive and negative behaviors, norms, and values of the capitalist society with a pluralistic constitutional government.

Relatedly, encoded constitutionalism (liberal democratic rule of law) in South Korean popular culture has the potential to informally raise North Koreans' awareness and understanding of their individual rights and protections—plus the legal accountability of government leaders and public officials. North Korea has a national constitution and numerous laws, but the absolutist system, leader-centered rights, and *Staatsrecht* displace rule of law for authoritarian rule, a government of party bureaucrats and army generals, and a police state. Under such circumstances, the great leader is not beneath the law. The great leader is the law, and the masses of the people are beneath the great leader. Consistent with the assessment, Kim Chŏng-il declared the following about his father in 1970: "What the great leader [Kim Il-sŏng] has said is law and the highest command" (Kim, 1990, p. 145). Likewise, when the son assumed party, army, and state leadership in 1994 to 1998, documents he sanctioned became undefiable law (Hwang, 2002b). Assimilating the themes, stories, and plots of South Korean popular culture, North Koreans (at home or defected) learn about an alternate political system, one that does not violate human rights through unaccountable authority and autocratic command. By the same token, the underground proliferation of South Korean popular culture in North Korea and the punitive hostility of the *chuch'e*-Stalinist state-regime indicate that a significant portion of the North Korean people is achieving awareness, beginning to understand its subjugation, and starting to grow into freedom.

Altogether, the situation of illegal foreign popular culture in North Korea is a site of pedagogical struggle through which different social layers intuitively pursue their self-interest, informally learn about the wider world society and themselves, and, in effect, militate against the political controls of the particularist and insular party-state. As belief in the ideology, the system, and the ruling family group is compromised, social consciousness transitions in a practical manner from passive/dependent to active/independent, and North Koreans come to prioritize concrete-individual human right over abstract-collective state right. While not all North Koreans may have the same impulse to personal freedom, and some partisan, patricentric, and privileged types may be reconciled to the absolutist system, exposure to the objective forms of foreign popular culture satisfies multiple needs and interests that are otherwise unfulfilled under economically impoverished and culturally oppressive conditions. In short, a transformative force, foreign popular culture in North Korea is an educational relationship that connects North Koreans to the global interdependence of nations and the universality of human rights.

CONCLUSION

This chapter has considered the problem of North Koreans' human rights awareness, through foreign popular culture, from a descriptive adult education perspective. Using the principles of Lindeman as the general theoretical framework, the exposition and analysis comprehend popular culture as a situation that satisfies the needs and interests of recreation and community and simultaneously provides informal learning experiences about life behaviors, norms, and values. Popular culture, which has serious/light, high/low, and complex/simple forms, is not merely a recipe of stereotypes, but encompasses professional varieties of creative expression intended for diverse audiences and sensibilities. North Koreans, who live in an absolutist, repressive, and poor country, find in illegal foreign popular culture unique opportunities to satisfy their individual needs, learn about international society, and develop modern autonomous personalities. The most notable consequence of their encounter with foreign popular culture is that, in the closed society, the cultural forms can motivate a desire for freedom, as North Koreans increasingly put their needs—their rights—before those of the authoritarian party-state.

Surveying the reality of human rights in North Korea, one finds that the WPK government perpetrates numerous human rights violations, puts the rights of the leader and the state above the rights of the people, and asserts hegemony and repression through ideology, law, and violence. In result, many North Koreans have an impaired awareness and understanding of their fundamental human rights. Still, as social human beings, different North Koreans find ways to circumvent ideological and political controls, and one of the ways is the underground distribution and consumption of foreign cultural commodities. Of these commodities, the profusion of illegal foreign popular culture, and especially South Korean popular culture, informally educates North Koreans about capitalism, constitutionalism, and pluralism. Social effects of the learning experience with popular culture are embodied in the ongoing development of North Korean civil society, as well as in economic and political defection from the country. In the case of North Koreans who defect to South Korea, their experience with South Korean popular culture proves crucial and necessary in the difficult process of adjusting to and succeeding in the competitive open society.

That said, two major implications are borne out from the descriptive investigation into North Koreans' human rights and the situation of foreign popular culture. First, external and internal forces are causing structural, cultural, and civil changes in the authoritarian society. Second, exposure to foreign popular culture is an integral element in the process of democratic transformation. Beyond descriptivism, there is finally a normative question: "Pedagogically, what is to be done to improve the human rights of North Koreans and end the violations of the absolutist state-regime?" Since many North Koreans are documented consumers of illegal foreign popular culture, and since foreign popular culture informally educates the people for personal growth into freedom, a continuous flow of foreign feature films and television shows (as well as portable multimedia players with replaceable backup batteries) is needed at the very least. Accordingly, international and civil rights organizations will have to make coordinated efforts to convey more popular culture into the country—ideally, the most accomplished, skillful, and tasteful forms of popular culture so as to educate and enrich feeling, thought, and behavior. In the process of transformation, the precise direction of things cannot be accurately predicted, but anticipatable effects of the popular cultural influx will be a mirroring of the democratic attitudes of contemporary society in North Korea and the preparation of intuition and consciousness for a democratic future.

ACKNOWLEDGMENT

I would like to thank Professor Alzo David-West for reading and commenting on the manuscript, bringing my attention to several sources, retranslating the Korean into English, and checking the references. I am grateful for his helping me express my ideas and perspective more precisely.

REFERENCES

Adorno, T. (2001). *The culture industry: Selected essays on mass culture* (J. M. Bernstein, Ed.). Routledge.

Alizadeh, H. (2011). A proposal for how to realize human rights at the national and regional level: A three-pillar strategy. *Human Rights Quarterly, 33*(3), 826–855. http://www.jstor.org/stable/23016002

Baek, J. (2018). Breaking through: North Korea's inform-ation underground and transnational advocacy network. In A. Yeo & D. Chubb (Eds.), *North Korean human rights: Activists and networks* (pp. 249–271). Routledge.

China's repatriation of North Korean refugees: Hearing before the Congressional-Executive Commission on China. (2012). HRNK. https://www.hrnk.org/uploads/pdfs/Congressional%20Hearings/China_Repatriation_March_5_2012.pdf

Cho, U. H. (2020, June 4). *"P'yohyŏn ŭi chayu" ranŭn maltwi e sumji malla* [Do not hide behind the words "freedom of expression"]. Uri minjok kkiri [Among our ethnic-race]. http://www.uriminzokkiri.com/index.php?ptype=cgisas&mtype=view&no=1193149

The criminal law of the Democratic People's Republic of Korea. (2009). HRNK. https://www.hrnk.org/uploads/pdfs/The%20Criminal%20Law%20of%20the%20Democratic%20Republic%20of%20Korea_2009_%20(1).pdf

Chung, K. Y. (2019). Media as soft power: The role of the South Korean media in North Korea. *Journal of International Communication, 25*(1), 137–157. https://doi.org/10.1080/13216597.2018.1533878

Daily NK. (2007, August 2). *North Korea's demand to cease scattering of flyers provides proof of their effectiveness.* Daily NK. https://www.dailynk.com/english/north-koreas-demand-to-cease-scatt/

David-West, A. (2011). What would Erich Fromm say about North Korea? A preliminary application of humanist psychoanalysis. *International Forum of Psychoanalysis, 22*(3), 176–187. http://doi.org/10.1080/0803706X.2011.622786

David-West, A. (2013). North Korea and the contradiction of inversion: Dictatorship, markets, social reform. *North Korean Review, 9*(1), 100–113. http://www.jstor.org/stable/43908909

Demick, B. (2014). *Nothing to envy: Real lives in North Korea.* Granta.

Fahy, S. (2019). *Dying for rights: Putting North Korea's human rights abuses on the record.* Columbia University Press.

Freedom House. (2020). *Freedom in the world 2020: North Korea.* https://freedomhouse.org/country/north-korea/freedom-world/2020

Ha, Y. A. (2018, October 2). *Despite crackdowns, South Korean media content remain popular.* Daily NK. https://www.dailynk.com/english/despite-crackdowns-south-korean-media-content-remains-popular/

Haggard, S., & Noland, M. (2007). *Famine in North Korea: Markets, aid, and reform.* Columbia University Press.

Hassig, R., & Oh, K. (2015). *The hidden people of North Korea: Everyday life in the hermit kingdom.* Rowman and Littlefield.

Ho, K. (2007). Structural violence as a human rights violation. *Essex Human Rights Review*, *4*(2), 1–17. University of Essex. http://projects.essex.ac.uk/ehrr/V4N2/ho.pdf

Human Rights Watch. (2020). North Korea. In *World report 2020: Events of 2019* (pp. 439–443). https://www.hrw.org/sites/default/files/world_report_download/hrw_world_report_2020_0.pdf

Hwang, J. Y. (2002a). The problems of human rights in North Korea (1). Columbia Law School. http://www2.law.columbia.edu/course_00S_L9436_001/North%20Korea%20materials/hwang%20jang1.html

Hwang, J. Y. (2002b). The problems of human rights in North Korea (2). Columbia Law School. http://www2.law.columbia.edu/course_00S_L9436_001/North%20Korea%20materials/hwang%20jang2.html

Hwang, J. Y. (2002c). The problems of human rights in North Korea (3). Columbia Law School. http://www2.law.columbia.edu/course_00S_L9436_001/North%20Korea%20materials/hwang%20jang3.html

Hwang, J. Y. (2002d). The problems of human rights in North Korea (4). Columbia Law School. http://www2.law.columbia.edu/course_00S_L9436_001/North%20Korea%20materials/hwang%20jang4.html

Hwang, J. Y. (2010, June 20). *Theoretical birth of the* juche [subject] *ideology*. Daily NK. https://www.dailynk.com/english/theoretical-birth-of-the-juche-ide/

Kim, H. C. (2020, March 4). *Chŏltaero yongnaphalsu ŏmnŭn kŭgagmudohan tobal haengwi* [Absolutely unacceptable, heinous provocative acts]. Uri minjok kkiri [Among our ethnic-race]. http://www.uriminzokkiri.com/index.php?ptype=cgisas&mtype=view&no=1188282

Kim, I. S. (n.d.). *Theses on socialist education: Published at the 14th plenary meeting of the fifth central committee of the Workers' Party of Korea, September 5, 1977*. Chosŏn ŭi ch'ulpanmul [Publications of the DPRK]. http://korean-books.com.kp/KBMbooks/en/work/leader1/00000278.pdf

Kim, I. S. (1965). On eliminating dogmatism and formalism and establishing *juche* [the subject] in ideological work: Speech to party propagandists and agitators, December 28, 1955. In *Selected works* (Vol. 1, pp. 315–340). Foreign Languages Publishing House.

Kim, J. I. (1990). On inculcating the revolutionary habit of creation in artists and writers: Speech to senior officials in the sector of art and literature and to artists, January 9, 1970. In *Accomplishing juche revolutionary cause: 1 (1964–1971)* (Vol. 1, pp. 142–149). Foreign Languages Publishing House.

Kim, J. I. (n.d.). *Socialism is a science: Treatise published in* Rodong sinmun *[Workers' daily], organ of the Central Committee of the Workers' Party of Korea, November 1, 1994*. Chosŏn ŭi ch'ulpanmul [Publications of the DPRK]. http://www.korean-books.com.kp/KBMbooks/en/work/leader2/3013.pdf

Kim, J. U. (n.d.). *Let us hasten final victory through a revolutionary ideological offensive: Speech at the eighth conference of ideological workers of the Workers' Party of Korean, February 25, juche 103 (2014)*. Chosŏn ŭi ch'ulpanmul [Publications of the DPRK]. http://www.korean-books.com.kp/KBMbooks/en/work/leader3/1212.pdf

Kim Kil-sŏn's P'yŏngyang mansa (2019, August 18). *2–63. Namhan ppira rŭl pon Pukhan chumin panŭng* [2-63. North Korean citizen reactions to South Korean leaflets]. YouTube. https://www.youtube.com/watch?v=qaX0lIq5WcQ

Kim, L. S. (2019). *2018-nyŏn samang wŏnin t'onggye* [2018 cause of death statistics]. T'onggye ch'ŏng [Statistics Korea]. http://www.kostat.go.kr/portal/korea/kor_nw/3/index.board?bmode=read&aSeq=377608

Korean News (2005, December 22). *Seminar held to mark anniversary of Kim Il Sung's famous work.* Korean News. http://www.kcna.co.jp/item/2005/200512/news12/22.htm#6

Korean News (2020, January 1). *Report on 5th Plenary Meeting of 7th C.C., WPK.* Korean News. http://www.kcna.co.jp/item/2020/202001/news01/20200101-01ee.html

Kretchun, N., Lee, C., & Tuohy, S. (2017). *Compromising connectivity: Information dynamics between the state and society in a digitizing North Korea.* Gwern. http://www.gwern.net/docs/technology/2017-kretchun.pdf

Lee, A. R., & English, D. A. (2016). Human rights violations in the North Korean education system: Voices of North Korean refugees in South Korea. *SNU Journal of Education Research*, 25(2), 21–38. S-Space. http://sspace.snu.ac.kr/bitstream/10371/110061/1/02.pdf

Lee, C. H. (2020). *Pukhan it'al chumin ŭi inkwŏn kamsusŏng e kwanhan yŏngu* [A study regarding the human rights sensibility of North Korean defector citizens (Master's thesis)]. Sogang University. http://dcollection.sogang.ac.kr:8089/dcollection/srch/srchDetail/000000065114

Lerner, M. (2015). Markets, movies, and media: The growing soft power threat to North Korea. *Journal of East Asian Affairs*, 29(1), 41–71. http://www.jstor.org/stable/43410714

Lindeman, E. C. (1926). *The meaning of adult education.* New Republic. Internet Archive. https://archive.org/stream/meaningofadulted00lind

McEachern, P. (2010). *Inside the red box: North Korea's post-totalitarian politics.* Columbia University Press.

Ministry of Foreign Affairs (2019, November 15). *Third committee of UN General Assembly adopts resolution on situation of human rights in DPRK.* Ministry of Foreign Affairs, Republic of Korea. http://www.mofa.go.kr/eng/brd/m_5676/view.do?seq=320829

Country Security Report [OASC]. (2020). *South Korea 2020 crime and safety report.* OSAC. https://www.osac.gov/Country/SouthKorea/Content/Detail/Report/55d33eb7-21b6-4b2f-8ccb-18618d06536b

Reporters Without Borders. (2020a). *North Korea.* RSF. https://rsf.org/en/north-korea

Reporters Without Borders. (2020b). *2020 World Press Freedom Index.* RSF. https://rsf.org/en/ranking

Scalapino, R., & Lee, C. S. (1972). *Communism in Korea: Part II: The Society* (Vol. 2). University of California Press.

Scobell, A. (2008). *Projecting Pyongyang: The future of North Korea's Kim Jong Il regime.* Strategic Studies Institute. Defense Technical Information Center. https://apps.dtic.mil/sti/pdfs/ADA478744.pdf

Silberstein, B. K. (2010). North Korea: Fading totalitarianism in the 'hermit kingdom.'" *IFN Working Paper*, *836*, 1–21. EconStor. https://www.econstor.eu/bitstream/10419/81397/1/wp836.pdf

Storey, J. (2018). *Cultural theory and popular culture: An introduction* (8th ed.). Routledge.

Strinati, D. (2004). *An introduction to theories of popular culture* (2nd ed.). Routledge.

Thae, Y. H. (2019). The Korean wave as a powerful agent: Hidden stories from a North Korean defector. In Y. Kim (Ed.), *South Korean popular culture and North Korea* (pp. 54–66). Routledge.

Tisdell, E. J., & Thompson, P. M. (2006). "Crash"-ing into pop culture in dealing with diversity: Adult education and critical media literacy about movies and television. In *2006 conference proceedings (Minneapolis, MN)* (pp. 397–402). Adult Education Research Conference. http://newprairiepress.org/cgi/viewcontent.cgi?article=2548&context=aerc

General Assembly of the United Nations [UNGA]. (n.d.). *Universal declaration of human rights*. United Nations. http://www.un.org/en/universal-declaration-human-rights/

United Nations Human Rights Council. (2014). *Report of the commission of inquiry on human rights in the Democratic People's Republic of Korea*. United Nations Digital Library. https://digitallibrary.un.org/record/766464?In=en

United Nations Human Rights Council. (2020). *Situation of human rights in the Democratic People's Republic of Korea: Report of the special rapporteur on the situation of human rights in the Democratic People's Republic of Korea*. United Nations Digital Library. https://digitallibrary.un.org/record/3864990?In=en

World Council of Human Right. (2020). *Vienna declaration and programme of action: Adopted by the World Conference on Human Rights in Vienna on 25 June 1993*. United Nations Human Rights office of the High Commissioner. https://www.ohchr.org/EN/ProfessionalInterest/Pages/Vienna.aspx

World Health Organization. (2020). *Suicide data*. http://www.who.int/mental_health/prevention/suicide/suicideprevent/en/

Williams, R. (2010). *The divided world: Human rights and its violence*. University of Minnesota Press.

Yoon, J. S. (2020). *Number of drug smuggling cases in South Korea from 2015 to 2019*. Statista. https://www.statista.com/statistics/1056772/south-korea-drug-smuggling-cases/

Yoon, S. (2020). Mobile media and its impacts on social change and human rights in North Korea. *International Journal of Communication,14*(2020), 1480–1497. https://ijoc.org/index.php/ijoc/article/view/10903

Zhang, W., & Lee, N. (2019). Black markets, red states: Media piracy in China and the Korean wave in North Korea. In Y. Kim (Ed.), *South Korean popular culture and North Korea* (pp. 83–95). Routledge.

SECTION II

ECONOMIC EMPOWERMENT: LABORING TO LEARN, LABORING TO EARN

A HUMAN CAPABILITIES DEVELOPMENT PERSPECTIVE IN ADULT EDUCATION

Elizabeth A. Roumell and Bora Jin
Texas A&M University, United States

Even while education is understood to have an overall positive effect on human development, quite a bit of debate exists as to what avenues of development are most important and should be prioritized. For decades, the field of adult education has been caught in a tension between humanistic and instrumental approaches to adult learning (Rubenson, 2006). Since the turn of the century, adult education policy has been primarily framed using human capital development theory (Holford & Mohorčič-Špolar, 2012; Schuetze, 2006), and yet, the historical underpinnings of the field in a philosophy of humanism and social justice remain alive and well. We consider this dueling dichotomy between humanism and human capital theory in adult education to be unproductive, and suggest an alternative lens for understanding human development.

We assert that, to date, the *human capabilities approach* (which we will refer to simply as *capabilities*) to human development is the most convincing. The theorization of human development in terms of capabilities, as freedoms and functionings, articulated by Sen (2005) and Nussbaum (2000), captures and subsumes the imperative for economic development and

Advancing the Global Agenda for Human Rights, Vulnerable Populations, and Environmental Sustainability: Adult Education as Strategic Partner, pp. 139–156

human capital formation "within a wider and ethically inclusive frame in which people's wellbeing individually, in nations and globally, is the end purpose of development, rather than profit or GDP" (Boni & Walker, 2016, p. 55). It also offers perspectives on how adult learning might contribute to per capita income, visions for democratic civic culture, means toward correcting social injustices, and ways for promoting sustainable human growth and well-being. The capabilities lens also explores the relationship between individual capabilities and sociocultural contexts, local and large-scale. We believe that, by applying a capabilities approach to the context of adult education and workplace learning, we can contribute to a collective reimagining of adult education, and build a promising agenda for adult learning and growth in the 21st century and onward.

In this chapter, we present a general approach of *human capabilities* development, derived from international development and critical theory scholarship (Boni & Walker, 2016; Finnegan, 2016; Nussbaum, 2000; Sen, 2005; Walker, 2006). In order to successfully present this perspective, we must lay a foundation of concepts and contextualize the necessity for such an approach to adult learning. First, we explore the notions of international development, globalization, and the human capital perspective. Next, we present critiques of human capital theory, and then introduce the notions of humanism, sociocultural approaches to adult education, and the capabilities perspective. We then offer examples to illustrate possibilities for the approach within adult learning contexts. Our aim is to illuminate and move toward commonly held principles, both humanistic and instrumental, as they inform adult learning.

INTERNATIONAL DEVELOPMENT

The industrial revolution spurred massive efforts at industrializing and building large-scale economies organized in nation-state units. Over the 19th and 20th centuries, societies rapidly transformed across the globe due to imperialist ambitions and the expansion of Western nations, and through the increasing amount of international trade. Correspondingly, nation-states developed large-scale institutions like government bureaucracies, public social services and health care, and national school systems (Robertson, 1992). Also, in response to these transformations, social sciences emerged to facilitate learning about and help control and predict human progress.

Among these, the field of "international development" emerged as a means for theorizing how nation-states and societies successfully develop into modern, industrialized economies that can compete in globalizing markets. Broadly speaking, this notion of "development" implied that nation-states had achieved varying levels of modernization. International development drove theorization regarding how nation-states should pursue the modernization project. The notion of development was also situated within the supposition that economic development in a capitalist market precedes other forms of social and cultural development (Arnove & Torres, 2007). Thus, economic measures served as markers for international comparison. At the same time, many less-develop nations struggled under the crisis of international "structural adjustment programs," which were based on neoliberal economic principles that required countries to prioritize economics over other social matters (Kubow & Fossum, 2007). As developing countries struggled in an increasingly globalized world, the heavy-handed focus on prioritizing economic development was questioned.

GLOBALIZATION

Broadly understood, *globalization* is the acceleration of international exchanges (social, political, cultural, business, economic, and the like) that affect the way people live, work, and relate to their own and everyone else's lifeworlds globally. Functionally speaking, globalization is understood as the transformation of economies in terms of investment and capital, production and distribution, and consumption (Stromquist, 2002). Robertson (1992) defined globalization as "the compression of the world and the intensification of the consciousness of the world as a whole" (p. 8) and described it as the blurring of the global and the local. Castells (1996) argued that globalizing forces both homogenize societies, making them more similar over time, and fragment societies, where each society differently conceives of their end goals.

In the 1990s, many theorized that globalization would bring the world together making it stronger and better developed overall. Authors depicted visions of a global village where an increasing number of people would be able to pursue prosperity and freedom, and a world with less warfare and strife, as societies cooperated to form institutions and agreements that would reinforce peaceful trade and interdependence (Giddens, 2002). Spanish sociologist Manuel Castells (1996) catapulted the term "network society" into international scholarship, illustrating the effects of increasing global interconnectedness. Authors such as Pinker (2018) and Rosling (2019) have written extensively on the windfall of Western enlightenment, science, medicine, and the modernization project. Their work offers detailed charts to illustrate how the world has incrementally been becoming healthier, less violent, more prosperous, better educated, and more democratic.

In contrast, Robertson (1992) contended that there was a real possibility globalization could lead to deep fractures in societies and between people. While many argued globalization was leveling the development playing field (Friedman, 2005), in many dimensions the gaps between the "haves" and "have-mores" have increased (Maskin, 2015), and a growing body of literature addresses "globalization and its discontents" (Stiglitz, 2003, 2013). Eisenberg (2020) challenged the unacknowledged utilitarianism that has become a form of distributive injustice, where decision makers render discrete populations worse off in the name of helping "everyone."

Nation-states face an ongoing paradox that must be negotiated for balanced development to occur. Countries must pursue economic growth, manage the effects of internationalization, and maintain social order. As global elites appropriate massive resources to maintain the global status quo, societies are accompanied with heavy social, political, and economic costs, which are continuously contested and protested. Thus, when contemplating the "global order" and how societies "should be" organized, we must also assume that disorder accompanies globalization (Body-Gendrot, 2016). These order/disorder, economic/social dialectics also play out in the education sector in the form of the human capital views of education versus humanistic and social development perspectives. As in any sector, adult education has been caught betwixt and between these visions and purposes of development in the face of globalization.

KNOWLEDGE-BASED ECONOMIES AND HUMAN CAPITAL PERSPECTIVES

From a human capital perspective, human workers are seen as a key variable in the function and predictive equation of modernization in terms of contributing to economic growth and competition. This translates into a productivity paradigm where the individual is calculated as a contributing unit in the larger national economic calculus. From this perspective, the education, training, and development of individuals are understood as means for supplying competitive economic units that can contribute to production, innovation, and consumption in order to continuously generate an increasingly economically active population. Correspondingly, adult education is presented as a mechanism contributing to the economic development of societies (Stromquist, 2002).

This economic rationale also serves as a foundation for investing in education with the expectation of financial return. Underlying these notions is also the assumption that individuals are primarily motivated by monetary reward in exchange for their efforts and participation (Holford & Mohorčič-Špolar, 2012). Just as development and modernization demand

greater participation and integration of nation-states into the global economy, so, too, it follows that individuals, as economic units, are expected to
invest in education as a means toward improved economic participation
and societal integration. In both views, individually and writ large, education serves as a means to an economic end.

Assumptions derived from human capital theory underlie large-scale
economic return on investment (ROI) studies. For example, in 2020, an
ROI study for adult education in the United States revealed that "getting
all US adults to at least a Level 3 of literacy proficiency would generate
an additional $2.2 trillion in annual income for the country. That is 10%
of the gross domestic product" (Rothwell, 2020, p. 4). The calculations
for arriving at such estimates are quite complex, but ROI studies provide
a powerful economic argument for promoting adult literacy and education. Such ROI research findings provide numbers and practical evidence
to support the notion that elevating adults' education levels and making
skills training widely available is central economically. An increased level
of economic output can also reduce the need to draw on costly social benefits (Boeren, 2016). Where the generation of new skills and knowledge
can result in monetary profits, individuals and society are also assumed to
benefit. Torres (2013) referred to this as *instrumental rationality*, referring to
the suppression of social costs and the maximization of growth and profit.
In this view, education is understood as a prerequisite for the development
of a human as a means to improve their economic participation and ability
to integrate into the workforce.

Findings from national economic studies also reveal how many people
are being left out. For example, Carnevale and associates (2019) at the
Georgetown University Center on Education and the Workforce released
a report titled, "The Unequal Race for Good Jobs: How Whites Made
Outsized Gains In Education and Good Jobs Compared to Blacks and
Latinos." Their report spelled out the differences in education attainment
levels and subsequent earnings averages, as compared between demographic groups. They detailed the differences in education and income
levels, suggesting that earnings inequality is systemic. Earnings inequality
and income insecurity are illuminated as material barriers faced by marginalized individuals, putting adults and their children at higher risk for
additional social disadvantages. Compounding inequities often result in
generational cycles of ill-health and financial fragility. What is more, Carnevale and team (2019) asserted that economic, workforce development,
and educational policy are social justice concerns that must be addressed,
especially in light of Industry 4.0.

Survival in a knowledge-based economy in the 21st century is deeply
embedded in economic rationale. Today's "networked society" is a combination of social media, cultural, and economic networks, giving shape

to the prime mode of organization and structure to interact, trade, communicate, produce, and consume, and create an unlimited amount of "fusion" worldwide (Friedman, 2016; Giddens, 2002). The accumulation, use, and commodification of knowledge is among the principal factors of economic growth and national development processes, and serves as the foundation for competitive advantages. To be left out of today's networked society and its rapid advancements is to simply be shut out of economic, social, and civic opportunities. When adults cannot fully participate in the networked society because they do not have access to technology, information, or digital skills building, they have fewer choices and options for sustaining themselves and their families. In light of the deep economic recession accompanying 2020's COVID-19 global pandemic, matters of digital equity and inclusion were foregrounded and brought into sharper focus (DigitalUS, 2020). The world was able to see, nearly in real time, just how inseparable economic justice and social justice have become, and that social and health needs cannot be solely tied to economic participation.

Clearly, the economic "rationale" and instrumentalism have been grossly oversimplified. Financial, social, and health benefits must be considered in parallel at both the individual and societal levels (Walker, 2006). As Finnegan (2016) wrote,

> The idea that market exchange between individuals is the basic building block of human interaction and that such exchanges somehow organically coalesces into complex forms of social organisation is remarkably simplistic and not at all credible in either historical or anthropological terms. (p. 48)

In the field of adult education, this instrumental view of learning has long been critiqued as inadequate (Torres, 2013). Human capital theory does not accurately reflect the social, structural, and cultural complexities of individuals' lives and contexts. A more human-centric philosophy, one that sees people as the ends and not mere economic means for profit, is needed to counterbalance neoliberal profit logic.

HUMANISM

Humanistic and progressive perspectives of adult education grew in popularity in the 1950–60s following World War II, resulting from the public's growing distrust of behaviorism and science. The Civil Rights Movement and midcentury counterculture brought people to question blinkered and discriminatory societal norms, and to explore avenues for egalitarianism and self-fulfillment focusing on more open, individualized, and learner-centered practices. The aim of humanistic education is the promotion of the freedom, equity, dignity, autonomy, integrity, well-being, and the inimitable potential of individual learners. The ultimate goal of humanistic education is for adults to grow emotionally and intellectually and become independent, self-directed learners who have the freedom and opportunity to develop their unique talents (Elias & Merriam, 2008). Humanistic philosophy focuses on self-awareness and reflection, as well as becoming more socially conscientious. Humanism also holds a lot in common with notions of liberal education, which aims for the cultivation of the free human being, open discourse, civic literacy, and broadening of the mind through exposure to varied ideas.

Humanistic education has also been heavily critiqued as Eurocentric, elitist, patriarchal, overly individualistic, impractical, and vague in terms of actual learning outcomes (Hansman & Mott, 2010; Merriam & Bierema 2014; Sandlin, 2005). Historically, liberal education has also reproduced dominant narratives of Western society, and offered little acknowledgement of diversity, subcultures, and other worldviews. Another concern is that it is not clear how such learning translates into employability, and often does not result in tangible qualifications. It is also criticized for not developing practical, "real-world" skills (Entwistle, 1997). Thus, its value in promoting economic mobility and equity has also been doubted.

Whether instrumentalist or humanist, either approach on its own is inevitably reduced to an incomplete vision of adult learning, distancing adult education from adult learners' complicated, lived realities. The historicity and contextualization of learners and the curriculum must be taken into account. Similarly, policy and practice from either perspective seem disconnected from the reality and complexities of adults' everyday lifeworld experience. However, when individual flourishing is promoted, recognizing the importance of sociocultural context and lifeworlds, this, in itself, can help remove barriers, reduce economic and social inequalities, and promote individual and global well-being.

SOCIOCULTURAL UNDERSTANDINGS OF ADULT LEARNING

A sociocultural approach takes the previous knowledge and experiences of individuals, families, and communities seriously to inform educational practice. When applying a sociocultural lens to learning, adult education begins with an analysis and understanding of the social and living conditions of the adult learners and the problems and needs they identify for themselves, acknowledging learning needs are embedded in a person's cultural, social, and economic context. Alfred (2002) argued that sociocultural understandings of adult education are necessary, because (1) adult learning is more complex than ossified and anti-human economic calculations, and

(2) it is important to recognize and validate the humanity and diversity of adult learners and their lifeworlds. She asked, "How can adult educators, practicing within a Eurocentric dominant institutional culture, validate the myriad social and cultural contexts from which learners' experiences emanate? These experiences have value intrinsically" (p. 4). Not only do these experiences and varieties of knowledge have intrinsic value in their own right, but adults, as individuals, too, have intrinsic value as human beings in their own right, separate from their ability to align with global economic aims.

Adult education and human development perspectives both hold in common democratic, educative practice, and a human rights focus. Education is understood to be an individual right and social good that should not be renounced, assuming a moral imperative when it comes to each individual's right to learn, grow, and thrive. Finnegan (2016) explained,

> Democratic practice has been a constitutive feature of adult education and it is one of the things that unifies a seemingly disparate field across continents and through time. Both desire and practice are bound to an ideal and the hope that education can play a part in creating societies which provide people with the conditions and resources necessary to live dignified and flourishing lives. (pp. 52–53)

Adult learning should be grounded in experience and should engender personal meaning as well as practical application. This also echoes contemporary human development perspectives, which define human development as "a process of enlarging human capabilities and functionings" (UNDP, 2016, p. 1). The *human capabilities development* (capabilities) perspective, where the departure point is that individuals are both the means and the end for learning and education, presents an integrated perspective of adult learning and development.

HUMAN CAPABILITIES DEVELOPMENT

Here, the *human capabilities approach*, as drawn from Sen's (2005) and Nussbaum's (2000) seminal works, is presented as an integrative framework for understanding human development and adult education. The United Nations Development Program (UNDP) has annually published the Human Development Report since 1990, which aligns with the capabilities approach. The UNDP defines human development as "a process of enlarging people's choices," which is achieved "by expanding human capabilities and functionings" (UNDP, 2016, p. 1). The United Nations also explicitly connects inalienable human rights and education in the five foundational human rights: the right to education, the right to take part in cultural life, the right to enjoy the benefits of scientific progress, the right to freedom of opinion and expression, and the right to water and sanitation. Within these rights, both instrumental and economic rights are coupled with social and cultural rights, which are promoted as a means for meeting the fundamental needs of all people. Over the past 30 years, this perspective has come to play a central role in economic and social theory, international development, education, and many other fields.

The human capabilities approach is also central in the Sustainability Developments Goals (SDGs) that were adopted by the members of the United Nations in 2015. The UNDP website clearly states, "The 17 SDGs are integrated—that is, they recognize that action in one area will affect outcomes in others, and that development must balance social, economic and environmental sustainability" (2020, para. 2). The SDGs employ an integral view embedded in a framework of human rights and social justice. We explore the capabilities approach primarily in relationship to SDG Goal 4, to "Ensure inclusive and equitable, quality education and promote life-long learning opportunities for all" (Department of Economic and Social Affairs, n.d., para 1). We also understand all 17 SDGs to be interdependent, and the following as essential to adult education: Goal 1, No poverty; Goal 2, Zero hunger; Goal 3, Good health and well-being; Goal 5, Gender equality; Goal 8, Decent work and economic growth; Goal 10, Reduced inequalities; Goal 11, Sustainable cities and communities; Goal 16, Peace justice and strong institutions; and Goal 17, Partnerships for the goals (Department of Economic and Social Affairs, n.d., para. 1).

Recognizing the narrow economic focus of past development frameworks, a human capabilities approach recenters people in the process of learning and human development, but also acknowledges the importance of social, cultural, and economic contexts. It asks what policies, approaches, and educational processes promote both economic development and individual thriving in a broader conception of human flourishing (Boni & Walker, 2016). Sen (2005) defined capabilities as "the opportunity to achieve valuable combinations of human functionings—what a person is able to do or be" (p. 153) and argued that well-being is best understood in terms of plural capabilities, meaning the greater a person's capabilities, the more likely they will achieve improved life circumstances and well-being.

Human development is understood as the enablement of people to achieve and extend the central life capabilities they value. Sen (2005) articulated capabilities through two core notions: functioning and freedom. *Functioning* ranges from the ability to meet basic needs, such as nourishment, shelter, health, and safety, to more complex social needs, such as self-respect, belongingness, meaningful participation in one's community, and dignified work. *Freedom* essentially entails an individual's ability to systematically pursue or achieve that which they choose and is meaningful to them. Sen intentionally left the articulation of capabilities broad, so it would apply to a wide range of contexts and subject areas.

Building on Sen's work, Nussbaum (2000) aimed to make human rights and social justice more explicit, and so further elucidated 10 human capabilities. Nussbaum's central human functional capabilities included: "Life; Bodily health; Bodily integrity; Senses, imagination, and thought; Emotions; Practical reason; Affiliation; Other species; Play; and Control over one's environment" (pp. 78–80). In this view, learning is a vehicle for improving quality of life; promoting health and extending one's life expectancy; obtaining shelter, food, and financial security; managing lifestyle and planning one's life; making career choices and gaining employment; pursuing self-expression and creativity; and belonging to and participating in one's chosen affiliations and community (Mousavi et al., 2015). Learning and capabilities development also contribute to the freedom to: move about freely; be free of abuse and oppression; have voice and express feelings; have meaningful relationships and improve communication; participate in democracy and governance; establish a relationship with one's environment and its many creatures; freely express spirituality as one would define it; pursue joy, entertainment, play and leisure; and to adapt to one's environment and be as independent as possible (Mousavi et al., 2015).

The capabilities approach subsumes both instrumental and humanistic approaches to adult learning and human development and extends them with the values of human rights and social justice, supporting both economic freedom as well as individual quality-of-life and social well-being. The capabilities approach also explicitly promotes the human values and rights that underlie the expansion of functionings and freedoms, making social justice aims more explicit. It follows, adult learning is understood as a multiplier for general capabilities in support of human flourishing. The approach also attends to the development of individual agency in relationship to individuals' contexts and lifeworlds, acknowledging complexity and interdependencies.

HUMAN CAPABILITIES AND SUSTAINABILITY

In using a human capabilities lens, educational arrangements are assessed by the extent to which they advance abilities, help learners develop agency and voice, support functionings and freedoms, engender respect and dignity, provide instrumental skills and tools, as well as develop individual efficacy and social belongingness. By the very nature of the functionings and freedoms, both humanistic (learning) and instrumental (performance) approaches to adult education are necessary, complimentary, and integrated.

A capabilities approach to adult education and learning implies and depends upon balanced economic, environmental, and social sustainability (Purvis et al., 2019). A tripart view of sustainability acknowledges the interdependent nature of economies, healthy environments, and social equity (Gibson, 2006). These three elements are interdependent and mutually reinforcing, and they all contain aspects of human rights and social justice. Economic empowerment is essential for the well-being and social integration of marginalized populations. However, economic development must also be environmentally and socially sustainable for it to truly improve and maintain the well-being of all people. Environmental and social sustainability are also interdependent, where people equally have access to necessary resources, but are also equally protected from the potentially harmful side effects of economic development. A socially sustainable development is also conscious of environmentally responsible citizenship and promotes economic justice as complimentary and necessary for social justice. Thus, adult education and learning can have a multiplier effect for individual as well as collective capabilities. Applying a capabilities approach can help reframe policy and research, democratize knowledge, as well as inform teaching and learning practice toward sustainable development.

HUMAN CAPABILITIES APPLIED

In the face of increasing global interdependencies, capabilities are crucial in maintaining social cohesion and mutual understanding, and promoting "the good life" (Finnegan, 2016). A human capabilities approach to adult educational practice aims to build social equity and inclusion, but also to create economies that are socially, economically, and environmentally sustainable (Langhelle, 2000). Most importantly, a capabilities approach asserts that education and ongoing learning improves people's opportunities and creates new options to choose from. It is also centered on building a sense of dignity, the ability to more critically read one's lifeworld, and a sense of agency in addressing pressing needs and problems (Torres, 2013). Hoskins and colleagues (2010) presented seven core dimensions as a more holistic model for learning outcomes: earnings and income, productivity, employment, health, life satisfaction and happiness, social cohesion and democracy, and sustainability. Within a capabilities approach, adult learning practice attends to each of these dimensions, promoting complementarity and interdependence. As applied to adult education, a capabilities framework could provide useful methodologies and practices across a wide variety of contexts.

Adult Community Learning

An instrumentalist perspective promotes a constricted view of adult learning, especially for marginalized groups. Schuller and Watson (2009) criticized contemporary lifelong learning policies for focusing on already advantaged populations (e.g., able-bodied, young, and paid employees). Such a narrow understanding of variance in adult learners may inadvertently devalue people with disabilities, especially when their various ways of learning are evaluated as cognitive/physical limitations (Florian et al., 2008). Many scholars in education have advocated and incorporated a capabilities approach as a framework that more broadly acknowledges and accommodates human diversity by applying a "freedom-based evaluative framework for assessing human wellbeing" (Ridley & Watts, 2014, p. 422).

Ridley and Watts (2014) illustrated how a capabilities approach can be used to evaluate the well-being of adult learners with disabilities. From a policy standpoint, people with disabilities are often not fully accorded autonomous status, acknowledging that some people with disabilities may have a limited capability set in some domains. Ridley and Watts explained how people with disabilities require unique support to enhance their quality of life and well-being, emphasizing that "goods are of value only insofar as the individual is able to make use of them, but people do not have the same abilities to utilize the same possessions" (p. 423). When it comes to the capabilities of people with disabilities, the *adaptive preference problem* presents a challenge where a lack of access to specialized equipment leads individuals to moderate their life expectations, and thus to demote their personal aspirations (Ridley & Watts, 2014). To address the problem of adaptive preferences, Sen (2005) posed the counterfactual question of what an individual with disabilities would desire to do if they were able-bodied. Aligned with Sen's emphasis on interpersonal variations, Ridley and Watts (2014) asserted that special resources are needed for people with disabilities to actualize "the same valued outcome of mobility" (p. 423).

Watts and Ridely (2007) illustrated an application of a capabilities approach in an evaluation of a music project for adults with disabilities, as the framework is more inclusive of human diversity. Existing evaluative approaches for adults with disabilities often focus on the individual's physical and musical limitations, largely based on a biological and social construction model (Watts & Ridely, 2007). A capabilities approach, however, shifts to valuing the lives and identities ("being" and "doing") of musicians with disabilities when assessing their personal well-being ("having"). In this view, learners' individual abilities are considered in conjunction with their environmental circumstances, and adjustments are made in order to provide what is necessary for them to pursue personal fulfillment as valued by the individual learner. For vulnerable communities, it is imperative to take the variation of individual capabilities, as well as the limitations of environment and context, into consideration in order to develop more equitable educational opportunities.

Vocational Education and Training/Workplace Learning

Generally, vocational education and training (VET) prepares learners for future occupations and workplace learning (WL) improves employee performance by generating economically valued skills and knowledge. As VET and WL play a critical role in bridging school education with the professional workplace (Draycott et al., 2011), the primary departure point has traditionally been based on human capital theory. Despite VET and WL's concerted efforts to cultivate learners' qualifications for future work, "the problem of a skills mismatch between the educated youth and the needs of industry" may still exist (Morselli, 2017, p. 286). This potentially presents a predicament where either employer cannot find labor with the desired skillset, or individuals are placed in positions that are misaligned with their abilities and qualifications (Cedefop, 2015).

A capabilities approach moves away from a central focus in VET and WL of providing individuals with instrumental workforce skills, toward developing social capabilities related to being able to read one's context, exercising critical thinking, and making complex judgements across a variety of future contexts. Harreveld and colleagues (2012) described the vulnerability of learners as they transition from school to work, applied a capabilities approach to assist young adults into the workforce, and evaluated educational policies based on equality/inequality outcomes in student transitions. The approach places more emphasis on "the conditions individuals need to engage in work and to progress through a career with the requirements of broad occupations" (Wheelahan & Moddie, 2011, p. 2).

Capabilities are not only an individual attribute, but also deeply relate to equitable participation in education and the necessary resources to pursue lives in accordance with their values and increase the number of real choices and opportunities (Sen, 2005). A capabilities approach underlines the importance of access to quality VET and opportunities that cultivate wider professional capabilities for diverse individuals and groups. Tikly (2013) addressed possible implications for students who have varied backgrounds and sociocultural identities, as well as the potential inequitable distribution of resources for quality VET. Morselli (2017) presented how a capabilities approach can contribute to WL through workshops for learners in hospitality programs to address such resource and social inequities. In the workshop meetings, trainees received targeted occupational training, but also discussed issues of personal value in order to enhance their agency freedom. Learners participated in a series of boundary crossing activities that included content on how learners can improve their professional qualifications as well as nurture personal capabilities valued in their own communities.

What is emphasized is that educational materials need to be contextualized in relation to the learners' sociocultural identities including their cognitive levels, language proficiencies, and learning environments. In terms of VET curriculum design, Muller (2009) highlighted the importance of curricular differences as "there is clearly not just one kind of professional practice and these differ in ways that are critical for curricular planning" (p. 217). A more holistic approach not only enables different students to improve their vocational qualifications, but also recognizes and cultivates individual capabilities that learners, their communities, and society at-large also have reason to value.

LEARNING SOCIETY

Williams (1961) described democratic society necessarily as a "learning society," one that works to self-correct and exercises the collective capacity to learn. In a learning society, through reflexive learning, adjustment, and approximations we can reorganize social institutions and cultural practices in ways to promote and improve human flourishing. Williams argued that if we believe in the human capacity to learn, create, communicate, self-monitor, adapt, and change, then these human capabilities should be foregrounded and become the focus of adult learning, as these capabilities are the most valuable renewable resource available to humankind.

Learning to Be, by Edgar Faure (1972), is widely recognized for the diffusion of the notion of the "learning society" as a mechanism for maintaining our humanity in the face of rapid change and as a way to maintain individual autonomy and the right to be able to solve our own problems, make our own decisions, and carry our own responsibilities. Faure wrote,

> If learning involves all of one's life, in the sense of both time-span and diversity, and all of society, including its social and economic as well as its educational resources, then we must go even further than the necessary overhaul of 'educational systems' until we reach the stage of a learning society. (Faure et al., 1972, p. xxxiii)

Adult education can play a critical role in building the necessary partnerships that can contribute to the development of human capabilities toward more inclusive, humane, equitably prosperous, and sustainable learning societies.

CONCLUDING THOUGHTS

What has become clear in the 21st century is that what globalization has helped realize for some has yet to be realized for many others. We presented the *human capabilities development* perspective as a possible framework for re-imagining adult education's role in human development. This approach offers a much needed and deeper understanding of the interplay between education and lifeworlds, learning and earning, and social and economic development. We believe that adult education can help in generating human-centered solutions for growing inequalities and moral urgencies.

Identifying touchstones, or the aspects that are held in common between competing visions, will be necessary for finding common values and developing a more collaborative approach to adult learning. It is the human desire for emancipation and the development of human capabilities that can bring adult education's dueling perspectives together. Finnegan (2016) wrote: "This work … is impossible without a multidimensional conception of equality which explores how access to cultural and economic resources and valued social practices contribute to human development" (p. 54). It is not a matter of whether one approach or the other supports *the* ideal curriculum, but rather how they can be integrated and carried out and, ultimately, to what end. A capabilities approach to adult education is a way of joining forces to face these challenges together.

We are not claiming education as a panacea for the world's "wicked" problems (Rittel & Webber, 1973). We do believe that education and learning across the lifespan, in the spirit of *human capabilities development*, can contribute to better societies with improved and ongoing human development, so that more people can live dignified and fulfilling lives. Only through deliberate action can any approach result in the realization of human capabilities, reconciling the various voices, approaches, intentions, and purposes.

REFERENCES

Alfred, M. V. (2002). The promise of sociocultural theory in democratizing adult education. *New Directions for Adult and Continuing Education, 96*, 3–13.

Arnove, R. F., & Torres, C. A. (eds.). (2007). *Comparative education: The dialectic of the global and the local* (3rd ed.). Rowman & Littlefield.

Body-Gendrot, S. (2016). *Public disorder and globalization.* Taylor & Francis Group.

Boeren, E. (2016). *Lifelong learning participation in a changing policy context: An interdisciplinary theory.* Palgrave Macmillan.

Boni, A., & Walker, M. (2016). *Universities and global human development: Theoretical and empirical insights for social change.* Routledge.

Carnevale, A. P., Strohl, J., Gulish, A., van der Werf, M., & Campbell, K. P. (2019). *The unequal race for good jobs: How Whites made outsized gains in education and good jobs compared to Blacks and Latinos.* Georgetown University Center on Education and the Workforce.https://1gyhoq479ufd3yna29x7ubjn-wpengine. netdna-ssl.com/wp-content/uploads/Full_Report-The_Unequal_Race_for_ Good_Jobs.pdf

Castells, M. (1996). *The information age: Economy, society and culture, Vol. II, The power of Identity.* Blackwell.

Cedefop. (2015). *Tackling unemployment while addressing skill mismatch: Lessons from policy and practice in European Union countries.* Publications Office of the European Union, Luxembourg.

Department of Economic and Social Affairs. (n.d.). *SDG goals.* United Nations. https://unstats.un.org/sdgs/report/2017/Goal-01/

DigitalUS Coalition. (2020, May). *Building a digitally resilient workforce: Creating on-ramps for opportunity, Annual Report.* https://digitalus.org/wp-content/ uploads/2020/05/DigitalUS-PreviewReport-May5-2020.pdf

Draycott, M. C., Rae, D., & Vause, K. (2011). The assessment of enterprise education in the secondary education sector: A new approach. *Education & Training, 53*(8–9), 673–691.

Eisenberg, A. M. (2020). Distributive justice and rural America. *Boston College Law Review, 61*(1), 190–251.

Elias, J. L., & Merriam, S. B.. (2008). *Philosophical foundations of adult education* (3rd ed.). Krieger.

Entwistle, H. (1997). Liberal education: Elitist and irrelevant to everyday life? *Liberal Education and Democratic Citizenship, 11*(1), 7–17.

Faure, E. Herrera, F., Kaddoura, A. D., Lopes, H., Petrovsky, A. V. Rahnema, M., & Ward, F. C. (1972). *Learning to be.* UNESCO.

Finnegan, F. (2016). *The future is unwritten: Democratic adult education against and beyond neoliberalism.* https://files.eric.ed.gov/fulltext/EJ1117510.pdf

Florian, L., Devecchi, C., & Dee, L. (2008). How can the capability approach contribute to understanding provision for people with learning difficulties? *Prospero: A Journal of New Thinking in Philosophy for Education, 14*(1), 24–33.

Friedman, T. L. (2005). *The world is flat: A brief history of the twenty-first century.* Farrar, Strauss, Giroux.

Friedman, T. L. (2016). *Thank you for being late: An optimist's guide to thriving in the age of accelerations.* Farrar, Strauss, Giroux.

Gibson, R. B. (2006). Beyond the pillars: Sustainability assessment as a framework for effective integration of social, economic and ecological considerations in significant decision-making. *Journal of Environmental Assessment Policy and Management, 8*(3), 259–280.

Giddens, A. (2002). *Runaway world: How globalisation is reshaping our lives.* Profile Books.

Hansman, C. A., & Mott, V. W. (2010). In Adult Learners. In C. E. Kasworm, A. D. Rose, & J. M. Ross-Gordon (Eds.), *Handbook of adult and continuing education: 2010 edition,* (pp. 13–23). SAGE.

Harreveld, R. B., Singh, M., & Li, B. (2012). A capability approach to cultural diversity in school-to-work transitions: Amartya Sen and young adults' diversely different education and work communities. In G. Tchibozo (Ed.), *Cultural and social diversity and the transition from education to work* (pp. 113–127). Springer.

Holford, J., & Mohorčič-Špolar, V. A. (2012). Neoliberal and inclusive themes in European lifelong learning policy. In S. Riddell, J. Markowitsch, & E. Weedon (Eds.), *Lifelong learning in Europe: equity and efficiency in the balance* (pp. 39–61). Policy Press.

Hoskins, B., Cartwright, F., & Schoof, U. (2010). *Making lifelong learning tangible: the ELLI index Europe 2010*. Gutersloh, Bertelsmann Stiftung.

Kubow, P. K., & Fossum, P. R. (2007). *Comparative education: Exploring issues in international context* (2nd ed.). Pearson Merill/Prentice Hall.

Langhelle, O. (2000). Sustainable development and social justice: Expanding the Rawlsian framework of global justice. *Environmental Value, 9,* 295–323.

Maskin, E. (2015). Why haven't global markets reduced inequality in emerging economies? *The World Bank Economic Review, 29,* 48–52. doi:10.1093/wber/lhv013

Merriam, S. B., & Bierema, L. L. (2014). *Adult learning: Linking theory and practice.* Jossey-Bass.

Morselli, D. (2017). Boundary crossing workshops for enterprise education: A capability approach. In P. Jones, G. Maas, & L. Pittaway (Eds.), *Entrepreneurship education: New perspectives on entrepreneurship education* (pp. 283–306). Emerald.

Mousavi, T., Forwell, S., Dharamsi, S., & Dean, E. (2015). Do Nussbaum's ten central human functional capabilities extend occupational therapy's construct of occupation? A narrative review. *New Zealand Journal of Occupational Therapy, 62*(1), 21–27.

Muller, J. (2009). Forms of knowledge and curriculum coherence. *Journal of Education and Work, 22*(3), 205–226.

Nussbaum, M. (2000). *Women and human development: The capabilities approach.* Cambridge University Press.

Pinker, S. (2018). *Enlightenment now: The case for reason, science, humanism, and progress.* Viking.

Purvis, B., Mao, Y., & Robinson, D. (2019). Three pillars of sustainability: In search of conceptual origins. *Sustainability Science, 14,* 681–695. https://doi.org/10.1007/s11625-018-0627-5dsa

Ridley, B., & Watts, M. (2014). Using the capability approach to evaluate the well-being of adult learners with dis/abilities. In L. Florian (Ed.), *The SAGE handbook of special education, Vol. 2* (pp. 421–434). SAGE.

Rittel, H. W. J., & Webber, M. M. (1973). Dilemmas in the general theory of planning. *Policy Sciences, 4,* 155–169.

Robertson, R. (1992). *Globalization: Social theory and global culture.* SAGE.

Rosling, H. (2019). *Factfulness: Ten reasons why we are wrong about the world—and why things are better than you think.* Flatiron Books.

Rothwell, J. (2020). *Assessing the economic gains of eradicating illiteracy nationally and regionally in the United States.* Gallup. https://www.barbarabush.org/wp-content/uploads/2020/09/BBFoundation_GainsFromEradicatingIlliteracy_9_8.pdf

Rubenson, K. (2006). Constructing the lifelong learning paradigm: competing visions from the OECD and UNESCO. In S. Ehlers (Ed.), *Milestones towards lifelong learning systems* (pp. 151–170). Danish School of Education.

Sandlin, J. (2005). Andragogy and its discontents: An analysis of andragogy from three critical perspectives. *PAACE Journal of Lifelong Learning, 14*, 25–42.

Schuetze, H. G. (2006). International concepts and agendas of lifelong learning. *Compare: A Journal of Comparative and International Education, 36*(3), 289–306.

Schuller, T., & Watson, D. (2009). *Learning through life: Inquiry into the future for lifelong Learning.* Leicester, UK: National Institute of Adult Continuing Education.

Sen, A. K. (2005). Human rights and capabilities. *Journal of Human Development, 6*(2), 151–66.

Stiglitz, J. (2003). *Globalization and its discontents.* Norton.

Stiglitz, J. (2013). *The price of inequality: How today's divided society endangers our future.* Norton.

Stromquist, N. (2002). *Education in a globalized world: The connectivity of economic power, technology, and knowledge.* Rowman & Littlefield.

Tikly, L. (2013). Reconceptualizing TVET and development: A human capability and social justice approach. In UNESCO-UNEVOC (Ed.), *Revisiting global trends in TVET: Reflections on theory and practice* (pp. 1–40). Unesco-Unevoc.

Torres, C. A. (2013). *International issues in adult education: Political sociology of adult education.* Sense.

United Nations Development Program (UNDP). (2016). *Human development report 2016: Human development for everyone.* United Nations Development Programme. http://hdr.undp.org/sites/default/files/2016_human_development_report.pdf

United Nations Development Program (UNDP). (2020). *What are the sustainable development goals?* United Nations Development Programme. https://www.undp.org/content/undp/en/home/sustainable-development-goals/background.html

Walker, M. (2006). Towards a capability-based theory of social justice for education policy-making. *Journal of Education Policy, 21*(20), 565–572.

Watts, M., & Ridley, B. (2007). Evaluating musical dis/abilities: operationalizing the capability approach. *International Journal of Research & Method in Education, 30*(2), 149–162.

Wheelahan, L., & Moodie, G. (2011). *Rethinking skills in vocational education and training: from competencies to capabilities.* NSW Department of Education and Communities, 13.

Williams, R. (1961). *The long revolution.* Pelican.

CHAPTER 10

UNREALIZED POTENTIAL

Marginalized Youth Around the Globe, With a Focus on Turkey

Aydın Yücesan Durgunoğlu and Fatoş Dayıoğlu
University of Minnesota Duluth, United States

In this chapter we discuss a global concern, marginalized youth *Not in Education, Employment, or Training* (often referred to as NEET). NEET status usually describes a highly heterogeneous group of individuals aged 15–29 who are not employed or in school (Carcillo et al., 2015; Eurofund, 2016; Mauro & Mitra, 2015; Serracant, 2014). Some are women who are not in the labor market because of family responsibilities, some are individuals who are discouraged by long, fruitless employment searches, and some are recent college graduates who are looking for work and are in NEET status for a short period of time. In this chapter, we are focusing on disadvantaged youth whose education was interrupted before completing high school because of economic and sociocultural reasons, such as poverty or girls not being allowed to continue with their education.

This group of young people constitutes a serious unrealized potential for their countries, with their marginalization and poverty reverberating for generations (Cardenas et al., 2015). As young people are shut out of opportunities to further develop themselves and contribute to their communities,

Advancing the Global Agenda for Human Rights, Vulnerable Populations, and Environmental Sustainability: Adult Education as Strategic Partner, pp. 157–171

there are serious costs both to their communities and to themselves (Carcillo et al., 2015; Mauro & Mitra, 2015; Serracant, 2014; Susanli, 2016). In addition to the economic costs of limited employment and wages, youth's mental health is also impacted, as they may experience hopelessness, isolation, and uncertainty. This can lead to disengagement and risky behaviors, thus making it a public health concern as well (Eurofund, 2012; Thompson, 2011). The NEET group is also less likely to participate in civic life compared to the non-NEET group (Erdoğan et al., 2017; Eurofund, 2012).

In such contexts of uncertainty and disengagement, individuals tend to both associate with more extremist groups and to support more autocratic leaders, thus constituting a threat to democratic institutions (Hogg, 2019). Research on radicalization of youth indicates that initially, it is not political ideology that attracts youth to extremist causes. Rather, the initial reasons are perceived injustices, searching for personal significance, and trying to find a way to reduce the uncertainty in one's life (Moghaddam et al., 2013). All individuals want to improve their lives, but in many societies, upward social mobility is limited by political, social, and economic restrictions (Moghaddam et al., 2013; Wilkerson, 2020), making individuals feel uncertain and hopeless about their future. During times of uncertainty, people identify more strongly with groups that claim to provide clarity, simplicity, and a sense of certainty. After identifying with such groups, it is a short jump to viewing the world through an "us versus them" prism. In addition, social exclusion (as in the case of NEET youth) seems to sharpen the ideological perspectives and move individuals towards extremism (Pretus et al., 2018).

Although NEET youth may be stigmatized and perceived as withdrawing from society because of their personal disposition or choices (Thompson, 2011), across the globe, it is the societal inequalities and structural barriers that make it very difficult for marginalized young people to break out of this vicious cycle (Gökşen et al., 2016; Mauro & Mitra, 2015; Serracant, 2014; Thompson, 2011). In the next section, we will first discuss the predictors of NEET status at the individual level and then place these characteristics within the broader sociocultural context of inequalities (e.g., sexism, poverty), followed by an examination of the situation in Turkey and sharing some recommendations given by the NEET youth themselves.

PREDICTORS OF NEET STATUS

Across the globe (with the exception of East Asia and Northern and Baltic States in Europe) more women than men are in NEET status, especially if they are married (Eurofund, 2012, 2016; Katz, 2013; Mauro & Mitra, 2015; Tamesberger & Bache, 2014). Women also show longer periods of inactivity between their current status and starting education or work (Cardenas et al., 2015). Disadvantages faced by women as compared to men start early and expand across the life span (Gökşen et al., 2016).

Level of education completed is another strong predictor of NEET status (Eurofund, 2012). In Latin America, 51% of NEET youth had not completed primary school, and 33% had not completed lower secondary school (the first three years postprimary). In Austria, 50% of the NEET population but only 5% of the non-NEET population had left school early (Tamesberger & Bacher, 2014). These data suggest that interrupted education at an early age increases the probability of being part of this vulnerable group.

Another predictor is migration and minority status. For example, in Europe, the probability of a young person becoming NEET is 70% higher for immigrants than for nonimmigrants (Eurofund, 2012; Mauro & Mitra, 2015; Tamesberger & Bacher, 2014). Migration can also occur internally, especially in cases of families moving from rural to urban areas, which can interrupt the schooling of youth (Kurtaran, 2014). In the United States, the percent of young people (ages 16–29) in NEET status is higher for Blacks and Hispanics (22 and 20%, respectively) as compared to 16% for Whites (https://www.pewresearch.org/fact-tank/2016/01/28/us-eu-neet-population/).

Health issues are also correlated with NEET status. In Europe, young people with a disability are 40% more likely to become NEET compared to others (Eurofund, 2012, 2016). Reading disabilities and undiagnosed learning and reading difficulties play a big part in students dropping out of school. Across 15 countries, children with physical disabilities are much more likely to be out of school, compared to those without disabilities (Mizunoya et al., 2018). In addition, adverse childhood experiences, low academic levels, and disengagement also predict leaving school (Thompson, 2011).

SYSTEMIC FACTORS

Although individual characteristics such as gender and education level are predictors of NEET status, they reflect the inequities in the broader social context. For example, interrupted formal education is higher for women than men across the globe, as families value education much more for boys than for girls (Gökşen et al., 2016), leaving women with limited opportunities for further education and employment. Gender also affects the distribution of family responsibilities, with young women taking on a disproportionate share of unpaid domestic labor (Katz, 2008; Mensch et al., 2004). Overall, young women constitute 88% of all 15–24-year-olds who are NEET due to family responsibilities, such as taking care of their children or other family members (Eurofund, 2016; Tamesberger & Bacher, 2014). This leaves them with no time to study or work outside of the home.

Another crucial factor is poverty, as it affects education completion rates and can lead to a downward spiral across generations. In an analysis of the 18 countries in Latin America, Cardenas et al. (2015) found that on the average, 54% of NEET youth lived in households in the poorest 40% of the population, while only 10% of NEET youth lived in the richest 20% of households. Hence the researchers labeled household income as the "crucial determinant" of NEET status (p. 34). Moreover, in Latin America, after household income, the second and third strongest predictors of NEET status were the two characteristics of the household head, namely their employment status and education level, which are, of course, interrelated with household income (see also Eurofund, 2012; Thompson, 2011 for similar data in Europe). Poverty and class-based differences also affect educational choices and the level of support provided to students to prevent their disengagement from school (Carcillo et al., 2015; Thompson, 2011).

To summarize, even characteristics that seem to be personal (gender, educational attainment) are closely related to proximal social causes. Despite this, the marginalization of youth can be described as consequences of personal characteristics, creating what Thompson (2011) calls "the individualization of social risk" (p. 785). Consequently, it is misleading to only focus on young people's individual characteristics without addressing underlying economic and social inequalities (Thompson, 2011) because race-, class- and gender-based inequalities affect the social, economic, and cultural capital available to marginalized young people as they navigate the systems of education and labor.

SITUATION IN TURKEY

Turkey has the highest overall NEET rate (32%) among the youth of all OECD countries (Erdoğan et al., 2017). Although the NEET numbers are steadily declining (Susanli, 2016), one concern is the wide gap that remains between the rates for men and women. In 2014, NEET rates were 17% for men and 46% for women, implying that the NEET problem is, to a large extent, due to the exclusion of young women from both education and the workplace. The patriarchal society creates barriers for women from a very early age. These include not allowing young girls to continue with their education, thus leaving women with limited skills to participate in the workforce. In addition, enabling women to get married at a young age and putting family caregiving responsibilities—for their own children, siblings, elders—mainly on their shoulders are additional barriers. Marriage affects men and women's NEET status differently. Single women are *less* likely to be in NEET status compared to married women, whereas single men are more likely to be NEET than married men (Susanli, 2016). Tamesberger and Bacher (2014) argued that married women (in Austria) should not be considered as NEET as they voluntarily choose not to work because of family responsibilities. Of course, if affordable childcare and supportive workplaces are available, and women choose to remain at home to take care of their families, this conjecture is true. However, if women stay at home because their society expects women to leave school and get married early and does not provide support such as childcare and family-friendly workplace policies (Gökşen et al., 2016; Kurtaran, 2014), then it cannot be considered a voluntary choice. Consequences of such restraining socio-cultural practices are very hard to remediate without serious changes in perspectives and systems.

Like gender, ethnicity in Turkey also exhibit patterns similar to what is found in other countries. Those reporting a minority ethnicity (e.g., Kurdish) have a higher NEET rate as compared to those reporting Turkish ethnicity, 45% versus 22%, respectively (Erdoğan et al., 2017). As in other countries, educational attainment shows a linear connection with NEET status for women in Turkey. Compared to university graduates, women with less than five years of education are 10 times more likely to be NEET. However, for men there is a curvilinear relationship between education and NEET status, because of high unemployment among college graduates (Erdoğan et al., 2017).

Finally, as is true in many other countries, poverty and class differences are serious risk factors in Turkey as well. For both men and women, those with below-average economic resources tend to be at a higher risk of having NEET status (Erdoğan et al., 2017; Gökşen et al., 2016), with economic inequality intersecting with many other factors. In economically disad-vantaged families, parental education tends to be low as well, and that affects physical, social, and cultural resources available to the youth. These resources range from having money to buying books, to helping children with schoolwork, and having a network to assist with job search.

Turkey has another insidious and systemic factor that disproportionately affects youth from economically disadvantaged families, namely the differ-ent tracks and admission processes in the secondary education system. In a European macro-analysis, it was shown that as the percent of secondary students who are in private schools increases, education level of 18-year-olds decreases (Alegre & Benito, 2014), implying that when public schools bear a larger burden to educate the poorest and less-prepared students, they may not be as effective in keeping students in school.

In Turkey, the quality of education differs greatly between private and public schools. Çelik (2015) eloquently summarized how the poor become poorer within the Turkish educational system. On the national entrance exam for secondary school placement, students from poorer families fare worse. The very rich can afford both tutoring for the exams as well as the tuition for the high-status private schools. For those who cannot afford such private schools, the exams determine which the type of secondary schools their children can attend. Students who have parents with modest means but strong academic support, can attend primary schools in their neighborhoods, and get into strong secondary schools, such as magnet schools. Youth who have limited support and resources at home tend to score low on the exams and can only enter vocational and religious schools that do not require exam scores. If the vocational schools in Turkey prepared youth for 21st century jobs, the situation would not be as severe, and youth would be prepared for employment. Unfortunately, based on his observations, Çelik described vocational schools as having very low prestige, with a high percentage of poor students who are not academically prepared. In addition, the classrooms were crowded, with limited hands-on opportunities to learn trades. In sum, poverty accompanied by such systemic barriers can lead to student disengagement and limit both the overall quality of education they receive and the ultimate grade they can complete.

Although NEET youth is an active topic of study, most studies analyze large national databases such as household budgets, living standards, and labor force surveys, conducted by governmental or international agencies. However, directly talking with the marginalized youth provides more detailed and nuanced data. Hence, we conducted an in-depth survey with NEET youth in Turkey to accomplish this goal. Reaching these young men and women is difficult as they are not clustered in schools or workplaces. Therefore, using an innovative approach, we relied on peer researchers to reach them in their own neighborhoods. The peer researchers were women who had successfully completed our literacy and empowerment programs (Durgunoğlu, 2018; Durgunoğlu et al., 2003). They received training on the ethics and the procedures of research before reaching out to the youth in their own neighborhoods and interviewing them. The in-depth surveys asked youth about their life histories, goals, aspirations, as well as the barriers and obstacles in their lives, and finally their suggestions for what would help them.

The sample included 126 people between 14–25 years old (87 women and 39 men; women were oversampled on purpose as they represent the majority of NEET youth). Most were unmarried (71%) and reported growing up in households with average or below average economic means (91%). Most had fathers who were laborers or farmworkers (57%). The mothers were predominantly homemakers (94%). Many of the participants had completed 8th grade (78% of men and 72% of women), but only 27% attended any kind of class or continuing education program since then. Although currently unemployed, 74% of men and 58% of women had some work experience, but these jobs had been inconsistent, short-term, and mostly as unskilled work running errands, rather than learning a vocation. Men and women reported different reasons for why they were not able to work. For men, the two main reasons were insufficient education (22%) and lack of jobs (42%). For women, family was the main reason for not working (36%), which included reports of family responsibilities and the husband/family not allowing them to work. Women also reported unhappiness with the work (19%), which indicated that workplaces were unwelcoming toward women.

When asked why they could not continue with their education, men and women reported poverty as the main reason, 48% and 42%, respectively. The second reason was disengagement (36% for men, 30% for women), which included disinterest in school, bad grades, or absenteeism. As the last reason, 28% of women but only 16% of men mentioned family barriers. When asked about future educational aspirations, 16% of women and 18% of men stated that they were no longer interested. The rest wanted to continue and get a diploma but did not know how to proceed. They described the obstacles to accomplishing their dreams. For men, the main obstacle was economic hardship (70%). They reported personal and academic difficulties as the second obstacle (11%). For women, the main obstacle was family responsibilities, including children (35%), followed by economic hardship (29%), and academic challenges (22%).

In their responses to the open-ended survey questions, participants offered the following recommendations for reaching and supporting marginalized youth: (a) a fair, free, and effective educational system, (b) support for economically disadvantaged students, (c) career counseling and vocational education, (d) creating jobs and opportunities, (e) addressing the psychological needs of the youth, (f) raising the awareness of the families to enable young girls to stay in school, (g) having classes outside of the formal educational system to provide foundations of academic and career skills. These concrete recommendations voiced by the marginalized youth themselves can be a guide to policy development and implementation.

POLICY IMPLICATIONS

The suggestions by the marginalized youth summarized above have implications for two global policy realms: (a) preventing students from leaving school early and (b) supporting those who had to leave school early.

Preventing Students From Leaving School Early

At a systemic level, some general initiatives are extremely important to overhaul the education enterprise to help students succeed. Among these are investing in education, reducing class sizes, preparing quality teachers, and paying teachers better salaries. While these are critical to school success, they are beyond the scope of this chapter and will not be discussed further.

Students leave school for myriad reasons (Lehr et al., 2003). Individual reasons such as academic challenges, disengagement, and lack of interest in school are closely intertwined with poverty, cultural and economic capital (Archambault et al., 2017), and the stresses youth experience at home and at school (Dupéré et al., 2018). Bowers and Sprott (2012) identified that in a national sample in the United States, there was a large subgroup of students who seemed to enjoy school, but did not have the necessary support and could quickly slip through the cracks when pressured by the challenges in their lives. They had low grades and attendance problems, but they were not necessarily disruptive or disaffected by school. They were also more likely to be from low socioeconomic status (SES) backgrounds. This group needed more academic as well as financial support to increase their academic performance. Likewise, in a study of 27 European countries, financial aid to students was a strong predictor of young people staying in school (Alegre & Benito, 2014). The students at risk for leaving school also needed counseling and support to cope during the breaking points in their lives.

In Turkey and some other countries, another important factor is the family decisions that either take the girls out of school early or do not allow them to continue their schooling once they complete the mandatory eight years of schooling. In addition to providing scholarships to reduce the financial burden of a child's educational expenses to the family, a systemic effort to raise awareness is needed, such as highlighting the long-term negative consequences of interrupted education and early marriage for women (Katz, 2013).

Vocational and technical education as an alternative to purely academic secondary education can be a way to reduce NEET rates (Carcillo et al., 2015; Eurofund, 2012). Nonetheless, vocational education is less effective in places where it is low in prestige and not supported to keep up with current labor force needs and trends (Çetin, 2015). This requires making the vocational education a valued and viable alternative to classical academic paths. Lavrijsen and Nicaise (2017) found that in 13 European countries with well-established vocational education systems, a narrowly focused vocational training was useful for employment in the short term. However, programs that also build a more general academic foundation were more effective in equipping students for lifelong learning and changing employment conditions.

Supporting Those Who Had to Leave School Early

Reaching youth who remain outside of the formal education system is where adult education and lifelong learning can play a prominent role, by using a two-pronged approach. In what is sometimes called "second-chance programs" (Carcillo et al., 2015; Eurofund, 2012), youth are encouraged to complete their missed educational years through open education systems, and thus "catch up," get their diplomas, and eventually continue their education further in the formal education system. Although getting their primary or secondary diplomas is a goal, these needs are usually tied to more pragmatic concerns such as finding employment or getting a driver's license. Therefore, programs should also include components that can lead to more concrete outcomes, such as workforce skills and apprenticeships (Carcillo et al., 2015). Career counseling, assisting with job searches, and job placement also must be part of these efforts.

The second prong, which has been studied more extensively, is to provide vocational, technical, and business training to youth as a mechanism for workforce development and employment. These are usually short-term programs outside of the formal education systems (Tripney et al., 2013). One study in Turkey showed that it is very difficult to get good returns on investment in vocational educational programs, as the effects of training on employment were modest and tended to dissipate over time (Hirshleifer et al., 2016) [It must be noted that this particular program did not include several components that could have improved outcomes, such as a life skills curriculum, internships and job placement help, and attention to the gender-specific needs of women, as will be discussed below].

Several reviews illustrated that gender-specific barriers (Gökşen et al., 2016) have to be addressed to make the programs more effective for women (Chinen et al., 2018; Katz, 2008, 2013; Kabeer, 2018). For example, recruiting family support is quite important for women to be able to attend courses, such as convincing fathers/brothers to allow young women to leave their homes or encouraging family members to share the domestic responsibilities. Women are also more likely to attend if programs are available in safe spaces in their neighborhoods. Also, programs with a strong gender focus are more effective, as they can challenge the gender norms that contribute to occupational segregation and biases against women as employees.

In some countries, the sociocultural constraints on women, such as limited mobility outside of the house, early marriage and high fertility, and heavy domestic responsibilities (Stavropoulou, 2018) make these programs very difficult to implement. Another promising approach is to target adolescent girls early on and provide them with workforce and life skills in a safe space in their neighborhoods (Chinen et al., 2018; Kabeer, 2018; Katz, 2008, 2013). These skills may cover topics such as reproductive health, workers' rights, and access to financial information and capital, as well as "soft skills" such as conflict resolution, self-control, effective communication, teamwork, and problem solving.

Successful programs in Latin America (Katz, 2008) combined on-the-job training with classroom instruction. They were decentralized programs in neighborhoods that were responsive to local labor-market demands and could directly connect program participants with employers. The programs also assisted women by providing peer support, mentoring and childcare.

In a program in Nepal, upon completing the vocational training, often lasting from one to four months, the participants were connected to on-the-job paid employment for six months. In addition, women completed 40 hours of life skills training, which included such topics as negotiation strategies, reproductive health, and workers' rights. Evaluation data showed that there were significant gains in employment and income, mostly driven by women's self-employment (Chakravarty et al., 2019).

Programs in Turkey provide a window as to why life skills are relevant, especially for women. We have developed programs to facilitate young women's empowerment by providing them with opportunities to practice their literacy, numeracy, and critical thinking skills while learning about their rights and the pathways to continue with their education or to find employment (Cantürk et al., 2019; Durgunoğlu, 2018). These programs were quite effective in developing cognitive and communication skills, as well as the self-efficacy of young women. The women also reported an increased understanding of their rights, and they participated more fully in the decision-making processes in their homes. A majority also started making plans and took steps to continue with their education using open education programs. Although some reported a desire to establish their own business, they reported family and childcare responsibilities as a serious obstacle to employment and education. In sum, the program yielded significant positive change in the individuals and in their close relationships, but without broader sociocultural support—for example, childcare, more equitable distribution of domestic responsibilities, social mobility—their growth and participation at the societal level was more limited.

CONCLUSIONS

Overall, promising programs for marginalized youth tend to have some common characteristics. Encouraging youth to stay in school is an important first step. This requires close monitoring of students, understanding the pressures in their lives, supporting them financially, mentoring, providing psychological and career counseling, and involving parents and families.

- As for vocational, technical, and business training programs for youth who are no longer in school, certain practices have been found to be effective:
- Include both classroom and on-the-job training for youth to develop work experiences in the form of apprenticeships, internships, preferably paid.
- Collaborate closely with the employers, keeping local demand for workforce in mind. In economies with weaker wage-paying employment, provide youth with business and entrepreneurship skills and possibly cash grants to start a business to facilitate self-employment.
- Strengthen basic academic skills (literacy, numeracy, critical thinking) in addition to vocational skills.
- Cover life skills in the programs, such as how to apply for a job, teamwork, communication, problem-solving.
- Develop programs with gender-sensitivity for both men and women, thus facilitating an awareness of societal barriers against women in education and work settings.
- Provide strong mentoring by knowledgeable and trusted individuals.
- Offer stipends to cover transportation and other expenses.

Some additional considerations are especially relevant for women in such training programs (Chakravarty et al., 2019; Chinen et al., 2018; Katz, 2008; 2013; Kabeer, 2018; Stavropoulou, 2018): (1) Offer childcare arrangements, either in the form of on-site care or subsidies/vouchers, (2) enlist family support in reducing sociocultural pressures on women and sharing their domestic responsibilities, (3) hold training programs in safe spaces within neighborhoods, especially for women whose mobility is limited by sociocultural constraints, (4) offer peer groups to provide support for the unique challenges faced by women at school, work, and home, and (5) provide instruction at flexible times convenient for the participants, taking their family responsibilities into consideration.

Finally, the adult education community can also adopt an advocacy role to address systemic barriers, such as gender and income inequalities that leave some youth with limited opportunities. Some systemic changes have been shown to relate to NEET rates. Strong coordination between unions, employers, and governments helps reduce NEET rates (Eurofund, 2012). At a global level, the NEET rate is lower in countries that have a larger proportion of funds dedicated to Active Labor Market Participation (ALMP) expenditures, such as job search assistance, training courses, and subsidized work that supports the transition of youth to the labor market.

Of course, the overall economic health of a country is the biggest factor in employment rates and the available resources. Given that the traditional approaches of targeting individual participants and providing skills training and job search assistance have only modest impacts, one very obvious solution is to focus on improving the economy and job creation (McKenzie, 2017). Although this seems like a straightforward goal, it is complicated by how income is distributed in a country and the kind of wages the newly created jobs bring. Even when new jobs are created, youth from families with limited economic and human capital are less likely to benefit if these youth do not have the necessary educational preparation for these new jobs or if the jobs that they are eligible for do not pay fair living wages. When life prospects of youth depend on their parents' income and education, intergenerational poverty is perpetuated, limiting mobility along class and race lines (Piketty & Saez, 2014; Stiglitz, 2016; Wilkerson, 2020). As we work toward improving the lives and prospects of youth who are systematically socially and economically disenfranchised, it is helpful to keep in mind both the characteristics of these individuals, as well as the broader sociocultural and economic forces that affect them.

REFERENCES

Alegre M. A., & Benito, R. (2014). Youth education attainment and participation in Europe: The role of contextual factors and the scope of education policy. *European Journal of Education, 49*(1), 127–143. https://doi.org/10.1111/ejed.12045

Archambault, V. I., Janosz, M., Dupéré, V., Brault, M.-C., & Andrew, M. (2017). Individual, social, and family factors associated with high school dropout among low-SES youth. *British Journal of Educational Psychology. 87*(3), 456–477.

Bowers, A. J., & Sprott, R. A. (2012). Why tenth graders fail to finish high school: A Dropout typology latent class analysis. *The Journal of Education for Students Placed at Risk, 17*(3), 129–148. https://doi.org/10.1080/10824669.2012.692071

Cantürk, M., Aşık, D., Şahinkaya, A., Durgunoğlu, A., & Öztan, E. (2019). *Empowering young women not in education or employment*. Paper presented at European Conference on Literacy, Copenhagen, Denmark.

Carcillo, S., Fernández, R., Königs, S., & Minea, A. (2015). NEET youth in the aftermath of the crisis: Challenges and policies. *OECD Social, Employment and Migration Working Papers*, No. 164. OECD. http://dx.doi.org/10.1787/5js6363503f6-en

Cardenas, M., de Hoyos, R., & Szekely, M. (2015). Out-of-school and out-of-work youth in Latin America: A persistent problem in a decade of prosperity. *Economía, 16*(1), 3–40.

Çelik, Ç. (2015). Eğitim sistemi yoksulu nasıl yoksul bırakıyor? [How the educational system leaves poor even poorer], T24, interview.

Chakravarty, S., Lundberg, M., Nikolov, P. & Zenker, J. (2019). Vocational training programs and youth labor market outcomes: Evidence from Nepal, *Journal of Development Economics, 136*, 71–110.

Chinen, M, De Hoop, T., Balarin, M., Alcázar, L., Sennett, J., & Mezarina, J., (2018). Vocational and business training to improve women's labour market outcomes in low- and middle-income countries: A systematic review. *3ie Systematic Review, 40.* London: International Initiative for Impact Evaluation (3ie). https://doi.org/10.23846/SR71094

Dupéré, V., Dion, E., Leventhal, T., Archambault, I., Crosnoe, R., & Janosz, M. (2018). High school dropout in proximal context: The triggering role of stressful life events. *Child Development, 89*(2), 107–122.

Durgunoğlu, A. Y. (2018). *Observations from programs of adult literacy, numeracy and empowerment in Turkey.* European Literacy Policy Network Association meeting, Cologne, Germany.

Durgunoğlu, A. Y., Öney, B., & Kuşcul, H. (2003). Development and evaluation of an adult literacy program in Turkey. *International Journal of Educational Development, 23*, 17–36.

Erdoğan, E., Yentürk, N., Akyüz, A., Kurtaran,Y., Yurttagüler, L., Dursun, K., & Oy, B. (2017). Being a NEET in Turkey: Determinants and consequences. *Power2Youth Working Paper*, No. 30.

Eurofund. (2012). *NEETs-Young people not in employment, education or training: Characteristics, costs and policy responses in Europe.* Publications Office of the European Union, Luxembourg.

Eurofund. (2016). *Exploring the diversity of NEETs.* Publications Office of the European Union, Luxembourg.

Gökşen, F., Filiztekin, A., Smith, M., Çelik, Ç., Öker, İ., & Kuz, S. (2016). Vulnerable Youth and Gender Mainstreaming. *STYLE Working Paper WP 10.2*, CROME, University of Brighton, Brighton. http://www.style-research.eu/publications/working-papers

Hogg, M. A. (2019). Radical change. Uncertainty in the world threatens our sense of self: To cope, people embrace populism. *Scientific American, 321*(3), 85–87.

Hirshleifer, S., McKenzie, D., Almeida, R., & Ridao-Cano, C. (2016). The Impact of vocational training for the unemployed: Experimental evidence from Turkey, *Economic Journal, 126*, 2115–2146.

Kabeer, N. (2018). *Gender, livelihood capabilities and women's economic empowerment. Reviewing the evidence over the life course.* Gage (Gender and Adolescent Global Evidence) report. https://www.gage.odi.org/publication/gender-livelihood-capabilities/

Katz, E. (2008). *Programs promoting young women's employment: What works?* Adolescent Girls Initiative Launch Report. http://citeseerx.ist.psu.edu/viewdoc/download? 10.1.1.536.6068&rep=rep1&type=pdf

Katz, E. (2013). *Identifying Research Gaps and Priorities for Women's Economic Empowerment: Gender and Youth Employment.* Unpublished Report. http://womeneconroadmap.org/sites/default/files/Katz_Youth_Employment.pdf

Kurtaran, Y. (2014). Türkiye Gençlik İzleme Raporu 2009-2012 (Youth Monitoring report for Turkey 2009-2012). In L. Yurttagüler, B. Oy, & Y. Kurtaran (Eds.),

Youth Policies in Turkey. Youth and Participation Project Publications, No. 8. Bilgi University Press.

Lehr, C., Hansen, A., Sinclair, M., & Christenson, S. (2003). Moving beyond dropout towards school completion: An integrative review of data-based interventions. *School Psychology Review, 32*(3), 342–364.

Lavrijsen, J., & Nicaise, I. (2017). Returns on vocational education over the life cycle: Between immediate labour market preparation and lifelong employability. *International Review of Education / Internationale Zeitschrift für Erziehungswissenschaft, 63*(2), 257–280.

Mauro, J. A., & Mitra, S. (2015). *Understanding out-of-work and out-of-school youth in Europe and Central Asia* (English). World Bank Group. http://documents.wor ldbank.org/curated/en/103971468187482224/Understanding-out-of-work-and-out-of-school-youth-in-Europe-and-Central-Asia

McKenzie, D. (2017). How effective are active labor market policies in developing countries? A critical review of recent evidence. *World Bank Research Observer, 32*(2), 127–154.

Mensch, B., Grant, M. J., Sebastian, M. P., Hewett, P. C., & Huntington, D. (2004). The effect of a livelihoods intervention in an urban slum in India: Do vocational counseling and training alter the attitudes and behavior of adolescent girls? *Population Council Working Papers*, No. 194. Population Council. https://knowledgecommons. popcouncil.org/departments_sbsr-pgy/52/

Mizunoya, S., Mitra, S., & Izumi, Y. (2018). Disability and school attendance in 15 low- and middle-income countries. *World Development, 104*, 388–403. https://doi.org/10.1016/j.worlddev.2017.12.001

Moghaddam, F. M., Warren, Z., & Love, K. (2013). Religion and the staircase to terrorism. In R. F. Paloutzian & C. Park (Eds.). *Handbook of the Psychology of Religion and Spirituality* (2nd ed., pp. 632–648). The Guilford Press.

Piketty, T., & Saez, E. (2014). Inequality in the long run. *Science, 344*(6186), 838–843.https://doi.org/10.1126/science.1251936

Pretus, C., Hamid, N., Sheikh, H., Ginges, J., Tobeña, A., Davis, R., Vilarroya, O., & Atran, S. (2018). Neural and behavioral correlates of sacred values and vulnerability to violent extremism. *Frontiers in Psychology, 9*, 1–12, 10.3389/fpsyg.2018.02462

Serracant, P. (2014). A brute indicator for a NEET case: Genesis and evolution of a problematic concept and results from an alternative indicator. *Social Indicators Research, 117*(2), 401–419.

Stavropoulou, M. (2018). *Interventions promoting adolescent girls' economic capabilities: what works? A rapid evidence review.* Overseas Development Institute, London.

Stiglitz, J. (2016). Inequality and economic growth. In M. Jacobs & M. Mazzucat (Eds.), *Rethinking capitalism: Economics and policy for sustainable and inclusive growth* (pp. 134–155). Wiley-Blackwell. https://bit.ly/2JPP6wy

Susanli, Z. B. (2016). Understanding the NEET in Turkey, *Eurasian Journal of Economics and Finance, 4*(2), 42–57. https://doi.org/10.15604/ejef.2016.04.02.004

Tamesberger, D., & Bacher, J. (2014). NEET youth in Austria: a typology including socio-demography, labour market behaviour and permanence. *Journal of*

Youth Studies, 17(9), 1239–1259. http://dx.doi.org/10.1080/13676261.2014.901492

Thompson, R. (2011). Individualisation and social exclusion: The case of young people not in education, employment or training. *Oxford Review of Education, 37*(6), 785–802. http://doi.org/10.1080/03054985.2011.636507

Tripney, J., Hombrados, J., Newman M., Hovish, K., Brown, C., Steinka-Fry, K., & Wilkey, E. (2013). *Technical and Vocational Education and Training (TVET) interventions to improve the employability and employment of young people in low- and middle-income countries: A Systematic review.* Campbell Systematic Reviews. https://doi.org/10.4073/csr.2013.9

Wilkerson, I. (2020). *Caste: The origins of our discontents.* Random House.

CHAPTER 11

ADULT STUDENTS IN COMMUNITY COLLEGES AND ECONOMIC JUSTICE

Kyung-Hwa K. Yang
Prairie State Community College, United States

This chapter focuses on the role that community colleges can play in advancing the United Nations (UN) agenda for economic justice. My discussion draws on a qualitative study about adult students' higher education experience. It was conducted in a community college located in an economically marginalized metropolitan suburb in the United States. The purpose of the study was to better understand barriers adult college students face in search for institutional support.

As discussed throughout this volume, the implications of the United Nations Sustainable Development Goals (SDGs) for adult education are significant. The SDGs build on the Millennium Development Goals (MDGs), but there are some differences. While the MDGs focus squarely on universal primary education, the SDGs shed light on adult education by making lifelong learning prominent, as articulated in Sustainable Development Goal 4 (SDG 4): "Ensure inclusive and equitable quality education and promote lifelong learning opportunities for all" (UN, 2015, p. 19). In doing so, the UN suggests that every country, including those that achieved universal primary education, has a role to play in achieving global education goals.

Advancing the Global Agenda for Human Rights, Vulnerable Populations, and Environmental Sustainability: Adult Education as Strategic Partner, pp. 173–188

Further, the SDGs foreground economic justice, as indicated in the eighth goal (SDG 8), "promote sustained, inclusive and sustainable economic growth, full and productive employment and decent work for all" (UN, 2015, p. 21). The implication of lifelong learning for economic justice is made clear in one of the target statements for SDG 4, which underscores the need to provide adults with meaningful skills training. Adult education is acknowledged as key to achieving economic justice in the statement. How adult education is conceived, and how that concept paves the groundwork for economic justice are, however, at stake. As Orlovic Lovren and Popovic (2018) sharply pointed out, the SDGs define adult education narrowly, primarily focused on literacy and vocational education. While lifelong learning is set at the forefront of the UN's global goals, adult education for economic justice remains on the outskirts.

The rapid growth of community colleges during the postwar period played a pivotal role in promoting adult education in the United States (Pfal et al., 2010). By offering a variety of programs, including adult basic education, workforce development, and technical education, community colleges have catered to a broad range of adult students (Ross-Gordon et al., 2017). Career education, in particular, which began to flourish in the 1960s, has driven the growth of the institutions (Cohen & Brawer, 2008). Adult students' experience of learning and its implications for economic justice, however, are yet to be explored. In what follows, I offer a brief overview of college enrollment for adults and their experiences, and go on to introduce the study from which the chapter draws. Based on analysis of study results, I discuss the role that community colleges can play in advancing adult education for economic justice.

ADULT STUDENTS' COLLEGE ENROLLMENT AND BARRIERS FOR THEIR LEARNING

Adult students are often called nontraditional students, who are defined as individuals who meet one of the following nontraditional characteristics: being financially independent, working full-time while studying part-time, having no high school diploma, delayed entry into college, being a first-generation college student, and being a single caregiver (Choy, 2002). In the 2011–2012 academic year, approximately 74% of all undergraduate students were, by definition, nontraditional students, possessing at least one of the above nontraditional characteristics (National Center for Education Statistics, 2015). While age is not a defining factor, practically, learners whose age is 25 or older are considered nontraditional students.

According to a recent survey on community college enrollment (American Association of Community Colleges, 2019), traditional-aged students (18 to 21 years of age) made up 41% of community college students, followed by students aged 22–29 (26%) and students aged 30–49 (17%). Community college students are older than overall undergraduate students (Ma & Baum, 2016), but the number of adult students in community colleges has decreased over recent years. The same survey shows that between 2010 and 2017, the enrollment in the 30–49-year-old group declined by 34% whereas the overall community college enrollment decreased by 14% during the period; in contrast, the enrollment for the under-18-year-old group increased by almost 65%, largely due to a growth in the number of high school students enrolled in high school–college dual programs. While community colleges still serve a diverse student body, the faces of community college students have become younger. This can have implications for adult college education.

Age matters. Kasworm (2005) argued adult students in community college classrooms construct their student identities through interactions with faculty and younger students. As she suggested, adult students might undergo difficulty adjusting to college environments; once they adjust, however, they can enrich younger students' experience of learning by adding their existing knowledge and skills to the classroom. However, their participation in the classroom is often hampered for various reasons. Multiple roles they assume as parents, employees, and community members, for instance, keep them away from participation (Ross-Gordon, 2011). Time management challenge is also a deterrent to participation for many of them (MacDonald, 2018). As Bowl (2001) posited, even with the intention to participate, some adult students become frustrated due to a lack of guidance and support from institutions.

Cross (1981) categorized barriers adult students face into three groups: situational, institutional, and dispositional barriers. *Situational barriers*, according to the author, are those arising from one's situation, for example, lack of time and money, or issues of childcare and transportation. *Institutional barriers* refer to institutional practices that discourage adult students, such as location, schedules, and fees, whereas *dispositional barriers* are a student's attitude toward learning, or self-perception about oneself as a learner. As Cross noted, dispositional barriers are elusive, especially in surveys, due to the issue of social desirability. For instance, it can be easier for adult students to point to the cost of education rather than their lack of interest in learning when asked to talk about barriers for learning. In-depth interviews can be immensely helpful to understanding adult students' perceptions of barriers for learning.

STUDY

The study presented in this chapter was conceived primarily to identify barriers that adult students encounter in pursuing their educational goals at community colleges. Cross's (1981) classification of barriers were used as the framework for the inquiry. To better understand the barriers, I examined adult students' motivations for learning as well. Social cognitive theory informs that one's belief in their ability forms the basis of the individual's motivation (Bandura, 2001). Expressed motivations for learning, however, do not necessarily indicate a college student's ability to acquire knowledge when devoid of self-regulated efforts (Liao et al., 2014). Thus, in my inquiry into dispositional barriers, I scrutinized adult students' self-efficacy (i.e., beliefs in their abilities to learn), motivations, and self-regulated efforts.

At the community college where the study was conducted, a vast majority of students are Black or African American and receive federal financial assistance. Of all students in its credit programs, 40% are 25 or older with near 60% female. The target population of the study were students aged between 25 and 50, who were currently enrolled in a credit course and had taken one or more classes in the college. The upper limit was chosen to highlight age-related shared experience. The number of students who are older than 50 was significantly less than that of the target population. Furthermore, a small set of interviews that I had conducted prior to the study at the institution suggested that members of the older population have distinctively different experiences than the target population and share few barriers with them. A call for research participants was sent out across campus in multiple ways to reach out to the population as widely as possible. Posters and handouts were distributed throughout campus, and an email notice was sent out to all students.

Of the 17 students who showed interest in participating in the study, those who did not meet the participation eligibility requirements were eliminated from the list. In addition, some were not available for interviews. To make the sampling as proportionate to the college adult student body as possible, I finally selected six female and four male students. Individual interviews were conducted, lasting up to one hour per participant. Based on the interviews, I prepared a narrative sketch (Connelly & Clandinin, 1990) for each interviewee to offer potential readers, namely college faculty and administrators, a picture of who they are as individuals. For member checking, each interviewee was given a chance to read and modify or confirm his or her narrative sketch. The sketches were then used as a source for my preliminary analysis to formulate questions in a focus group that followed.

I invited all the students who had showed interest in participating in the study and met the eligibility requirements to the focus group. Eight of the 10 interviewees were able to participate, and one non-interviewee volunteered to join the group. Their ideas about what the college could do to support adult students were sought through participatory activities. They shared the most pressing challenges they faced and made suggestions for the college to consider.

PARTICIPANTS

Five interviewees were in the 28 and 32 age range, and the others were in their 40s. The overall education level of the participants is of note. Four in the younger participant group are returning students who had graduated or attended the college in the past and came back for other credit programs. In contrast, only one in the older participant group had an associate degree, and the others were pursuing one for the first time. In what follows, I offer a brief narrative sketch for each interviewee. Pseudonyms, chosen by either the interviewees or me, are used to protect their privacy.

Blu, in her mid-40s, was pursuing her second associate degree in early childhood education full-time in hopes of opening her own child daycare center someday. She had earned an associate degree in psychology from the same institution years ago.

Constance, in her early 40s, was pursuing her associate degree in psychology to transfer to a university within a year. She was working full-time, taking care of a preteen daughter, and actively participating in her community to mentor girls and young women at risk.

Debbie, in her late 40s, was a first-year college student. A recent illness prompted her to pursue college education. Soon after recovery, she registered for classes and hoped to transfer to a university.

Mary, in her early 30s, was pursuing her second associate degree in nursing. She attended the college immediately after graduating from high school and later obtained a bachelor's degree. She returned to the college in hopes of finding a financially secure job.

Mom, in her late 40s, was studying full-time to transfer to a university in order to accomplish her long-sought dream of becoming a preschool teacher.

Nancy, in her late 20s, was pursuing her second associate degree in nursing. A few months prior to the interview, she earned her associate degree in general studies from the college. Her low self-esteem kept her from enrolling in the nursing program. Her graduation, however, offered the confidence she needed to enroll.

David, in his late 40s, began his program in manufacturing technology after the closure of a company where he had worked throughout his adulthood. He came to the college after realizing that he would not be able to earn decent income without a college degree. He was working toward an associate degree for the first time.

Ken, in his early 30s, was studying liberal arts and hoped to obtain an associate degree within a year. As he started working recently for the first time, he was juggling his schedule to be able to both work and study. But he embraced the new challenge and believed his college degree would bring him more job opportunities.

Mansa, in his early 30s, was pursuing a certificate in industrial electricity. After graduation from the college, he opened a small business. His experience, however, was not satisfactory. In exploring other career options, he returned to the college to become an electrician.

Sam, in his early 30s, was also studying industrial electricity. Like Mary, he attended the college and transferred to a university. After obtaining a bachelor's degree, he joined the U.S. military. Five years of service were long enough for him to conclude that he wanted to do something else for his career. As he believed industrial electricity would be useful to landing a job, he returned to the college.

ANALYSIS OF PARTICIPANTS' STORIES

Ten one-on-one interviews and a focus group discussion are the sources of my analysis. It centers on barriers that the participants face and issues that they believe contribute to the barriers. The findings are organized by prominence along the following themes: returning students, feelings of disorientation and disconnection, latent financial hardship, poor course management, and issues of time and space.

Returning Students

Of the 10 interviewees, three female and two male students held an associate or bachelor's degree. Four of them were aged between 28 and 32, and three of them had no dependents, worked part-time, and lived with their parents. Their profile was distinct from that of traditional students discussed earlier (Choy, 2002). The barriers they encountered also differ. They focused on a lack of financial aid and course-related issues. Mary expressed her frustration in accessing financial aid, saying:

If you are coming back to school as an adult learner, I don't have many options. That's pretty much how it is. I understand that priority is made for first-time students coming to this college for the first time. So then what do the rest of us do? Do we just go on to a secondary or master's program?

Blu similarly argued, "Why don't I qualify [for a scholarship]? I am here as a learner." The college offers scholarships to selected students. Credit hours are one important criterion for determining the qualification. Because most returning students are likely to have exhausted the credit hour limit, they are not eligible for the scholarships. Campus financial assistance available to them is significantly less, compared with first-time college students. In general, they pay tuition out of pocket or take out student loans. As the participants stated, although the lack of campus financial aid does not necessarily deter their educational pursuits, some aid, such as textbook awards or fee waivers, however trivial, can be helpful and encouraging.

Poor course management and unaccommodating course requirements were also mentioned by returning students. Sam said, "One of the classes, its environment is too relaxed. The class always starts late, like 15 minutes late. It's like why you even need to show up on time." Cancelation of classes was so frequent that he even considered leaving the college entirely at times. For Mansa, taking a first-year college experience course (a seminar course designed for first-time college students) was the least enjoyable part of his experience. He skipped the course when he first came to the college because it was not required then. Years after having earned an associate degree, he had to take the course because it was required in his current program. The course requirement delayed his certification process, and he had to pay for the delay.

Feelings of Disorientation and Disconnection

Feelings of disorientation and disconnection are prominent for the participants who recently started their college education. Debbie became a college student for the first time several months before the interview was conducted. Soon after her first visit to the college, she received a phone call from the admission office. As she described:

They said, "Come and register." When I came ... they said, "You can go and get your books and register for classes.... You pick your major." No one explained to me like, "This class is a prerequisite [and so on.]" I was right there picking classes with them.

Feeling disoriented in the rushed enrollment process, Debbie walked into the First Year Experience office to get help and registered for classes in that office. A few days later, she sat in her first college classroom. As she recalled, she made a series of quick decisions without deliberation over the decisions she had to make. She has since tried to orient herself in the college environment on her own. She has selected courses on her own and has visited the First Year Experience office for course registrations. She has never met an academic advisor because no one recommended it. During the interview, she asked me what the advisors are for. At the time of the interview, Debbie still felt unsettled. Surely, a sense of disorientation can be felt by any first-year college student regardless of age. Age, however, matters for orientation from an adult students' perspective. Debbie thought that she had not been guided step-by-step as a young traditional college student might have been. She said, "Because you are an old adult and because people are your age or younger, they don't engage with you like [a traditional college student.]" She believed that her age puts her at a disadvantage in the process of college orientation.

Debbie's feeling of disorientation resonated with David's experience. David started college education after having been away from school for nearly 30 years. Sponsored by the State unemployment office, he was sent to the college's career advising office for enrollment. Amid a stack of paperwork sent back and forth between the offices, his enrollment was done in a rush. In that process, as happened to Debbie, his college orientation took a back seat. As he recalled:

> I didn't know [about the orientation]. It was never brought up. I think it's because there was such a rush. I mean the program head and an advisor were trying to get me to sign up for the classes that I needed to get it going.

In retrospect, David wished he had attended a student orientation to make full use of his time in the college. Becoming a student was not easy for him. The interview took place several months after he began his program. Yet, feelings of isolation and disconnection were still lingering. As he argued, adult learners, unlike recent high school graduates, come from all over the place and thus lack a basic network to begin with. This can delay the process of acclimation to college environments and even contribute to alienating some adult students from the environments.

Constance attended a new student orientation before starting her program three years ago, but it took quite some effort for her to become adjusted to the college environment. As she put it, "You have to research. I walked around the school in my second semester, just to try to figure out where things were so that I don't have to come in to be lost." She emphasized that adult students should put themselves out to actively seek information on college resources. This is what both Debbie and David tried to an extent. Debbie paid attention to announcements, notices, and flyers to inform herself of campus events. Her thirst for connection and information, however, was not quenched. She hinted at her frustration, saying "I still don't know because I didn't really have time to pursue looking [for information]. But I shouldn't have to pursue all by myself. Some of those things, information should get to students, to me." First-time adult college students make efforts to orient themselves in the college and to make connections with others. Yet, their feelings of disorientation and disconnection can continue and even hamper their college education.

Latent Financial Hardship

Financial hardship was a common issue among the participants. Interestingly, however, only one was explicit about it. As the mother of three young children, Nancy stopped working immediately after having started her current program to afford more time to study. But financial stress soon became a reality for her, as she described:

> This almost makes me not want to continue the program because I don't have money to continue ... I don't have anything left in my loan. So now it's really stressful. I want to work again, but I know for a fact that if working, doing the nursing program and taking care of three children, something is going to be lacking.

The participants hinted at varying degrees of financial difficulty. Younger participants chose to live with their parents to manage their financial situations. Meanwhile, an older participant lived with her relative after having experienced foreclosure. Regardless of their circumstances, however, most of them did not describe financial hardship as a challenge to their studies. Rather, they seemed to think of it as an inevitable trade-off that they need to cope with personally while pursuing education. Blu, for instance, said, "I make sacrifices to take these courses because in the long run, it will benefit me." They believed that financial hardship was only temporary and eventually would pay off. Their belief motivated them to endure the hardship. However, Constance suggested that financial hardship can erupt at any moment to derail their educational journey. Recalling the moment when she felt like leaving college, she said:

> They [previous employer] laid me off and then let me go. The job that I am working on now, I absolutely love it. It doesn't pay me, though, what I used to be getting paid. So even though my pay is different, my bills are still the same. I own a car and different things. Things just got backed up and backed up and backed up because I am not paying all my bills. I am

paying half of this bill. I am paying half of that bill. So … my head got a little under the water.

One day, Constance found a campus scholarship opportunity. As a first-time college student, she met the criteria for the scholarship and succeeded in securing it. This helped her regain momentum to continue her educational journey.

Poor Course Management

Most of the participants mentioned course-related issues as a barrier for learning. As discussed earlier, the returning students were particularly critical about this matter, but the participants who are first-time college students were not quite different. Pointing to underutilized class time, David said, "There is only one machine in a class of 10 students." He spent his class time waiting for his turn to practice with a machine. As an experienced machinist, he had already gained significant hands-on practice at work. What he needed and enjoyed more was learning about theories behind the work he had done for nearly three decades. Yet, he was wasting a chunk of class time standing in line. Surely, his age did not put him at a disadvantage. Every student, regardless of age, equally stood in the line. David's work experience, however, made much of the class time particularly irrelevant to his learning because neither standing in line nor hands-on practice was conducive to his learning. It is questionable whether his work experience was considered in designing the course and whether the course responded adequately to his needs. Debbie also talked about course-related challenges. She referred to a five-week long summer course on communications as the most challenging part of her experience at the college. She taught herself about PowerPoint presentations and spent many nights preparing to deliver a speech in class. She only wished that the course had spanned a longer period so as for her to develop skills more gradually. The course was challenging to her because it pushed her capacity. Unlike what David described above, it was a productive challenge and only solidified her determination to pursue higher education. In sharp contrast, the type of challenge that frustrated her was a lack of rigor in instruction. She found it in most online courses she has taken. In her observation, instructors were much less involved than in-class instructors, as if teaching were their "side gig." When she felt that way, she rethought about the value of college education. Poor course management did not stop the participants from pursuing their education goals. It, however, tarnished their higher education experience.

Time and Space

Issues of time and space stood out among parenting female participants. Constance and Debbie frequented a cafe to study because at home, they often found themselves looking for something else to do, such as cleaning or cooking. To avoid distraction, they chose to leave their homes. Meanwhile, Nancy always felt like she was running out of time. She carried course material with her most of the time and opened it whenever possible between appointments or between classes. Mom, raising two teenagers, described the difficulty in prioritizing her time for herself as follows:

> Being a mom is a choice and school is a choice. But for me being a mom is a top priority.... [I make] sure that my kids don't suffer in any way because I am going to school. It's because this is their time to be in school.... I had my time. I didn't make good use of it. I didn't do what I needed to do. So the time has gone now. It's their time. So my schooling takes the second seat to them.

At home, Mom normally began to study late at night. She thus tried to make use of daytime. On campus, however, it was extremely challenging for her to find a place to study because of noises. Even small chats in the library were so disturbing that she chose to leave the college building to study in her car.

Her argument for space on campus resonated with other participants in the focus group discussion. Suggesting that the campus is primarily reserved for young, traditional college students, they called for a quiet zone where they could study, or simply be relaxed, away from noises, house chores, and other distractions. A college campus can be the most convenient, time-saving place for some adult students to study. According to the participants, however, it is not adequate for them to use, and at times, prompted them to feel like outsiders.

DISCUSSION OF BARRIERS

In this section, I discuss the participants' stories from the perspective of dispositional, situational, and institutional barriers (Cross, 1981). First, none of the participants exhibited any signs of dispositional barriers. None of them signaled a lack of either interest or confidence in learning. They all invested their time and money in higher education. This is somewhat predictable because participation in the study itself suggests the participants' high-level of engagement in education. Some participants, however, indicated having experienced dispositional barriers in the past. Mom, who enrolled in college programs three different times, stated that she was not mentally ready to pursue college education in the past. Ken, who first enrolled into college more than a decade ago, had no intention to continue his education for a long time. He was in and out of college until recently. It is worth noting, though, that their dispositional barriers often coincided with situational barriers, such as pregnancy, illness, or death in the family. These findings suggest that the complexity of barriers—different barriers combined—lead to disruption in college education among adult students.

The study also suggests that dispositional barriers can be developed externally while at college. Debbie, for instance, hesitated to pursue college education for some decades because of her self-perception that she was not smart enough. Even after she was enrolled in college, however, she constantly reminded herself of her ability not to be discouraged. As she put it:

> They [People] are going to ask you all the time, "Why do you go there [to college]?" You do not get encouragement like 18 years old or 20 when you go to school. You have to encourage yourself to continue. That's what I have to do. If I were 18 or 19, everybody would be rallying around me, "You can do it." Instead, people around me would say, "You chose this. This is what you chose. You don't have to do this. You decided to do this."

Adult students, especially those who are from low-income families, often bring psychological, physical, intellectual, and other types of wounds to their sites for learning, and those wounds interfere with their education (Lange et al., 2015). Such wounds can persist, or even be reproduced, in higher education institutions to inflict microaggression (Locke & Trolian, 2018). This situation can create or aggrandize existing dispositional barriers.

Second, situational barriers exist, but can stay latent. Most participants in the study did not pinpoint financial hardship as a barrier. Rather, they regarded it as an unavoidable part of being a student, or simply as an inconvenience to their educational pursuits. Many adult students could be struggling financially, or feeling engulfed by competing responsibilities as parents, caregivers, and employees (MacDonald, 2018; Ross-Gordon, 2011). However, because they tend to think of handling situational barriers as a personal responsibility, they do not describe it as a barrier. Although those barriers might not impose an immediate hurdle to their educational journey, they can become a primary reason for some adult students to leave college if not dealt with appropriately. The study affirms the necessity for financial aid reform that can better meet adult students' needs. It should include providing targeted financial aid for adults, revising financial aid eligibility standards, and funding for life expenses (Van Noy & Heidkamp, 2013). The reform can play a crucial role in helping adult students with low income overcome their situational barriers and succeed in higher education.

Third, most participants pointed to institutional barriers. Returning students, those who earned college degrees and came back for additional credentials, were particularly vocal about this issue. Career development was the primary reason why they returned to college. However, their presence on campus, let alone their needs, are hardly recognized in community colleges. The fact that half of the participants held a college degree should also be a wake-up call. They might be a growing student population that community colleges have failed to notice. Institutional barriers were also noted by first-time college students. Poor course management or instructional quality disappoints students who aspire to higher education, especially when they attend college after having gained significant work experience. Courses designed primarily with inexperienced, traditional-aged college students in mind can render adult students' college education largely pointless.

Institutional barriers are not limited to course-related issues. The feelings of disorientation and disconnection that the study participants talked about are also institutional barriers. Those who were first-time college students showed a strong interest in joining campus events and activities along with each other and younger students. Calling for attention to their desire, Debbie argued, "This is my first time at college. I want a full college experience. That's why I am here." Mom claimed, "I matter!" A college degree matters to adult students, but they also want to *experience* college as traditional-aged college students would. They want to be involved in activities and opportunities colleges offer and capitalize on campus resources. Surely, this finding might not represent every adult student. This study suggests, however, that the desire of adult students who wish to participate in campus activities and intermingle with other students is often suppressed due to a lack of information and connections. Community colleges may need to consider how to reach out to them. In this regard, as the participants championed, colleges should consider having an adult student liaison who can act on behalf of adult students and interact with the administration to voice their needs and concerns.

IMPLICATIONS FOR ECONOMIC JUSTICE

The UN defines economic justice as "the existence of opportunities for meaningful work and employment and the dispensation of fair rewards for the productive activities of individuals" (Department of Economic and Social Affairs, 2006, p. 14). The organization regards it as a key element of social justice, which is broadly described as the fair distribution of economic gain. Whereas economic gain takes the center stage of economic justice, social justice focuses on distribution. What knits them together in the name of justice is "environmental consciousness" (p. 8), or sustainability, which refers to the intention to create a safe environment for all. From this view, without sustainable growth, there is neither economic justice nor social justice. Stated differently, even the economic gain of a historically marginalized social group will not amount to economic justice if devoid of sustainability.

For sustainability, individuals' fair participation in productive activities is at the heart of the UN's economic justice. That participation requires equitable distribution of material resources and institutionalized recognition of culturally defined social orders and hierarchies (Fraser, 1999). Without recognition of hierarchical social relationships and unfair treatments for different cultural groups based on race, gender, class, and other social markers, fair participation in economic activities cannot be fulfilled. In a sense, economic justice builds on social justice and demands structural change in society.

What, then, can community colleges do to contribute to economic justice? The study hints at some of the roles that community colleges can play. Every study participant aspired to obtain a college degree or credential, and some of them returned to the college explicitly for that, even after having achieved a higher degree. They perceived their education as a vehicle to their economic gain. Having a credential can be crucially important to the gain, especially for those having lived with limited resources.

To respond to their motivations and objectives, first, community colleges need to be aware of barriers that adult students face and to address them. In this regard, the study highlights a need for financial aid reform, among others. Second, community colleges should be aware of the work experience, knowledge, and skills adult students bring to classrooms and take them into consideration in designing courses and programs. Lastly, but most importantly, it is critical to invite students to engage in conversations on justice and sustainability. Without awareness of them, aspirations for individual economic gain can disguise the social structure that maintains unfair social orders and even glorify the ideology of merit-based social mobility (Littler, 2017). Without efforts to promote justice, community colleges can brand themselves as institutions to embolden the myth of meritocracy (Liu, 2011). Community colleges should make efforts to reach out to adult students to tap into their aspirations for college experience. They should create activities and events in which adult students can participate to allow them to examine unfair social structure and shape their ideas about economic gain and development from a justice perspective.

REFERENCES

American Association of Community Colleges. (2019). *Community college enrollment crisis? Historical trends in community college enrollment.* https://www.aacc.nche.edu/wp-content/uploads/2019/08/Crisis-in-Enrollment-2019.pdf

Bandura, A. (2001). Social cognitive theory: An agentic perspective. *Annual Reviews of Psychology, 52,* 1–26.

Bowl, M. (2001). Experiencing the barriers: Non-traditional students entering higher education. *Research Papers in Education, 16*(2), 141–160.

Choy, S. (2002). *Findings from the condition of education 2002: Nontraditional undergraduates.* National Center for Education Statistics. https://nces.ed.gov/pubs2002/2002012.pdf

Cohen, A. M., & Brawer, F. B. (2008). *The American community college.* Jossey-Bass.

Connelly, M., & Clandinin, D. J. (1990). Stories of experience and narrative inquiry. *Educational Researcher, 19*(5), 2–14.

Cross, K. P. (1981). *Adults as learners.* Jossey-Bass.

Department of Economic and Social Affairs. (2006). *Social justice in an open world: The role of the United Nations.* United Nations. https://www.un.org/esa/socdev/documents/ifsd/SocialJustice.pdf

Fraser, N. (1999). Social justice in the age of identity politics: Redistribution, recognition, and participation. In L. Ray & A. Sayer (Eds.), *Culture and economy after the cultural turn* (pp. 25–52). SAGE.

Kasworm, C. (2005). Adult student identity in an intergenerational community college classroom. *Adult Education Quarterly, 56*(1), 3–20.

Lange, E. A., Chovanec, D. M., Cardinal, T., Kajner, T., & Smith Acuna, N. (2015). Wounded learners: Symbolic violence, educational justice, and re-engagement of low-income adults. *The Canadian Journal for the Study of Adult Education, 27*(3), 84–104.

Liao, H.-A., Edlin, M., & Ferdenzi, A. C. (2014). Persistence at an urban community college: The implications of self-efficacy and motivation. *Community College Journal of Research and Practice, 38*(7), 595–561.

Littler, J. (2017). *Against meritocracy: Culture, power and myths of mobility.* Routledge.

Liu, A. (2011). Unraveling the myth of meritocracy within the context of US higher education. *High Education, 62,* 383–397.

Locke, L. A., & Trolian, T. L. (2018). Microaggressions and social class identity in higher education and student affairs. *New Directions for Student Services, 162,* 63–74.

Ma, J., & Baum, S. (2016). *Research brief: Trends in community colleges.* College Board Research.

MacDonald, K. (2018). A review of the literature: The needs of nontraditional students in postsecondary education. *Strategic Enrollment Management Quarterly, 5*(4), 159–164.

National Center for Education Statistics. (2015). *Demographic and enrollment characteristics of nontraditional undergraduates: 2011–12.* U.S. Department of Education. https://nces.ed.gov/pubs2015/2015025.pdf

Orlovic Lovren, V., & Popovic, K. (2018). Lifelong learning for sustainable development–Is adult education left behind? In W. Leal Filho, M. Mifsud,

& P. Pace (Eds.), *Handbook of lifelong learning for sustainable development* (pp. 1–17). Springer.

Pfal, N. I., McClenney, K. C., O'Brian, T., Sullivan, L. G., & Wilson, C. M. (2010). The learning landscape in community colleges. In C. E. Kasworm, A. D. Rose, & J. M. Ross-Gordon (Eds.), *Handbook of adult and continuing education: 2010 edition* (pp. 231–241). SAGE.

Ross-Gordon, J. M. (2011). Research on adult learners: Supporting the needs of a student population that is no longer nontraditional. *Peer Review, 13*(1), 26-29.

Ross-Gordon, J. M., Rose, A. D, & Kasworm, C. E. (2017). *Foundations of adult and continuing education.* Jossey-Bass.

United Nations (UN). (2015). *Transforming our world: The 2030 agenda for sustainable development.* https://sustainabledevelopment.un.org/content/documents/21252030%20Agenda%20for%20Sustainable%20Development%20web.pdf

Van Noy, M., & Heidkamp, M. (2013). *Working for adults: State policies and community college practices to better serve adult learners at community colleges during the great recession and beyond.* NTAR Leadership Center. http://www.heldrich.rutgers.edu/sites/default/files/products/uploads/WorkingForAdults.pdf

CHAPTER 12

LOOKING FOR EDUCATIONAL NEEDS IN THE COMMUNITY

Adult Educators' Roles Matter

Isaac Kofi Biney
University of Ghana, Ghana

Adult learning is becoming increasingly important in societies fueled largely by the advancement of information communication technology (ICT). The digital era has connections with adult learning, and technology is key to conquering relentless accompanying waves of change (King, 2017). Hence, adult educators have responsibility for working with and helping people identify educational needs in their communities. Regmi (2015) argued that the 2000 millennium development goals (MDGs) failed because adult education was not considered. Meanwhile the 2015 sustainable development goals (SDGs) are underway, with GOAL 4—Quality Education, aimed at promoting inclusive, quality, and lifelong learning among people to engender sustainable communities. "Sustainable communities" is used here connote communities that maintain and improve the economic, environmental, and social characteristics of their areas to enable people to lead healthy and productive lives (Frank & Smith, 1999). To Reynolds (2010), sustainability is conditioned on an environmentally

Advancing the Global Agenda for Human Rights, Vulnerable Populations, and Environmental Sustainability: Adult Education as Strategic Partner, pp. 189–206

literate society; hence sustainable development is defined as development that "meets the needs of the present without compromising the ability of future generations to meet their own needs" (World Commission on Environment and Development, 1987, p. 44).

The goal of community education is community development (Bidwell & McConnell, 1990; Ross, 2017), and "working together is key in community development because it allows for results than working as isolated units" (English & Mayo, 2012, p. 138). The term community is defined as a geographical location where people live and work and share the same basic culture, psychological ties, and interests (Robinson & Green, 2011). For example, villages are important because there is a relationship between community and the individual (Robinson & Green, 2011). Adult educators have to address educational needs in the community; educational needs exist at several levels: individuals have personal needs, organizations have needs, and the community-at-large has needs (Brookfield, 1995). The people of Ghana in the 1960s and 1970s were noted for their strong self-help spirit, initiating development projects on their own (Biney, 2009). The same cannot be said today because the strong self-help spirit of the people seems to be waning. Some communities' water bodies and arable lands appear unsustainable due to "galamsey" activities (Biney, 2019). According to Biney, "galamsey" connotes gathering of rich mineral resources, particular gold for sale. These situations require deepening of community education to rekindle the self-help spirit in the people to make communities sustainable. Poverty and unemployment constitute the bane of people in communities (Biney, 2009), yet there are opportunities in communities, and given the needed support through education, the people can improve livelihoods. Low education and lack of skills among the people are making it difficult to identify opportunities in communities (Baah-Boateng, 2018; Oduro-Mensah, 2009). It is argued that the inability to identify educational needs in communities serves as barrier to improvement of communities. This gap can be filled when community educational needs are identified and leveraged because educational programs can provide skills to people to improve their circumstances and enjoy quality of life within their communities.

The globalization phenomenon seems to increase the competitive spirit, resulting in a race for business and material gains, rather than education (Oduro-Mensah, 2009); as the world shrinks, the gap between the rich and the poor widens, and the marginalized become more marginalized. This chapter makes a case that educational needs can become visible through the services of adult educators. In this chapter, I explore the following questions: What is community education? What are community educational needs? Can connection between international development and community drive adult education in communities? The chapter examines roles of adult educators in identifying educational needs in communities. It proposes that if adult educators are supported by governments in community education work, they could, together with community leadership groups, identify educational needs in communities. Adult educators, according to United Nations (1986) are an *educating force,* and a *source of education* for the community. This role they play, I argue, is not receiving the support of governments in developing countries. Hence, the influence of adult educators is not felt much in communities and that could account for the low levels of development (Mera, 2004). This is a gap to be explored within this chapter to open opportunities for societies in developing countries to start experiencing sustainable communities. This chapter is organized in the following sections: community education, community educational needs and resources, the case of community education in Ghana, strategies for promoting community education, and practical implications for teaching and learning practice.

COMMUNITY EDUCATION

Community education represents all forms of educational processes, programs, and activities organized by the community, in collaboration with organizations, to address educational needs (Bidwell & McConnell, 1990; Brookfield, 1995). Community education is not just a matter of improving the individual's position in society; it is a matter of enabling the society to survive (Cole, 1979). Connolly (2011) sees community education as an extension of a pragmatic education service designed to target hard-to-reach people and integrate them into the mainstream through employment and further education. It is interpreted as a dimension of community development empowering powerless people to address educational needs. Though the term "community" suggests a collective for the education process, it runs through community education where a strong emphasis is placed on the development of the individual, inherent in a concept like *consciousness raising* (Brookfield, 1995). Murphy (2014) perceived community education and development broadly as "a process of communal education towards empowerment, both at an individual and a collective level, an interactive, challenging process, not only in terms of its content but also in terms of its methodologies and decision-making processes" (p. 12).

Community education is at the heart of human development, and it has played a vital role throughout the history of adult education. It is an instrument of change in community climate that results in a change in home environment, and a positive change in adults' attitudes and achievements (Engelbrecht, 2005). One distinguishing feature of community education is the interplay between developing consciousness and autonomy of people to change with a potential for learning (Bidwell & McConnell, 1990). Community education is a constantly evolving process of interaction between the needs of people and educational resources of the community. A common feature is that programs are developed in dialogue with communities (Brookfield, 1995). The purpose is to build the capacity of individuals, groups, and communities to improve the quality of life of people. Central to this is the ability to participate in democratic processes (Bidwell & McConnell, 1990). Community education is a developmental process of lifelong learning and social action relevant to the problems, and needs of individuals, groups, and society. Community education and community development are two integrated and inseparable parts of a process that allows communities to develop their consciousness, integrate more successfully, and contribute toward developing their communities (Frank & Smith, 1999). The idea of community education first addresses itself to the involvement of the community, in determining its needs, not only educational needs, but economic, social, and political needs (Brookfield, 1995). Unfortunately, this educational approach to identifying community needs and addressing them has not been deepened enough in the communities. In Ghana, community education provided to the people includes services by agricultural extension officers to farmers. The government has initiated agricultural programs, including *"Planting for food and jobs," "Planting for export and rural development,"* and *"Rearing for jobs and development"* in creating job opportunities to farmers, agricultural extension officers, and players in agricultural value chain. Since the inception of the programs, over 2,700 extension officers have been recruited by the Ministry of Food and Agriculture (Government of Ghana, 2019).

Extension education enables rural people to improve their level of living by aided self-help education (Kumar, 1979); however, self-help education is facilitated by adult educators through community education programs. The organization of educational programs for farmer's groups helps in fostering the "can-do" spirit among farmers involved in the agricultural programs. Extension education combines adult education in educating farmers to adapt techniques of raising crops and animals in better combinations (Kumar, 1979). Village problems can be conceived as educational problems, so building skills of farmers is crucial.

As facilitators in community education programs, adult educators cultivate the rural communities as farmers cultivate their fields of corn. Their task in community education involves communicating with an illiterate majority and helping them in changing the attitudes to bring about continuous improvement (Kumar, 1979). Adult educators play critical roles in improving communities because adult education emerged in response to widespread concerns about poverty and exploitation (Woelke, 2017). If we choose education for liberation, as Freire observed, educators need to love the people and trust them in equal measure (Crowther, 2015). However, the success of government's initiatives hinges on identification of educational needs of the people and supports to achieve the goals of the programs.

Health and environmental awareness programs on COVID-19, degradation of forest vegetation and arable lands, pollution of water bodies, and education on democracy and constitution of Ghana are community education programs. These programs utilize partnerships and collaborative roles played by international development organizations to include non-governmental organizations, civil society organizations, community-based organizations, faith-based organizations, charities, and foundations. Hence, community education is to empower community members to work together to identify problems and seek out solutions in their respective communities (Bidwell & McConnell, 1990). This indicates that community education should be linked to community action geared to securing a greater degree of local community control over the bureaucratic system to deliver services and offer people a greater say in defining their needs and meeting the needs. Brookfield (1995) argued that for community action to be effective, it has to be informed by the spirit of critical awareness on the part of the people undertaking it. This demonstrates that community education is a lifelong learning venture; however, implicit in this change is the belief that there should be equality of access to education in our communities throughout the life stages (Bidwell & McConnell, 1990). When this happens, the education system can become more open, flexible, and diverse to Ghanaians.

COMMUNITY EDUCATIONAL NEEDS AND RESOURCES

The identification of community educational needs and resources in empowering people for development constitutes the initial task of adult educators working in communities. This section examines community educational needs. It looks at needs, educational needs, and resources to improve lives in communities.

Needs

Needs are viewed as gaps between what is and what should be, as felt by an individual, a group or a community (Gajanayake & Gajanayake, 1993). It can be as concrete as the need for food and water, or as abstract as improved community cohesiveness (Brookfield et al., 2003). The educational needs of African people are as varied as the different types of the communities, arising from a combination of local challenges posed by economic, scientific, and technological factors (Indabawa & Mpofu, 2006). In Ghana, people are faced with problems of poverty and unemployment. It is the researcher's view that people overcome these challenges by engaging in adult education to improve their life circumstances through provision of skills and attitudes to fit into the dynamics of change. Ghana's developmental challenges require adult educators to facilitate education programs among the poorest and least educationally privileged enabling people to learn skills and trades thus becoming useful in the spaces they occupy. If we accept that all human needs have implications for education, then Ghana needs to develop good adult educators to drive its development, using education as a tool.

Educational Needs

McConnell (2002) argued that any society, democratic or not, cannot afford to have large parts of its population unproductive to meet new challenges in the labor market. Educational activities are embedded in and directed toward activism, community organizing, and civic participation (Prins & Drayton, 2010). Hence adult educators must place value on the people, support them, and work with them to address their needs within those roles. This desire to address an educational need might have informed the government's policy initiative of making senior high schools (SHS) free of charge. It is hoped that when the youth become educated, the knowledge and skills acquired would drive development in their personal lives, their communities, and the economy at large.

Low education and lack of skills development during adult life could cause the citizenry to be at risk of being excluded from participation in the social, political, and cultural spheres of their community, and their potential employability could be reduced (Iniquez-Berrozpe et al., 2019). This requires imaginative adult educators to help the people reach out to their goals in life. The point is that educational needs grow out of the roles, responsibilities, and functions of individuals, groups, and communities. As adults play roles in the spaces they occupy, they require education to address these needs. This makes identification of educational needs in communities important because one critical skill that matters in keeping a job is the ability to keep learning (The Economist, 2017). Adults in our communities need to develop the desire to be lifelong, lifewide, and life-deep learners (Belanger, 2016) and become effective in the spaces they occupy.

Community-based organizations, faith-based organizations, youth groups and "Asafo companies" (self-help voluntary groups established in communities to undertake development projects) have roles and functions to play. Their operations add to improvement in communities. Needs exist and problems arise, and they are dealt with by addressing the people's educational needs. The provision of community education by adult educators serving as community animators aids people to learn about self-help projects and build leadership skills to improve communities. Building these roles requires identification of educational needs; after all, building the capacity of the wider community is critical to improving quality of life of people (Ross, 2017).

Adult educators appreciate that the important key to success of programs is that they are known to people in the community. This implies that the process of undertaking needs assessment in a community should be one through which media publicity is deepened. I employ the services of the media to promote educational programs at Accra Learning Center to build the capacity of adult learners in a lifelong learning fashion. The Accra Learning Center, the biggest of the University of Ghana Learning Centers, has nearly 9,000 students reading degree and diploma programs through distance education. It runs pre-access, access/mature, and continuing professional development programs marketed through media platforms. The Center buys airtime and talks about community education and outreach programs live on radio and television stations. These media outlets are used to promote, inform, and educate the public on Annual New Year School and Conference, a flagship program of the University of Ghana. Using adult education as a strategy for building the "can-do" spirit in people is one approach adult educators can adapt in helping people learn initiatives and implement programs.

Resources

Resources include individuals, organizations and institutions, buildings, and equipment. It involves anything that can be used to improve the quality of life. Essentially, there are two main resources of community education—human and nonhuman resources. The human resource is what is referred to as human capital. The adult educators, resource persons, and the people with varied knowledge and skills belong in this category. Examples include a mother in Ghana who volunteers to organize games for neighborhood children after school or the Kenyan farmers' cooperative that makes it possible for farmers to buy seed and fertilizer cheaply and send their produce directly to market without a middleman. These are resources that enhance community life. The nonhuman resources consist of financial, logistics comprising vehicles, learning materials like chairs, projectors, and accommodation for resource persons (Knowles et al., 2012; Nafukho et al., 2011). Every individual is a potential community asset that can be tapped into and used for community building. The community itself is made up of a web of experts whose ideas, skills, and knowledge can lead to the improvement of communities. Adult educators must look for them through community forums, workshops, seminars, and other spaces.

THE CASE OF COMMUNITY EDUCATION IN GHANA

Connolly (2011) asserted that any discussion of community education must consider that perspectives vary from context and place. In Ghana, community education is found in agriculture and food, fisheries, trade and industry, manpower development, rural development, social welfare, and education ministries. The National Commission for Civic Education (NCCE), Electoral Commission (EC), Non-Formal Education Division of Ministry of Education (NFED), Non-Governmental Organizations (NGOs), and Faith-Based Organizations (FBOs) are all involved in community education. These organizations have programs; unfortunately, they are not resourced (Baidoo, 2019) to deliver them to the people to address their needs. If community education institutions were well funded, they could empower the people to build sustainable communities.

Ghana has educational institutions like schools, universities, and colleges that open their doors to adults for a first, second, or further chance to learn. The School of Continuing and Distance Education, University of Ghana, is noted for providing adult basic and distance education opportunities to adults. There are voluntary bodies and interest groups like churches, charities, and political parties involved in community education. There are private organizations that earn their living by providing education for adults. If you walk down the streets of Accra, the capital of Ghana, you will find different banners informing the public about continuing education programs of all types. These programs are designed to help adults learn; however, they require regulatory policies to guide the organizations operations.

Beyond these, there are other self-help groups providing a chance for people to learn from one another. There are community-based organizations (CBOs) representing community character, including "Kroye kuo," Asafo Groups, Nnboa Groups, Youth Clubs, and Reading Clubs—all of which are made up of people providing community education. Such programs include health education, vocational education, civic education, financial literacy education, and environmental education. These types of education are provided to community members to improve quality of life. The awareness created as a result of participating in community education is indispensable because the impact on health, nutrition, income-generation, food production, women's empowerment, environmental sustainability and human resource development is enormous.

INTERNATIONAL DEVELOPMENT, COMMUNITY DEVELOPMENT, AND ADULT EDUCATION

From an international perspective, Chekki (1979) observed that community development (CD) has been one of the most significant social forces in the process of planned change. The United Nations (UN) and its affiliate organizations—United Nations Educational, Scientific and Cultural Organization (UNESCO), International Labor Organization (ILO), Food and Agricultural Organization (FAO), World Health Organization (WHO), and United Nations Children's Fund (UNICEF) promoted community development throughout the developing world as a means of raising standards of living among the poor (Campfens, 1997). However, the assumptions upon which CD and national development were based by UN organizations and its affiliate expert groups were challenged for their contradictory and culturally biased nature (Alldred, 1976, as cited in Campfens, 1997; Biddle, 1966; Galbraith, 1962).

It was apparent that the basic concepts of CD such as human needs, community, participation, and development required thorough reexamination. Alldred (1976) drew attention to the complexities and unequal realities of rural and urban communities and questioned the popular notion of unrestrained self-reliant development by local communities. He argued that politically disquieting inequalities emerge because of different communities pursuing their own development priorities at their own pace and with unequal resource bases. To achieve a balanced development at the community and national levels, some directive planning by central authorities is necessary.

The UN agencies, including UNESCO, United Nations Development Program (UNDP), UNICEF, ILO, and notable international development agencies such as United States Agency for International Development (USAID), United Nations Population Fund (UNFPA), Joint United Nations Program on HIV and AIDS (UNAIDS), Department for International Development (DFID), and Danish International Development Agency (DANIDA) have been funding adult education programs in the communities to improve quality of life. Adult education is a key component of worldwide collaborative efforts to achieve social justice aims such as the UN's Sustainable Development Goals (Zarestky & Ray, 2019). These international agencies work by navigating complex political, financial hurdles and cultural differences they experience in their line of duty, demonstrating that adult education has a lot to offer in making the global economy a better place to live in. It plays an important role in a period of social, economic, and political change (Moreland & Lovett, 2006). Lange (2015) argued that adult educators can help address profound issues of global dynamics by organizing education programs, encourage learners, and promote change based on the social, political, and cultural situation and priorities in the society. Adult educators take responsibility for being open; they ensure the individual's development, and promote social interventions in communities by increasing interaction with the people based on the democratic values by helping them take initiatives to better communities.

International development programs are carried out in communities in the global south in partnership with community groups; however, much success is realized through training of local leadership groups. When leadership groups dialogue, think through ideas, and take initiative in developing their communities, their influences are felt in communities. This requires "all hands on deck" to achieve sustainable development goals in the remaining 10 years. When people educate themselves about their community needs, identify available opportunities, and mobilize resources, they can work together to address them. In Ghana, there are number of agricultural initiatives being implemented by governments, including planting for export and rural development which require the buy-in of the people and international development partners to succeed. The partnership of international development organizations and local organizations engaged in community education is a necessary requirement in improving communities in the global south (the developing countries) in ensuring peace in the global north (the developed countries). When jobs are created in the global south, young adults are less likely to embark upon perilous trips to the global north countries for sometimes nonexistent greener pastures. Zarestky and Ray (2019) argued that the inter-connectedness of all nations is more apparent than ever through the effects of globalization; one nation's progress, or lack thereof, is integral to its relationships with other nations. Partnership in achieving global peace and development should receive attention of adult educators, using community education as a development strategy.

Globalization is the way in which nations work together to address global social justice issues such as the marginalization of women and girls through initiatives like the United Nations' (UN) Agenda for Sustainable Development, and Sustainable Development Goals (UN, 2015); and the ongoing International Conference on Adult Learning and Education (CONFINTEA) series (Zarestky & Ray, 2019). Although globalization presents challenges, it provides opportunities for addressing issues of global and local development. Zarestky and Ray (2019) argued that the current political climate and uneven efforts in the international community around common challenges, including sustainable development and climate change, make it important to consider dialogue around social justice. The social justice orientation of the SGDs, according to the United Nations (2017), centers on combatting inequality within and among countries. This informs countries in the global south to place more emphasis on partnerships and collaborations in developing communities because the world is inter-connected and interdependent, such that the rippling effect of a major challenge in one country is felt in the global community. Campfens (1997) advocated for a more participatory approach to planning in which state agencies increasingly function in partnership with NGOs and CBOs.

In Ghana, NGOs funded by donor agencies, including Adventist Relief Agency, World Vision International, and Care International, have been using community education approaches to empower people in diverse areas. Corporate institutions in the extractive industries (e.g., mining materials such as gold, bauxite, and manganese), energy sector (oil and gas), financial sector (banking institutions), and telecommunication subsector (mobile and Internet-providing services) are using community education to train young adults and build infrastructure for economic growth, particularly in agribusiness. As Adu-Gyamerah (2019) noted, Eni Ghana, an Italian Oil and Gas company, has constructed a multipurpose agribusiness campus facility named "Okuafo Pa Project" at Kyeremasu in the Bono Region in Ghana. The company aims to train 150,000 youth in various models in agribusiness. This partnership between Eni Ghana and the government of Ghana intends to reach about one million people across Africa over four years to trigger economic diversification in the agricultural sector (Adu-Gyamerah, 2019). Technical skills will be transferred through vocational training, labor, new investments, and local entrepreneurship in sub-Saharan Africa will be stimulated (Adu-Gyamerah, 2019). Kosmos Energy Ghana, Goldfields, and Newmont Ghana are building entrepreneurial capabilities of young adults in Ghana. Kosmos Innovation Center Alternative Livelihoods Programs is addressing unemployment in host communities. The difficulty is lack of replication of the initiatives in other deprived communities in Ghana.

Other difficulties faced by the people of Ghana include a poor culture of maintenance of facilities. State-owned enterprises built in the 1960s were allowed to deteriorate and placed on the divestiture lists. The local people, when empowered through community education programs, would take control of their own development. The culture of maintenance can be promoted among the people through the power of community education, using group learning approaches (Imel, 1997). There are civil society organizations (CSOs) working in the areas of health, education, energy, democracy, and economic empowerment through community education programs. Churches, charities, and foundations are contributing to educating citizenry and constructing vocational, technical, and secondary schools to build the human capital base of young adults. Participatory democracy in Ghana is spearheaded by the CSOs in grassroots communities through education. Media outlets support undertaking educational programs, and people have learned to take up leadership roles and work with the assemblies to deliver services. Young adults have acquired trades, skills, and knowledge of varied dimensions to enrich their lives and improve communities.

STRATEGIES IN PROMOTING COMMUNITY EDUCATION

Since the field of adult education is expanding, the role of the adult educator is becoming more complex and demanding (TIME Project Partnership, 2016). Adult educators, as generalists and specialists (Rogers, 1993), promote learning in the communities. As change agents, adult educators can drive improvements in communities. They are referred to as instructors, trainers, extension workers, animators, promoters, consultants, and facilitators and play multiple roles in improving communities (Rogers, 1993). They help in deepening the leadership qualities of the local groups and strengthening partnerships and social networking with organizations operating within communities. Networking and partnership with organizations are keys to success in community education programs. As adult educators reach out to partner organizations, they can dialogue, discuss, and reach agreement on a viable way forward in improving education programs. This supports Freire's (1972) thinking that through dialogue, the difference between the teacher-of-the-students and the students-of-the teacher ceases to exist. Both deliberate on learning endeavors and become jointly responsible for community development. As we work together, no obstacle is insurmountable, and "we are what we are because of our interaction with others" (Jeffs & Smith, 1996, p. 27). As adult educators consult with local leadership groups, peace is built to push forward development in communities.

As change agents work democratically with communities to analyze their environment and improve situations, they reflect on their experiences through gathering of information about the community's environment in which people live and work (Brookfield et al., 2003). Adult educators seek information and data on services, facilities, and learning opportunities, cultural traditions, and living conditions of community members in terms of economic, business, and industry. When adult educators become immersed in the community and come to know its problems, and work with the people to experience what is happening in their lives, progress is achieved (Brookfield et al., 2003). More needs assessments are to be carried out by adult educators to get a better view of the communities they work with. In so doing, they get to know people in the localities and work with them for the betterment of the communities.

Adult educators should find ways to bring people together with common interests by nurturing the development process of community groups.

Mobilizing people into meetings and encouraging them to form groups can facilitate the discussion of problems their communities face. In all this, the adult educator may assist groups in identifying innovative ways to improve prevailing conditions in their neighborhoods, and opportunities for people to learn and research ways to address their needs. As adult educators work with groups, they collectively act in carrying out projects to address identified needs. Tett (2012) opined that community education can play a role in creating a more democratic and equal society. Hence, adult educators should not impose ideas on the community groups, but rather encourage them to explore solutions to address problems.

Knowles et al. (2012) gave the adult educator the role of "encourager" who plans and coordinates the educational process in building relationships, detecting, and diagnosing needs, and involving learners. This is important because the people are insiders, but adult educators are usually outsiders. The people know their communities better than the adult educators do; therefore, the educators can help groups develop organizational and mobilization skills. Together, they can establish objectives for identified projects. The educators can assist in raising funds for projects, keeping finances, negotiating, and building group skills (Nafukho et al., 2011). As training opportunities are created, the groups are strengthened, and community participation increases.

Adult educators can also help build relationships with people in policy making. According to Jeffs and Smith (1996), educators must help in negotiating relationships of power, and rejuvenating communities by providing support to ongoing projects. They should know of stakeholders and people to contact regarding projects, and gain access to physical resources and sources of funds for projects. Adult educators can also help initiate projects where people can do things for themselves, but this requires flexibility informed by cultural settings, ages of participants, and capabilities (Brookfield et al., 2003). Educators must accept the challenge of building communities and listening to their feedback (Kokkos, 2005) to improve environments where adults learn and live.

PRACTICAL IMPLICATIONS FOR TEACHING AND LEARNING

The Economist (2017) asserted, "if the 21st century economies are not to create a massive underclass, policy-makers urgently need to work out how to help all citizens learn while they earn" (p. 9). King (2017) argued that adult learning has become essential in the digital age, yet it seems one of the best kept secrets. Technological innovations require people to learn across the lifespan and independently use critical thinking and problem-solving skills. This means that education must be placed at the center of policy strategies to drive development, because the current focus on producing skilled workers rather than well-educated adults can lead to policy that undervalues adult education, missing the benefits that it can bring to individuals, communities, and society (Mallows, 2018). Bowl (2014) admitted that adult and community-based educators have been rendered almost invisible by policy pronouncements. Meanwhile, developing countries are confronted with high unemployment rates, suggesting they should take adult education more seriously. This requires that adult education policies, promulgated in developing countries, empower people, and make them relevant in the economies. Through lifelong learning, people can appreciate challenges facing their communities and strategize to address them.

It is hoped that when appropriate policies are developed for adult education in Ghana, it will attract funding from governments and international development organizations to implement programs, leading to community development. Adult education can no longer remain the marginalized and a "poor cousin" of general education (Findsen, 2014); it must be centered within the mainstream of education. The holistic approach of adult education is central to development and improvement of communities and must be upheld in teaching, learning, and development programs. Adult educators can focus attention on engaging communities in lifelong, life wide, and life-deep learning (Belanger, 2016) to improve their life conditions. Learning should not be limited to the individuals' development, but include that of groups and communities.

Adult educators' use of dialogue, discussions, conversations, and storytelling are keys to active civic participation in community education programs. Increased partnership, networking, and involvement in decision-making are important in community education. Adult educators can form citizen advisory groups to identify sources of educational needs. As Imel (1997) asserted, adult education has a long tradition of working in groups, meaning learning should be conceived of as an interactive process, thus transforming experiences to improve communities. When there is cross-fertilization of ideas between people as they brainstorm and share views on educational needs in their communities, they become informed in implementing programs. As adult educators adapt a facilitative approach to learning, this may help put communities on the path of improvement.

CONCLUSION

This chapter examined community educational needs in communities in Ghana. It analyzed the terms community education and community educational needs and resources. It also examined community education practices in Ghana. It highlighted the importance of investing in community education, international development, community development, and adult education in building strong communities. It discussed strategies adult educators adapted in creating awareness in the people to become empowered in developing leadership qualities in improving communities. The chapter, finally, examined teaching and learning practice in adult education. The extensive roles of adult educators in deepening community education with the people to develop themselves, groups, and communities received attention. This chapter noted that adult educators work with people to identify educational needs in communities. However, the effort of adult educators in improving communities has to be supported by governments in developing countries. It means policy decision-making has to be made for adult education, with community education as component part, to be anchored in development frameworks of Ghana. Gajanayake and Gajanayake (1993) argued that the central focus of adult educators is to get full participation of target groups and empower them to become partners in the decision-making process. Communities can realize improvements when the people are empowered to pursue sustainable development. An integrated approach to community development should receive the attention of adult educators. Organizations that are a part of and external to communities can partner to ensure holistic development. Finally, building local leadership qualities among working groups in communities should also be supported by governments. By this process, the people may learn to become architects of development in their own communities.

REFERENCES

Adu-Gyamerah, E. (2019, December 3). Agribusiness campus for Kyeremasu: Aims at training 150,000 youth in various models. *Daily Graphic*, p. 23.

Alldred, N. (1976). Some contradictions in community development: The need for stronger community approach. *Community Development Journal, 11*(2), 134–140.

Baah-Boateng, W. (2018, February 27). Jobless growth is Ghana's biggest youth challenge. *African Center for Economic Transformation*. https://acetforafrica.org/highlights/jobless-growth-is-ghanas-biggest-youth-challenge/

Baidoo, F. A. (2019, October 19). Resource community development adequately. *Daily Graphic*, p. 26.

Biddle, W. (1966). The fuzziness of definition of community development. *Community Development Journal, 2*, 5–12.

Bidwell, L., & McConnell, C. (1990). *Community education and community development.* Dundee College of Education.

Belanger, P. (2016). *Self-construction and social transformation: Lifelong, lifewide and life-deep learning.* UNESCO Institute of Lifelong Learning.

Biney, I. K. (2009). *Factors influencing participation in alternative livelihood programmes in the mining communities of the Western Region in Ghana.* University of Ghana.

Biney, I. K. (2019). Exploring the power of the media in promoting lifelong learning and popular mobilisation drive against 'Galamsey' in Ghana. *Australian Journal of Adult Learning, 59*(3), 435–467.

Bowl, M. (2014). *Adult education in changing time: Policies, philosophies and professionalism.* The National Institute of Adult Continuing Education (NIACE).

Brookfield, M., Jeff, T., Larkins, R., Pye, C., & Smith, M. K. (2003). *Community learning* (2nd ed.). YMCA George Williams College.

Brookfield, S. (1995). *Adult learners, adult education and the community.* Open University Press.

Campfens, H. (Ed.). (1997). *Community development around the world: Practice, theory, research, training.* University of Toronto.

Chekki, D. (1979). *Community development: Theory and method of planned change.* Vikas.

Cole, C. R. A. (1979). The adult learner. In L. Bown & S. H. Olu-Tomori (Eds.). *A handbook of adult education for West Africa* (pp. 29–42). Hutchison University Library for Africa.

Connolly, B. (2011). Community based adult education. In K. Rubenson (Ed.). *Adult Learning and Education* (pp. 133–139). Elsevier.

Crowther, J. (2015). Preface. In E. Lucio-Villegas (Ed.), *Adult education in communities: Approaches from a participatory perspective* (pp. vii–ix). Sense.

Engelbrecht, L.K. (2005). Perspectives on the community education model of social work: Implications for education and practice. *Social Work/Maatskaplike Werk, 41*(2), 143–154.

English, L. M., & Mayo, P. (2012). *Learning with adults: A critical pedagogical introduction.* Sense.

Findsen, B. C. (2014). Adult education from "the bottom up:" An analysis of an educational journey from an adult educator in Aotearoa, New Zealand. *PAACE Journal of Lifelong Learning, 23,* 1–17.

Frank, F., & Smith, A. (1999). *Introduction to community development.* Human Resource Development Canada.

Freire, P. (1972). *Pedagogy of the oppressed.* Penguin.

Gajanayake, S., & Gajanayake, J. (1993). *Community empowerment: A participatory training manual on community project development.* Northern Illinois University.

Galbraith, J. K. 1962, September). The poverty of nations. *Atlantic Monthly.*

Government of Ghana. (2019, October 26). Government has employed 2,700 extension officers since 2017. *GhanaWeb.* https://www.ghanaweb.com/GhanaHomePage/NewsArchive/Government-has-employed-2-700-Agric-Extension-Officers-since-2017-Kennedy-Osei-Nyarko-793513

Imel, S. (1997). Adult learning in groups. *Review of Educational Research, 52*(3), 421–445.

Indabawa, S., & Mpofu, S. (2006). *The social context of adult learning in Africa.* Pearson Education, South Africa.

Iniquez-Berrozpe, T., Elboj-Saso, C., Flecha, A., & Marcaletti, F. (2019). Benefits of adult education participation for low-educated women. *Adult Education Quarterly,* 1–25. https://doi.org/10.1177/0741713619870793

Jeffs, T., & Smith, M. K. (1996). *Informal education- conversation, democracy and learning.* Education Now.

King, K. P. (2017). *Technology and innovation in adult learning.* Jossey-Bass.

Knowles, M. S., Holton, E. F., & Swanson, R. A. (2012). *The adult learner: The definitive classic in adult education and human resource development.* Routledge.

Kokkos, A. (2005). *Adult education: Detecting the field.* Metaichmio.

Kumar, A. (1979). Education for rural development. In L. Bown & S. H. Olu Tomori (Eds.). *A handbook of adult education for West Africa* (pp. 203–220). Hutchinson University Library for Africa.

Lange, E. (2015). (Re)igniting a sociological imagination in adult education: The continuing relevance of classical theory. *International Journal of Lifelong Education, 34*(5), 1–23. http://dx.doi.org/10.1080/02601370.2015.1028574.

Moreland, R., & Lovett, T. (2006). Lifelong learning and community development. *International Journal of Lifelong Education, 16*(3), 201–216.

Mallows, D. (2018). Guest forward: Adult learning, upskilling pathways, and the adult learner. *Irish Journal of Adult and Community Education: The Adult Learner, 2018,* 10–15.

McConnell, C. (Ed.). (2002). *Community learning and development. The making of an empowering profession* (3rd ed.). Community Learning Scotland.

Mera, C. Z. (2004). Reflections on challenges facing adult education movement. *Journal of Adult Education and Development, 63,* 103–110.

Murphy, K. (Ed.). (2014). *Development education in adult and community settings: Guidelines for good practice.* IDEA Community Sector Working Group.

Nafukho, F. M., Wawire, N. H. W., & Lam, P. M. (2011). *Management of adult education organizations in Africa.* Pearson Education South Africa.

Oduro-Mensah, D. (2009). Adult education for community development: Case of the Forikrom community adult education and development program. *Journal of Literacy and Adult Education, 4*(1), 14–45.

Prins, E., & Drayton, B. (2010). Adult education for the employment of individuals and communities. In C. E. Kasworm, A. D. Rose, & J. M. Ross-Gordon (Eds.), *Handbook of Adult and Continuing Education* (pp. 209–219). SAGE.

Regmi, K. D. (2015). Adult education and sustainable development goals. *Proceedings of the 2015 Annual Conference of CASAE.* University of Montreal.

Reynolds, H. L. (2010). Core learning goals for campus-wide environmental literacy: Overview. In H. L. Reynolds, J. M. Eduardo, S. Brondizio, J. M. Robinson, D. Karpa, & B. L. Gross (Eds.), *Teaching environmental literacy across campus and across the curriculum.* (pp. 17–27). Indiana University Press.

Robinson, J. W., & Green, G. P. (2011). Developing communities. In J. W. Robinson & G. J. Green (Eds.), *Introduction to Community Development* (pp. 1–34). SAGE.

Rogers, A. (1993). *Adult learning for development.* Cassell.

Ross, C. (Ed.). (2017). *Influencing change: Community learning and development in Scotland, 2001-2015: The making of an empowering profession (Vol. 2).* International Association for Community Development.

Tett, L. (2012). *Community education, learning and development* (3rd ed.). Academic Press.

The Economist. (2017). *Lifelong learning: How to survive in the age of automation* (A Special Report), January 14–20, 2017.

TIME Project Partnership. (2016). *Adult training methodology and techniques.* European Commission, Erasmus+.

United Nations. (1986). *Non-formal education for integrated rural development.* United Nations Document Office.

United Nations. (2015). *Transforming our world: The 2030 Agenda for Sustainable Development. A/RES/701.* Retrieved June 14, 2020, from https://w.w.w.un.org/ga/search/view_doc.asp?symbol+NRES/70/1&Lang+E

United Nations. (2017). *The sustainable development agenda.* http://www.un.org/sustainabledevelopment/development-agenda

World Commission on Environment and Development. (1987). *Our common future.* Oxford University Press.

Woelke, L. (2017). *The role of adult education.* University of the Fraser Valley.

Zarestky, J., & Ray, S. M. (2019). Adult education programmes of NGOs operating in non-Western contexts: A review of literature. *International Journal of Lifelong Education,* 1–16. https://doi.org/10.1080/02601370.2019.1693437

CHAPTER 13

LEVERAGING CONTINUING MEDICAL EDUCATION IN ADDRESSING HEALTH DISPARITIES

Case Studies from the Republic of Ghana

Linda D. Caples and Christopher M. Dodgion
The Medical College of Wisconsin, United States

We would like to dedicate this chapter to Professor Jacob Plange-Rhule, Rector of the Ghana College of Physicians and Surgeons who lost his life to COVID-19. Prof. Plange-Rhule dedicated his life to medicine and medical education.

When attempting to address health disparities, one of the challenges clinical educators face globally is the disconnect between the use of evidence-based clinical practice guidelines and medical practice. For years, the prevailing belief was that if healthcare workers (HCWs) knew more, their practice of medicine would improve. The result is volumes of redundant continuing medical education (CME) content aimed at changing behavior by providing information "on safety, efficacy and cost-effectiveness of intended behaviours" (Rashidian et al., 2008, p. 150).

Advancing the Global Agenda for Human Rights, Vulnerable Populations, and Environmental Sustainability: Adult Education as Strategic Partner, pp. 207–222
Copyright © 2021 by Information Age Publishing
All rights of reproduction in any form reserved.

Sub-Saharan African countries provide CME similar to the global practice of CME. However, the body of research of CME in Sub-Saharan Africa is primarily limited to the degree to which HCWs acquired new knowledge and HCWs education delivery preferences such as online learning or instructor-led (Desalu et al., 2011; Entsua-Mensah et al., 2012). As CME is a major component of HCW's education, educators should consider factors such as culture, context, and the interplay of Indigenous medicine with western medicine when developing and providing clinical education in the developing world.

This chapter describes theoretical, cultural, and contextual considerations in the development and delivery of continuing medical education interventions in the Republic of Ghana. By investigating culture and context in a medical pluralistic environment such as rural Ghana, adult educators may develop CME interventions that are perceived as meaningful and clinically applicable by HCWs. To begin, it is helpful to first understand medical pluralism and its influence on how HCWs utilize what they learn from CME.

Medical Pluralism

Gabe et al. (2004) defined medical pluralism as "the coexistence in a society of differing medical traditions, grounded in different principles or based on different-world views" (p. 183). In the context of Ghana, medical pluralism manifests as the coexistence and utilization of both Indigenous (traditional) medicine and western (biomedical) medicine by HCWs and patients alike. Adult educators and medical educators should (a) consider the attributes and influences of Indigenous medicine and (b) integrate western medicine in culturally and contextually relevant ways. This is a critical step, as Indigenous medicine practitioners constitute a large portion of the health care community throughout the African continent for several reasons.

First, these practitioners have been the primary medical providers for centuries all over the globe well before the invention of western medicine. Second, Indigenous medicine continues to be practiced globally and typically referred to as alternative or complementary medicine. Third, the significant shortage of western trained HCWs leaves many living in Africa with no other option but to seek medical care from Indigenous medicine practitioners (Saluja et al., 2020). Fourth, limited financial resources for many in the Sub-Saharan African population make purchasing pharmaceutical medicines difficult. Some patients may need multiple medications to get a medical condition "controlled." In a 2012 study of the cost of blood pressure control in Nigeria, researchers reported "52.8% [of patients] spending ≥ 10% of their income on treatment" (Ilesanmi et al., 2012, p. 1). Many Africans in rural areas may need to travel great distances (sometimes on foot) to access western medical care.

These factors support findings from a Tanzanian study that found the lives of people in Sub-Saharan African countries "were characterised by poverty, insecurity, uncertainty, and hence unpredictability. According to our observations, this suggests that the possibilities for health-seeking behaviour were often assessed on a day-to-day basis" (Kolling et al., 2010, p. 5). Therefore, when addressing the Sustainable Development Goal 3— good health and wellbeing, using CME—adult and medical educators may wish to consider a theory-based approach that supports cultural and contextual realities that medical pluralism presents.

To illustrate a theory-based approach to the development and delivery of CME in Sub-Saharan Africa, this chapter presents two case studies from the Republic of Ghana. The first case describes a CME in hypertension where the theory of planned behavior is incorporated. The second case is a CME in primary trauma training that utilized social constructivism and shared mental models.

Case Study: Hypertension CME

This case looks at the implications of Ghanaian primary care physicians' beliefs on the management of hypertension, particularly how those beliefs influence clinical knowledge translation (CKT). CME is a major conduit for CKT as the primary purpose of CME is to educate HCWs to improve patient care. Graham et al. (2006) referred to the Canadian Institutes of Health Research definition of clinical knowledge translation as

> The exchange, synthesis and ethically-sound application of knowledge— within a complex system of interactions among researchers and users—to accelerate the capture of the benefits of research for Canadians through improved health, more effective services and products, and a strengthened health care system. (p. 15)

What clinical knowledge translation does not take into consideration is the influence of beliefs.

One strategy to increase the effectiveness of CME in Sub-Saharan Africa is the consideration and incorporation of beliefs into the CKT process. As primary care physicians are on the front line of hypertension management, Caples's (2019) qualitative study utilized the theory of planned behavior and gathered data from 10 Ghanaian primary care physicians who had participated in a hypertension CME within the 12 months prior to being interviewed and who practice medicine in Ghana. Findings derived from the thematic analysis of participant interviews revealed six overarching themes. The resulting implications for CME are discussed here as well.

Beliefs are complex constructs for which the theory of planned behavior (TPB) subsumes into three major categories: behavioral beliefs, normative beliefs, and control beliefs (Ajzen, 2019). Each category of beliefs is dynamically influenced by one another and by background factors to varying degrees and magnitudes. Ajzen (2019) described behavioral beliefs as beliefs about the real or potential consequences of a belief. Normative beliefs are described by Ajzen as group or shared beliefs of others, and perceived control beliefs are the factors that support or inhibit performing a behavior. Background factors include such constructs as formal and informal knowledge systems, spiritual systems, biosocial status, socioeconomic status, Indigenous heritage and culture, and political ideology (Ajzen, 2019). Background factors such as Indigenous knowledge, medical education, years of clinical practice as well as other background factors can be intentionally addressed using TPB allowing for a culturally and contextually relevant approach to the creation of a CME activity designed to address hypertension in Ghana.

In this case study, some participant background factors included primary care physicians from both urban and rural areas of Ghana and represented both public and private sector healthcare. Three of the 10 physicians were women, and a background factor of note was that eight of the participants attended medical school in Ghana. Ghana is a lower-middle income country, according to the 2020 World Bank data, and has both public and private medical schools and teaching hospitals, which enables the country to produce many of its own physicians. While the background factors of the physician learners is important, it is also important to consider the background factors of their patients.

Hypertension is a lifestyle disease and therefore heavily influenced by culture including diet, exercise, smoking, and other lifestyle choices. In Caples's (2019) study, participants noted that many in Ghana associate wealth with being overweight or obese. Smoking tobacco products significantly declined among patients, but some of the elderly patients had smoked in their youth. Ghanaians tend to live a sedentary lifestyle, and a lack of exercise is a contributing factor to hypertension. Caples reported that "people will laugh at you if you are walking to work or to the market instead of sitting in a taxi or a motorbike. They will laugh at you for using a basket and walking" (p. 79).

Caples (2019) found three cultural factors that had an impact on health outcomes including hypertension were skin bleaching, herbal medications, and family relationships. Skin bleaching is pervasive in Ghana and many countries in West Africa (Fokuo, 2009). These products have a number of ingredients that are harmful and excessive use of skin bleaching products introduces high volumes of steroids into a patient's system and is a known contributing factor to hypertension (Peppa et al., 2011).

Next, given the medically pluralistic nature of healthcare in Ghana, most Ghanaians use some form of herbal medicine, as do many Americans. However, the notable difference is American herbal medicines (dietary supplements) are required to list their ingredients. In Ghana, the ingredients of herbal medicines, the quantities of each ingredient, and the potential herb-drug interactions remains largely not known. Therefore, patients could be taking an herbal supplement that counteracts the hypertension medicine prescribed by their physician. Patients may take herbal medicine because they are less expensive than prescription medicine and many herbalists guarantee their medicines cure diseases for which Western medicine currently has no cure, such as hypertension.

Lastly, the study found that family and spiritual relationships of patients play a role in health. Wives who are good cooks are greatly prized. The head of the household is given more food than others, and pregnant women eat for two as in-laws expect her to remain sedentary for nine months while they cook and feed the pregnant women extra amounts of food. When patients are very ill, seeking medical assistance from Christian prayer camps, Islamic priests, Fetish priests, or all three can occur regardless of the patient's religious practice.

Based on these background factors, Caples (2019) identified six themes that illustrate the importance of culture and context in shaping the beliefs of how primary care physicians saw their patients and how they translated clinical knowledge into medical practice. Thematic analysis was used with line-by-line coding of physician participant interview transcripts. The first round of coding utilized the theory of planned behavior's behavioral, normative and control beliefs. Physicians believed:

1. My patients are highly complex (behavioral and control beliefs).
2. The cost of care impedes my practice (control belief).
3. Other healthcare professionals benefit from local guidelines more than physicians (normative belief).
4. Ghanaian clinical trials are critically needed for local guideline development and clinical practice (behavioral, normative, and control beliefs).
5. CME should be relevant to local practice and interprofessional in nature (normative and control belief).
6. Patient education about the facts of hypertension and aspects of lifestyle modifications is greatly needed in Ghana (normative and control beliefs).

Findings suggest it was not sufficient to reiterate clinical practice guidelines from various parts of the world; it was essential to specifically address the realities "on the ground." Findings also highlight the patient-centered, evidenced-based, and interprofessional approach primary care physicians in Ghana use in their medical practice. Upon reflecting on their most recent hypertension CME course, each participant shared an appreciation for learning the latest advancements in hypertension management; however, the content that seemed to resonate with participant physicians was content that focused on improving patient interactions.

Implications for CME

The CME content that spoke to practicing with a high degree of suspicion for hypertension and its complications was mentioned along with taking a more involved medical history. The CME content that also covered the secondary courses of hypertension, again requiring a more involved medical history, was highlighted, along with the importance of CME content that addressed the need to take time to counsel/educate patients on specific aspects of hypertension. These aspects of clinical knowledge were the things participants were interested in implementing into their practice. Seven participants acknowledged that given the high volume of patients, taking the time to talk with patients would be challenging. Furthermore, considering the cultural realities surrounding patient perspectives about hypertension, the Ghanaian diet, and Ghanaian concepts of wealth and beauty, CME content that addresses how to deal with these issues (patient history and counseling) were useful to primary care physicians.

The findings in this research suggests a disconnect between how physicians manage hypertension and how other healthcare professionals do. Primary care physicians are part of a care team, and participants shared the importance of interprofessional continuing education. Many patients' hypertension was managed by physician assistants or community health workers (nurses). At least four participants mentioned the need for their colleagues to engage in CME so that all persons on the care team would be equally informed as to best practices in hypertension management.

CME should not solely be in the form of lectures. There is an opportunity for interprofessional continuing medical education in Ghana and throughout Sub-Saharan Africa in the form of hypertension case review conferences that could include the physicians, physician assistants, nurses, dietitians, and clinical pharmacologists. In regular intervals (e.g., monthly), the care team could meet to review and discuss cases of complicated hypertension, hypertension with co-morbidities, and stroke patients. The academic institutions in Ghana do have clinical meetings that include the case review conference format; however, this format of CME should be extended to other healthcare facilities and be disease focused.

Case Study: Primary Trauma Training

This case looks at the utilization of shared mental models and social constructivism in the design and evaluation of a CME course in primary trauma held in Ghana. One of the assumptions of social constructivism is that the concept of truth or reality "is a matter of consensus among informed and sophisticated constructors, not of correspondence with objective reality" (Patton, 2015, p. 123). For example, in this case, factors such as the level of self-efficacy among the care team, the role each person plays, and how they perceive their practice environment may work together and shape their collective reality of the healthcare environment. A second assumption of social constructivism claims that what constitutes facts or knowledge "have no meaning except within some value framework, hence there cannot be an 'objective' assessment of any proposition" (Patton, 2015, p. 123). In this case study, what knowledge the care team believed to be accurate about trauma recommendations and injured patients within the context of their medical practice is considered. Third, social constructivism assumes that "phenomena can only be understood within the context in which they are studied" (Patton, 2015, pp. 123–124). The context of clinical practice varies significantly within countries and across the world. Resources HCWs have access to, in terms of clinical knowledge, technical support, clinical support, medications, and equipment vary widely.

Further, social constructivism assumes that "data derived from constructivist inquiry have neither special status nor legitimation; they represent simply another construction to be taken into account in the move toward consensus" (Patton, 2015, p. 124). Consensus of meaning is a moving target and warrants study. Patton (2015) examined the work of Thomas Kuhn as Kuhn described communities coming to consensus. According to Patton, Kuhn argues that people are organized by certain traditions, practices, or beliefs. Occasionally, the constructs of organizations are challenged (for example, new drugs, new technology, and new techniques) and old ways of thinking no longer work. New meanings are constructed, and a new consensus is created (Patton, 2015).

Constructivist learning environments emphasize authentic tasks in a meaningful context rather than abstract instruction out of context, and these environments encourage reflection on experience. It can be said that shared mental models are socially constructed where learning is more than the assimilation of new knowledge by learners; it is the process by which learners are integrated into a knowledge community. Social constructivism in this case study was paired with the methodology of shared mental models. Baker et al. (2006) reported the definition of shared mental models as "an organizing knowledge structure of the relationships between the task the team is engaged in and how the team members will interact" (p. 1582).

According to Westli et al. (2010), shared mental models developed from military tactical operations where effective teamwork is critical for success and depends on individual team members' mutual understanding of the tasks, their role, and the nature of the team. This holds true for trauma teams in healthcare settings as well. Members of the project team for this case study included an academic emergency medicine physician and trauma surgeon that utilized shared mental models in their practice of trauma management as it supports the team construct meaning in order for teams to become of "one mind." In their experience, this enables members of the trauma team to anticipate needs of other team members and tasks without the need for specific instructions. In addition to the emergency medicine physician and trauma surgeon was a medical education researcher who used social constructivism and shared mental models to approach teaching primary trauma management to address the clinical needs of injured patients in Ghana.

The project team based the content of their training on the American College of Surgeons Trauma Evaluation and Management (TEAM) training. This was for a few reasons. First, the Advanced Trauma Life Support (ATLS) course is the curriculum used to train trauma teams in high-resourced countries. It is cost prohibitive for the low-to-middle income countries for this proprietary course and many countries, such as Ghana, may not have sufficient technological resources to execute the trauma care according to what is taught in ATLS. Second, in 2016, Stewart et al. (2016) published a serial assessment regarding the capacity of trauma care in Ghana. Findings from Steward's 2016 study indicated significant improvement in trauma care capacity, yet there remain notable deficiencies that must be addressed to save lives.

The viability and appropriateness of the TEAMS course was discussed with the local staff of Africa Partners Medical-Ghana (AMPG), a nonprofit organization that locally coordinated a variety of CME offerings in 2017 including a primary trauma training course Wenchi, Ghana. APMG proved a critical partner as the organization has extensive experience conducting CME throughout Ghana. The U.S. team in collaboration with APMG conducted an educational needs assessment including the culture and context of the community. Wenchi, Ghana was the first location; it has a population of approximately 40,000 and is in the Brong Ahafo Region. It is a rural small-scale farm community with yams as their primary crop. Christians, traditional faith practitioners, and Muslims live peacefully together and receive care at the Methodist hospital.

Daily outpatient services include prenatal care and critical care for diabetes, hypertension, and HIV/AIDS. Less than two percent of all Ghanaians are living with HIV/AIDS. The catchment area for the hospital is approximately 100 miles, and patients typically seek care for maternity care, lifestyle diseases such as hypertension and diabetes, and infectious diseases, namely malaria (Institute for International Medicine, n.d.). The second location of the training was in Ankaase, Ghana at another Methodist hospital with similar demographics. However, it should be noted that at the time of this project, Wenchi had nine physicians on staff and Ankaase only had one.

Having a limited number of physicians requires the entire care team regardless of their role, to be knowledgeable in how to care for an injured patient and work together effectively. WHO's (2016) Sustainable Development Goal 3.6 focuses on reducing the number of global deaths and injuries due to road traffic accidents by 50%. Data from the Agenda for International Development (Harshe & Afful-Mensah, 2019) report that within a year of the SDGs, the National Road Safety Commission of Ghana (2018) reported a 15.65% increase in deaths from road crashes. In 2015, 1,802 people died, which increased to 2,084 people in 2016. Road deaths may have steadied in 2017; however, they rose again in 2018 by 12.76%. In order for Ghana to achieve the SDG 3.6 to reduce the number of global deaths and injuries from road accidents, Ghana would need to see a 53.01% decrease in road deaths by the end of 2020 (Harshe & Afful-Mensah, 2019).

The government of Ghana is the primary source of financing as part of the national health insurance scheme. The Methodist church supports their hospital system including Wenchi and Ankaase to a modest extent. The hospitals depend on nongovernmental organizations (NGOs) and nonprofits such as Africa Partners Medical-Ghana for additional financial support and training. Patients pay out of pocket and in some cases in advance for services such as X-rays, laboratory tests, and medications. Most of the residents are living below the poverty line. Those who are inpatient at the hospital rely on family members to bring food, as the hospital cannot afford to provide daily meals to all patients.

The two nearest urban centers are Kumasi to the southeast and Tamale to the northeast. Kumasi has a large hospital and teaching center. Komfo Anokye Teaching Hospital (KATH) in Kumasi developed the first formal accredited Emergency Medicine program in 2010, yet there persisted greater demand for these professionals than the program produced. This program was developed in collaboration with the University of Michigan–Ann Arbor who continues to have a highly engaged presence at KATH. In 2017, Wenchi was without an Emergency Medicine physician, and Ankaase had one who was trained at KATH. All patient referrals that Wenchi or Ankaase cannot manage may be sent to KATH. Additionally, the National

Ambulance Service of Ghana was created in 2004 and expanded in 2008 (Ministry of Health, 2008). Wenchi and Ankaase had one ambulance each in 2017 to transport patients and was staffed with one driver and one medical personnel. The hospitals have an Accident and Emergency Unit with an open ward layout. They receive traumas and poly-traumas mainly from motor vehicle accidents. There are not many sidewalks and pedestrian traffic along the roads is heavy causing numerous accidents.

The Clinical Problem

In the case narrative presented above, multiple issues in the management of trauma were identified. For example, neither hospital had a CT scanner, and there was a lack of ventilators. During exploratory discussions led by the project team emergency medicine physician with hospital frontline staff, the project team learned that it could take a physician up to 30 minutes to arrive at the Emergency Unit to treat a trauma patient. While on-site housing is provided for physicians and nursing staff, the shortage of physicians means that a doctor may be in surgery or delivering a baby and unable to immediately assist with an injured patient. In the case of a trauma or poly-trauma, available nurses are called from the wards to assist. The project team agreed that given the realities of limited staff, lack of key equipment, and the distance between hospitals, the purpose of this project would be to create training focused on providing effective clinical care during the first 30 minutes of a trauma or until a physician arrives. The rationale of the project was to take an asset approach and recognize that HCWs who work effectively together as a team are more likely to have better health outcomes for the injured patient. Therefore, our strategy was to tailor the TEAMS course content to fit the local context while incorporating social constructivism and shared mental models into the instructional design and evaluation components of the learning in order to foster more effective teamwork. Data were collected through subject matter expert observations during the training from our emergency medicine physician and trauma surgeon as well as an analysis of pre/posttest data and evaluation data by our medical education researcher.

The Learners

Primary trauma training learners included physicians, dentists, nurse practitioners, anesthetists, community health workers, midwives, nurses, and physician assistants. While the training was designed to address care before the physician arrives, the physicians needed to know what the care team had been trained on, as they would serve as trainers for refresher courses and to train new staff. In many cases, the nursing staff are the first responders. This includes nurses assigned to the emergency unit as well as other nursing staff as they could be called upon to assist. The nursing programs are robust in Ghana and there is a school of nursing at a local institution in Wenchi. Thus, the Wenchi Hospital has a number of nursing students who would be called to assist in a trauma as well. The nursing staff included both men and women. Those who were more experienced showed more confidence and were more engaged in our discussions, while the student nurses were more reserved. Nursing is a highly respected profession in Ghana, and nurses are highly educated and well trained. Yet there is still a hierarchical structure to medical care in Ghana, with clear limits to nursing care and what was considered appropriate tasks based on the level of professional training. A nurse could potentially be trained to perform a lifesaving procedure like a chest tube placement. If she or he were to perform it for a patient and if it went well all would be fine; however, if it went poorly, either due to the patient's concomitant injuries or the procedure, the nurse would be heavily criticized. This cultural difference serves as a further barrier to care for the trauma.

Educational Intervention

In partnership with APMG, six physicians and one physician assistant were identified as participants in a train-the-trainer program. The physicians were generalists and emergency medicine physicians. The day-long program was based on the American College of Surgeons Trauma Evaluation, Assessment, and Management (TEAM) training, which was created to be an introductory trauma education course for U.S. medical students; it has been adapted previously into target low resource environments (Berndtson et al., 2019). Keeping in mind the social constructivist approach, the adaptations of the course slides and materials, including the addition of a hands-on case scenario simulation, was developed with feedback from the Ghana physicians and the APMG clinical education leadership. Consensus was critical, not only to the social constructivist model, but also to ensuring buy-in and to allow the course to become more contextually appropriate and reinforce trauma management skills using the local resources available. Additionally, the cost of the TEAMS course is more economically viable for lower resourced areas compared to other primary trauma courses.

Local trainers shadowed the project team through both the didactic session and hand-on skills sessions. Debriefings were held with the trainers throughout the day discussing specific pedagogical strategies to increase the retention and impact of course for the learners. The following day, the local trainers facilitated the TEAMS training with the project team observing and providing real-time feedback. A second round of training occurred at another rural hospital and educational outcomes data were collected for all sessions. After the initial training-the-trainer course, additional CME accredited sessions were conducted by APMG with the trainers using the TEAMS course materials and evaluation tools provided by the project team.

Educational Outcomes

There is no electronic health record system in the hospitals as most of the health records are paper based. This makes evaluating the patient outcomes associated with the project difficult, as it would be cumbersome to pull data from paper files to verify clinical outcomes related to the TEAMS training. The project team did not want to create yet another record keeping burden; therefore, the focus of the content and design of the evaluation tools was to capture data on aspects of shared mental models, self-efficacy, as well as knowledge acquisition. A 20-item pre- and posttest assessment was created using ACS TEAM curriculum and distributed to three cohorts of HCWs, mostly non-physicians. Of the HCWs, 65% were physician assistants and 34% were nurses. Among the participants, 44% reported being in their 30s, with 52% stating they have 1–5 years of clinical experience. Furthermore, 36% of HCWs trained work primarily in the in-patient setting, with another 28% of HCWs trained working primarily in the emergency unit. On average, the cohorts improved their test scores by 3.175 points. The project team critiqued each test item relative to content taught and clinical context to determine if certain test items should be replaced. At least one question was replaced, and in follow-up discussions with the local trainers, the project team shared the need to go more in-depth on certain topics.

The evaluation instrument included inquiries into self-efficacy at executing the TEAM learning objectives. Shared mental model data was gathered during the hands-on skills lab evaluation process as participants in the skills lab had more direct responsibility for primary trauma management. Using the revised version of the Anesthetists' Non-Technical Skills Behavioral marker system as described in Westli et al. (2010), this system was created from "incident analyses, team observation, and attitude surveys of effective teamwork skills, first for anesthetist, and later for other clinicians" (p. 2).

Implications for CME

Key lessons learned and essential principles for creating a locally resourced, contextually appropriate trauma education course in a resource-limited environment are as follows:

1. Know your resources (hospital and personnel) and those of hospitals around you.
   a. Do you have specialists?
   b. What is the transport time to the nearest facility with more resources?
   c. What are you capable of caring for?
   d. What are the skill sets of your providers?
   e. Early transport is key if you don't have the resources to care for someone.
2. Collaborate with local medical leaders to make the course contextually relevant.
   a. What cases do they see?
   b. What resources are readily available to care for common problems seen in trauma patients—chest tube, oxygen, intubation, etc.?
3. Emphasize the importance of early access to care.
   a. Which should be included in an appropriate prehospital care/transport and community education campaign?
4. Reinforce the assessment and treatment of life-threatening injuries first.
   a. (Airway, Breathing, Circulation, Disability)
5. Create a hands-on, skill-based curriculum that reinforces the key learning principles that is easily reproducible and allows for modification and repetition.
6. Identify local champions to lead long after the course is completed.
   a. Allows for one/several people to be the local experts, which will improve the longevity of the course, and allows for directed follow up for outcomes assessment and impact.

Future investigations need to be conducted to determine the durability, sustainability, and impact of this novel education program. Such investigations could answer questions such as: Has the course continued to be taught? How often does it need to be retaught? Do people remember the material? Has the culture of trauma management changed? Has mortality improved?

CONCLUSION

In both the noncommunicable disease (hypertension) case and the injury (primary trauma) case, the learners were HCWs who live and work throughout Ghana. They serve as the gatekeepers as to what knowledge is or is not translated into clinical practice. In addition to the knowledge they acquire through CME, it is their beliefs, their ability to work effectively as a team, and the daily realities of the patients that shape how they practice and what new knowledge or skills they will seek. Incorporating culture and context into the development of CME content was important for effective clinical knowledge translation and improved health outcomes. The process of knowledge translation helps HCWs construct knowledge along with interactions with other healthcare professionals, their patients, and the communities they serve. This is particularly important in medically pluralistic societies such as Ghana, where clinically trained healthcare professionals are few and traditional medical practitioners are prevalent.

REFERENCES

Ajzen, I. (2019). *Icek Ajzen: Theory of planned behaviors with background factors*. https://people.umass.edu/aizen/tpb.background.html

Baker, D. P., Day, R., & Salas, E. (2006). Teamwork as an essential component of high-reliability organizations. *Health Services Research*, *41*(4p2), 1576–1598. https://doi.org/10.1111/j.1475-6773.2006.00566.x

Berndtson, A. E., Morna, M., Debrah, S., & Coimbra, R. (2019). The TEAM (Trauma Evaluation and Management) course: Medical student knowledge gains and retention in the USA versus Ghana. *Trauma Surgery & Acute Care*. https://doi.org/10.1136/tsaco-2018-000287

Caples, L. D. (2019). An investigation into Ghanaian primary care physicians' beliefs and their influence on clinical knowledge translation. (13863459) [Doctoral Dissertation University of Wisconsin-Milwaukee]. Open Access Publishing PLUS

Desalu, O. O., Onyedum, C. C., Iseh, K. R., Salawu F. K., & Salami, A. K. (2011). Asthma in Nigeria: Are the facilities and resources available to support internationally endorsed standards of care? *Health Policy*, *99*(3), 250–254.

Entsua-Mensah, K., Doku, A., & Adzamli, I. (2012). The national cardiothoracic centre, Accra Ghana: Proceedings of the second international update course in cardiology—improving the coverage of cardiology services. *The Pan African Medical Journal*, *11*(8).

Fokuo, K. (2009). The lighter side of marriage: Skin bleaching in post-colonial Ghana. *African and Asian Studies*, *8*(1–2), 125–146. https://doi.org/10.1163/156921009X413180

Gabe, J., Bury, M., & Elston, M. A. (2004). *Key concepts in medical sociology*. SAGE.

Graham, I. D., Logan, J., Harrison, M. B., Straus, S. E., Tetroe, J., Caswell, W., & Robinson, N. (2006). Lost in knowledge translation: time for a map? *The Journal of Continuing Education in the Health Professions*, *26*(1), 13–24. https://doi.org/10.1002/chp.4

Harshe, N., & Afful-Mensah, G. (2019). *Health - A-id: Agenda for international development*. A-id. https://www.a-id.org/research/topics/health/

Ilesanmi, O. S., Ige, O. K., & Adebiyi, A. O. (2012). The managed hypertensive: The costs of blood pressure control in a Nigerian town. *The Pan African Medical Journal*, *12*, 96.

Institute for International Medicine. (n.d.). *Ankaase Methodist Hospital—Ghana*. https://www.inmed.us/training-sites/ankaase-methodist-hospital-ghana/

Kolling, M., Winkley, K., & Deden, M. V. (2010). "For someone who's rich, it's not a problem". Insights from Tanzania on diabetes health-seeking and medical pluralism among Dar es Salaam's urban poor. *Globalization and Health*, *6*(1), 8. https://doi.org/10.1186/1744-8603-6-8

Ministry of Health. (2008). National Ambulance Services. http://nas.gov.gh/

National Road Safety Commission—Ghana. (2018). http://www.nrsc.gov.gh/index.php/statistics

Patton, M. Q. (2015). *Qualitative research & evaluation methods: Integrating theory and practice* (4th ed.). SAGE.

Peppa, M., Krania, M., & Raptis, S. A. (2011). Hypertension and other morbidities with Cushing's syndrome associated with corticosteroids: A review. *Integrated Blood Pressure Control*, *4*, 7–16. https://doi.org/10.2147/IBPC.S9486

Rashidian, A., Eccles, M. P., & Russell, I. (2008). Falling on stony ground? A qualitative study of implementation of clinical guidelines' prescribing recommendations in primary care. *Health Policy*, *85*(2), 148–161. https://doi.org/10.1016/j.healthpol.2007.07.011

Saluja, S., Rudolfson, N., Massenburg, B. B., Meara, J. G., & Shrime, M. G. (2020). The impact of physician migration on mortality in low and middle-income countries: An economic modelling study. *BMJ Global Health*, *5*(1), e001535. https://doi.org/10.1136/bmjgh-2019-001535

Stewart, B. T., Quansah, R., Gyedu, A., Boakye, G., Abantanga, F., Ankomah, J., Donkor, P., & Mock, C. (2016). Serial assessment of trauma care capacity in Ghana in 2004 and 2014. *JAMA Surgery*, *151*(2), 164. https://doi.org/10.1001/jamasurg.2015.3648

Westli, H., Johnsen, B., Eid, J., Rasten, I., & Brattebø, G. (2010). Teamwork skills, shared mental models, and performance in simulated trauma teams: An independent group design. *Scandinavian Journal of Trauma, Resuscitation and Emergency Medicine*, *18*(1), 47.

Wenchi Methodist Hospital—Ghana | INMED. (n.d.). Wenchi Methodist Hospital—Ghana. https://www.inmed.us/training-sites/wenchi-methodist-hospital-ghana/

World Health Organization [WHO]. (2016). *Sustainable development goals (SDGs): Goal 3. Target 3.6: By 2020, halve the number of global deaths and injuries from road traffic accidents [poster]*. https://iris.wpro.who.int/handle/10665.1/12878

CHAPTER 14

STRATEGIES OF ENGAGEMENT AND SUPPORT

Addressing the Holistic Needs of Veterans Pursuing Higher Education

Yvonne Hunter-Johnson
Southern Illinois University (Carbondale)

Sharlene Smith, Rutgers
The State University of New Jersey, United States

Geleana Alston
North Carolina A&T State University, United States

Aynur Charkasova
University of Arkansas Fayetteville

The United Nations Educational, Scientific and Cultural Organization (UNESCO) was formalized in 1945 and initiated formal agreement with the United Nations in 1946. The foundational platform of this distinct governing body is its contribution to ensuring world peace and security

Advancing the Global Agenda for Human Rights, Vulnerable Populations, and Environmental Sustainability: Adult Education as Strategic Partner, pp. 223–241
223

utilizing the tool of collaboration across a multiplicity of nations regarding education, science, culture, and communication (United Nations [UN], 2015). In addition to this overarching global initiative, world leaders of the UN recognized the need for strategic initiatives, specifically regarding economic sustainability, meanwhile addressing the global concerns of education, health, human rights, and environmental protection. Hence, the United Nations 2015 Sustainable Development Goals were introduced encompassing 17 broad goals (United Nations 2015).

Within this chapter, we focus on student veterans, a vulnerable population. Goal 4 emphasizes the need for inclusive and equitable quality education and promotes lifelong learning opportunities for all. More specifically, Goal 4.3 highlight equal access to technical/vocational and higher education. Emphasis is placed on defining the student veteran and its classification as a vulnerable population within the field of adult education. We address the challenges this marginalized group encounters to obtain higher education, relevant support systems to ensure educational success, and discuss institutional strategies that align with the designation of being veteran—friendly higher learning institute.

Veterans are often characterized as mature, motivated, and experienced students (Navarre-Cleary & Wozniak, 2013) who are goal-driven (Hinton, 2012) and mission-oriented (Hart & Thompson, 2013). According to Brown and Gross (2011), a student veteran is anyone who is on active duty in reserve, who has retired from the military, or who has completed military service and entered post-secondary education. Vacchi (2012) defined student veterans as "any student who is a current military member or was one previously, National Guard or Reserves regardless of deployment status, combat experience, legal veteran status, or GI Bill use" (p. 17). For this chapter, we propose using Vacchi's definition of student veterans because of the emphasis on both current military members and those who have previously served.

According to Hembrough et al. (2018), 85% of student veterans are nontraditional students (ages 24 to 40), while only 15% are traditional students (ages 18 to 23). However, there are instances of veteran students over the age of 40. Regarding their marital status, nearly half of student veterans are married and have children (NCSL, 2017), and 42% work full time (American Council on Education, 2014). Most veteran learners are pursuing bachelor's degrees (48%), but some are obtaining more advanced degrees, such as masters (16%), and doctoral degrees (2%). Compared to traditional nonmilitary students, veteran learners are more likely to major in engineering, applied, and social sciences rather than in arts and communications (Durdella & Kim, 2012). Borsari et al. (2017) reported that 43% of veteran students attend public two-year colleges, 21% attend public four-year colleges, 13% attend private non-profit institutions, and 12% attend private for-profit universities. However, there is limited literature about veterans attending technical training. Additionally, military and veteran students are more likely to be first-generation college students from lower-income backgrounds (Kirchner, 2015). Despite veteran student military background, demographics, and discipline of choice, many veteran students use the opportunities presented to them to obtain higher education.

HISTORY OF MILITARY SERVICE PERSONNEL IN U.S. COLLEGES AND UNIVERSITIES

U.S. universities and colleges have been serving military personnel since the early 1800s. The 1862 Morrill Act formally integrated military training into higher education (Griffin & Gilbert, 2015). However, during the World War II, American policymakers realized the economic consequences of the end of the war, recognizing a need for a policy for thousands of veterans soon to be returning from overseas (McMurray, 2007). In 1944, Congress approved the first GI Bill of Rights, officially titled the Servicemen's Readjustment Act of 1944. This bill included financial assistance for tuition and books, monthly stipends, low-interest home mortgages, business loans, and health benefits (Tinoco, 2014). As early as 1950, 6.6 million World War veterans had used their GI Bill benefits by enrolling in higher education (Breedin, 1972). The GI Bill of Rights has been amended several times.

Approved in 1984, the Veterans' Educational Assistance Act (Montgomery GI Bill) aimed to increase the high school graduation rate among veterans (McMurray, 2007) and included monthly checks that covered educational and living expenses (Radford, 2009). The Post-9/11 Veterans Educational Assistance Act was signed in 2008 and provided more money to military undergraduates compared to the Montgomery GI Bill. Beginning January 1, 2016, The Veterans Access, Choice, and Accountability Act (2016) mandated all public higher education institutions offer in-state tuition to qualified veterans and their dependents, notwithstanding their residency status (Fulton & Sponsler, 2015). As a result, as of 2013, more than one million veterans received Veterans Affairs educational benefits at over 6,000 institutions (Fulton & Sponsler, 2015; Tinoco, 2014), and two million military veterans are expected to attend higher education institutions by 2020 (Tinoco, 2014). Due to the troop reductions, more veterans are expected to pursue a college degree as the post-9/11 GI Bill has made higher education an attractive and financially affordable option (Brown & Gross, 2011; Kirchner, 2015; Olsen et al., 2014). GI Bill benefits have led to accelerated growth in the numbers of veteran students at universities, increased higher education access, and increased student diversity.

The introduction of such acts provided a pathway for veterans and active-duty military personnel to the archways of academia. Utilizing their active-duty service history as an underpinning, veterans are eligible for a variety of financial support while obtaining their education. Such support includes tuition and fees, allowances for books and supplies, and in specific cases, monthly housing stipends (U.S. Department of Veteran Affairs, 2017). According to the National Conference of State Legislature (NCSL, 2017), more than a million veterans have enrolled in college. Most of them (79%) are enrolled in public institutions (Cate et al., 2017), with an estimated 52% completion rate in four to five years (Cate, 2014). In 2016, approximately 790,090 beneficiaries were recipients of educational assistance totaling $11,583,408.00 (U.S. Department of Veterans Affairs, 2017). As a result of The Colmery Veterans Educational Assistance Act (also known as the Forever GI Bill), which was passed in the U.S. Congress in 2017, opportunities are available for service members and their families and survivors.

MOTIVATION FOR PURSUING HIGHER EDUCATION

Although there is significant research in the field of adult education in particular regarding nontraditional students' motivations to pursue higher education (Chu et al., 2007; Hunter-Johnson, 2017), there is inadequate academic literature that focuses specifically on veterans' motivations to pursue higher education. However, among the limited academic literature that exists, the motivations of veterans to pursue higher education include job-related reasons such as "job or career enhancement and job stability" (Patterson & Paulson, 2016, p. 13); career enhancement and promotion (Brauchle, 1997; Brown, 1993); opportunity to receive mental health and social service while enrolled in college (McCaslin et al., 2013); educational benefits such as Post-9/11 G.I. Bill (Vacchi, 2012); the anticipation of the transition to civilian life (Wilson et al., 2013); and self-improvement for a career change, obtain a degree, experience college, and for financial gain (Hunter-Johnson, 2018).

Aikins et al. (2015) stated that "attending higher education represents an opportunity for many veterans to readjust to civilian life, although they often require special help to enter and persist in postsecondary settings" (p. 482). Despite veterans' motivations to pursue higher education, they are often faced with a multiplicity of unique challenges when compared to other traditional and nontraditional learners. Such challenges require institutions of higher learning, specifically those marketing their institutions as "veteran-friendly," to make available relevant support services to assist veterans with their unique needs. Additionally, it is incumbent upon institutions to ensure their policies and best practices not only align with the designation of "veteran-friendly," but also embrace principles of adult learning while ensuring equitable access to technical/vocational and higher education as outlined in Goal 4.3 of the United Nations Sustainable Development Goals.

TRANSITIONAL CHALLENGES OF VETERANS IN HIGHER EDUCATION

Within institutions of higher education, transitional challenges for veterans can include navigation of governmental and institutional bureaucracies, namely, (a) understanding and application of benefits and support systems, (b) feelings of being overwhelmed and dismayed if not provided mechanisms of support as a result of acculturation (Bonar & Domenici, 2011; Brown & Gross, 2011), (c) social, cognitive, physical and psychological readjustment challenges when transitioning to college environments (Aikins et al., 2015), (d) addressing personal family issues (Johnson et al., 2014), and (e) feeling apathetic concerning their future outlook (Morin, 2011). Despite the vast amount of overarching challenges veterans encounter when transitioning to higher education, veterans also embrace transitional challenges that are unique to the learning environment that can have an impact on their learning experience and overall student success while enrolled in higher education.

Learning Environment Transitional Challenges

Considering the vast differences in purpose and structure between the military and institutions of higher education, some student veterans find it difficult to adapt to academic life (Naphan & Elliot, 2015). Examining the higher education learning environment through the lens of military training creates great dismay because of the difference in foundational theories. Within adult higher education, the foundational theories are humanism and andragogy compared to military training, which is grounded in behaviorist theory (Hunter-Johnson & Closson, 2012). Hence, such theoretical differences inform the structures of the two institutions with implications for the learning environment that include instructional methods and techniques, student role (passive vs. active), student/teacher interaction, student expectations, assessment techniques, and the overall learning climate.

Hunter-Johnson's (2018) qualitative study on veterans' motivations and adjustments to higher education further highlighted major challenges veterans encounter when transitioning to higher education. Table 14.1

compares the learning environments in higher education to those in the military, which expand on the transitional challenges of the student veteran.

Moreover, in the learning environment, veterans' interactions with civilian students in the classroom can present additional challenges with

Table 14.1

Comparison of Learning Environments: Higher Education Versus Military

Impact on Veteran Student	Higher Education Learning Environment	Military Learning Environment
Passive versus Active Student Role	In a higher education learning environment, the adult learner is expected to be more engaged and an active participant in the learning process.	In the military learning environment, adult learners assume the role of a passive participant and assume the role of the recipient of knowledge/information.
Pace of Learning	In higher education, to obtain a degree—depending on the type and discipline—will take a few years, incorporates a variety of subjects and at a slower pace compared to military training;	Within a military learning environment, the pace of receiving knowledge is fast-paced, task focused, and usually a shorter length of time for training (i.e., training sessions, seminars)
Instructor's Role	Within a higher education learning environment, the instructor is perceived as a facilitator or knowledge and more collaboration is welcomed by adult learners.	Within the military training environment, the instructor is perceived as an authority figure, subject matter expert, and not to be challenged.
Individualism versus Collectivism	Within higher education, the emphasis is placed on individualism and individual success.	Within the military and military training environment, the emphasis is placed on team building.
Institutional Structure and Protocol	The overall structure and protocol with institutions of higher education are less structured than those of the military. As a result, the expectations to follow different protocols from that of the military to which they were accustomed (Cipher et al., 2018) create additional challenges for veterans enrolled in higher education (Livingston et al., 2011).	Emphasis is placed on the hierarchical structure within the military, which is transferred to the learning environment. Overall, there is more institutional structure, commands/orders that must be adhered to without challenge.

traditional and nontraditional students. According to Bellafiore (2012) and Rumann and Hamrick (2010), the different life circumstances and larger world experiences of combat veterans cause them to feel separated from their civilian student peers and alienated from staff and faculty. This can create a challenge when socializing with traditional and nontraditional civilian students, particularly when collaborating on assignments, presentations, and networking.

Mental and Physical Health Challenges

Veterans face mental and physical health challenges as they transition to higher education. Several factors that contribute to the challenges military and veteran learners face during the transition, such as the feeling of isolation on campuses; reluctance to seek social support (Olsen et al., 2014); a range of mental health diagnoses such as posttraumatic stress disorder (PTSD), anxiety, depression, suicide attempts, military sexual trauma (Borsari et al., 2017); traumatic brain injury (TBI, Church, 2009); risk of redeployment while enrolled in college (Livingston & Bauman, 2013); difficulties in managing education-related finances (Borsari et al., 2017); and viewing school environment as chaotic and unstructured (Durdella & Kim, 2012). The absence of a coherent social network may also bring an additional struggle while adapting to new expectations (DiRamio et al., 2008).

Both mental issues and physical disabilities can interfere with veteran students' academic success; therefore, they require special support systems established by colleges and universities (Borsari et al., 2017). Depressive symptoms, aggression, anxiety, PSTD, and suicidal thoughts are of particular concern among this student population. According to the Department of Defense Task Force on Mental Health (2007), 27% of returning veterans suffer from significant depression, whereas 24% report alcohol abuse issues, and 43% report problems dealing with anger. These mental health issues are associated with less identification with campus and lower social support (Weber, 2012). Several physical disabilities (e.g., traumatic brain injury or spinal cord injury) may result in social and communicational deficits with peers and faculty (Church, 2009). Redeployment is also a big transitional challenge for the active-duty personnel as it may result in loss of course credit and loss of scholarship (Ackerman et al., 2009). Although 82% of universities established some form of support system to address redeployment issues (e.g., reimbursement of college credit, an extension of incomplete status for courses), more persistent and long-term measures will be required to encourage military learners to complete their degrees after the interruption (Cook & Kim, 2009).

Social Adaptation Challenges

Social adaptation to the civilian world brings an additional burden to veteran learners who often reflect an unwillingness to ask for help and, among other things, experience difficulty with time management (Borsari et al., 2017). Transitioning from a highly hierarchical lifestyle to civilian or student life (Messina, 2014) brings several challenges, such as feeling lost or isolated (Campbell & Riggs, 2015). Many students have reported feelings of frustration and confusion while navigating college campuses (Mechur-Karp & Klempin, 2016). A world of multiple choices, freedom, and ambiguity can be daunting for some veteran/military students who are accustomed to the regulated and organized military culture (Kappell, 2017). All these unique challenges create barriers for military students and their nonmilitary peers (Osborne, 2014a). Military/veteran students continue to struggle while managing both academic (López et al., 2016), and nonacademic responsibilities (Hitt et al., 2015). Although military/veteran students bring diverse experiences to college campuses, they continue to struggle with the transition into the social aspects of student life and contributing in the classroom (Osborne, 2014b). Additionally, military/veteran students believe that universities and colleges are not prepared to assist them (Hitt et al., 2015), and unsupported military students are less likely to interact with their nonmilitary peers and instructors (Osborne, 2014a).

The underlying question of why veterans encounter such challenges in higher education when transitioning to civilian life provokes much thought. Veterans, specifically aging veterans who opt to enroll in higher education, have unique characteristics based on their military experiences (Cipher et al., 2018). As a result, they are equipped with a multiplicity of skills that were developed during their military career and are later transferred to their academic experience. These prior career skills contribute to their perseverance, value for teamwork, global awareness, and increased self-efficacy (Allen et al., 2014; Dyar, 2016), making the challenge of academia more manageable. Despite such challenges, veterans utilize higher education as a transitional tool to readjust to civilian life (Aikins et al., 2015) and as a means of preparation for the civilian workforce.

SUPPORT SERVICES FOR VETERANS AND MILITARY SERVICE MEMBERS PURSUING HIGHER EDUCATION

Veteran students encounter considerably more challenges than do the civilian traditional and nontraditional students while pursuing higher education. On this premise, it is paramount that institutions of higher education provide support systems specific to the veteran student. In addition, in an effort not only to recruit but to retain and ensure veteran student success, many institutions of higher education market their institutions as veteran-friendly and provide specific programs for veteran students.

Institutional Support for Veteran Students

Although each military division offers some form of transitional assistance, only 36% of veterans described the transition from military to college to be "easy" (Kurzynski, 2014). Several authors (Borsari et al., 2017; Durdella & Kim, 2012) documented a need for a support system in classrooms to help alleviate challenges veterans encounter while in higher education. Various techniques should be embraced to target the needs of military and veteran students to make their transition from the military to civilian life easier and more productive. Among these supports include (a) creating a military-friendly campus, (b) establishing a veterans affairs office, (c) providing financial aid services, tuition incentives, support transfers of credits toward a degree, and (d) foster veteran-friendly engagement.

Creating a Military-Friendly Campus

Many colleges and universities are creating a military-friendly campus to assist veterans and active military members in transitioning to higher education, complete college programs, and obtain career-ready skills (Griffin & Gilbert, 2015). According to the U.S. Department of Education (2013), the designation "military-friendly" is used to identify colleges that have embraced practices that recognize the unique needs and characteristics of student veterans. To that end, the Departments of Veteran Affairs (VA) and Education created a joint program called the eight keys to veteran's success. This program encourages colleges to register as military-friendly with the Department of Education if they implement programs that assist veterans in transitioning to the college environment, completing degrees, and obtaining new job skills (U.S. Department of Education, 2013). The eight key components are as follows:

1. Create a culture of trust and connectedness across the campus community to promote well-being and success for veterans.
2. Ensure consistent and sustained support from campus leadership.
3. Implement an early-alert system to ensure all veterans receive academic, career, and financial advice before challenges become overwhelming.

4. Coordinate and centralize campus efforts for all veterans, together with the creation of a designated space (even if the space is limited in size).
5. Collaborate with local communities and organizations, including government agencies, to align and coordinate various services for veterans.
6. Utilize a uniform set of data tools to collect and track information on veterans, including demographics, retention, and degree completion.
7. Provide comprehensive professional development for faculty and staff on issues and challenges unique to veterans.
8. Develop systems that ensure the sustainability of effective practices for veterans. (U.S. Department of Education, 2013)

Establish a Veteran Affairs Office

One of the first steps toward implementing the eight keys to creating a military-friendly campus is the establishment of a veteran's affairs office. This office is designed to support military and veteran students' academic and social transition to the college/university and is managed by a staff that understands military and veteran students' unique issues and concerns (Griffin & Gilbert, 2015; Osborne, 2014a). Military and veteran students can receive admissions, financial aid/scholarship, health services, tutoring, and all other services through this office (Griffin & Gilbert, 2015; O'Herrin, 2011; Osborne, 2014a).

Provide Financial Aid Services/Tuition Incentives

Providing tuition incentives is another strategy for recruiting veterans and active military personnel, while promoting equitable access for this vulnerable student population. Colleges and universities participate in government programs, such as the Post-9/11 GI Bill and the Yellow Ribbon Program. The Yellow Ribbon Program makes funding available for tuition, tuition assistance, and in-state tuition to veterans and active-duty military personnel pursuing higher education. These financial benefits assist student veterans with funding to defray tuition and housing costs. Therefore, one way to assist student veterans with transitioning to college is to create financial packages to accompany acceptance letters. When a veteran student applies to a college, the financial aid office, in collaboration with the veteran office, could determine the financial aid/scholarship available to the student. Once that is determined, the information could be indicated in the acceptance letter. This process will allow the veteran student to gain a clearer understanding of the financial assistance available and eliminate the stress of seeking this information.

Support Transfer of Credits Toward a Degree

Many veteran students earn credits through various military training programs. Colleges and universities can allow American Council on Education (ACE) credit for military experience, awards credit for the College Level Examination Program (CLEP), and offer the Reserve Officers' Training Corps (ROTC) program, which offers students an opportunity to focus on receiving credits for completion of their degrees and serve upon graduation. The ACE military evaluations program evaluates formal military training in terms of academic credit, allowing military personnel to earn credit for college-level learning acquired through training and experience. The CLEP exam allows veterans to receive college credit by earning qualifying scores on any one or more of 34 assessments, thus enabling them to move directly into higher-level courses, which will save time and money. Additionally, ROTC is one of the best opportunities for military members to gain invaluable experience while earning a college degree.

Foster Veteran Students' Engagement

Student engagement is very important for success, and support from campus personnel and peers can enhance students' learning experiences (Griffin & Gilbert, 2015). Some of the best practices and strategies for implementing student engagement for military and veteran students include social and cultural support and interactions with peers, faculty, and staff. This can be presented as veteran students' support groups (via special media or on-campus), veteran mentoring programs, veteran academic support services, and transitional programs specifically for veterans upon initial entry to higher education. Similarly, experiential learning settings, such as job placement assistance, are beneficial. There should be a representative within career services who works directly with veterans to address their unique needs as it relates to career preparation (resume writing, interviewing techniques, identifying transferable skills from the military to the civilian workforce, and communication skills). Additionally, academic programs can incorporate internships, practicums, and field experiences that provide an opportunity for the veteran student to obtain experience working within the civilian sector while completing their degrees.

According to Hunter-Johnson (2018), it is critical for higher education administrators to demonstrate a commitment to promoting a veteran-friendly environment. While higher education institutions have made significant strides in supporting students who are veterans, the authors present the following considerations for fostering or enhancing effective engagement while supporting veteran students (see Table 14.2).

Table 14.2

Considerations For Fostering or Enhancing Effective Engagement While Supporting Veteran Students

Club Association for Veterans (Ackerman et al., 2009; Bauman, 2009; Military.com, 2020)	Create a supportive, student-centered space where student veterans interact and connect with other student veterans for support and engagement.
Campus Student Veteran Association (SVA) Chapter (Heine, 2020)	Establish Student Veteran Association Chapters—student-veteran groups that formed on college and university campuses to provide peer-to-peer networks for veterans who are attending those schools. The chapters are designed to be advocates for student veterans and to help bridge the campus to career transition.
Career Industry Partnerships (Osborne, 2014a; University of South Florida, 2020)	Leverage partnerships with local industries. For example, consider developing a program to assist veteran students with understanding more about the career they wish to pursue upon graduation. Program goals could focus on providing student veterans with opportunities to develop relationships with successful local business and community leaders to enhance their ability to transition from college/university to the workforce; increase their knowledge of the local job market, employer expectations, and skills necessary to be successful; and increase the student veterans' confidence in their knowledge, skills, and abilities to succeed in the civilian workforce. The program could include components such as mentoring, networking, employment/internship, and job shadowing.
Veterans Recognition Ceremony (Osborne, 2014a)	Commit to and financially support an annual ceremony around Veterans' Day to honor and recognize veterans and invite the campus community.

(Table continued on next page)

Table 14.2 (Continued)

Considerations For Fostering or Enhancing Effective Engagement While Supporting Veteran Students

Veteran Upward Bound Program	Pursue extramural funding to support a program focused on motivating and assisting veterans in the development of academic and other requisite skills necessary for acceptance and success in a program of postsecondary education.
Orientation Program for Veterans (Osborne, 2014a)	Organize a separate orientation program for incoming student veterans to provide them with information regarding support services on campus and within the community. The program can include information pertaining to VA benefits, academic support such as tutoring, mental and health services; educational and career endeavors, vocational exploration and assistance in selecting a suitable career/major; assistance in applying for healthcare benefits; referrals for medical and mental health; help to access, understand, and apply for VA benefits; referrals for readjustment counseling services for eligible veterans and their families.
Veteran Success Course (University of South Florida, 2020)	Develop a course that can assist student veterans with a successful transition into college/university, and to successfully launch into a meaningful career. The Transition topics could include resume writing, interviewing skills, network strategies, career exploration and preparation, identity development, civic engagement, campus resources, and so forth.
Veteran Ally Training (Osborne, 2014a); O'Herrin, 2011)	Commit to and financially support a training to develop a knowledgeable and supportive network of faculty and staff members who will serve as veteran liaisons in their colleges or administrative offices (Osborne, 2014a; O'Herrin, 2011).

IMPLICATION FOR ADULT EDUCATION PRACTICE: SUPPORT FOR VETERAN STUDENTS

With the increase of veteran student enrollment in higher education, it is paramount that institutions of higher education ensure that the learning environment is conducive for learning and adhere to adult learning theories and practices. On this premise, it is recommended that the institution partner with the department/division of adult education to help facilitate the transition of military and veteran members to higher education. The partnership with the adult education department is threefold: (a) emphasizing the needs of the military student utilizing the lens of adult education, (b) training and development of faculty with responsibility for teaching in the online program, and (c) coaching and mentoring the liaison within the veteran affairs office. It is important that an educator (with an academic background in adult education) assist with the development and facilitation of a transitional course that prepares the military student for courses online or face-to-face. It is critical to consider the training background of the military student, which is grounded in behaviorism. The learning environment in higher education is grounded in humanism and reflective of andragogical approaches (Hunter-Johnson & Closson, 2012). Therefore, this could be a culture shock for military students. On this premise, the transitional course should be research-based and reflect best practices relative to the application of adult learning theories, strategies for military students as they transition from "being directed" to "self-directed," and understanding the differences between the military and higher education learning environments.

In relation to the partnership between the adult educator and the veteran affairs office, this individual could be responsible for training their respective liaisons in the application of principles of adult learning when engaging in any learning process with military/veteran students. Further, the adult educator can serve in the capacity of a mentor/coach for the liaison in areas of program development, academic advising, and an academic resource. The adult educator responsible for the training and development of faculty will emphasize the art of teaching adults and raise awareness between the military and higher education learning environments. Such training should involve comparing and explaining the roles relative to students versus teachers, strategies for providing a culturally sensitive pedagogy, military versus civilian culture, and exploration of a multiplicity of online instructional methods that align with the learning styles of veteran students to the adult education approach.

The higher education landscape will continue to change, and this will influence how veteran and military-friendly environments are fostered within institutions, and especially with considerations of supporting students deployed internationally. For example, a faculty member may need to be more open-minded about scheduling a time to meet virtually with a military/veteran student who may be in a time zone with a seven hour difference. Additionally, there may be times when an active military student may not be able to access the learning management system while abroad because it could potentially yield a technological security breach. All in all, institutions of higher education should be mindful of how to be flexible in supporting the unique needs of military/veteran students when they are abroad.

CONCLUSION

Education is classified as a human right and a force for sustainable development and peace (United Nation, 2015). Education, and more specifically, equitable access to education also serves as an empowerment tool for people specifically regarding knowledge, skills, and values that serve as an underpinning for people to live in dignity while building their lives which by extension contribute to the overall development of societies (United Nations, 2015).Veterans, a vulnerable population in adult education, also perceive the attainment of higher education as an empowerment tool not only for self but the upward mobility of society. Hence, the enrollment in higher education for veterans and active-duty military personnel is often utilized as a transitioning tool to the civilian world (Hunter-Johnson, 2018) and an opportunity to positively contribute to society. However, although motivated and resilient, veterans and military personnel encounter myriad challenges compared to traditional and nontraditional students. Within this chapter, the authors discussed the challenges veteran students encounter while pursuing higher education. Additionally, the authors emphasized strategies and best practices to support and engage veteran students. However, it is important for higher education institutions to exhibit an institutional culture that exhibits a military-friendly institution. Hence, policies, practices, and support services should reflect this. As the enrollment of military service members and veterans increases, it is hoped that higher education institutions will continue to identify innovative strategies to best support veteran students.

REFERENCES

Ackerman, R., DiRamio, D., & Mitchell, R. L. (2009). Transitions: Combat veterans as college students. *New Directions for Student Services, 126,* 5–14.

Aikins, R. D., Golub, A., & Bennett, A. S. (2015). Readjustment of urban veterans: A mental health and substance use profile of Iraq and Afghanistan veterans in higher education. *Journal of American College Health, 63*(7), 482–494.

Allen, P. E., Armstrong, M. L., Saladiner, J. E., Hamilton, M. J., & Conard, P. L. (2014). Opportunities, hurdles, solutions, and approaches to transition military veterans into professional nursing programs. *Journal of Professional Nursing, 30*(6), 474–480.

American Council on Education. (2014). *Undergraduate student veterans.* https://www.acenet.edu/Documents/Higher-ed-spotlight-undergraduate-student-veterans.pdf

Bauman, M. (2009). The mobilization and return of undergraduate students serving in the National Guard and Reserves. *New Directions for Student Services,* (126), 15–23.

Bellafiore, M. (2012). Combat to campus. *Bridgewater Review, 31,* 12–14.

Bonar, T. C., & Domenici, P. L. (2011). Counseling and connecting with the military undergraduate: The intersection of military service and university life. *Journal of College Student Psychotherapy, 25*(3), 204–219.

Borsari, B., Yurasek, A., Miller, M. B., Murphy, J. G., McDevitt-Murphy, M. E., Martens, M. P., Darcy, M. G., & Carey, K. B. (2017). Student service members/veterans on campus: Challenges for reintegration. *American Journal of Orthopsychiatry, 87*(2), 166–175. https://doi.org/10.1037/ort0000199

Brauchle, K. C. (1997). *United States armed forces' voluntary education program: The effect on enlisted service member retention* [Unpublished doctoral dissertation]. University of Alaska.

Breedin, B. (1972, March 1). Research currents: Veterans in college. *American Association for Higher Education* (ED058467). ERIC. https://eric.ed.gov/?id=ED058467

Brown, J. L. S. (1993). *Participation of U.S. Army enlisted personnel in off-duty college degree programs* [Unpublished doctoral dissertation]. Kansas State University.

Brown, P. A., & Gross, C. (2011). Serving those who have served managing veteran and military student best practices. *Journal of Continuing Higher Education, 59*(1), 45–49. https://doi.org/10.1080/07377363.2011.544982

Campbell, R., & Riggs, S. A. (2015). The role of psychological symptomatology and social support in the academic adjustment of previously deployed student veterans. *Journal of American College Health, 63*(7), 473–481.

Cate, C. A. (2014). *Million Records Project: Research from Student Veterans of America.* Student Veterans of American.

Cate, C. A., Lyon, J. S., Schmeling, J., & Bogue, B. Y. (2017). National veteran education success tracker: A report on the academic success of student veterans using the post-9/11 GI Bill. *Student Veterans of America,* Washington, DC.

Chu, H. C., Hsieh, M. C., & Chang, S. C. (2007). *A study of career development, learning motivation, and learning satisfaction of adult learners in unconventional scheduling graduate programs* [Paper presentation]. Academy of Human Resource Development (AHRD) International Research Conference, Indianapolis, IN. https://files.eric.ed.gov/fulltext/ED504762.pdf

Church, T. E. (2009). Returning veterans on campus with war related injuries and the long road back home. *Journal of Postsecondary Education and Disability, 22*(1), 43–52.

Cipher, D., Urban, R., Boyd, J., & Mancini, M. (2018). Online course engagement among undergraduate nursing student veterans. *Journal of Veterans Studies, 4,* 1–14. http://doi.org/10.21061/jvs.v4i1.65

Cook, B. J., & Kim, Y. (2009). *From soldier to student: Easing the transition of service members on campus.* American Association of State Colleges and Universities.

Department of Defense Task Force on Mental Health. (2007). *Achievable vision: Report of the Department of Defense Task Force on mental health, June 2007.* Psychological Health Center of Excellence. https://www.pdhealth.mil/strategy-policy-library/achievable-vision-report-department-defense-task-force-mental-health-june-2007

DiRamio, D., Ackerman, R., & Mitchell, R. L. (2008). From combat to campus: Voices of student-veterans. *NASPA Journal, 45*(1), 73–102.

Durdella, N., & Kim, Y. K. (2012). Understanding patterns of college outcomes among student veterans. *Journal of Studies in Education, 2,* 109–129. https://doi.org/10.5296/jse.v2i2.1469

Dyar, K. L. (2016). Veterans in transition: Implications for nurse educators. *Nursing Forum, 51*(3), 173–179.

Fulton, M., & Sponsler, B. A. (2015). *In-state tuition policies under the Veterans Access, Choice and Accountability Act.* Education Commission of the States. https://files.eric.ed.gov/fulltext/ED555524.pdf

Griffin, K. A., & Gilbert, C. K. (2015). Better transitions for troops: An application of Schlossberg's transition framework to analyses of barriers and institutional support structures for student veterans. *The Journal of Higher Education, 86*(1), 71–97.

Heine, H. (2020). *Which college have the best veterans program?* https://www.military.com/education/finding-a-school/which-colleges-have-the-best-veterans-programs.html

Hart, D. A., & Thompson, R. (2013). 'An Ethical Obligation': Promising practices for student veterans in college writing classrooms. *Results of a 2011 CCCC Research Grant,* 1–19.

Hembrough, T., Madewell, A., & Dunn, K. (2018). Students veterans' preference for traditional versus online course formats: A case study at two Midwestern universities. *Journal of Veterans Studies, 3*(2), 57–93.

Hinton, C. E. (2012). *The experiences of Marine student veterans in undergraduate composition courses: A phenomenological study* [Doctoral dissertation]. Saint Louis University.

Hitt, S., Sternberg, M., MacDermid-Wadsworth, S., Vaughan, J., Carlson, R., Dansie, E., & Mohrbacher, M. (2015). The higher education landscape for U.S. student service members and veterans in Indiana. *Higher Education, 70,* 535–550. https://doi.org/10.1007/s10734-014-9854-6

Hunter-Johnson, Y. (2017). Demystifying educational resilience: Barriers of Bahamian nontraditional adult learners in higher education. *The Journal of Continuing Higher Education, 65*(3), 175–186.

Hunter-Johnson, Y. (2018). Promoting veterans in higher education: Motivation and adjustments to their learning environments. *International Research Journal of Curriculum and Pedagogy, 4*(1), 66–79.

Hunter-Johnson, Y. O., & Closson, R. B. (2012). Learners' educational orientation as a design tool for human resource development professionals in law enforcement: A Caribbean context. *Human Resource Development International, 15*(2), 193–208.

Johnson, W. B., Bertschinger, M., Snell, A. K., & Wilson, A. (2014). Secondary trauma and ethical obligations for military psychologists: Preserving compassion and competence in the crucible of combat. *Psychological Services*, *11*(1), 68.

Kappell, J. (2017). Student veterans' participation in high-impact practices: Veterans' experiences at three institutions of higher education in southeastern North Carolina. *Journal of Veterans Studies*, *2*(1), 29–49.

Kirchner, M. J. (2015). Supporting student veteran transition to college and academic success. *Adult Learning*, *26*(3), 116–123. https://doi.org/10.1177/1045159515583813

Kurzynski, K. (2014). Veteran services in higher education. *Career Planning & Adult Development Journal*, *30*(3).

López, O. S., Springer, S. B., & Nelson, J. B. (2016). Veterans in the college classroom: Guidelines for instructional practices. *Adult Learning, 27(4),* 143–151.

Livingston, W. G., Havice, P. A., Cawthon, T. W., & Fleming, D. S. (2011). Coming home: Student veterans articulation of college re-enrollment. *Journal of Student Affairs Research and Practice*, *48*(3), 315–331.

Livingston, W. G., & Bauman, M. C. (2013). Activations, deployments, and returns. In F. A. Hamrick & C. B. Rumann (Eds.), *A handbook on student veterans and higher education* (pp. 41–68). Jossey-Bass.

McCaslin, S., Leach, B., Herbst, E., & Armstrong, K. (2013). Overcoming barriers to returning veterans: Expanding services to college campuses. *Journal of Rehabilitation Research & Development*, *50*(8), vii–xiv. https://doi.org/10.1682/jrrd.2013.09.0204

McMurray, A. J. (2007). College students, the GI Bill, and the proliferation of online learning: A history of learning and contemporary challenges. *The Internet and Higher Education*, *10*(2), 143–150.

Mechur-Karp, M., & Klempin, S. (2016). Improving student services for military veterans. *Community College Research Center*. http://ccrc.tc.columbia.edu/publications/improving-student-services-for-military-veterans.html

Messina, V. (2014). *In and out of uniform: The transition of Iraq and Afghanistan war veterans into higher education* [Doctoral dissertation]. City University of New York.

Military.com (2020). *17 key veteran benefits offered by colleges*. www.military.com/education/finding-a-school/which-colleges-have-the-best-veterans-programs.html.

Morin, R. (2011, December 8). *The difficult transition from military to civilian life*. Pew research Center https://www.pewresearch.org/social-trends/2011/12/08/the-difficult-transition-from-military-to-civilian-life/

Navarre-Cleary, M., & Wozniak, K. (2013). Veterans as adult learners in composition courses. *Composition Forum*, *28*. https://files.eric.ed.gov/fulltext/EJ1016751.pdf

Naphan, D., & Elliot, M. (2015). Role exit from the military: Student veterans' perceptions of transitioning from the U.S. military to higher education. *The Qualitative Report*, *20*(2), 36–48. https://nsuworks.nova.edu/tqr/vol20/iss2/4

National Conference of State Legislatures (NCSL). (2017). State renewable portfolio standards and goals. https://www.ncsl.org/research/energy/renewable-portfolio-standards.aspx

O'Herrin, L. (2011). Enhancing veteran success in higher education. *Peer Review*, *13*, 15–18.

Olsen, T., Badger, K., & McCuddy, M. D. (2014). Understanding the student veterans' college experience: An exploratory study. *U.S. Army Medical Department Journal*, 101–108.

Osborne, N. J. (May 2014a). Veteran ally: Practical strategies for closing the military-civilian gap on campus. *Innovation Higher Education*, *39*(3), 247–260.

Osborne, N. J. (2014b, June). Student veteran discussion panels: Deconstructing the traumatized veteran stigma on campus. *About Campus*, *19*(2), 24–29. https://doi.org/10.1002/abc21153

Patterson, M. B., & Paulson, U. G. (2016). Adult transitions to learning in the USA: What do PIAAC survey results tell us? *Journal of Research and Practice for Adult Literacy, Secondary, and Basic Education*, *5*, 5–27. https://eric.ed.gov/?id=EJ1098806

Radford, A. W. (2009). *Military service members and veterans in higher education: What the new GI Bill may mean for postsecondary institutions*. American Council on Education.

Rumann, C. B., & Hamrick, F. A. (2010). Student veterans in transition: Re-enrolling after war zone deployments. *The Journal of Higher Education*, *81*(4), 431-458.

Tinoco, E. M. (2014). Student veterans in higher education: A transitional challenge. *Community Investments*, *26*(3), 28–44.

UNESCO. (1946). *Agreement between the United Nations and the United Nations Educational, Scientific and Cultural Organization*. http://portal.unesco.org/en/ev.php-URL_ID=48886&URL_DO=DO_TOPIC&URL_SECTION=201.html

U.S. Department of Education. (2013). *President Obama applauds community colleges' and universities' efforts to implement 8 keys to veterans' success* [Press release]. http://www.ed.gov/news/press-releases/president-obama-applauds-community-colleges'-and-universities'-efforts-implement-8-keys-veterans'-success

United Nations. (2015). *History of the UN: 70th Anniversary*. https://www.un.org/un70/en/content/history/index.html

University of South Florida. (2020). *Services*. http://www.usf.edu/student-affairs/veterans/services/index.aspx

U.S. Department of Veteran Affairs. (2017). *G.I. bill comparison tool*. https://www.va.gov/gi-bill-comparison-tool

Vacchi, D. T. (2012). Considering student veterans on the twenty-first-century college campus. *About Campus*, *17*(2), 15–21. https://doi.org/10.1002/abc.21075

Weber, D. (2012). *Academic success and well-being following OEF/OIF deployment*. Arizona State University.

Wilson, K. B., Smith, N. L., Lee, A. L., & Stevenson, M. A. (2013). When the Army post is the campus: Understanding the social and academic integration of soldiers attending college. *Journal of College Student Development*, *54*(6), 628–642.

CHAPTER 15

THE STATUS AND PROSPECTS OF COMMUNITY EDUCATION WORKERS IN CHINA

Lixin Sun, Shuo Li, and Yuxin Song
Ningbo University, China

In 21st-century China, community education plays an important role in moving toward a learning society and building a lifelong education system as an avenue for community members to study and gradually enhance their knowledge and personal prospects. According to Chinese scholar Liu Xuelian (Liu, 2007), community education entails community-based educational activities and processes that promote improvement of all community members and community social development. In recent years, with the continuous expansion of the scope and content of community education work, the professionalization of community educators has become an imperative task in promoting learning communities in China. In terms of the UN's Sustainable Development Goals 2030, the social value and contribution of community education falls within the following goal areas: (3) good health and well-being, (4) quality education, (8) decent work and economic growth, (11) sustainable cities and communities, and (16) peace, justice, and strong institutions. However, the current circumstances of community education in China and the low professional status of its community educators are hindering their ability to effectively meet the needs of their communities.

Advancing the Global Agenda for Human Rights, Vulnerable Populations, and Environmental Sustainability: Adult Education as Strategic Partner, pp. 243–256

In this chapter, we cover the current state of community education in China and analyze some of the contributing factors that influence the social status and professional prospects of Chinese community educators. This chapter is organized along the following sections: defining community education worker; characteristics of community education workers; training and professional development of community educators (including professional status of community educators and the government and public support for community education); context, design, and study findings; discussion; and recommendations for the professionalization of community education.

DEFINING COMMUNITY EDUCATION WORKER

Community education workers are the main agents and organizers of community education. However, at present, a clear definition of the concept and connotation of *community educators* has not yet been agreed upon by scholars in China. Shi and Zhuo (2005) stated that community educators mainly include those who specialize in providing community education at all levels, career management and school management personnel, and full-time teachers engaged in community education and teaching work: "Community educators have both the basic requirements of educators and the working nature of social workers" (p. 8).

Within the context of professionalizing community education, Murrell (2001) differentiated the main roles of the community educators as analytical thinking, creativity within the community, and curating the legacy community educators' work (Guadalupe & Delgado, 2017). However, Guoliang (2010) asserted that "community education workers" and "community educators" are simply different terms for the same thing. Creyton (2004) noted it may be more appropriate to consider all those who contribute to such work as "community members" (Creyton, 2004). In our presentation, the term "community educators" refers to the people who plan and organize community education work to better serve community development.

CHARACTERISTICS OF
COMMUNITY EDUCATION WORKERS

In a study based on data obtained from 207 learning teams, Ning et al. (2015) further explored the social function of community education and denoted a team value orientation. All teachers and paraprofessionals need a clear demonstration of instructional processes so they can learn how to focus on improving their educational practice and create a vision to help all individuals learn and pursue personal development (Cansoy & Parlar, 2017).

THE TRAINING AND PROFESSIONAL DEVELOPMENT OF COMMUNITY EDUCATORS

F. Liu (2007) noted China's Ministry of Education suggested that local education departments should strengthen the composition of community education teams in 2004. Recent research introduced a blueprint for establishing new communities of learning. This professional development framework emphasized the importance of community educators. Similarly, Schmoker's (2004) concept of (PLCs) underscored collaboration between teachers and paraprofessionals working in teams where educators can borrow and collaboratively generate ideas that contribute to learner success (Brown et al., 2018; Hoaglund et al., 2014).

In the adult education community, both individual motives and external demands influence the process of professionalization. A common theme in the extant literature on professional development of community education has discussed how community educators learn through their involvement in PLCs (Schmoker, 2004). Fitzsimons (2010) expressed concern that the value of personal and life experiences that community educators bring to their work is often overlooked and underestimated because it utilizes tacit, local knowledge and direct involvement. These concerns conflict with the emphasis on the importance of community educators' lived experience identified elsewhere in the literature.

Based on narrative interviews with 29 individuals who were training to become adult educators, Andersson et al. (2013) analyzed the qualification paths and learning trajectories of prospective adult educators in Sweden and Denmark. Their findings revealed that many adult educators circumstantially lack the background and credentials as professional educators. It is suggested that the qualification level of adult educators represents a central predictor for the quality of adult education provided (Hord, 1997, 2004; Wilson, 2016). Another theme in the literature about professionalization has focused on training needs and provisions. In Australia, Broadbent and Papadopoulos (2009) discussed the requirements of community workers, especially volunteers who need training and on-going support. Their findings suggested program coordinators and governments should work to ensure mentors are aware of best practice principles. From the literature, we found that community educators may also tend to be more focused on the community work (Adams, 1992). According to Volunteering Australia

(2007), the professional status of community education professionals is often regarded as less reputable than teaching in formal education settings.

Professional Status of Community Educators

The term "status" can be interpreted as a current professional situation and refers to the comprehensive state formed by individuals in the process of survival as a result of the personal and external factors. Divides in socioeconomic status and negative social perceptions of community work are inherent in community education. Whelan (1990) identified a tension between community workers residing in disadvantaged areas and went on to challenge the appropriateness of professionalizing community work, arguing that to do so could further exacerbate tensions between disparate groups.

Public Support for Community Education

Strong communities understand and work with their most disadvantaged populations to ensure good quality service provision for all. For example, the Department of Planning and Community Development can help build stronger communities at the local level (Creyton, 2004). Similarly, governments can implement benchmarks within programs to ensure quality programming (Broadbent & Papadopoulos, 2009).

Peng (2017) investigated government attitudes towards community education. Peng found that government intervention in community educational opportunities can improve the lifelong education system and overall educational level of the population. Unfortunately, much of the public is unaware of the need for adult and community education, making it difficult to obtain and maintain necessary community resources. We now turn to our research study where we aimed to fill this knowledge gap.

PROFESSIONAL STATUS OF COMMUNITY EDUCATORS IN CHINA

Community educators are the main driving force of community education. Therefore, the study of community education is inseparable from the study of community educators. We present the main themes and findings from the research study we conducted pertaining to the community educators in Ningbo, China. In our research, we were primarily interested in identifying the characteristics and roles of part-time staff, their level of satisfaction with existing training and preparation, and their perceptions of a module system for training (Munn et al., 1989). We also discuss the disconnect between Chinese community education polices and the independent career development system. The purpose of our research was to uncover community education workers' perceptions of professional status and problems related to their occupation.

CONTEXT OF THE STUDY

Ningbo is a coastal city in eastern China, where the economy is well developed. Promotion by government departments has resulted in the rapid development of community education of Ningbo, giving it a leading position in China. We interviewed 24 community educators from Ningbo using semistructured interviews to retrieve a high volume of authentic and detailed information. The purpose of the study was to investigate occupational status and problems of community educators, including their salaries, working conditions, professional-qualification foundations, professional training systems, external attention, and planning and career development opportunities.

At present, there are three main groups of community educators in Ningbo: full-time staff in community education, community workers who manage community education, and volunteers. Since volunteers are unpaid, they were not included in the interviews. The community education workers in this study were mainly represented in three groups: graduate university students, former primary school teachers (including those who were unsatisfied with their original work and those who had retired), and staff who were temporarily recruited from the labor market.

The content of the interviews focused on four aspects. First, we explored whether the living standards of community educators met their expectations and improved their conditions. Second, we investigated whether the working environment adequately provided for the professional development of community educators. Third, we studied whether the subject background and professional achievement of community educators were appropriate for their professional role. Fourth, we evaluated community educators' vision and plans for their overall development within community education. In order to protect the privacy of the respondents, pseudonyms replace the names of the participants.

Analytic Framework

In our examination, we apply an ecological framework to study the system of community education and human development. Extant literature has discussed the pivotal roles of community educators in developing an ecology of community education (Fettes, 1998). An ecological approach to community education aims to establish a reasonable environment inside and outside the school, improve teaching efficiency, and promote the healthy growth of the next generation. The approach also advocates for social change and providing educational activities.

STUDY FINDINGS

Findings from this study are organized around the following themes: lack of professional training; improving professional skills; the disconnect between Chinese community education policies and practice; low occupational status of community educators; and lack of an independent career development system.

Lack of Professional Training

Most of the interviewed community education workers had no professional knowledge and no professional training before securing their current position. When some full-time community educators were asked if they had any prior understanding of adult or community education, their responses reflected that the professional training of community educators is insufficient. Interviewee Huang stated, "Before I was a community education worker, I did not know what community education was or what it does," and Ma added, "I came here with one piece of white paper." Xu noted that "The professional knowledge of some primary school teachers and people who are about to retire from adult schools is not very comprehensive."

As a baseline, these statements conveyed that most of the full-time community education workers had experienced similar problems, noting particularly that their jobs were not matched with their specialties and overall professional preparation was weak. An interviewee summarized:

> The reality of community education today is too complex and the recruited social workers are too unprofessional. There is no specialization in community education. In fact, what needs to be specialized is not the social workers, but the professionals in community education.

When asked about the specialization of his social work, Mr. Xu said, "It is not limited to your field." Further, in response to the question "[Do] they have previous knowledge when workers started to manage community education?" he answered, "No, I don't think they have any professional knowledge of it at all."

At present, the complexity and lack of professional preparation in community education work in China represents systematic reasons for the low professional quality of workers in the field. Zhao, a community teacher, expressed her views on the current situation of community education. She said, "Now, the real situation is that it is too complicated and there is no specialization in community education."

There are different requirements for community education managers and front-line social workers in terms of their understanding of the content of community education work. However, workers rarely complete a project or carry out an activity by themselves. The real executors of community education are specialized community staff, while other community education workers believe that full-time community education employees should carry out this educational work.

Improving Professional Skills

Two types of training were available for community education workers in China. This kind of training is organized by community colleges on behalf of the community workers who are responsible for community education. However, such training is offered infrequently. Therefore, most workers have limited opportunities to attend. A teacher named Huang reflected on a similar professional training problem: "At present, the professional skill levels of the staff are not adequate, and the training opportunities are few, which makes it hard for their professional ability to significantly improve." Overall, the lack of investment in professional training for community education reflects that community education is not very important to the public or the government.

The Disconnect Between Chinese Community Education Policies and Practice

Another theme noted from the interviews was that community education is undervalued by the Chinese government. In the early 1970s, the modern concept of lifelong education and policies began to develop in China, and the government published many policies to develop a *learning society*. The 2015 "Regulations on Promoting Lifelong Education in Ningbo" was the fifth published local regulation on the Chinese mainland, which was widely marketed and highly praised by the authorities. During the interviews, we discovered that it conflicted with the intent of the regulation to promote continuing education.

When asked whether the implementation of the regulations regarding the promotion of lifelong education in Ningbo had helped the professional assessment of community education workers, Feng, a dean, replied:

> Since it was published in 2015, there have been concrete measures on the promotion of lifelong education. In terms of jobs, this regulation should enact professional law, just like educational law, and formulate specific implementation rules to promote these jobs. However, during these years, there has been nothing except for the file. So, it is useless.

Although the Regulations on Promoting Lifelong Education in Ningbo mentioned the technical qualifications for workers, it has not been implemented. To solve this problem, Mr. Xu suggested:

> With the development of community education, both maintaining the stability of ranks and promoting their professionalism need to be perfected via a system of professional and technical titles. A relatively independent and open channel for promotion should also be set up.

There are many aspects of community education work, but the problem of insufficient personnel is particularly highlighted in practical work in the community. The source of this problem is that government departments pay little attention to this work, as Yao, a teacher, observed: "Leaders always focus on so-called key projects, which are acknowledged as people's livelihoods. Community education is not a key project because leaders can't see the effects." Xu added, "Community work is on the wrong track. It is not included in the government's work schedule." This issue of governmental neglect also emerged in the opinions of community education workers.

Low Occupational Status of Community Educators

Another dominant theme that emerged from the interviews was the low social and professional status of community educators. Most community education workers in this study did not believe that their jobs are important. Ms. Jing said, "Many community workers are responsible for six jobs, including health, civil administration, community education, and so on, which puts big pressure on them." The neglected status of community education work leads to lower salaries and limited recognition by society. The phenomenon of rapid turnover was also frequently mentioned among interview participants.

Lack of an Independent Career Development System

The vocational system for professional and technical teaching positions in China was implemented in 1986, but even to the present, a separate system still has not been implemented to promote the professional roles of full-time community education teachers in China. The professional positions of full-time community educators in Ningbo are mainly assessed by their former school units where they previously taught, not by community providers.

Our study revealed differing opinions on career development planning for community education workers. However, work intensity was not found to be directly proportional to salary, and lack of support for promotion caused negative effects on professional development and future planning. Pay is not proportional to professional gains, which causes the slow professional progress of workers, especially for the staff employed to work with the general public and who do not hold official positions.

This situation differed for those who had already achieved a higher professional level. The problems that exist in career development planning for community education workers is that promotion channels are limited when compared to those within the general education system, causing negative effects on the efficient construction of community educator teams, and negatively impacting the willingness of community educators to remain in the career.

DISCUSSION

Presently, the diverse context of community education work in China and the lack of professionalism represents the systemic reasons for the low professional quality requirements of employees in the field. Although school education and community education belong to the overall scope of education, there are great differences in the professional knowledge and skills required by each. Teachers transferred from the general education system to community education face distinctive differences in teaching content and objectives, and the professional qualities acquired in general education are not suitable to meet the needs within the community education ecology. Additionally, there were no professional restrictions and requirements on social workers recruited to deliver community education.

Cultivating Professional Community Educator Talent

The professional development of community educators depends on the overall progress of and their access to adult education training. While the overall progress of community education depends on the development of more practice and the cultivation of professional community education. Furthermore, countries should not ignore the exploration of related academic fields and promote professional talent development within the area of specialization. Lindeman, the adult educator first introduced "adult education" to the United States in 1926 with *Andragogik: The Method of Teaching Adults* (Chen, 2010, p. 68–73). Later, Knowles proposed a conceptual model of adult education based on the model of andragogy, which provided theoretical guidance for the cultivation of adult education professionals.

In 1964, the United States Commission for Professors of Adult Education (CPAE) published *Adult Education: Outlines of an Emerging Field of University Study*. Likewise, *The Handbook of Adult Education* was written by Smith, Aker, and Kidd in 1970. These have become classic texts in the field, providing rich academic insights for the development of adult education research and practice (Chen, 2010, pp. 68–73). Thus, more developed countries have made outstanding contributions to this specialized discipline and the professional development of adult education.

In China, the development of adult education and theoretical research on the subject began relatively late. Community education in the country is also in its initial stages of development. As such, there is a lack of professional talent in the area. At present, there is no community education major offered in undergraduate education in China's universities. Unfortunately, professional talent in community education is still quite sparse. Universities, colleges, and community colleges should jointly manage schools and implement internships in community colleges to allow students to apply their theoretical knowledge of community education in practice (Lin, 2017).

RECOMMENDATIONS FOR THE PROFESSIONALIZATION OF COMMUNITY EDUCATION

Based on the findings from the study and information drawn from the extant literature, we make the following recommendations for the professionalization of community education in China: (a) improve training systems for the professional development of educators and (b) establish and improve policy systems and regulations.

Improving the Training System for Community Educators

Community education training content is underdeveloped in China and more importance is placed on theory than practice. At present, the majority of the instructional content is relatively singular. In addition, government officials are lacking knowledge about community education. The culture of government includes a low level of organizational commitment to community engagement within many government agencies, a multitude of pressures and constraints on public servants, and limited training opportunities for public servants to develop their knowledge and skills in community engagement (Tobias, 2009, p. 20).

Within the global development of adult education, many countries and regions have realized the importance of adult education. In March 1985, the first committee of the Fourth International Conference on Adult Education, held in Paris, stated in its report: "Many representatives emphasized the importance of training adult educators as a major concern of many countries. Many speakers noted the importance of preservice training and continuing education" (Zhang, 1990, p. 377). According to this report, adult educators should establish their own training system and carry out targeted professional development. Even though adult education shares some similarities with general educators, there are also many obvious differences. Murrell took community language teachers as the object of his research and proposed the establishment of corresponding situational factors to improve the professional quality of community educators' preparation and promote their continuing education. The training of adult education and community educators with high professional standards has long been requested and realized throughout the world.

Thus, Chinese professional training for community educators should incorporate knowledge derived from international experience. First, the format of training should be flexible and diverse. Theoretical courses should be combined with lectures, discussions, and practical experience. Practical courses should be augmented with more placement and exchange activities, which should be combined with theoretical knowledge. Second, training content should be more targeted. The professional background and working ability of community educators from a "one-size-fits-all" training approach is inefficient; training should reflect community differences and diversity. During training, previous experience should be respected, and educators should be instructed according to workers' aptitude, prior knowledge, and ability. Finally, pre-service training should be strengthened. As the level of most community educators in China is not aligned with the specialty of community education, it is necessary to strengthen orientation training for these workers to address gaps in professional knowledge.

Establishing and Improving Policy Systems and Regulations

A sound system of policies and regulations is not only the key to the professional development of community education workers, but also an important guarantee for community education to obtain social recognition and long-term future development. Western developed countries have long supported the training of adult education providers with policies and regulations. France was the first country globally to implement adult continuing education legislation. In 1919, the French government promulgated the *Loi Astier* law and began to recognize adult basic education (Zhang, 2007). Since the 1950s, France has legislated more than ten further adult education laws based on its national reality. In Britain, legislation has been passed to ensure that adult education administrators enjoy the same social status, benefits, opportunities for further study, and other welfare benefits as general school staff. In 1968, the *Leisure Time Education Act*, a Danish adult education act, was passed, which stipulated that the main supervisor of an adult education provider must study related management courses. Further, in 1966, the United States implemented the *Adult Education Act*, which made comprehensive provisions for the institution, content, and funding of adult education training (F. Liu, 2007). In Japan, the social education law was designed to give clear and detailed conditions for the training and qualification opportunities for adult education management personnel. These developed countries have made corresponding provisions for adult education managers in law so that their professional qualifications and social status can be clearly defined. Since these measures have greatly promoted the professional development of adult education globally, this strategy is especially worthy of attention in China.

Thus, to realize the long-term and orderly development of community education, it is necessary to have the guarantee of a legal system and ensure its practical implementation. We propose some specific measures. First, the state should introduce relevant legal regulations to provide general guidance for community education work. Local governments should also formulate policies and regulations with high relevance and conduct regular inspections and supervision on the implementation of such policies. Second, according to the contribution of individual workers, the relevant departments should offer different social benefits, bonuses, and corresponding employment standards. Third, the establishment of a separate professional evaluation system for community education should be expedited, and it should be ensured that community educators can clearly define their career development plans. The existing professional hierarchy for teachers should be revised, making room for a series of special and independent professional titles for community educators to ensure the professional evaluation is appropriate for and suitable to teachers in community education. And finally, in order to let adult education and community education to be perceived as on par with the other education sectors, consistent public and government support will be necessary.

REFERENCES

Adams, C. F. (1992). "Finding psychic rewards in today's schools": A rebuttal. *The Clearing House*, *65*(6), 343–347.

Andersson, P., Kopsen, S., Larson, A., & Milana, M. (2013). Qualification paths of adult educators in Sweden and Denmark. *Studies in Continuing Education*, *35*(1), 102–118.

Broadbent, R., & Papadopoulos, T. (2009). Community education and youth mentoring: How to build good practice? *Australian Journal of Adult Learning*, *49*(2), 319–351.

Brown, B. D., Horn, R. S., & King, G. (2018). The effective implementation of professional learning communities. *Alabama Journal of Educational Leadership*, *5*, 53–59.

Cansoy, R., & Parlar, H. (2017). Summary of H.R.1031-115th Congress (2017–2018) *Malaysian Online Journal of Educational Sciences*, *5*, 13–27.

Chen, F. (2010). A historical study of the foreign adult education. *Journal of Hebei Normal University (Educational Science Edition)*, *12*(3), 68–73.

Creyton, M. (2004). *Working with: Collaborative approaches for engaging and leading volunteers (Capacity Volunteer Programs)*. htttp://www.volqld.org.au/resources/vq_papers.shtml

Guadalupe, P., & Delgado, M. A. (Eds). (2017). *Narratives of community education and community development*. Perla Delgado.

Fettes, M. (1998). Indigenous education and the ecology of community. *Indigenous education and the ecology of community*, *11*, 250–271.

Fitzsimons, C. (2010). Professionalising community work and its implications for radical community education. *Adult Learner the Irish Journal of Adult & Community Education*, 53–71.

Guoliang, W. (2010). *Research on Teachers' Team Construction in Shanghai Community Schools*. Shanghai Normal University.

Hoaglund, A., Birkenfeld, K., & Box, J. (2014). Professional learning communities: Creating a foundation for collaboration skills in pre-service teachers. *Education*, *134*(4), 521–528.

Hord, S. (1997). *Professional learning communities: Communities of continuous inquiry and improvement*. Southwest Educational Development Laboratory. http://www.sedl.org/pubs/change34/2.html

Hord, S. M. (Ed.). (2004). *Learning together, leading together: Changing schools through professional learning communities*. Teachers College Press.

Lin, J. (2017). *The study on construction of teachers team of Chengdu community education*. Sichuan Normal University.

Liu, F. (2007). Characteristics of continuing education for adult education administrators abroad. *Chinese Vocational Education*, *262*, 16–18.

Liu, X. (2007). *Research on the specialization of community educators*. East China Normal University.

Munn, P., Castelino, C., & Hamilton, D. (1989). *Part-time community development workers and training: A study of needs and provision*. The Scottish Council for Research in Education.

Murrell, P. C. (2001). *The community teacher: A new framework for effective urban teaching.* Teachers College Press.

Ning, H. K., Lee, D., & Lee, W. O. (2015). Relationships between teacher value orientations, collegiality, and collaboration in school professional learning communities. *Social Psychology of Education, 18*(2), 337–354.

Peng, Y. (2017). *On development and reform of community colleges in the United States.* East China Normal University.

Schmoker, M. (2004). Learning communities at the crossroads: Toward the best schools we've ever had. *Phi Delta Kappan, 86*(1), 84–88.

Shi, Y., & Zhuo, S. (2005). *Community Education and Learning community.* China Social Press.

Tobias, R. (2009). Is adult and community education for active citizenship important for community engagement by government? *Adult Learning Aotearoa New Zealand, 37*(1), 16–26.

Volunteering Australia. (2007). *Practical Guide: Involving volunteers from diverse cultural and language backgrounds in your organisation.* https://www.volunteeringaustralia.org/wp-content/files_mf/1377046067VAPracticalGuideInvolvingvolunteersfromCALDbackgrounds2007.pdf

Whelan, R. J. (1990). Education of students with behavior disorders: Theories and practices. *National Forum of Special Education Journal, 1*(1) 11–17.

Wilson, A. (2016). From professional practice to practical leader: Teacher leadership in professional learning communities. *International Journal of Teacher Leadership, 7*(2), 45–62.

Zhang, P. (2007). The adult education laws of France and the enlightenment to our Country. *Adult Education, 3,* 87–88.

Zhang, W. (1990). *Introduction to world adult education.* Beijing Publishing House.

SECTION III

ENVIRONMENTAL SUSTAINABILITY AND ADULT EDUCATION

CHAPTER 16

LEARNING TO RECREATE THE WORLD

Adult Education for Environmental Sustainability

Wendy Griswold
University of Memphis, United States

Humanity is overdue for a global shift in our worldview when it comes to the relationships between humans and nature. This relationship should recognize the limits of our environment and guide us in developing approaches to guarantee that we both stay within our limits and that all beings have a healthy environment and access to the resources they need to thrive. We have the knowledge to address our environmental problems; we know the science and we have the technology. What we lack is the will, the motivation, the determination to implement the solutions (Gore, 2019). This is where adult education has a crucial role to play in facilitating this transformation in our collective mindset (Griswold, 2017a; McDonald, 2006; Milana et al., 2016). As stewards and creators of a body of knowledge on adult development, perspective transformation and adult learning, adult educators are well positioned to help people learn to recreate our world into one that values its natural and human resources. But what does adult

Advancing the Global Agenda for Human Rights, Vulnerable Populations, and Environmental Sustainability: Adult Education as Strategic Partner, pp. 259–276

learning in such a context look like, and how can adult educators support these efforts?

What follows is a brief overview of the global environmental issues facing us and the 50-year history of the global conversation toward sustainable development. This conversation informed the development of the United Nations Sustainable Development Goals (UN SDGs), adopted by all UN member countries in 2015. Achieving these goals will require global change. Being able to make these changes requires EfS (Seddon, 2016), which is an education that prepares people to be far-seeing enough, flexible enough, and wise enough to contribute to the regenerative capacity of the physical and social systems upon which they depend (Meadows et al., 1992). Many people in many places are already participating in EfS.

Drawing from my research and practice in EFS, this chapter continues by highlighting the insights, wisdom, and truths from EfS learners, situated in several adult education contexts such as community, informal, and higher education. These include possible avenues for broadening adult education practice to support EfS, such as ensuring that learner's environmental experiences and contexts are acknowledged as sources of wisdom; focusing on informal science learning to support democratic rule; making clear connections between environmental, economic and social equity; increasing the use of participatory practices, and understanding the complexity of the issues and solutions required to achieve the UN SDGs.

This chapter concludes with policy implications that will help ensure that our reach toward sustainability has a greater chance of succeeding. There are two policy implications for achieving the UN SDGs that the adult education field can play a role in: participatory processes for developing partnerships and informal learning around science, technology, engineering, and mathematics (STEM). Partnerships are essential to achieving the UN SDGs, and progress toward developing the types of partnerships needed is stagnating (Stibbe et al., 2019). We also need to create increased opportunities and support for informal STEM learning. Educating and involving the public in STEM learning and decision-making is an investment we can no longer afford not to make.

A GLOBAL CONVERSATION

Some of us have lives where environmental contamination and threats are invisible and thus not readily apparent to us. Many of us do not, and those numbers will increase as climate change becomes more disruptive. Until very recently, 2050 was the predicted year for when we would be living in an ecosystem that is uncomfortable at best and hostile to our survival at worst (Intergovernmental Panel on Climate Change, 2014). At the end of

2019, several researchers and the United Nations concluded that climate change is accelerating at a faster rate than predicted (Fountain, 2019). In April 2020, a group of international researchers reported that large areas of ecosystems are on track to collapse abruptly before 2030 (Trisos et al., 2020).

To address the approaching crises, the United Nations adopted 17 goals that, if reached, would significantly move us toward global sustainability. They focus on addressing social, economic, and environmental inequities and are an urgent call to action worldwide (United Nations [UN], n.d.-b). The UN SDGs are the culmination of several decades of conversation, concern, and research on the environment and human impact upon it. The first Earth Day in 1970 and the 1972 UN Conference on the Human Environment in Stockholm, Sweden, marked the beginning of this global conversation. By the 1992 UN Conference on Environment and Development in Rio De Janeiro, Brazil, our understanding and ability to address environmental threats had developed significantly. Most participating nations had established environmental agencies, and scientific and technological understanding of the human impacts on the environment had grown tremendously (Conca & Dabelko, 2010).

Scientists, economists, and public health experts have been sounding the alarm about climate change since the 1970s, but global leadership has by-and-large continuously declined to take serious action (Rich, 2018). In the intervening years, scientists have continued to collect data and conduct research that further illuminates the threat of climate change on humans and the environment and have developed technological solutions. We are now at the point where we have the scientific and technological knowledge to implement solutions, but in many countries, leaders still lack the political will to institute significant changes (Gore, 2019). "To make the shift away from carbon to non-carbon energy sources, we need to change beliefs and perceptions and foster mind sets that facilitate the transition. Energy infrastructure by itself will not result in the appropriate changes" (UNESCO, 2015, p. 28).

To push for a sustainable world, centered around economic, environmental, and social equity, how we think about and utilize education must change. The United Nations calls for

> a learning process (or approach to teaching) based on the ideals and principles that underlie sustainability ... concerned with all levels and types of learning to provide quality education and foster sustainable human development —learning to know, learning to be, learning to live together, learning to do and learning to transform oneself and society. (UNESCO, 2017, as cited in Pedersen, 2017, p. 682)

The time for business as usual has come to an end. To paraphrase poet Audre Lorde, we cannot tear down the master's house using the master's tools (Lorde, 1984). It is time for us to arm ourselves with new tools, and EfS can facilitate their development.

EDUCATION FOR SUSTAINABILITY

If we approach the concept of sustainability as "the possibility that human and other life will flourish on the planet forever" (Ehrenfeld, 2008, p. 49), we must recognize that humanity's current ways of being are moving us further away from this possibility. To move ourselves toward a sustainable world, we require learning philosophies and lived practices that "prepare people to be far-seeing enough, flexible enough, and wise enough to contribute to the regenerative capacity of the physical and social systems upon which they depend" (Meadows et al., 1992, p. 209). This is EfS, and it should lead us toward figuring out "how to fundamentally change the social conditions which have led to environmental degradation" (Räthzel & Uzzell, 2009, pp. 264-265). EfS should equip learners with a systemic understanding of our planet and humanity's relationship with it. This learning needs to be lifelong and life-wide, necessitating its infusion in formal, nonformal, and informal contexts (Blewitt, 2006). EfS should be transformative and lead us to perspectives and actions that incorporate planet-wide consideration of impacts and outcomes (O'Sullivan & Taylor, 2004). Ideally, it should blend content and skill knowledge (instrumental learning) with new perspectives on the relationship of humanity to the universe (transformative learning) and the ability to subvert the dominant paradigm (emancipatory learning) to bring about the changes needed to create systems that are just, equitable, and kind to all the species inhabiting the earth (Papenfuss et al., 2019).

What follows is a look at EfS through the experiences and wisdom of five different learners. People in many places and spaces are participating in learning to recreate the world. Each has different motivations and experiences, and they represent engagement with EfS in formal, nonformal, and informal realms. Their learning is connected to a variety of practices and theories that we should look to for guidance in further developing adult focused EfS theory and practice, including local knowledge, informal science learning, equity, participatory action research, and contemplative education. Each of their learning contexts has implications for the future of adult learning that will lead us toward a sustainable and equitable world. The learners introduced below are identified by pseudonyms; their quotes are from interviews and documents collected via various research projects.

Climate Justice: Incorporating Local Knowledge to Improve Human and Environmental Health

Estrella lives in Chicago. A former Marine, she and her family live in a historically mixed Latinx and Eastern European immigrant neighborhood. The neighborhood is nestled among industrial activity, such as petroleum coke storage piles, asphalt recyclers, and other activities that contribute to an unhealthy environment. Many of her neighbors suffer the health impacts of breathing polluted air, such as respiratory ailments, strokes, and heart disease (Erickson et al., 2017). To help communities understand the air quality impacts of these activities and to engage residents in developing action to respond to threats to their local air quality, several community-based environmental advocacy organizations participated in an air quality monitoring research project using low-cost air monitors (Griswold, 2017b). Estrella was a participant, joining a team of volunteer monitors who, during a humid summer and frigid winter, walked set routes in their neighborhood for three weeks each season, collecting air quality data and noting possible pollution sources. The overall aim of the UN SDGs are to achieve climate justice. The types of activities Estrella and her neighbors participated in represent learning toward UN SDG 3: Good health and well-being, which seeks to "ensure healthy lives and promote well-being" and 13: Climate action, which calls for taking "urgent action to combat climate change and its impacts" (UN, n.d.b). When I asked Estrella what she hoped to learn by participating in this work, she responded, "I have a brain tumor, and I'm wondering if where I live contributed to that."

Estrella provides us with a very stark reminder that many people live in places that are not environmentally healthy, and poor environmental health translates directly to poor human health. Communities with a high number of people of color and/or economically challenged residents often experience environmental injustice, which means they have a dispropor-tionate share of environmental burdens (Katz, 2012). According to Robert Bullard, considered the father of the environmental justice movement,

> Zip code is still the most potent predictor of an individual's health and well-being. Individuals who physically live on the "wrong side of the tracks" are subjected to elevated environmental health threats and more than their fair share of preventable diseases. (Bullard, 2018, para. 1)

Addressing environmental inequity requires that communities experi-encing it are full participants in crafting solutions and approaches. Local knowledge is often crucial to understanding the socio-environmental con-text of a problem. However, crafting workable solutions require full and genuine participation (Corburn, 2005). Local knowledge is "practical, collective, and strongly rooted in a particular place," resulting in an "organized body of thought based on immediacy of experience" (Geertz, 1983, as cited in Corburn, 2005, p. 48). Incorporating local knowledge and lived experience into community learning about science and technology and local environmental concerns results in new cocreated knowledge, which in turn can inform action and advocacy efforts to address environmental justice issues (Corburn, 2005). Opening ourselves and our institutions to acknowledging and incorporating local knowledge will help move toward UN SDG 16: Peace, justice and strong institutions. This goal seeks to "promote peaceful and inclusive societies for sustainable development, provide access to justice for all and build effective, accountable and inclusive institutions at all levels" (UN, n.d.b).

An issue with accessing local knowledge for environmental solutions often lies with traditional (business as usual) practices that do not allow or value local knowledge and the people who hold it. For adult educators, the intersection of community and scientific/technical knowledge is a space in which we can be of immense service and value. Our role here is twofold. We can serve as on-the-ground mediators between technical and community experts and ensure equitable processes honoring all sources of knowledge are used. We can also direct our efforts toward training scientists and technical experts in our practices and traditions. Achieving the UN SDGs will require opening the realm of science to a broader base of participants and sources of knowledge than have traditionally been allowed.

Democratizing Science Through Informal Learning

Calum is an informal science educator. He develops and delivers programming for public audiences, primarily using astrobiology to connect learners to global environmental issues and local actions. These types of activities help engage the public in UN SDG 13: Climate action using the possibility of life on other planets as a hook toward learning about and taking care of life on our planet. He is a sustainability-minded young professional, and his career has now bridged two U.S. presidential administrations. He has witnessed the shift from an administration that improved environmental and human heath using science as a basis for decision-making to one that seemingly rejects the role of science in governing. When I asked him what he has learned from leading informal science programs, he said

> Scientific literacy is necessary so people can pursue environmentally conscious policy decisions. You see that with the anti-science attitudes right

now in our government and what they are doing to our policies. If we had a better educated populace, it'd be harder to elect people like that.

Environmental challenges can have an impact on human health, economic resiliency and vitality, and community strength and well-being (Brunekreef & Holgate, 2002; Shy & Finklea, 1973). Communities need to understand the science and technology surrounding the environmental challenges that affect their neighborhoods, which will be exacerbated by climate change. They need to be informed decision-makers when developing or advocating policies to address these challenges and electing representatives responsible for enacting and enforcing policy. This is especially important for environmental justice communities, where the most vulnerable segments of our populations reside. We need to critically question why those currently in power in many countries seek to downplay and diminish science and scientists. Democratizing science and opening participation and cultivating interest through informal science learning is essential for creating a world that is truly sustainable and equitable.

Informal learning, particularly when rooted in our everyday lived experiences, is becoming recognized as a crucial facet of EfS, despite being insufficiently researched and not well documented (Blewitt, 2006; Garrecht et al., 2018). This is a key area for contribution from adult education researchers and practitioners. What would be most helpful toward these efforts is helping learners connect global environmental, economic, and social equity issues to their everyday lived experiences, struggles and concerns, such as connecting localized flooding events to climate change (Blewitt, 2006). This (dis)connection is slowing EfS progress (Seddon, 2016) and preventing us from recognizing the inherent inequities in our current approaches to addressing our shared challenges. However, bringing personal relevance to big ideas is a phenomenon endemic to adult education

Solutions That Work for All: The Intersections of the Environment, Society, and Economy

Caleb works for a nonprofit organization that addresses food insecurity, directly contributing toward progress on UN SDG 2: Zero hunger, which strives to "end hunger, achieve food security and improved nutrition and promote sustainable agriculture" (UN, n.d.b). When I interviewed him about his experiences as a sustainability-minded young professional, he was serving as an associate director charged with providing training for anti-hunger organizations nation-wide on best practices in anti-hunger and anti-poverty solutions. In discussing his learning about food insecurity and global sustainability through his professional and informal learning, he shared what he considered to be a key learning outcome: "If we have a solution that is not a solution for everyone, then we have to rethink it. That is basically what equity is all about."

Economic, social, and environmental equity for ALL must be the standard for a sustainable world and the UN SDGs are designed to move us toward that reality. Moving toward equity for all requires us to have a better understanding of the intersections of the environment, society, and economics, both in terms of their interrelationships and the intertangled inequities infecting them. These are not separate, independent realms, but nested, interdependent relationships. The environment is that space in which the social and the economic reside. Without a healthy, stable environment, a society could not exist. Society in turn is what necessitates the need for economy. Allowing inequity to flourish has made it easy for those with economic power to dominate the decision-making around how we utilize our natural and human resources, which is currently exploitative and extractive. Let us learn together to create economies that sustain societies and societies that in turn sustain our environments.

For too long, we have been locked into the mindset that a healthy environment comes at the price of a healthy economy, forcing us to sacrifice human and environmental health to maintain an inequitable economic system. The job of adult educators concerned with reducing inequity (UN SDG 10) is to counter this false dichotomy. We need to help learners uncover the intersections of the environment, society, and economy in their own lives and the lives of others around the globe, with a focus on who benefits from our current inequitable systems. By gaining clarity on these relationships and the institutionalized inequities currently within them, we will uncover the ways to dismantle them and build just economic and social structures that sustain the environment. The use of participatory processes can provide mechanisms for this kind of learning to proliferate.

Participatory Processes Supporting Collaborative Learning and Decision-Making

Ella is an advocate for solar energy, focusing her work toward achieving UN SDG 7: Affordable and clean energy, which is concerned with "ensuring access to affordable, reliable, sustainable, and modern energy for all" (UN, n.d.b). She continues to develop her role through formal and non-formal educational experiences, which include involvement in community solar energy projects as an undergraduate and earning a master's degree in public policy with an emphasis on sustainable development. She also spent two years as a Department of Energy fellow tasked with promoting solar energy grants to communities in several states across the United States.

Her learning outcomes from that experience included transforming her attitude toward politics and its role in creating sustainable societies. She shared,

> I did not care about politics until the last two years … I thought it was worthless actually, but now I realize that my views on sustainability have changed to governmental action. Individual action is great, but we really need to push government either through research, through our voices, or even writing the policies for them.

It is time we—especially those of us steeped in Western identities—release ourselves from privileging the individual over the collective, particularly regarding governance and policy decisions. Such perspectives serve only to isolate us from each other, which not only dilutes the power of a collective voice but also prevents us from making decisions and changes that benefit us collectively, perpetuating the practices that now threaten our existence. "The individual benefits as an individual from [the] ability to deny the truth even though society as a whole, of which [one] is a part, suffers" (Hardin, 2010, p 39). We will not achieve the UN SDGs as individuals; it requires a collective approach.

Community education, which is education with and for communities (Tett, 2010), is an approach that can help facilitate the shift toward collective thought and action. While these practices have many names—participatory action research, community-based participatory action research, community-based learning, and research—their common elements include a focus on usefulness, employ diverse methods, and emphasize collaboration (Stoecker, 2013). Making such practices the norm will help us to give voice to marginalized peoples, helping us to also address UN SDG 5: Gender equity, which entails "achieving gender equity and empowering all women and girls" (U.N., n.d.b) and UN SDG 10: Reducing inequity wherein we will "reduce inequity within and among countries" (UN, n.d.b). Infusing these approaches throughout the movement toward sustainability will also equip broader segments of the public with the tools necessary for wide-scale empowerment and agency not only to demand social, economic, and environmental justice but also to participate in research to identify local solutions to global problems. In turn, this will lead us toward policy solutions that have a much better chance at serving all of us, rather than just some of us.

Our role as adult educators is to infuse community and participatory processes throughout our practice and teaching. This body of knowledge should be a fundamental component of every formally trained adult educator. It is the heritage left to us by Myles Horton and still employed by the Highlander Research and Education Center. I challenge adult educators to incorporate a community educator identity into their self-concepts and recognize that we each have "an important role to play in assisting communities to understand, operate within, and challenge their political environment" (Tett, 2010, p. 90). The use of participatory learning processes can also aid learners in navigating the complexity of achieving the UN SDGs, as making room for multiple perspectives is needed to both explore problems and develop solutions. Contemplative education practices are means to develop skill in navigating complexity.

Contemplation on Complexity and Systems-Thinking

Alison is an adult education doctoral student and a talent management professional focusing on recruiting health professionals for government programs, which contributes to UN SDG 3: good health and well-being. As part of a course on global education, she participated in contemplative reading and writing about *Rethinking Education*, a UNESCO publication on the role of education and learning in sustainability. Derived from *lectio divina* (divine reading), the practice "is a method of deep reading, study and reflection, leading students to a transformative experience" (Keator, 2018, p. 10). In a class discussion, she shared this insight: "We haven't been taught how to intellectually navigate the complexity of our current lives."

Education for Sustainability is an evolving pedagogy, in both practice and theory. Learning to recreate the world requires meaning making and knowledge creation that is both emancipatory and transformative (Papenfuss et al., 2019), which can be difficult to accomplish. Such learning, particularly in formal contexts like higher education or nonformal government-funded programs, is often constrained by institutions, which are generally resistant to change. Adult educators must counter this by creating opportunities for learners in all settings to challenge "institutional and classroom authority that can lead to shifts in power" (Papenfuss et al., 2019, p, 10). It is practice with exactly these types of experiences and skills future leaders and decision-makers need.

Adult educators must make space for deep emancipatory and transformative learning around economic, social, and environmental sustainability issues for positive change to occur. The relationships between economic, social, and environmental injustices are complex and intertangled, forming a system of oppression within which the bulk of the world's human population resides. The UN SDGs are also complex and interdependent of each other. Absorbing, processing, and gaining clarity about all of this is not an easy task. Creating and experimenting with possible solutions is even harder. Adult educators can make space for this work. It is less about adding more content and more about making space for connections to be made and new ways of thinking about being to emerge. Modeling complex, interdependent, and critical thinking for our learners is another important support function of the adult educator, as well as designing scaffolded tasks that provide opportunities to build foundational skills that will culminate in higher order skills.

One pathway toward this is the use of contemplative education. Contemplative education practices, particularly those seeking to facilitate "connection between our internal lives and environmental degradation" (Wapner, 2016, p. 67), are useful in formal, nonformal and informal learning contexts. According to Barbezat and Bush (2014), the benefits of contemplative practices include increased concentration and attention; improved mental health and psychological well-being; increased connection, generosity, and loving kindness; deepened understanding of learning content; and increased creativity and insight. A burgeoning body of research on the use of contemplative practices support these claims, all of which support both transformative and emancipatory learning, as well as EfS (Papenfuss et al., 2019). Tapping into the interconnected nature of our individual and collective existence, accessing the deep wells of compassion that reside in each of us, and questioning and gaining clarity on what we actually need versus what we desire and think we deserve is crucial to creating a sustainable future for all. This is how we will harness the will to articulate and demand change. Doing this for ourselves is the first step. The second is helping our learners along the same path. Third is developing their capacity to, in turn, help their learners. This is how we adult educators will help recreate the world. While our actions as individuals can help support movement toward the UN SDGs, we must also engage in collective advocacy to develop policy that supports our individual practices.

POLICY IMPLICATIONS FOR ACHIEVING SUSTAINABLE DEVELOPMENT GOALS

Two policy implications that the adult education field can contribute to and advocate for with respect toward achieving the UN SDGs are the development of partnerships that utilize participatory processes and increased opportunities for informal STEM learning. Participatory processes can facilitate the development of the types of partnerships needed to reach the UN SDGs. Informal STEM learning can prepare learners to participate in decision-making, advocacy, and policy development that will lead to environmental, social, and economic equity.

Participatory Processes and Partnerships

Partnerships are recognized as the means by which the UN SDGs will be achieved. It is Goal 17: Strengthen the means of implementation and revitalize the Global Partnership for Sustainable Development. "Goal 17 further seeks to encourage and promote effective public, public-private and civil society partnerships, building on the experience and resourcing strategies of partnerships" (United Nations, n.d.-a). Such partnerships need to be characterized by cooperative, integrated efforts that pool financial resources, knowledge and expertise (UN, n.d.-a).

A 2019 report on UN SDG partnerships noted that so far, such partnerships are not the norm, and there are no mechanisms in place to develop the needed scale of such partnerships. Existing partnerships are not as effective as they need to be, likely because they are not run in effective and efficient manners or they do not use approaches aligned with the context (Stibbe et al., 2019). Achieving the UN SDGs requires a "fundamental shift in thinking, explicitly acknowledging the interconnectedness of prosperous business, a thriving society and a healthy environment" and will "require an unprecedented level of cooperation and collaboration among civil society, business, government, NGOs, foundations and others for their achievement" (Stibbe et al., 2019, p. 6).

The partnerships needed to meet UN SDGs are transformative, meaning they are created with the intent of making systemic change through innovation and multifaceted approaches (Stibbe et al., 2019). These partnerships will be charged with finding their way through

> a complex environment, where the problem definition may be unclear, and partners bring differing world views and perspectives to the issue. The problem and path to follow to address must be negotiated with the different stakeholders. Partners will need to iterate and adapt to collectively find a solution that is feasible and politically acceptable to all. (Stibbe et al., 2019, p. 8)

This is a clarion call to make participatory processes the norm for partnerships, at least for the types of partnerships expected to be transformative and produce outcomes that are significant departures from business as usual. We need to promote and advocate for the use of participatory processes in as many places as we can. Using the generative and iterative processes common to participatory strategies, partners will participate in meaning making, constructing new understandings derived from their collaborative learning experiences (Bandura, 1976; Vygotsky, 1978). Educational policy is a place we can start, as "policy dialogue to define educational goals must be participatory and inclusive. Curriculum policy and content must both be guided by the principles of social and economic justice, equality and environmental responsibility" (UNESCO, 2015, p. 42).

However, we cannot stop at the border of educational policy. Rather, we must push for participatory processes throughout local, state, national, and international governance as well as civil society. Opportunities to utilize collaborative decision-making and knowledge-creation opportunities will also create a path for the inclusion of voices and interests most commonly marginalized in traditional partnership models. Their use

> involves identifying and stressing areas of commonality and the creative development of links and alliances between groups that might otherwise see themselves as being in competition. It also involves recognizing the rights of those who experience problems to define appropriate solutions and campaign for their implementation often against the vested interests of the powerful. (Tett, 2010, p. 90)

Increased use of participatory processes is also useful to informal STEM learning, particularly to facilitate the involvement of underrepresented populations.

Informal STEM Learning

Humans have been practicing and benefitting from science, technology, engineering, and mathematics (STEM) for millennia. Our modern lives are heavily reliant upon STEM fields and their resulting innovations, from the computers that power much of our work and entertainment to the vaccines that save our lives. An increasingly complex and technical world that aspires toward democratic rule as a norm requires a higher level of STEM knowledge among the populous than we currently have in many nations. We also must address the inequities in the STEM professions to expand the perspectives of these fields for improved human and environmental health outcomes. There are many populations who are underrepresented in both decision-making involving environmental and STEM-related issues as well as in STEM careers (Bevan et al., 2018). Several studies have identified challenges and barriers that prevent underrepresented groups from participating in STEM learning, which include inadequate school STEM instruction, lack of identification with STEM or STEM careers, and unfamiliarity with specialized language (National Research Council [NRC], 2009). These two pressing issues can be addressed in tandem through informal STEM learning at the community level that is driven by and focused on learner issues, interests, and concerns. Moreover, more opportunities, increased participation, and more research in informal STEM learning are needed. Connecting informal learning opportunities to skills that environmental justice communities can use to improve their economic opportunities is an issue ripe for exploration.

Broadly speaking, informal learning "takes place outside of a dedicated learning environment and arises from the activities and interests of individuals or groups ... in a wide range of social contexts through families, workplaces, communities, and leisure activities" (Golding, 2011, p. 104). Informal STEM learning is "learner-motivated, guided by learner interests, voluntary, personal, ongoing, contextually-relevant, collaborative, non-linear, and open-ended" (NRC, 2009, p. 11). Informal STEM learning presents an opportunity to focus learners' natural curiosity about their interests with new understandings about science and technology to create new meaning and knowledge about their individual and community-lived realities.

It is crucial that informal STEM learning be rooted in participatory processes, as that ensures learning and solutions are informed by local knowledge that is relevant to learners' lives and interests. Community residents motivated to participate in informal STEM learning bring local, lived experience about the neighborhood and its environmental threats and challenges. The use of participatory informal STEM learning will result in learning that honors local knowledge and places STEM learning in the hands of communities. Engaging in STEM learning that is reflective of their lived experience and honors local knowledge (their own and that of their community and culture) helps to develop their personal STEM identities (Stake & Mares, 2005). This is an opportunity for community-based learning about how science and technology can be utilized to develop and advocate for policy change to address environmental challenges. This process will also help create the next generation of decision-makers with higher levels of STEM literacy and interest in STEM careers.

Informal STEM learning is happening, but more opportunities are needed. While a lot of valuable research has been conducted and incorporated, the field could use an infusion of adult learning theory and practice. This would improve the learning experiences of adults and guide the use of participatory practices. The potential of informal STEM learning for developing and advocating for policy change to address environmental challenges is a recognized yet underresearched phenomenon (Igalla et al., 2019; NRC, 2009). Adult educators, particularly those with significant interest and experience with informal learning, have a great deal to contribute to this process.

CONCLUSION

The UN SDGs are the culmination of decades of research, conversation, and education about the impacts of humans on their environment. Achieving the

UN SDGs requires an educational shift in how we humans learn to recreate our world to be environmentally, socially, and economically sustainable for current and future generations. Education for sustainability is developing as the framework for this learning challenge. To facilitate and support adult learning around EfS, adult educators can both influence the development of EfS by infusing our knowledge and traditions into existing EfS practices as well as bringing EfS into the learning spaces that we inhabit. Possible adult learning practices relevant to the challenge include the incorporation of local knowledge, informal learning, addressing inequity, participatory practices and helping learners navigate complexity. We can also engage and advocate for policies that prioritize truly participatory partnership development and increase opportunities for engaging in informal STEM learning. We, as adult educators, have a major role to play in EfS. We are the stewards of the wisdom of how to make change and how to develop strong learners and leaders who can demand and create change. We are the ones who develop learners who are far-seeing … flexible … and wise.

REFERENCES

Bandura, A. (1976). Modeling theory. In W. S. Sahakian (Ed.), *Learning: Systems, models, and theories* (2nd ed., pp. 391–409). Rand McNally.

Barbezat, D. P., & Bush, M. (2014). *Contemplative practices in higher education: Powerful methods to transform teaching and learning.* Jossey-Bass.

Bevan, B., Calabrese Barton, A., & Garibay, C. (2018). *Broadening perspectives on broadening participation in STEM.* Center for Advancement of Informal Science Education.

Blewitt, J. (2006). *The ecology of learning: Sustainability, lifelong learning and everyday life.* Earthscan.

Brunekreef, B., & Holgate, S. T. (2002). Air pollution and health. *The Lancet, 360*(934), 1233–1242.

Bullard, R. (2018). *Learn about environmental justice.* https://drrobertbullard.com/learn-about-environmental-justice/

Conca, K., & Dabelko, G. D. (Eds.). (2010). *Green planet blues: Four decades of global environmental politics* (4th ed.). Westview Press.

Corburn, J. (2005). *Street science: Community knowledge and environmental health justice.* The MIT Press.

Ehrenfeld, J. R. (2008). *Sustainability by design.* Yale University Press.

Erickson, L. E., Griswold, W., Maghirang, R. G., & Urbaszewski, B. P. (2017). Air quality, health, and community action. *Journal of Environmental Protection, 8*(10), 1057–1074. https://doi.org/10.4236/jep.2017.810067

Fountain, H. (2019, December 4). Climate change is accelerating, bringing world 'dangerously close' to irreversible change. *New York Times.* https://www.nytimes.com/2019/12/04/climate/climate-change-acceleration.html?searchResultPosition=2

Garrecht, C., Bruckermann, T., & Harms, U. (2018). Students' decision-making in education for sustainability-related extracurricular activities—A systematic review of empirical studies. *Sustainability, 10,* 3876. https://doi.org/10.3390/su10113876

Golding, B. G. (2011). Social, local, and situated: Recent findings about the effectiveness of older men's informal learning in community contexts. *Adult Education Quarterly, 61*(2), 103–120.

Gore, A. (2019, September 20). The climate crisis is the battle of our times, and we can win. *New York Times.* https://www.nytimes.com/2019/09/20/opinion/al-gore-climate-change.html?searchResultPosition=1

Griswold, W. (2017a). Sustainability, ecojustice, and adult education. In A. Dentith, & W. Griswold (Eds.), *Special Issue: Ecojustice adult education: Theory and practice. New directions for adult and continuing education, 153* (pp. 7–15). Wiley Periodicals.

Griswold, W. (2017b). Breathing together: Learning locally to address air quality globally. In M. Boucouvalas, & M. Avoseh (Eds.), *Proceedings of the 2017 International Pre-conference* (pp. 107–118). Commission for International Adult Education of the American Association for Adult and Continuing Education.

Hardin, G. (2010). The tragedy of the commons. In K. Conca, & G. D. Dabelko (Eds.), *Green planet blues: Four decades of global environmental politics* (4th ed., pp. 38–45). Westview Press.

Igalla, M., Edelenbos, J., & van Meerkerk, I. (2019). Citizens in action, what do they accomplish? A systematic literature review of citizen initiatives, their main characteristics, outcomes, and factors. *VOLUNTAS: International Journal of Voluntary and Nonprofit Organizations, 30,* 1176–1194. https://doi.org/10.1007/s11266-019-00129-0

Intergovernmental Panel on Climate Change. (2014). *Climate change 2014: Synthesis report. Contribution of working groups I, II and III to the fifth assessment report of the Intergovernmental Panel on Climate Change* [Core Writing Team, R. K. Pachauri & L.A. Meyer (Eds.)]. IPCC.

Katz, C. (2012, November 1). Unequal exposures: People in poor, non-white neighborhoods breathe more hazardous particles. *Scientific American.* https://www.scientificamerican.com/article/people-poor-neighborhoods-breathe-more-hazardous-particles/

Keator, M. (2018). *Lectio divina as contemplative pedagogy: Re-appropriating monastic practice for the humanities.* Routledge.

Lorde, A. (1984). The master's tools will never dismantle the master's house. *Sister outsider: Essays and speeches.* Crossing Press.

McDonald, B. (2006). Adult education on the environmental margin. In S. Merriam, B. C. Courtenay, & R. M. Cervero (Eds.), *Global issues and adult education: Perspectives from Latin America, Southern Africa, and the United States* (pp. 278–290). Jossey-Bass.

Meadows, D. H., Meadows, D. L., & Randers, J. (1992). *Beyond the limits: Global collapse or a sustainable future.* Earthscan.

Milana, M., Rasmussen, P., & Holford, J. (2016). The role of adult education and learning in fostering societal sustainability. *International Review of Education, 62,* 523–540. https://doi.org/10.1007/s11159-016-9588-z

National Research Council. (2009). *Learning science in informal environments: People, places, and pursuits.* The National Academies Press. https://doi.org/10.17226/12190

O'Sullivan, E., & Taylor, M. (2004). *Learning toward an ecological consciousness: Selected transformative practices.* Palgrave Macmillan.

Papenfuss, J., Merritt, E., Manuel-Navarrete, D., Cloutier, S., & Eckhard, B. (2019). Interacting pedagogies: A review and framework for sustainability education. *Journal of Sustainability Education, 20.*

Pedersen, K. W. (2017). Supporting collaborative and continuing professional development in education for sustainability through a communities of practice approach. *International Journal of Sustainability in Higher Education, 18*(5), 681–696.

Räthzel, N., & Uzzell, D. (2009). Transformative environmental education: A collective rehearsal for reality. *Environmental Education Research, 15*(3), 263–277.

Rich, N. (2018, August 1). Loosing earth: The decade we almost stopped climate change. *New York Times Magazine.* https://www.nytimes.com/interactive/2018/08/01/magazine/climate-change-losing-earth.html?searchResultPosition=3

Seddon, T. (2016). Sustainable development and social learning: Re-contextualizing the space of orientation. *International Review of Education, 62*, 563–586. https://doi.org/10.1007/s11159-016-9592-3

Shy, C. M., & Finklea, J. F. (1973). Air pollution affects community health. *Environmental Science & Technology, 7*(3), 204–208.

Stake, J. E., & Mares, K. R. (2005). Evaluating the impact of science-enrichment programs on adolescents' science motivation and confidence: The splashdown effect. *Journal of Research in Science Teaching, 42*(4), 359–375.

Stibbe, D. T., Reid, S., & Gilbert, J. (2019). *Maximizing the impact of partnerships for the SDGs.* The Partnering Initiative and UN DESA. https://sustainabledevelopment.un.org/index.php?page=view&type=400&nr=2564&menu=35

Stoecker, R. (2013). *Research methods for community change: A project-based approach.* SAGE.

Tett, L. (2010). *Community education, learning and development.* Dunedin Academic Press.

Trisos, C. H., Merow, C., & Pigot, A. L. (2020). The projected timing of abrupt ecological disruption from climate change. *Nature.* https://doi.org/10.1038/s41586-020-2189-9

UNESCO. (2015). *Rethinking education: Towards a global common good?* United Nations.

UNESCO. (2017). *Improving measurement of gender equality in STEM.* Gender and Science. http://www.unesco.org/new/en/natural-sciences/priority-areas/gender-and-science/improving-measurement-of-gender-equality-in-stem/

United Nations (n.d.-a). *Multi-stakeholder partnerships and voluntary commitments.* https://sustainabledevelopment.un.org/sdinaction

United Nations. (n.d.-b). *Sustainable development goals.* https://sdgs.un.org/goals

Vygotsky, L. S. (1978). *Mind in society: The development of higher psychological processes.* Harvard University Press.

Wapner, P. (2016). Contemplative environmental studies: Pedagogy for self and planet. *Journal of Contemplative Inquiry, 3*(1), 67–83.

CHAPTER 17

CITIZEN SCIENCE

Adult Education for Environmental Sustainability and Conservation

Jill Zarestky and Lauren Vilen
Colorado State University, United States

Issues of conservation and sustainability are closely linked to the general public's understanding and buy-in of scientific findings and recommendations. Consider, for example, the Trump administration's U.S.-Mexico border wall, which could destroy sensitive ecosystems and skirt important environmental laws (Peters et al., 2018). Other examples include deforestation's unexpected consequences for human infectious diseases (Bloomfield et al., 2020), mining's impact on local economies, ecological systems, and indigenous communities (Pearson et al., 2019), and renewable energy industry growth (Penn, 2020).

Given the large number of sociopolitical activities with environmental impacts, it is critical to help the general public worldwide understand the scientific assessments and subsequent conservation implications of our behaviors and civic engagement. One way to help laypersons understand science and make better-informed personal and political choices is by providing opportunities for positive learning experiences grounded in current scientific knowledge and approaches to sustainability. UNESCO

Advancing the Global Agenda for Human Rights, Vulnerable Populations, and Environmental Sustainability: Adult Education as Strategic Partner, pp. 277–290
Copyright © 2021 by Information Age Publishing

(2016) recommended "Scientists, policy-makers, and societal leaders should strongly advocate for public awareness of science as a public good and for public understanding of scientific knowledge and methods" (p. 13). Yet, the means through which scientists and science educators reach the general public remain underexplored.

Certainly, many adults leverage the knowledge and skills gained through formal schooling, but in developed countries such as the United States, people spend less than five percent of their lives in school and even less in science class (Falk & Dierking, 2010). In nations with less educational infrastructure, there is even less science education. This worldwide lack of science learning opportunities creates fundamental challenges in helping people understand how human actions impact the natural environment and what we can collectively do to diminish those impacts. Participation in a contemporary, globalized society requires continued out-of-school science learning, and science learning directed at pressing societal issues, such as the United Nation's (UN) Sustainable Development Goals (SDGs; UN, 2015).

Sustainable Development Goals

One focus area of the SDGs is the health of the natural environment and mitigation of climate change. While sustainability and conservation are threaded throughout several specific SDGs, environmental concerns are most directly addressed in Goals 13, 14, and 15, calling for climate action and protection of "life below water" and "life on land," respectively:

> Goal 13. Take urgent action to combat climate change and its impacts.
>
> Goal 14. Conserve and sustainably use the oceans, seas, and marine resources for sustainable development.
>
> Goal 15. Protect, restore, and promote sustainable use of terrestrial ecosystems, sustainably manage forests, combat desertification, and halt and reverse land degradation and halt biodiversity loss (UN, 2015, p. 14).

To address these three SDGs, we need clear scientific understanding of the impacts of human actions and a means of bringing people into the scientific conversation and helping them to apply that science to their everyday lives.

Citizen Science

One way to help laypersons understand science and make better-informed personal and political choices is by providing opportunities for positive learning experiences grounded in current scientific knowledge and approaches to sustainability. One such opportunity is *citizen science*, in which "the public participates voluntarily in the scientific process, addressing real-world problems in ways that may include formulating research questions, conducting scientific experiments, collecting and analyzing data, interpreting results, making new discoveries, developing technologies and applications, and solving complex problems" (U.S. General Services Administration, 2020, para. 3). Through citizen science, learners are exposed to and interact with nature, science, and scientists, ideally building interest, understanding, and practice around issues of conservation and sustainability. Interacting with a scientist or STEM professional can result in positive learning outcomes such as increased interest in science (Bonney et al., 2009), key factors for motivation and transfer of learning.

In connection to the SDGs, this chapter presents and integrates three main topics: (a) adult science education, (b) the value and impact of citizen science projects worldwide, and (c) the contributions of adult education and citizen science to address issues of conservation and sustainability as indicated in the SDGs.

OVERVIEW OF ADULT SCIENCE EDUCATION

Lifelong and life-wide science learning means that individuals develop science-related understanding, appreciation, and identity through an accumulation of experiences and utilize different sources at different times based on personal relevancy and interest (Falk et al., 2007; Falk, Dierking et al., 2016). Consequently, most adults engage in science learning through free-choice environments outside of formal education and workplace contexts, such as visiting science centers and zoos, reading books and magazines, watching television, talking with friends and colleagues, and perusing the internet (Falk et al., 2007; Miller, 2010). Falk et al. (2007) described *free-choice learning* as settings where learning is voluntary, intrinsically motivated, and the learner has "a clear understanding of why, where, how and with whom it occurs" (p. 456). Free-choice learning encompasses the ubiquitous, informal learning that adults engage in through daily activities and facilitated, nonformal learning opportunities, such as extension programs.

Research on participation and science learning in free-choice contexts is growing but still primarily focuses on children (Falk & Dierking, 2019). The majority of studies attending to adult science learning are conducted at cultural institutions, such as museums (e.g., Sachatello-Sawyer et al., 2002) and science centers (e.g., Falk et al., 2016), where researchers explore why individuals visit these science-oriented venues and what and how they learn during their visit. For example, Falk et al. (2016) investigated the learning outcomes of science center visitors in 17 communities across Australia, Europe, North America, and South America. They found that individuals who visited science centers had a higher understanding, curiosity and interest, engagement, and identity related to science than individuals who did not visit science centers, even after accounting for prior interest, education level, and income. Less common are studies investigating participatory programs (e.g., Van Den Berg et al., 2011) or adult science learning predicated by a local environmental issue. For example, Shaughnessy et al. (2014) investigated the learning outcomes of a nonformal adult education course about shale gas development affecting the local community. Regardless of their original positions on shale gas development, participants reported increased scientific knowledge about the drilling process, a deeper understanding of scientific inquiry, heightened ability to be critical consumers of scientific information, greater confidence in sharing knowledge with others, and more frequent involvement in community events related to shale gas development (Shaughnessy et al., 2014). Although limited in scope, such localized studies complement macrolevel investigations and contribute to understanding how adults interact with and incorporate scientific knowledge into their lives and the contextual factors that support meaningful learning experiences.

Individual motivations to seek out and participate in free-choice science learning reflect the varied interests and needs of adults, such as membership in civic and social clubs, hobbies, family activities, intellectual curiosity, investment in social or ethical issues, and experiences that necessitate the need for information and problem-solving (e.g., Heimlich & Horr, 2010; Van Den Berg et al., 2009). Additionally, an adult's social role, developmental stage, and temporal identity have a powerful influence on motivation and learning outcomes, with the result that "most people selectively utilize [free-choice] settings to build upon, reinforce and strengthen their own preferred, pre-existing science understandings" (Falk & Dierking, 2019, p. 3).

These findings support recent research that suggests connecting adults to science-related issues relevant to their lives can increase interest, engagement, and enjoyment in science, which in turn increases scientific competencies (Pan et al., 2018; Phillips et al., 2019) and enables adults to use evidence-based knowledge to address social and environmental issues encountered in daily life (Tsai et al., 2017). Additionally, Kluttz and Walter (2018) advocated for place-based and situated learning for mobilizing individuals and groups towards action and advocacy on science-related issues such as climate change. *Place-based learning* is rooted in a particular community or environment and aims to foster local stewardship (Sobel, 2004). *Situated learning* emphasizes learning's relational nature, where learners engage with content in context and make meaning through this dynamic interaction (Lave & Wenger, 1991). Both approaches emphasize context's importance for fostering science learning that is integrated with adults' lives and communities.

A free-choice framework utilizes an asset-based approach to adult science learning by leveraging personal interests and motivation to develop scientific competencies in specific content areas important to an individual based on their sociocultural context, education, beliefs, and circumstances (Falk & Dierking, 2019; Falk et al., 2007). An *asset-based approach* challenges the traditional deficient-perspective, which frames science learning as a prescriptive set of concepts learners need to acquire in order to be scientifically literate. Often these key concepts are established by policy makers for formal education systems and reflect academic disciplinary boundaries incongruent with the free-choice, situated, interdisciplinary, and cumulative nature of adult science learning (Falk & Dierking, 2019).

Consider gardening, a common activity worldwide that draws on life experiences and ongoing adult science learning. An individual's gardening knowledge might represent cumulative learning from assisting a family elder with their garden, school-based plant biology, internet research, personal observations, and other sources. These experiences incorporate multiple scientific disciplines (e.g., biology, ecology, chemistry) without the individual's awareness, because learning is integrated seamlessly as the individual develops a deeper understanding of gardening over time. One cannot pinpoint when or where a particular scientific concept was learned, highlighting the incongruency between the contextual and cumulative nature of adult science learning and national science literacy measures (e.g., the National Science Board's *Science and Engineering Indicators* or the European Union's *Eurobarometer*).

This incongruency illuminates the need to increase coherence between the motivations and predispositions of adult learners and the educational offerings and associated learning agendas established by free-choice science learning institutions and programs (Heimlich & Horr, 2010). An asset-based approach can leverage adult education theory and practices to support public engagement in addition to practical and civic science literacy (Shen, 1975). This approach emphasizes an individual's ability to find, ask, or determine answers to questions derived from everyday experiences and personal interests (National Research Council, 1996) and is "not *incidentally* but *fundamentally* about identifying relevance: learning to see how science is or could be significant to the things you care about most" ([Emphasis added] Feinstein, 2011, p. 180).

As one means of addressing the SDGs, an asset-based approach to adult science learning recognizes the situated sociocultural, political, and economic complexities of learners and communities. Similarly, sustainable development is defined within a particular community or region's context. Thus, the contextual dependence of both adult science learning and sustainable development presents an avenue for mutually reinforcing approaches to sustainability education.

VALUE AND IMPACT OF
CITIZEN SCIENCE PROJECTS WORLDWIDE

Citizen science comes in many forms; project design is influenced by the intended outcomes, location, geospatial scope, resources, and degree and quality of participation by individuals and communities. Shirk et al. (2012) defined *degree of participation* as the extent to which individuals are involved in the scientific research process and conceptualize the quality of participation as the extent to which the project's activities and goals align with, are relevant to, and respond to the interests and needs of the participants. Degrees of participation can range from data collection and minimal interactions with scientists to full participatory planning (Shirk et al., 2012). While all citizen science projects aim to contribute to scientific research and/or monitoring, considering the degree and quality of participation can help clarify the relationship between participants, scientists, and desired outcomes for science, individuals, and communities.

The value of citizen science projects is multifaceted and broad. For large-scale international monitoring initiatives, citizen science projects across the continents provide essential data and human capital needed to track progress toward global biodiversity targets (Chandler et al., 2017). Additionally, many citizen science projects make their data publicly available, which increases knowledge sharing among scientists and contributes to peer-reviewed publications that inform the scientific community more broadly (Theobald et al., 2015). Although citizen science is often focused on ecological research, the impacts and outcomes of projects have contributed to discoveries in diverse disciplines, including gender patterns in nature recreation activities (Cooper & Smith, 2010), novel galaxies and astronomical objects (Clery, 2011), and applied human computation (Newman, 2014).

At the regional and community level, citizen science projects have been shown to increase social-ecological resilience by improving the relationship between communities and management agencies, providing public access to data used to address environmental degradation, and fostering adaptive comanagement strategies that are responsive to stakeholder knowledge and values (Shirk et al., 2012). Furthermore, participation in local citizen science projects contributes to accelerated participatory conservation decisions where individuals, community groups, and government collaboratively address natural resource issues using locally gathered data (Danielsen et al., 2005; Reid et al., 2016). Citizen science data may also help democratize science by empowering communities to use local knowledge and evidence to challenge harmful environmental policies and industry regulations (Ottinger, 2010).

At the individual level, participation in citizen science projects contributes to science literacy by providing opportunities to engage in scientific thinking, the process of inquiry (Trumbull et al., 2000), develop content-specific skills, such as species identification, and engage in pro-environmental behaviors (Crall et al., 2013). Citizen science projects also create "buy-in" by supporting social norms that value natural resources and conservation behaviors (Dickinson & Bonney, 2012; Schultz, 2011), resulting in heightened perceptions of the environment as a public resource (Van Den Berg et al., 2011). Although citizen science projects are not a new phenomenon, the extent to which projects are designed to support participants' learning varies considerably and warrants further exploration (Bonney et al., 2016).

Much of the research on citizen science programs has been conducted in North America and Europe, but efforts are underway to globalize the reach of programs. Designing citizen science projects in developing nations presents challenges that include prioritization of basic needs over volunteerism, low levels of basic science education, inconsistent access to technology, poor coordination among government and community organizations, distrust of outsiders or scientists, and perceived relevancy of the project to participants (Braschler, 2009).

In regions where livelihoods depend on environmental quality, citizen science has the capacity to support economic development and environmental sustainability. For example, the citizen science program *Scuba Tourism for the Environment* recruits eco-tourists in Egypt, Sudan, and Saudi Arabia to conduct Red Sea coral reef monitoring during recreational dives, providing ecological data that informs practices and policies for maintaining reef health and the ecotourism sector (Branchini et al., 2015). Other examples include data collection in India about the effects of climate change on biodiversity and forest degradation in a region where livelihoods depend on forest products (Chandler et al., 2012); changes in land ownership, pastoral herders, and the economic returns of conservation to pastoralists in four regions in East Africa (Reid et al., 2016); and hydrological monitoring projects (i.e., water levels, water quality, precipitation) in Kenya that assist in developing effective water management plans, especially in remote regions, to mitigate climate and land use changes (Weeser et al., 2018). Taken together, citizen science projects worldwide are creating access to scientific knowledge for communities and contributing data to our collective international conservation efforts.

BENEFITS TO NATURE AND SOCIETY: TACKLING THE ENVIRONMENTAL SDGS

Adult science education, and citizen science as one of its forms, has the power and potential to support the general public's capacity to address issues of conservation and sustainability, as indicated in the SDGs. The projects and studies described in the previous sections present a wide variety of learners, locations, and science content and skills. This variety suggests the power and breadth of citizen science, grounded in adult education, to impact learners, their local environments, and achievement of the SDGs.

Citizen science benefits to learners and local contexts also accrue to society as a whole, specifically regarding efforts to achieve the SDGs. Fritz et al. (2019) argued that traditional data sources are insufficient to measure progress towards the SDGs; the authors advocated for citizen science as one means of providing key data. In addition to the wide range of subject areas addressed by citizen science data, as previously discussed, citizen science can be used to collect spatial and temporal data otherwise unattainable but pertinent to the SDGs (Fritz et al., 2019).

Returning to the SDGs, we have seen how some projects (e.g., Chandler et al., 2012; Weeser et al., 2018) address climate change in general, stressing the issue's urgency as in Goal 13. The health of oceans and other bodies of water and the conservation and sustainable use of those resources, Goal 14, is studied by projects such as Branchini et al. (2015). Finally, for Goal 15, the conservation and careful use of land ecosystems, including forests, and attention to issues of biodiversity, is prevalent in studies such as Chandler et al. (2015) and Reid et al. (2016).

Opportunities

Adult science education through participation in citizen science creates several opportunities. First, trustworthy out-of-school science learning can be difficult to come by for adult learners. Citizen science projects create educational opportunities, grounded in experiential learning, that cannot be achieved at other free-choice venues, such as museums, nature parks, zoos, or aquaria. Second, citizen science provides personal contact with scientists, ensuring learners have access to accurate and deep content knowledge, and demystifies the scientific endeavor as a human endeavor. Third, given the localized data collection in citizen science, these projects address the direct needs and concerns of participants and their communities. Citizen science reinforces participants' understanding of the local impacts of climate change and environmental degradation and provides individuals an opportunity to make a difference. Finally, citizen science leverages the general benefits of interaction with nature and community, building connections between and among people and nature.

Challenges

Certainly, challenges exist for adult education through citizen science. First, citizen science is predominantly a volunteer activity. Learner capacity to participate is highly dependent on location, socioeconomic status, and the environmental stakes, among other factors. In developing and economically unstable regions, or nations with weak governance, environmental degradation is more likely to be severe, as judged by the Environmental Performance Index (Yale Center for Environmental Law & Policy, 2020). Projects in such locations are more likely to need to provide a financial or economic incentive to participants (e.g., Branchini et al., 2015; Chandler et al., 2012) or operate without governmental or institutional supports. Participants' livelihoods in such regions are more likely to depend on the environment (e.g., farming, fishing), which suggests that the related science should aim to increase or stabilize their incomes.

Second, a person's capacity to participate in citizen science correlates to their prior education and experience. Many citizen science participants, particularly in developed countries, already have strong scientific backgrounds and, therefore, are primed to handle more complex or sensitive scientific tasks. The amount of training prior to participation will necessarily vary depending on the complexity of data collection and sharing. Subsequently, the learning objectives for and evaluation of projects requires careful attention (Phillips et al., 2018).

Partnerships

From an academic perspective, insights from the research activities and data, including outreach gaps and best implementation practices, should be disseminated to citizen science project leaders and adult science educators. For adult educators, this work necessarily requires meaningful partnerships with environmental scientists and communities worldwide who are affected by or working to mitigate environmental changes. Much of the current citizen science work discussed in this chapter is progressing without the benefit of support from education professionals. For the expertise of

286 J. ZARESTKY and L. VILEN

adult education to come to bear, we must begin by building rapport with colleagues in the sciences at our home institutions and beyond. There are many scientists who wish to effectively educate or communicate with the public; our partnerships with them create opportunities to design and support adult science learning through citizen science.

The value of adult science education also requires understanding of local communities' scientific needs based on the issues they are facing, as in the work of Shaughnessy et al. (2014). Our field already values doing this, but the stakes of environmental and human health instill a renewed sense of urgency. People from all backgrounds have the fundamental capacity to recognize environmental degradation and seek scientific information. Scientists and educators need to view the general public as equal partners, not only data collection devices. Projects may be instigated or driven by community members who seek out scientific evidence to reinforce local knowledge. As adult science education and citizen science become community-driven, conservation and sustainability efforts begin to also address issues of ecojustice (Griswold, 2017), fundamental to the social justice values of adult education as a field.

RECOMMENDATIONS AND CONCLUSIONS

Citizen science and science literacy are important areas that will be necessary for sustainable development and environmental conservation worldwide. Key facets of impactful citizen science include: (a) local relevance, which is critical to addressing real problems and involving populations that might otherwise feel disenfranchised, (b) balancing economic and environmental concerns, particularly in locations where participants' livelihoods are affected, and (c) respecting the contributions of scientists and the general public to ensure quality scientific design and project execution. Combined, these three qualities support citizen science endeavors that span the breadth of environmental, scientific, and human concerns.

As adult educators, we are collectively concerned with where and how people learn, outside of school. It is tempting, particularly in science education, to dictate what and how people ought to learn. Yet, for meaningful and impactful science learning, approaches grounded in adult education can help scientists and citizen science projects leverage people's existing interests, concerns, and needs. We can use these as entry and connection points to the science happening in local contexts, thereby bringing in the community and leveraging our unique contributions as adult educators.

ACKNOWLEDGMENT

This work is partially supported by the National Science Foundation under Grant No. NSF-DRL 1713351.

REFERENCES

Bloomfield, L. S. P., McIntosh, T. L., & Lambin, E. F. (2020). Habitat fragmentation, livelihood behaviors, and contact between people and nonhuman primates in Africa. *Landscape Ecology*, *35*(4), 985–1000. https://doi.org/10.1007/s10980-020-00995-w

Bonney, R., Hellenga, R., Luke, J., Marcussen, M., & Palmquist, S. (Eds.). (2009). *Principal investigator's guide: Managing evaluation in informal STEM education projects.* Center for Advancement of Informal Science Education (CAISE). http://www.informalscience.org/evaluation/pi-guide

Bonney, R., Phillips, T. B., Ballard, H. L., & Enck, J. W. (2016). Can citizen science enhance public understanding of science? *Public Understanding of Science*, *25*(1), 2–16. https://doi.org/10.1177/0963662515607406

Branchini, S., Meschini, M., Covi, C., Piccinetti, C., Zaccanti, F., & Goffredo, S. (2015). Participating in a citizen science monitoring program: Implications for environmental education. *PLoS ONE*, *10*(7), 1–14. https://doi.org/10.1371/journal.pone.0131812

Braschler, B. (2009) Successfully implementing a citizen-scientist approach to insect monitoring in a resource-poor country. *BioScience*, *59*(2), 103–104. https://doi.org/10.1525/bio.2009.59.2.2

Chandler, M., Bebber, D. P., Castro, S., Lowman, M. D., Muoria, P., Oguge, N., & Rubenstein, D. I. (2012). International citizen science: making the local global. *Frontiers in Ecology and the Environment*, *10*(6), 328–331. https://doi.org/10.1890/110283

Chandler, M., Rullman, S., Cousins, J., Esmail, N., Begin, E., Venicx, G., Eisenberg, C., & Studer, M. (2017). Contributions to publications and management plans from 7 years of citizen science: Use of a novel evaluation tool on Earthwatch-supported projects. *Biological Conservation*, *208*, 163–173. https://doi.org/10.1016/j.biocon.2016.09.024

Clery, D. (2011). Galaxy zoo volunteers share pain and glory of research. *Science*, *333*(6039), 173–175. https://doi.org/10.1126/science.333.6039.173

Cooper, C., & Smith, J. (2010). Gender patterns in bird-related recreation in the USA and UK. *Ecology and Society*, *15*(4), Article 4. https://doi.org/10.5751/ES-03603-150404

Crall, A. W., Jordan, R., Holfelder, K., Newman, G. J., Graham, J., & Waller, D. M. (2013). The impacts of an invasive species citizen science training program on participant attitudes, behavior, and science literacy. *Public Understanding of Science*, *22*(6), 744–764. https://doi.org/10.1177/0963662511434894

Danielsen, F., Burgess, N. D., & Balmford, A. (2005). Monitoring matters: Examining the potential of locally-based approaches. *Biodiversity & Conservation, 14*(11), 2507–2542. https://doi.org/10.1007/s10531-005-8375-0

Dickinson, J. L., & Bonney R. (2012). *Citizen science: Public collaboration in environmental research.* Cornell University Press.

Falk, J. H., & Dierking, L. D. (2010). The 95 percent solution. *American Scientist, 98*(6), 486–493. https://doi.org/10.1511/2010.87.486

Falk, J. H., & Dierking, L. D. (2019). Reimagining public science education: The role of lifelong free-choice learning. *Disciplinary and Interdisciplary Science Education Research, 1,* Article 10. https://doi.org/10.1186/s43031-019-0013-x

Falk, J. H., Dierking, L. D., Swanger, L. P., Staus, N., Back, M., Barriault, C., Catalano, C., Chambers, S, C., Chew, L.-L., Dahl, S. A., Falla, S., Gorecki, B., Lau, T.-C., Lloyd, A., Martin, J., Santer, J., Singer, S., Solli, A., Trepanier, G., … Verheyden, P. (2016). Correlating science center use with adult science literacy: An international, cross-institutional study. *Science Education, 100*(5), 849–876. https://doi.org/10.1002/sce.21225

Falk, J. H., Storksdieck, M., & Dierking, L. D. (2007). Investigating public science interest and understanding: Evidence for the importance of free-choice learning. *Public Understanding of Science, 16*(4), 455–469. https://doi.org/10.1177/0963662506064240

Feinstein, N. (2011). Salvaging science literacy. *Science Education, 95*(1), 168–185. https://doi.org/10.1002/sce.20414

Fritz, S., See, L., Carlson, T. Haklay, M., Oliver, J. L., Fraisl, D., Mondardini, R., Brocklehurst, M., Shanley, L. A., Schade, S., Wehn, U., Abrate, T., Anstee, J., Arnold, S., Billot, M., Campbell, J., Espey, J., Gold, M., Hager, … West, S. (2019). Citizen science and the United Nations Sustainable Development Goals. *Nature Sustainability, 2*(10), 922–930. https://doi.org/10.1038/s41893-019-0390-3

Griswold, W. (2017). Sustainability, ecojustice, and adult education. *New Directions for Adult and Continuing Education, 2017*(153), 7–15. https://doi.org/10.1002/ace.20217

Heimlich, J., & Horr, E. E. (2010). Adult learning in free-choice, environmental settings: What makes it different? *New Directions for Adult and Continuing Education, 2010*(127), 57–66. https://doi.org/10.1002/ace.381

Kluttz, J., & Walter, P. (2018). Conceptualizing learning in the climate justice movement. *Adult Education Quarterly, 68*(2), 91–107. https://doi.org/10.1177%2F0741713617751043

Lave, J., & Wenger, E. (1991). *Situated learning: Legitimate peripheral participation.* Cambridge University Press.

Miller, J. (2010). Adult science learning in the internet era. *Curator: The Museum Journal, 53*(2), 191–208. https://doi.org/10.1111/j.2151-6952.2010.00019.x

National Research Council. (1996). *National science education standards.* The National Academies Press. https://doi.org/10.17226/4962

Newman, G. (2014). Citizen cyberscience—New directions and opportunities for human computation. *Human Computation, 1*(1), 103–109. https://doi.org/10.15346/hc.v1i2.2

Ottinger, G. (2010). Buckets of resistance: Standards and the effectiveness of citizen science. *Science, Technology, & Human Values, 35*(2), 244–270. https://doi.org/10.1177/0162243909337121

Pan, Y.-T., Yang, K.-K., Hong, Z.-R., & Lin, H.-S. (2018). The effect of interest and engagement in learning science on adults' scientific competency and environmental action. *Eurasia Journal of Mathematics, Science and Technology Education, 14*(12), Article No: em1609. https://doi.org/10.29333/ejmste/94225

Pearson, J., Ipsen, J., Sutherland, S., Wegerson, K., & Onello, E. (2019). Risks and costs to human health of sulfide-ore mining near the Boundary Waters Canoe Area Wilderness. *Human and Ecological Risk Assessment: An International Journal.* Advance online publication. https://doi.org/10.1080/10807039.2019.1576026

Penn, I. (2020, April 7). Oil companies are collapsing, but wind and solar energy keep growing. *New York Times.* https://www.nytimes.com/2020/04/07/business/energy-environment/coronavirus-oil-wind-solar-energy.html

Peters, R., Ripple, W. J., Wolf, C., Moskwik, M., Carreón-Arroyo, G., Ceballos, G., Córdova, A., Dirzo, R., Ehrlich, P. R., Flesch, A. D., List, R., Lovejoy, T. E., Noss, R. F., Pacheco, J., Sarukhán, J. K., Soulé, M. E., Wilson, E. O., Miller, J. R. B., & 2556 scientist signatories from 43 countries. (2018). Nature divided, scientists united: US–Mexico border wall threatens biodiversity and binational conservation. *BioScience, 68*(10), 740–743. https://doi.org/10.1093/biosci/biy063

Phillips, T. B., Ballard, H. L., Lewenstein, B. V., & Bonney, R. (2019). Engagement in science through citizen science: Moving beyond data collection. *Science Education, 103*(3), 665–690. https://doi.org/10.1002/sce.21501

Phillips, T., Porticella, N., Constas, M., & Bonney, R. (2018). A framework for articulating and measuring individual learning outcomes from participation in citizen Science. *Citizen Science: Theory and Practice, 3*(2), 1–19. https://doi.org/10.5334/cstp.126

Reid, R. S., Nkedianye, D., Said, M. Y., Kaelo, D., Neselle, M., Makui, O., Onetu, L., Kiruswa, S., Kamuaro, N. O., Kristjanson, P., Ogutu, J., BurnSilver, S. B., Goldman, M. J., Boone, R. B., Galvin, K. A., Dickson, N. M., & Clark, W. C. (2016). Evolution of models to support community and policy action with science: Balancing pastoral livelihoods and wildlife conservation in savannas of East Africa. *Proceedings of the National Academy of Sciences, 113*(17), 4579–4584. https://doi.org/10.1073/pnas.0900313106

Sachatello-Sawyer, B., Fellenz, R. A., Burton, H., Gittings-Carlson, L., Lewis-Mahony, J., & Woolbaugh, W. (2002). *Adult museum programs: Designing meaningful experiences.* AltaMira Press.

Schultz, P. W. (2011). Conservation means behavior. *Conservation Biology, 25*(6), 1080–1083. https://doi.org/10.1111/j.1523-1739.2011.01766.x

Shaughnessy, C., Prins, E., & Hopkins, M. (2014). Adults learning about shale gas development: Information sharing, community engagement, and critical science literacy. *Adult Education Research Conference,* 473–478. http://newprairiepress.org/aerc/2014/papers/81

Shen, B. (1975). Views: Science literacy: Public understanding of science is becoming vitally needed in developing and industrialized countries alike. *American Scientist, 63*(3), 265–268. http://www.jstor.org/stable/27845461

Shirk, J. L., Ballard, H. L., Wilderman, C. C., Phillips, T., Wiggins, A., Jordan, R., McCallie, E., Minarchek, M., Lewenstein, B. V., Krasny, M. E., & Bonney, R. (2012). Public participation in scientific research: a framework for deliberate design. *Ecology and Society, 17*(2), Article 29. http://dx.doi.org/10.5751/ES-04705-170229

Sobel, D. (2004). *Place-based education: Connecting classrooms and communities.* Orion Society.

Theobald, E. J., Ettinger, A. K., Burgess, H. K., DeBey, L. B., Schmidt, N. R., Froehlich, H. E., Wagner, C., HilleRisLambers, J., Tewksbury, J., Harsch, M. A., & Parrish, J. K. (2015). Global change and local solutions: Tapping the unrealized potential of citizen science for biodiversity research. *Biological Conservation, 181*, 236–244. https://doi.org/10.1016/j.biocon.2014.10.021

Trumbull, D. J., Bonney, R., Bascom, D., & Cabral, A. (2000). Thinking scientifically during participation in a citizen-science project. *Science Education, 84*(2), 265–275. https://doi.org/10.1002/(SICI)1098-237X(200003)84:2%3C265::AID-SCE7%3E3.0.CO;2-5

Tsai, C.-Y., Li, Y.-Y., & Cheng, Y.-Y. (2017). The relationships among adult affective factors, engagement in science, and scientific competencies. *Adult Education Quarterly, 67*(1), 30–47. https://doi.org/10.1177%2F0741713616673148

UNESCO. (2016). *The future of scientific advice to the United Nations: A summary report to the Secretary-General of the United Nations from the scientific advisory board.* https://unesdoc.unesco.org/ark:/48223/pf0000245801/PDF/245801eng.pdf

United Nations. (2015). *Transforming our world: The 2030 agenda for sustainable development.* https://sustainabledevelopment.un.org/post2015/transformingourworld

U.S. General Services Administration. (2020). *About CitizenScience.gov.* https://www.citizenscience.gov/about/#

Van Den Berg, H. A., Dann, S. L., & Dirkx, J. M. (2009). Motivations of adults for nonformal conservation education and volunteerism: Implications for programming. *Applied Environmental Education & Communication, 8*(1), 6–17. http://doi/10.1080/15330150902847328

Van Den Berg, H. A., Riley, S. J., & Dann, S. L. (2011). Conservation education for advancing natural resources knowledge and building capacity for volunteerism. *Society & Natural Resources, 24*(3), 205–220. https://doi.org/10.1080/08941920902960404

Weeser, B., Stenfert Kroese, J., Jacobs, S. R., Njue, N., Kemboi, Z., Ran, A., Rufino, M. C., & Breuer, L. (2018). Citizen science pioneers in Kenya—A crowd sourced approach for hydrological monitoring. *Science of the Total Environment, 631–632*, 1590–1599. https://doi.org/10.1016/j.scitotenv.2018.03.130

Yale Center for Environmental Law & Policy. (2020). *Executive summary.* https://epi.envirocenter.yale.edu/2018-epi-report/executive-summary

CHAPTER 18

MILLENNIUM FELLOWS AS CATALYSTS FOR GLOBAL CLIMATE CHANGE

Hilary Landorf, Yenisleidy Simon Mengana, and Birgitta Rausch-Montoto
Florida International University, United States

There are no gray areas when it comes to survival. Now we all have a choice. We can create transformational action that will safeguard the future living conditions for humankind, or we can continue with our business as usual and fail. That is up to you and me. (Thunberg, 2019, para. 6)

More than 10 years ago, Florida International University (FIU), a Hispanic serving institution with more than 55,000 students, launched Global Learning for Global Citizenship, a university-wide initiative that graduates global citizens ready to tackle the world's most pressing issues. The initiative encompasses a two-course global learning graduation requirement, participation in global learning cocurricular activities, and training for faculty to teach global learning courses. In 2014, we expanded the initiative to include the Global Learning Medallion (GLM) program. This medallion is conferred upon students who graduate having completed at least four global learning courses, a significant number of global learning cocurricular activities, a capstone project, and a personal reflection.

Advancing the Global Agenda for Human Rights, Vulnerable Populations, and Environmental Sustainability: Adult Education as Strategic Partner, pp. 291–306

As global initiatives leaders at FIU, we are always attentive to programs offered within and outside the university that can provide students with the tools to become global citizens. More specifically, we have made it our mission to empower the next generation of global citizens through a set of curricular and cocurricular opportunities, including globally focused internships, fellowships, and research projects. Thus, when, in late March of 2019 an email with the subject line "Recognizing your students' global leadership" came across our inboxes, it immediately caught our attention. The email was our very first introduction to the Millennium Fellowship, a one-semester program for undergraduates that convenes, challenges, and celebrates student leadership (Millennium Campus Network, n.d.). The Millennium Fellowship Program (MFP) is based on a collaborative model that places students' voices at the center of the changemaking process while exhorting them to find solutions for the world's greatest challenges. Given our definition of global learning as "the process of diverse people collaboratively analyzing and addressing complex problems that transcend borders" (Landorf et al., 2018, p. 32), the MFP was of great interest to us as educators and to our students as global citizens in the making.

As we looked into the program in detail, we were delighted to learn of its focus on the United Nations Sustainable Development Goals (SDGs), as they are of growing interest to students in higher education throughout the world (StudyPortals, n.d.) and particularly to students on our campus. As evidence of FIU's overall commitment to engaging with the SDGs, in 2020, the *Times Higher Education* ranked FIU among the top three universities in the United States in its work related to SDG 1 (No Poverty), SDG 8 (Decent Work & Economic Growth), SDG 14 (Life Below Water) and SDG 16 (Peace, Justice & Strong Institutions) (Hughes, 2020). The MFP requires that a minimum of eight students per campus apply to the program by submitting a plan to develop and implement, within one semester, a project associated with one of the SDGs. Another noteworthy feature of the program is that the application process is open to all undergraduate students around the world, making it inclusive of all learners, including adults.

Even though we only had five weeks to advertise, recruit, and help our students identify projects of interest for their applications, we enthusiastically accepted this challenge. We invited our entire Global Learning Medallion population of more than 1,200 students to submit applications and at least 18 students did so. We were thrilled when, in late July, our university president forwarded us the official email message from Sam Vaghar, the Executive Director and Cofounder of the Boston based nonprofit Millennium Campus Network (MCN). MCN and the United Nations Academic Impact present the Millennium Fellowship annually, and Vaghar's email informed us that FIU had been selected to host a cohort of Fellows! Working with the 13 accepted students during the fall of 2019 and seeing the strides they made through their participation in the program increased our interest in exploring the program as a site for adult learners' engagement with projects related to global climate change.

For this chapter, we explored the following research question: How can adult learners become catalysts for global climate change, particularly in the context of interdisciplinary and multifaceted partnerships? The focus on adult learners is particularly important since the vast knowledge and experience they bring to their curricular and cocurricular endeavors often goes unnoticed (Greene, 2006). Walter (2009) argued that the adult education field is deeply connected to social movements and well positioned to advance environmental action. Yet, as he pointed out: "Although there is a healthy and expansive world of 'green' educational practice for adults, and a strong network of committed environmental adult educators and activists on the ground, research and theorizing in academia are still largely in the infant stage" (p. 4). Finally, Milana et al. (2018) pointed out that adult learning and education play a key role in advancing the 2030 plan for sustainable development. Our work aims to contribute to this developing body of research.

In this chapter, we use Merriam and Brockett's (1997) definition of adult education as "activities intentionally designed for the purpose of bringing about learning among those whose age, social roles, or self-perception define them as adults" (p. 8). We like this definition as it is expansive and inclusive, and it acknowledges the agency of adult learners to self-define and self-evaluate their place in the world. As delineated below, according to this definition, all the participants in our case study are adults.

We have two interrelated aims in this chapter: to uncover the processes of a nonprofit organization that uses a collaborative leadership model in partnership with higher education institutions to engage adult learners in tackling environmental sustainability challenges, and to add these previously unheard adult learners' voices to the literature. First, we provide a brief history of the Millennium Campus Network and the creation of the MFP. We then describe the methods we used to explore our research question. We go on to discuss the themes we uncovered from our interviews with eight fellows who were in either the 2018 or 2019 Millennium Fellowship cohort. We conclude with implications for practice.

THE MILLENNIUM CAMPUS NETWORK AND THE MILLENNIUM FELLOWS PROGRAM

The Millennium Campus Network (MCN) was launched in 2008 as a global nonprofit organization dedicated to connecting and training social impact leaders. Through its flagship activities—the MFP, global campaigns, and conferences—this organization supports student leadership in advancing the UN SDGs and harnessing their power to bring about social change (Millennium Campus Network, n.d.).

The Millennium Fellowship program was created in 2013 with the purpose of convening, challenging, and celebrating student leadership. In 2018, MCN partnered with United Nations Academic Impact (UNAI) to expand the reach and impact of the MFP. The UNAI was launched in 2010 as a bridge connecting higher education institutions with the United Nations. The partnership between UNAI and MCN allows MCN to increase its network of colleges and universities across the globe (United Nations Academic Impact, n.d.). The fellowship now invites undergraduate students to develop and implement projects that address both the SDGs and UNAI principles. In an interview with Sam Vaghar, MCN's Executive Director, we learned that the decision to focus on the SDGs was deliberate. Mr. Vaghar had been inspired by the intentionality of the eight Millennium Development Goals (MDGs), a set of targets that all the countries around the world needed to address by 2015 (S. Vaghar, personal communication, April 9, 2020). These targets were followed by the 2030 development agenda, a plan centered around the 17 SDGs. Instead of reinventing fellowship goals, Mr. Vaghar chose to align the fellowship with the existing United Nations framework and leverage the knowledge, tools, and resources available to accelerate leadership development and increase the impact of students' projects. In addition to focusing on the SDGs, the fellowship also encompasses the 10 UNAI principles including global citizenship, access to higher education, and sustainability.

METHOD

The case study method is effective when the research question is designed to understand "how" or "why" a phenomenon occurs (Yin, 1994). In this study, the question is how do adult learners become catalysts for global climate change, particularly in the context of interdisciplinary and multi-faceted partnerships? The partnerships invoked in the question are those between MCN, the organization behind the MFP, and the various institutions of higher education around the world whose students were selected to be part of the program in 2018 or 2019. The focus of this case study was on the Millennium Fellows' leadership in addressing the following SDGs: affordable and clean energy (SDG 7), sustainable cities and communities (SDG 11), responsible consumption and production (SDG 12), and climate action (SDG 13).

Population, Sampling Strategy, Data Collection, and Sources of Evidence

For this case study, our population of interest consisted of (1) fellows who had completed the program in 2018 or 2019, (2) were 25 years of age or older, thereby meeting the first condition of Merriam and Brockett's (1997) definition of adult learner ("those whose age … define them as adults"; p. 8), and (3) had pursued projects related to SDGs 7, 11, 12, or 13. Once we had gotten permission from MCN Programs Director Noha Al-Khalqi to carry out this study (N. Al-Khalqi, personal communication, December 21, 2019), we devised a four-step sampling and data collection strategy. Our first step was to request a list from Ms. Al-Khalqi of all fellows who had completed the program in either 2018 or 2019 and were 25 years of age or older. We chose this criterion to identify adult learner fellows as the other two criteria for identifying adult learners were not made available to us before contacting the fellows. Once we received this list, with a total of 164 fellows, we moved to our second step of identifying the 40 fellows whose projects focused on SDGs 7, 11, 12, or 13. We further narrowed our pool in this step to 14 fellows, by choosing a comparable number of female and male fellows, as well as fellows from diverse geographic areas of the world. We chose these criteria to ensure gender and geographic equity. Ms. Al-Khalqi then sent an email to these 14 fellows, asking if they would be willing to participate in our study, and if so, requesting permission for us to contact them. She released the fellows' contact information to us only when they responded to her in the affirmative.

When, after 10 days, she had received affirmative responses from only two fellows, we went onto step three. In this step, we expanded our pool by 16 additional fellows who met all our sampling criteria. A total of 13 fellows confirmed interest in the project, and we contacted them all to confirm their interest in participating in our study and set up a time and date for an interview on Zoom, a video communication platform. To determine an adequate sample size, we followed the recommendation of Strauss and Corbin (1998), who suggested that the researcher stops collecting data once "saturation" is reached. Saturation is a somewhat subjective concept, but Strauss and Corbin suggested that it is the point where anything new being discovered in the data is not contributing to the overall story. After having interviewed six of the 13 fellows in our sample, the three authors agreed that we had reached saturation.

We also conducted interviews with two fellows who met the other two conditions of Merriam and Brockett's (1997) definition of adult learner ("those whose … social roles, or self-perception define them as adults"; p. 8). Importantly, these fellows' projects focused on SDG 3 (good health and well-being), and SDG 4 (quality education). These two fellows served as a comparison group to discover whether findings resulting from the interviews not only apply to projects centered around environmental sustainability and learners of age 25 or older, but also hold true for fellows who pursue nonenvironmental sustainability projects and who are by definition adult learners due to their social roles and self-perception. In full disclosure, the two fellows interviewed as the comparison group are enrolled and led projects at our home institution, Florida International University (FIU).

We conducted semi-structured in-depth interviews with all eight participants to explore in detail their experiences, motives, and opinions and see the world from their perspectives (Rubin & Rubin, 2012). We posed the same 10 questions to each participant, giving them ample opportunities to expound on their ideas, add new ideas, and ask questions of us. We used a combination of probing questions and follow up questions to tease out the perspectives of the participants. With the permission of the participants, all the interviews were recorded and transcribed via Zoom. The interviewers also took notes during the interviews.

In addition to conducting interviews with the fellows, we interviewed Sam Vaghar and Noha Al-Khalqi, MCN Executive Director and Program Director, respectively. The purpose of these interviews was to glean information about the creation, development, and implementation of the program, and to solicit their opinions about its successes, challenges, and future direction. Other than interviews, sources of evidence included web-based documents on the MFP and its partner programs, the MCN and the UNAI, as well as literature pertaining to adult education, environmental sustainability, and later, the four themes we uncovered.

Data Analysis and Integrity Measures

To start the data analysis, each of us separately coded the data into concepts or themes that we identified within the transcripts of and notes from the interviews (Rubin & Rubin, 2012). After coding all the interviews, we each consolidated the codes by creating major categories and put codes in each category, if they fit. Some new codes emerged in each interview and we went back to see if those codes were present in the previous interviews. Out of the main themes that answered our research question, we each identified which codes occurred the most for each participant, and which codes occurred most overall. As the last step, we compared and consolidated our separate results. This consolidation is represented by the themes we present in our findings below.

To ensure the overall accuracy of the findings for this case study, we used multiple credibility and transferability measures. We triangulated the data by examining the evidence from multiple sources and using that evidence to build coherent justification for the themes that were uncovered throughout the study (Creswell & Creswell, 2018). The evidence we examined included the university websites of all the participants, research literature, interview transcripts, and relevant documents that the participants sent to us as background information. All three authors checked the data to ensure that the information that we included in the findings were both coherent and factual. Likewise, we utilized rich, thick description when conveying the findings.

FINDINGS

In this section, we provide a description of the interviewees and their projects and discuss the four major themes we uncovered from our data analysis process. The themes that emerged speak to features of the fellowship that make it an ideal catalyst of climate change leaders. First, we discuss the collaborative leadership model, a staple of the fellowship. Then, we address the leadership development of the fellows. We continue discussing the effect of the fellowship in fellows' interest for social impact careers. We finish the section by addressing the connections between local engagement and global impact.

Description of the Fellows and Their Projects

Derick Nwasor (2018 cohort) is a student at the University of Benin, Nigeria, leading a project to tackle energy poverty in Sub-Saharan Africa in support of SDG 7 (Affordable & Clean Energy). He is the founder and serves as President and CEO of XIGMA, Inc., a center for advanced research and applied sciences, working on a zero-emission energy solution and hoping to create broader clean energy awareness.

Mandeg Djama (2019 cohort) is a native student of Djibouti completing her studies at the African Leadership University in Rwanda. She is a community organizer pursuing a project associated with SDG 11 (Sustainable Cities & Communities). Her aim is to mentor youth in her native Djibouti to become creative and innovative problem-solvers in their communities through environmental action and specifically every-day recycling practices.

Danielle Wolf (2018 cohort) is a student at the Western University of Sydney, Australia. She is the founder of P.E.A.C.E (Promotion, Education, Awareness, Campaigns, Empowerment) in Western Sydney, a framework for disrupting practices and current ideology within her on- and off-campus community aligned with SDG 12 (Responsible Consumption &

Production). She actively brought together multiple environmental initiatives to cultivate collaboration and accountability among leaders.

Duplicate Sambani (2019 cohort) is a native student of Tanzania pursuing her studies at EARTH University in Costa Rica. She is the founder of the AgroManitos project, associated with SDG 12 (Responsible Consumption & Production), which helps raise children's knowledge of food security and sustainability by engaging them in growing their own vegetables and using recycled materials in school gardens.

Emmanuel Yakhama (2019 cohort) is pursuing studies at Kenyatta University, Kenya and is the founder of the Adopt a Tree project. This project, bolstering SDG 13 (Climate Action), is aimed at sensitizing the community to the effects of deforestation and initiating forest restoration initiatives with locals, government officials and environmental organizations.

Wantoe Wantoe (2019 cohort) is a native of Liberia and a student at the College of Mount Saint Vincent, USA. He led Phins For Change, an SDG 13 (Climate Action) affiliated project, which seeks to educate students on the impact of climate change and inspire them to actively pursue sustainable environmental practices and prepare them as global leaders of tomorrow. Project activities included service, blogging, capacity building seminars, panel dialogues, and participation in the annual Youth Assembly at the United Nations Headquarters.

Kelly Nair Rojas (2019 cohort) is a student at Florida International University, USA, whose project centers around low-cost health monitoring methods. In the context of SDG 3 (Good Health & Well-being), she conducts collaborative research on different designs and characteristics of an affordable electrode system accessible by patients of all socio-economic backgrounds.

Melanie Rodriguez (2019 cohort) is a student at Florida International University, United States, who founded and serves as the director of the LIVE (Let your Voices Echo) project. In support of SDG 4 (Quality Education), this project consists of research on the community's school-to-prison pipeline and creative arts events for audiences to engage with the complexities of the issue.

Fellows' Perspectives of their Millennium Leadership Projects

In the descriptions of their projects, the fellows clearly articulated the following four themes: their enthusiasm for the collaborative leadership model, the MFP as a leadership incubator, their ambition to pursue a social impact career, and the connection between the local engagement and global impact of their projects.

The Secret to Success: The Collaborative Leadership Model

The very essence of the Millennium Fellowship's collaborative leadership model is encompassed by Rubin (2009):

> You are a collaborative leader once you have accepted responsibility for building—or helping to ensure the success of a heterogeneous team to accomplish a shared purpose. Your tools are (1) the purposeful exercise of your behavior, communication and organizational resources in order to affect the perspective, beliefs, and behaviors of another person (generally a collaborative partner) to influence that person's relationship with you and your collaborative enterprise and (2) the structure and climate of an environment that supports the collaborative relationship. (p. 4)

This approach is embedded throughout the fellowship from beginning to end. For instance, becoming a Millennium Fellowship campus requires the awarding of a minimum of eight fellows. Every campus must have two student campus directors that work together to lead their cohort. Moreover, the leadership and training sessions facilitated by the MCN are designed for cohort members to interact with, learn from, and lend support to one another as they implement their ideas. Additionally, MCN offers multiple opportunities throughout the semester for Millennium Fellows to collaborate not only with their peers on campus but also with fellows all around the world, which creates a global community of social impact leaders.

In responses to the question, "Why did you apply for this fellowship vs. others?", three of the fellows made specific reference to the collaborative leadership model enacted by the leaders of the program. Expressing her appreciation of this model, M. Djama said:

> I was very much pleased with the leadership model they proposed. It is a very participative model that involves us as youth. In other fellowships I have been to, they are more "you do this and you will get these results." But this particular program was more into "what are you guys passionate about" and "how can we help you achieve," and I really loved that.

D. Sambini also recognized the program's collaborative leadership, saying this:

> The idea that the fellowship program did not govern what we were going to do, the idea that we were supposed to come up with our own idea of what we want to do to change the world was the first thing that motivated me. As well, to connect with others of my age who were also doing projects on one of the 17 SDGs, I could get ideas on how to overcome challenges and how to share successes.

All the fellows interviewed responded that they were drawn to the program for its support of those with a desire to tackle complex social challenges and the recognition that individual action alone will limit their potential impact. Before becoming fellows, D. Sambini, D. Nwasor, M. Djama, and K. Nair Rojas were already engaged in projects in which they had real-life insights on how difficult effecting change can be. The others had a specific idea for an initiative and realized that forming alliances with others would be of great benefit.

All of the fellows also recognized that the program's model itself increased their opportunities to develop collaboration skills, especially with like-minded peers interested in social change. The idea of different program members supporting each other was appealing to the fellows, citing such reasons as that they would be more at ease to learn, train, share experiences, and support each other. K. Nair Rojas repeatedly stated that for her, learning best practices on how to collaborate with a team was critically important. In fact, she said that her main take-away was:

> I don't need to think that I am doing the project on my own but that there are a lot of people working to help society and that if I need help, I can find a group of people that can potentially contribute to my project or I can potentially contribute to their projects.

Overall, the fellows acknowledged that the program provided them with a unique platform for meeting, learning, training, sharing, supporting, and networking for emerging leaders who aspire to have a global impact. In this paradigm, the collaborative leadership model was applied through multidimensional learning experiences between fellow and fellow, fellow, and local teammates/campus supporters, fellow and the program leaders, as well as fellow and the United Nations.

Millennium Fellowship as Leadership Incubator

According to Greene (2006), "The existing power relationships in many classes, programs, and in society overall, place the student and particularly the adult student as the passive recipient of teacher knowledge not as an active subject engaged in social transformation" (p. 10). The MFP is a unique opportunity for adult learners to disrupt those dynamics by participating in a cocurricular program that believes in their ability to transform their communities and the world.

D. Nwasor, M. Djama, D. Sambani, and K. Nair Rojas, who already had initiatives underway before being selected for the fellowship, saw a unique opportunity to advance their project while putting their leadership abilities to the test. As D. Nwasor stated, "It presented a terrific opportunity for a student researcher and inventor like me to engage my team in product development during the idea stage and prior to the launch. It also gave us unprecedented access at our university."

As Smith and Nicolaides (2018) suggested, it is critically important to support adult students in the development of more sophisticated tools to gather and process knowledge, thereby increasing their awareness of the challenges facing the world and their success in tackling them. As the fellows reported, leadership skills that the program elicited include leading by example, communicating effectively, project management, being flexible and adjusting in times of adversity, listening intently, serving as a role model, and exercising patience. D. Sambini summed up what she learned from the program about leadership by saying, "Everyone is a leader. What you do as a leader is what makes you tick."

M. Djama, D. Wolf, D. Sambani, E. Yakhama, and M. Rodriguez acknowledged having to adjust their goals due to unexpected obstacles such as lack of time and resources, or adversity in the project community. Fellow M. Djama shared a particularly poignant example of needing to "create buy-in for environmental action" at the onset of her project, which was to bring community awareness of environmental impact of plastic waste. She was met with active resistance, and in conversations with local youths learned that they did not see the importance of protecting the environment when their daily struggle was focused on survival. Instead, they expressed an interest in learning English in order to enhance their employability prospects. The fellow, therefore, added to her project a focus on youth empowerment through learning English. Her project resulted in new English abilities in many of the 350 youth with whom she engaged. In addition, 50 out of these youth began to take their own, reusable shopping bag in place of single-use plastics. Such first-hand experiences with adjusting goals better prepare the fellows for future leadership challenges.

In summary, the fellows acknowledged that the program facilitated the development of leadership competencies in a real-life laboratory where they could practice new skills, and that they consciously selected the program as an opportunity to test their leadership abilities and gain new ones. Their perspectives are representative of the 2019 Millennium Fellows Class as a whole. According to the Class of 2019 Impact Report, 94% of the fellows would recommend the fellowship, and 92% found the training sessions and content useful for their leadership development (Millennium Campus Network, 2020).

As adults, the great majority of the fellows explicitly noted advantages that being an adult learner brought to their leadership capabilities and to the leadership potential of their younger colleagues. D. Wolf noted that, as an adult learner, she felt that she has greater self-esteem, confidence, and a greater understanding of how to engage and organize others than do younger learners. She added that younger fellows in the program and participants on campus—in recognition of her age and experience—looked up to her for guidance, which made leading much easier. W. Wantoe also talked about how, as an adult learner, he found it easier for him to communicate with others on campus. K. Nair Rojas and M. Rodriguez indicated that by having to carry out adult responsibilities such as working one or more jobs, taking care of ill family members, or having to pay for their own education taught them leadership skills such as multitasking, juggling multiple priorities, and effective time management.

Not only do the fellows acknowledge their own leadership advantages as adult learners, but they also think that they serve as a model for the leadership development of their younger colleagues. As D. Wolf put it, "Some of the younger students I suppose just feel out of depth in the uni experience itself, so my being there contributed to them gaining more confidence as leaders as well."

What's Next? Social Impact Careers

One of the explicit goals of the MFP is to "take your social impact to the next level" (Millennium Campus Network, n.d.) by having cohorts of students build unity on their respective campuses and within the Millennium Fellows worldwide network, and by each helping the other make one of the SDGs a reality in their local community. All the interviewees expressed their intent to pursue a career with a social impact focused on either the environment, health, or social justice. According to the Class of 2019 Impact Report, 90.6% of the fellowship cohort felt more prepared to pursue a career in social impact after completing the program while 94% acquired the skills to help others through social impact (Millennium Campus Network, 2020).

D. Sambani, who is determined to continue her project and start an agricultural manufacturing/education organization in her native Tanzania, stated that she "learned that the connection between research and making an impact on the world depends on action," and that she is now "even more determined to work with and teach farmers to grow sustainable agricultural products." E. Yakhama, who has earned his law degree and is preparing to practice law, has decided to follow his newly realized passion and "redirect his career from commercial law to environmental and humanitarian/international law." D. Nwasor avowed that the fellowship experience "turned us from job-seekers into human-centered entrepreneurs." Due to this transformation, he said that he has added human-centered aspects to his goals as an entrepreneur. For K. Nair Rojas, the program reinforced her desire to collaborate with other people on projects that improve the human condition "even if it's not in my field." M. Rodriguez explained that prior to the fellowship, she was uncertain if social entrepreneurship was a legitimate career path. She stated that, together with the global learning office on her home campus, the fellowship program "reassured me in pursuing a career focused on helping people and advancing social justice."

As a result of the program, all the interviewees report having developed a deeper desire to pursue social impact careers. They also all report recognizing that their newly gained status as Millennium Fellow program alumni provide them with unique credentials and legitimacy for future social impact leadership roles.

Global Citizenship in Action: Local Engagement and Global Impact

The fellows identified multiple avenues across which their local engagement would reach the global community via the fellow's home campus, through the global Millennium Fellowship alumni network, through setting an example, and through expansion or dissemination of the project's scope or outcomes. D. Sambini said that the cohort's diversity itself ensures a global impact. W. Wantoe, who is serving as a youth development representative at the United Nations, said that one of his goals is to leverage the fellowship as a credential to serve as a "generational changemaker" within the United Nations.

For D. Wolf, the program has cemented her aspirations "to work on global south/indigenous populations and how their world views can help the global north." She even delayed her time to graduation in order to continue her studies and better define her career path. E. Yakhama plans to expand his project from Kenya to Ghana, Tanzania, and the United States by reaching out to the global community through conferences. He explained that the U.N. Environmental Division invited him to write a white paper on his project for the U.N. Environment Assembly (UNEA), which will promote his work on the global stage. "We hope our work in Djibouti will set an example for others," M. Djama explained. She emphasized that "we don't have a Planet B." Her dream is for the people of drought-ridden Djibouti to make others in similar climates aware of the importance of environmental action.

Two fellows foresee that their research for technological solutions will be accessible by any society across the globe regardless of economic means. D. Nwasor is working on a new hydrogen electricity source that will produce electricity and gas to power light and cooking with zero emission. He says that this project "can be scaled to wide-reaching demand even beyond Africa and will bring us one step closer to global sustainability."

The fellows' reflections indicate that they have identified ways to multiply the impact of their local efforts to a global scale. Facilitated by the MFP, their projects and outcomes are planned with clarity and intentionality to allow for adaptation, expansion, and distribution beyond their home communities. Their desire for social impact and willingness to tackle complex problems and improve their leadership abilities have shaped the fellows into formidable global citizens.

IMPLICATIONS FOR PRACTICE

Our research contributes to the environmental adult education field of study in two significant ways. First, our findings confirm the critical role that collaboration plays in educating emerging leaders committed to enacting change. Brukardt et al. (2004) asserted that collaborative partnerships are essential in advancing the common good, and higher education is a critical player in this effort. This case study illustrates that higher education, in partnership with nongovernmental actors such as the United Nations, can promote healthy and sustainable communities globally. As outlined in the People's Sustainability Treaty on Higher Education 2011, to advance global sustainable development, higher education institutions are responsible for capacity building, including the provision of opportunities for experiential learning and collaboration (Clover & Hill, 2013). However, collaboration is not only a pivotal feature of the partnership between higher education institutions and external partners. As our findings suggest, collaboration should be a critical component of the programs in which the students, in this case adult learners, participate. The interviewees acknowledged that the Millennium Fellowship uniquely integrated leadership and collaboration in a way that expanded the fellows' networks locally and globally.

Secondly, our study emphasizes the importance of engaging adult learners in projects that have the potential to create visible positive change, in their communities and beyond. This approach to student engagement embodies Boyer's (1990, 1994) vision of institutions of higher learning as spaces that not only create knowledge but also emphasize the integration, communication, and application of knowledge through service. According to a report from the 4th UNESCO Chair Conference on Higher Education for Sustainable Development (Müller-Christ et al., 2014), higher learning institutions can contribute to sustainability efforts in multiple ways, including through student engagement with the real world. The authors argue that "learners must also experience interdisciplinary and transdisciplinary perspectives and learn to take into account different levels of scale, from local to global" (p. 136). This case study is a relevant example of how adult learners enact action beyond the classroom, first taking their projects into their local communities and then connecting them to the larger global stage. As Clover and Hill (2013) stated, "People are intervening, persevering, critically and creatively seeking social and environmental redress, and giving credence to alternative realities" (p. 56). This is the kind of conviction that the students bring to this fellowship that, in turn, becomes an inspiration for their social impact professional pursuits.

Lastly, our findings suggest that adult learners possess leadership advantages that allow them to enact social change effectively. As such, we recommend that organizations working to advance the sustainable development agenda provide flexible learning opportunities to accommodate adult learners' additional responsibilities. For instance, designing internships and fellowships that can be completed remotely or outside the traditional 9am-5pm work schedule would demonstrate an interest in and commitment to working with the adult learner population. Simultaneously, adult education programs can embed in their strategic plans the identification and promotion of leadership opportunities that connect to the SDGs. Adult education program faculty and staff can also make efforts to mentor adult learners in resume writing to facilitate their successful placement in these leadership positions. Both adult education programs and nongovernmental organizations involved in sustainable development work are responsible for the creation of the necessary conditions for adult learners to fully participate in social changemaking.

REFERENCES

Boyer, E. L. (1990). *Scholarship reconsidered: Priorities of the professoriate.* Jossey-Bass.

Boyer, E. L. (1994). Creating the new American college. *The Chronicle of Higher Education. 40*(27), 48.

Brukardt, M. J., Holland, B., Percy, S. L., & Zimpher, N. (2004). *Calling the question: Is higher education ready to commit to community engagement? A wingspread statement.* Milwaukee Idea Office, University of Wisconsin-Milwaukee.

Creswell, J. W., & Creswell, J. D. (2018). *Research design: Qualitative, quantitative, and mixed methods approaches.* SAGE.

Clover, D. E., & Hill, R. (2013). Adult learning, education, and the environment. *New Directions for Adult and Continuing Education, 2013*(138), 49–59. https://doi.org/10.1002/ace.20053

Greene, D. (2006) Against the tide: The role of adult student voice, student leadership and student organization in social transformation. *Convergence, 39*(1), 5–17.

Hughes, M. (2020). *FIU ranks among top 50 in world for positive impact.* FIU News. https://news.fiu.edu/2020/fiu-ranks-among-top-50-in-world-for-positive-impact

Landorf, H., Doscher, S., & Hardrick, J. (2018). *Making global learning universal: Promoting inclusion and success for all students.* Stylus.

Merriam, S. B., & Brockett, R. G. (1997) *The profession and practice of adult education.* Jossey-Bass.

Milana, M., Holford, J., Hodge, S., Waller, R., & Webb, S. (2018). Adult education and learning: Endorsing its contribution to the 2030 Agenda. *International Journal of Lifelong Education, 36*(6), 625–628. https://doi.org/10.1080/02601 370.2017.1405869

Millennium Campus Network. (n.d.). https://www.mcnpartners.org/

Millennium Campus Network. (2020). *Millennium Fellowship Class of 2019 Impact Report.* https://www.millenniumfellows.org/impact

Millennium Fellowship. (n.d.). https://www.millenniumfellows.org/ https://www.millenniumfellows.org/impact

Müller-Christ, G., Sterling, S., van Dam-Mieras, R., Adomßent, M., Fischer, D., & Rieckmann, M. (2014). The role of campus, curriculum, and community in higher education for sustainable development—A conference report. *Journal of Cleaner Production, 62*(1), 134–137.

Rubin, H. (2009). *Collaborative leadership: Developing effective partnerships for communities and schools* (2nd ed.). Orwin.

Rubin, H. J., & Rubin, I. S. (2012). *Qualitative interviewing: The art of hearing data* (3rd ed.). SAGE.

Smith, L. & Nicolaides, A. (2018). Mirror, mirror: Learning to "become" together. *New Directions for Adult and Continuing Education, 159,* 53–69. https://doi.org/10.1002/ace.20287

Strauss, A., & Corbin, J. (1998). *Basics of qualitative research: Techniques and procedures for developing grounded theory.* SAGE.

Studyportals. (n.d). Students from developing economies respond to need for Sustainable Development. https://studyportals.com/blog/growing-students-interest-in-sustainable-development/

Thunberg, G. (2019). Our house is on fire. *World Economic Forum.* https://www.fridaysforfuture.org/greta-speeches#greta_speech_jan22_2019

United Nations Academic Impact. (n.d.). https://academicimpact.un.org/

Yin, R. K. (1994). *Case study research: Design and methods* (2nd ed.). SAGE.

Walter, P. (2009). Philosophies of adult environmental education. *Adult Education Quarterly, 60*(1), 3–25. https://doi.org/10.1177/0741713609336109

CHAPTER 19

(MIS)PERCEPTIONS OF ABORIGINAL FISHING

Why Adult Education Must Confront the "Environmental Indian" Stereotype

Stanford T. Goto
Western Washington University, United States

> With repeated thrusts from steel harpoons and two finishing shots from a .50-caliber armor-piercing assault rifle, the Makah Indian tribe today conducted the first legal killing of a gray whale in American waters in nearly 75 years. It was described, in joyful terms by tribal leaders, as part of the proud resurrection of the Makahs' great seafaring traditions, but the kill of the 30-foot juvenile whale also enraged environmentalists, who had gathered in boats nearby to protest, and provoked a modern spectacle. (Verhovek, 1999, p. A18)

What are we to make of this event that occurred more than two decades ago on the western-most tip of Washington State? From the sensationalized first sentences of this *New York Times* article, we learn that a grey whale was killed by the Makah nation. In fact, this was the outcome of years of careful negotiation with the International Whaling Commission, the Clinton administration, and other branches of federal and state government

Advancing the Global Agenda for Human Rights, Vulnerable Populations, and Environmental Sustainability: Adult Education as Strategic Partner, pp. 307–322
Copyright © 2021 by Information Age Publishing
307

(Marker, 2006). The author mentions (almost in passing) that Tribal leaders were happy to revive a tradition. However, we do not get a sense of why whaling is so significant in Makah culture, nor do we hear about the loss of cultural traditions due to residential schools or other outside pressures. There is no mention of the Treaty of Neah Bay, signed in 1855, which greatly reduced Makah lands in exchange for a guarantee that the Makah Nation would have fishing and whaling rights in perpetuity (Roberts, 2010). Clearly, the article omitted or glossed over important facts. Instead, we hear in excruciating detail about the killing implements and the violence done to the animal, leaving little doubt about the author's editorial stance. The whale hunt of 1999 generated a violent backlash against the Makah Nation. Critics from across the political spectrum joined in condemnation (Marker, 2006).

Many in North America hold contradictory views of Aboriginal peoples in relation to the environment. Natives are often seen as victims of industrialization and environmental degradation (Agyeman et al., 2002). In some contexts, they are considered role models who offer a more mature way of understanding our relationship with the natural world (Sumner, 2008). In other instances, as the whale hunt illustrates, they are cast as traitors to an imagined Edenic past, when Aboriginal peoples supposedly lived in complete harmony with nature (Roberts, 2010). Colonialism across North America has led us to mythologize, lionize, demonize, and fetishize Aboriginal peoples of this continent. These conceptions of indigeneity get mixed and matched in our collective consciousness.

As we face an ever-growing list of environmental challenges across North America, our society must find ways to engage productively with all stakeholders, including Aboriginal groups. This will require mutual understanding, trust, and respect that extends beyond the organizations and governmental agencies that work directly with Tribal groups. How can we, as a society, alter our relationship with Native peoples and the environment? How can we engage in critical self-reflection with the aim of decolonizing our preconceptions? What role might adult educators play in facilitating such transformative learning?

These are important considerations for all who promote just sustainability in North America, whether or not they work directly with Native groups. A foundational assumption underlying environmental justice is that the protection of biological environments must occur in conjunction with the pursuit of human rights (Clover, 2003). When advocating for sustainable land use, educators must address historic injustices suffered by those who have inhabited those lands. Arguably, the most egregious violations of land rights in North America involved colonial seizures of Aboriginal territories (Hill, 2003). On rare occasions, present-day consequences of colonization come into public view, as evident in the Keystone

XL pipeline in North Dakota or the tragic toll of COVID-19 on the Navaho Nation. More often than not, however, the legacies of settler colonialism are ignored by the dominant society (Calderon, 2014). How many of us educators, for example, work in land-grant institutions? How often do we ask how the government "acquired" the land on which our campuses are built (see: langrabu.org)? Postcolonial scholars (e.g., Tuck et al., 2014) argued that Aboriginal histories and cultures have been systematically erased from public discourse in North America, effectively separating the pursuit of environmental sustainability from discussions of Aboriginal rights. If we truly embrace the principle of just sustainability, we must reintegrate these imperatives.

This chapter examines how settler colonialism has influenced dominant views of Aboriginal peoples and sustainable practices. These are hot-button topics around the Salish Sea, an inland marine area bordered by Victoria Island, lower British Columbia, and northwest Washington State. This region, which is larger than Connecticut, has a problematic history of colonial powers intruding on Aboriginal lands and appropriating natural resources (Boxburger, 1989). Central to the ecological and sociopolitical story are salmon, the lifeblood of the region. Millions of fish return to their natal rivers and streams each year, bringing food and nutrients to entire ecosystems. The five species of Pacific salmon have sustained Coast Salish peoples for millennia. These fish are essential to a billion-dollar recreational industry in British Columbia, as well as a 400-million-dollar commercial fishing industry (Sun & Hallin, 2018). Alarmingly, Pacific salmon stocks are in decline, with some populations classified as endangered or threatened (see Malick & Cox, 2016). Saving these fish is a monumental challenge requiring cooperation among multiple groups, including those who harvest salmon. Among West Coast fishing groups are non-Aboriginal sport anglers and First Nation fishers. Historically, relations between these groups have been contentious and fraught with mistrust (Boxburger, 1989). Declines in salmon populations have only complicated this tenuous relationship.

This discussion draws on findings from a participatory action research project (McIntyre, 2008) conducted in lower British Columbia. The study analyzed fishing-related discussion threads on two social media sites. Central to the analysis were instances of contentious interaction involving non-Aboriginal sport anglers and/or First Nation fishers. The original purpose of the study was to identify opportunities for educators to use social media as an instructional platform to address fishing-related challenges. For purposes of this chapter, I will not make recommendations for instruction via social media, as my research findings are not easily generalizable beyond the cultural/ geographic milieu of the Salish Sea. Instead, I will consider the broader question of why adult educators should include

Aboriginal perspectives in sustainability education. I will illustrate why educators should challenge the misguided stereotype of the "Environmental Indian" (Krech, 1999), which frequently underlies dominant perceptions of Aboriginal peoples and sustainable practices.

The topics of fishing and Aboriginal rights hit close to home for me. Yes, I am an associate professor of adult education with a scholarly interest in sustainability and social justice. But more pertinently, I am a fisherman who spends much of his recreational time on the rivers of southwestern British Columbia. I have one foot squarely in the sport fishing world, which is a product of a broader dominant culture of North America. At the same time, I am a non-Aboriginal person of color. My parents were among the Japanese Americans who were interned in American detention centers during World War II. Consequently, I feel a historic affinity for Aboriginal peoples of North America who were forced onto reservations and preserves. I present this chapter from an ideological third space (see Bhabha, 2004) that is neither Aboriginal nor entirely of the dominant culture.

History of Salmon Fishing and Intergroup Conflict on the Pacific Coast

Prior to colonization, Coast Salish tribes maintained a sophisticated system of boundaries and traditions that allowed all groups to have some level of fishing access at certain times and places. This system helped to protect salmon runs from over-exploitation (Wadewitz, 2012). Traditional practices were severely disrupted in the early 1800s, when increased contact with White traders brought waves of smallpox that decimated Native populations around the Salish Sea (Roberts, 2010). Whole communities were forced to reorganize and, in some cases, relocate, which severely tested their finely tuned, place-based fishing traditions. Still, Coast Salish peoples managed to adapt to a rapidly changing world.

As White occupation spread through the newly designated Washington Territory, Aboriginal leaders felt compelled to negotiate with the United States to ensure that at least some of their lands and rights would be protected. The territorial governor, Isaac Stevens, made no secret of his agenda to seize Native land for White settlement (Roberts, 2010). Between 1854 and 1857, Stevens conducted what Wadewitz (2012, p. 57) describes as "heavy-handed and questionable" treaty negotiations that resulted in the Treaty Tribes ceding more than 64 million acres. They were expected to relocate to eight reservations, mostly in coastal areas. In exchange, the treaties guaranteed that Native signatories would receive various token compensations, including the right to fish in their "usual and accustomed grounds" (Gates, 1955, p. 57).

The most significant test of the Nineteenth Century treaties came more than a hundred years later during the so-called Washington Fish Wars (Reyes, 2016). In the 1960s, Washington State initiated a series of legal cases, charging Coast Salish fishers with allegedly violating state fishing regulations. This was part of an increasingly aggressive campaign by the Department of Fish and Wildlife to enforce compliance with state-determined fishing seasons, locations, and gear restrictions. Aboriginal fishers in western Washington reported frequent harassment by state officers (Heffernan, 2013). From a Native perspective, these state actions were a direct violation of the sovereign right to fish. Aboriginal fishers began a campaign of non-violent resistance, deploying their fishing nets to protest state intrusion.

Resulting legal actions went to the state supreme court in 1974. In a landmark ruling, Judge George Boldt affirmed that Coast Salish fishers have the right to determine their activities within traditional fishing grounds. The judge went a step further in interpreting a particular phrase from the treaties, which specified that Treaty Tribes would be allowed "to fish in common" with White settlers (Boxburger, 1989, p. 155). Boldt understood this to mean that the fishery must be shared equally. He concluded that Aboriginal fishers of Washington were entitled to half of the state-wide salmon quota, while non-Aboriginal commercial fishers and sport anglers would share the other half (Knutson, 1987). With a gavel strike, the 50/50 mandate became the foundation of state fisheries management, continuing to this day.

The Boldt decision enraged non-Aboriginal fishers. A political cartoon of the era captured the predominant sentiment: A lightning "Boldt" strikes over a story sea. A Native fisher is depicted hauling in a net filled with salmon while, in the background, a non-Aboriginal boat captain yells, "The Indians are catching all the fish!" (Museum of the American Indian, 2020, April 8). On one level, the cartoon illustrated a common concern among non-Aboriginal anglers that the principle of 50/50 apportionment unfairly favored Natives, who are a numerically small minority. But there was more to it than that. A *Seattle Times* photographer captured another infamous image of the Boldt backlash. Pictured are commercial fishing vessels staging a floating protest. The boat in the foreground displays large, hand-painted signs declaring "Indians are racist!" and "Non-Indian and proud of it!" (Museum of the American Indian, 2020, April 8). The message was unambiguously spelled out: The Fish Wars were about race.

Research Methods

The research project was done in collaboration with the Fraser River Peacemakers (FRP), a coalition of Aboriginal fishers and sport anglers who promote peaceful coexistence among fishing groups in the lower Fraser River basin. As a FRP member, I proposed a study that might help the group to address tensions between fishing groups. The goal of the project was to explore the viability of using social media as an educational platform to address fishing-related conflict. FRP oversaw the design and analysis phases. Additionally, in reviewing the findings, the group provided critical feedback on the potential uses and limitations of social media for educational purposes. As a representative body of Aboriginal and non-Aboriginal fishers, the FRP group was ideally qualified to comment on the findings.

This work follows in the tradition of participatory action research (PAR). The methodology draws on the anthropological tradition of participant observation, wherein the researcher is an active collaborator in the social setting (Lawson, 2015). PAR takes this notion a step further. The PAR practitioner seeks to equalize the traditional asymmetry of power between researcher and participant (McIntyre, 2008). Rather than attempting to be a dispassionate and omniscient observer, the participant observer positions themself as a stakeholder in the social setting. Moreover, they may work collegially with study participants, who may serve as coresearchers and/or coauthors. In this respect, PAR subverts empirical traditions that privilege the position of researcher (Glassman & Erdem, 2014). This approach is particularly needed where scholarly understandings of colonized groups are informed by research conducted by outsiders who operate from positions of dominance.

Two social media sites were selected to illustrate contrasting discourse patterns concerning the topic of Aboriginal fishing in lower British Columbia. One case analysis was performed on a discussion thread accompanying a YouTube video showing Aboriginal fishing on a Fraser tributary. The second was done on a discussion forum devoted to sport angling in lower British Columbia. I identified references to Aboriginal fishing and then coded these references as positive, neutral, or negative. For those identified as negative, I analyzed discursive turns (Thurlow & Mroczek, 2011), noting how other participants responded to hostile comments directed at First Nation fishers. The following two sections summarize findings from the case studies.

Case One: Anatomy of a Toxic Exchange

This YouTube discussion thread was identified as a particularly troubling example of hostility directed toward First Nation fishers in British Columbia. The video shows individuals harvesting salmon using a stone weir, a traditional fishing method that is legal for Natives in the province.

The participants used dip nets to transport the fish to a station, where the fish were dispatched. The person who posted the video included an incendiary title and caption, implying that the fishers were willfully destroying the fishery. Responses were overwhelmingly negative toward Aboriginal fishing.

In general, complaints aligned with one of these themes: (a) Aboriginal fishers are not being good stewards of the land; (b) their fishing methods are not traditional; (c) they are not eating the fish; (d) they are killing for profit; (e) they are trying to catch all of the fish; and (f) fishing laws and standards are not equitable. Some of these complaints (e.g., e, f) echoed legal objections voiced in the Boldt era. The issue of killing for profit was more specific to Canadian law, which, until recently, restricted Aboriginal harvests to subsistence and ceremonial uses. As with the Boldt-era complaints, these critiques carried strong racialized connotations. The concern was not simply that any group was trying to catch all of the fish. It was that Natives supposedly were trying to do so. In general, these arguments were framed in relation to Aboriginal culture. The following excerpt shows a tag-team rant about how Aboriginal fishers are allegedly not true to their traditional ways. Individual participants are identified with pseudonymous initials:

TB: This an embarrassment to Canada and a shame necklace hung around the neck of our Government....

CG: embarrassing to your culture.

TR: One of the most pathetic things i have ever seen. You think a group of people who utalize [*sic*] something so much would show a little respect. It is actually funny just how pathetic it has gotten....

DS: ... You should be ashamed as your ancestors would be turing [*sic*] in their graves on the lazy methods you do in life....

AP: Fuck all u white guys our people the natives were here first and thats the way we did it even before the honkys were around so fuck u

FS: I have been fishing this river for over twenty years and this method has been used since I can remember. A weir is a traditional method (minus shopping carts) and is not easy to build. Most of the fishstock escapes slaughter in high water when the water surges the weir....

Those who complained about First Nation fishing in this video zeroed in on alleged violations of traditional Aboriginal values. Aboriginal fishers were criticized for supposedly showing "little respect" for the fish and for using "lazy (fishing) methods." These complaints fall in the broader categories of First Nation fishers not being good stewards and their fishing methods not being traditional. Implied (but not directly stated) in this excerpt are allegations that First Nation fishers are killing for profit and that they are trying to wipe out the fishery (actions that supposedly violate Aboriginal values).

It is important to recognize the presence of oppositional voices in the vitriolic storm. Aboriginal fishers and allies mounted a vigorous defense even though they were vastly outnumbered. Facing a barrage of racial insults from multiple fronts, AP fired back with his own epithets. FS responded with a more reasoned argument, rebutting an earlier claim (preceding the excerpted section) that weirs trap all salmon in the river. Unfortunately, oppositional voices tended to be drowned out in the sheer volume of negative allegations. The asynchronous nature of threaded discussions made it difficult for Aboriginal respondents or allies to respond to a specific comment.

Case Two: Hope for Changing Hearts and Minds

The Case Two analysis was conducted on a moderated fishing forum on a website dedicated to sport fishing in lower British Columbia. Of the 243 discussions referencing Aboriginal fishing, almost two thirds were identified as negative; about one third were positive, and the rest were neutral. The negative comments contained many of the same themes appearing in Case One, albeit with different frequency. The most common complaints had to do with (a) allegedly illegal fishing practices or (b) inequity of fishing regulations. Other comments alleged that (c) First Nations sell salmon for profit or that (d) they catch too many fish. Most striking about the discussions on the fishing forum were differences in tone and discursive style compared to the Case One discussion. Exchanges on the Case Two forum were more conversational and far less confrontational.

The following excerpt is illustrative. Here, a sport angler (identified below as RT) posted a wire service article stating that the sockeye salmon fishery would be closed on the Fraser River due to low returns. Several other sport anglers (identified as CM, FA, KM, and TF) lamented the closure and suggested that the fishery should be closed for several years in order to restore the run. The conversation continued:

RT: Shut it down completely for a few years at least- to let the runs rebuild cuz it's only going to get worse if they don't. Especially with the native fishery on the Fraser, they don't really care about us sports fishermen, that's obvious, they just want the fish No matter what....

Moderator: ... You have two choices: 1) Continue to point fingers at each group that utilize the resource and make the life of those who manage it difficult so we get our "fair" share of catch. 2) Forget what took place in the last couple of years, focus on rebuilding the stock and fishery by working cooperatively with FOC and other groups that share a common interest. Pick one....

CM (Addressing the moderator): you are right but memories are hard to forget thats why there [*sic*] memories continuing to point is fruitless but we do it in hopes that our voices maybe heard

FA: What happens if one user group decides not to participate and continues fishing 24/7?

KM: Yeah shut down the sockeye fishery.... Now with the river closed who will be there to monitor the illegal native netting

TF: It's pretty silly isnt it ... if you want springs (Chinook salmon), put aside the flossing gear and use bar rods! Almost 0 chance of hooking sockeye that way, catch springs and the river remains open. ::) (The moderator) is very right. If we all want to have a resource that is renewable and available for all, we all need to work together.

As in the Case One discussion, participants launched a litany of complaints about Aboriginal fishing practices being unfair or illegal. There were important differences, however. In the Case Two forum, participants were not single-mindedly intent on whipping up opposition to Aboriginal fishing (as was the case in the YouTube example). Rather, they left room for opposing perspectives. Obviously, the tone of this conversation differed markedly from that of the Case One discussion. While divergent viewpoints emerged, there was much less overt antagonism.

These differences were due, in part, to the active enforcement of participation rules. The site's login instructions specified that discussion participants were prohibited from posting "offensive or illegal information, files and pictures." As the moderator participated in the discussions, he reminded participants of this policy when they pushed the bounds of civil discourse. The moderator was not the sole rule enforcer, however. In some instances, discussion participants in Case Two policed themselves. In the excerpt, for example, TF attempted to soften the criticism of Aboriginal fishing by pointing out that all parties need to work together. Unlike the transient commentators in Case One, forum participants in Case Two tended to be regulars who wanted to remain members of the virtual community. Consequently, they were more willing to abide by a common set of rules. The community was developing a culture of civility, at least among sport fishers. However, Aboriginal voices were largely absent from this forum.

Moving Beyond Behavior Regulation to Address Stereotypical Perceptions

Case Two provides a glimmer of hope that stakeholders might adopt some civility in working through difficult topics such as fishing and Aboriginal rights. In particular, Case Two suggests that potentially volatile exchanges can be kept productive when a moderator enforces participation rules actively and when participants see value in maintaining their learning community. These conditions, however, do not guarantee that participants will achieve more enlightened insights. Despite their judicious use of language and their citation of sources, many of the Case Two participants fell back on the same faulty logic utilized by Case One participants and by sport anglers in the post-Boldt era. For example, while Case One and Case Two participants argued strenuously for equity between fishing groups, neither group questioned why First Nation fishers should be prohibited from selling salmon for profit while virtually anyone else can be licensed to do so.

At the heart of this faulty reasoning are persistent misconceptions about Natives in relation to the environment. Shepard Krech (1999) coined the term "Environmental Indian" to describe dominant perceptions of Aboriginal peoples and environmental sustainability. He noted anthropological evidence that Natives of North America had a mixed environmental record prior to First Contact. Presumably, the historic evidence contradicts a romanticized vision of Native stewardship of the natural world. In many respects, Krech's original argument aligns with criticism leveled by critics Aboriginal fishing and hunting. Since 1999, numerous scholars (including Krech, himself) have refined the interpretation (see Ranco, 2007). Harkin and Lewis (2007) put it succinctly:

> If one begins with the assumption that Indians lived in complete harmony with their environment, when it is not only possible but easy to find coun-

terexamples, the blaze that results when this straw man is ignited gener-
ates, as the cliché goes, heat but no light. (p. xxii)

The image of the ecological Indian upholds Native peoples as guardians of
the environment. At the same time, they are expected to remain in a state
of pre-contact purity, residing pastorally in an untouched natural world.
Presumably, living in "complete harmony with nature" involves hunting
with stone-age tools and killing just enough to avoid starvation. If modern
Natives do anything that violates these expectations (e.g., using modern
firearms, earning a livable wage from fishing), they are condemned by the
dominant society for allegedly betraying their culture. This is a pernicious
form of oppression dressed up as flattery.

This line of reasoning helps to explain some of the logical contradictions
underlying arguments against Aboriginal fishing articulated in the case
studies. Case Two participants were fixated on what they viewed as overly
aggressive fishing methods used by Aboriginal fishers. As RT put it, "They
just want the fish, no matter what." Interestingly, the same claim applied
to non-Aboriginal sport anglers (i.e., "Sport anglers just want the fish, no
matter what") would likely be interpreted as a compliment. In this context,
the statement implies that sport anglers are single-mindedly determined
in their sporting activity. Why would the same observation carry opposite
connotations when applied to different fishing groups? The answer, I sus-
pect, has to do with non-Aboriginal perceptions of the Ecological Indian
stereotype. If one assumes that Natives are culturally obligated to catch fish
solely for subsistence purposes, then one might feel justified in criticizing
those who harvest above some minimal threshold (a common complaint in
Case Two) or those who sell salmon for profit (another common complaint
in Case Two). This logic supports a racist double standard. The cultural
argument condemns Natives for engaging in fishing activities that non-
Natives can freely pursue.

Implications for Adult Education

Educators understand that promoting environmental sustainability cannot be separated from the pursuit of social justice. According to Agyeman
et al. (2002), this awareness grew in the 1980s and 90s as low-income communities and people of color mobilized across North America to fight
industrial polluters. There was mounting evidence that affluent populations consume a greater share of natural resources, while those in poverty
tend to suffer disproportional harms (Bowers, 2017). In light of these
inequities, adult educators have adapted their environmental curricula
to include analyses of how human activities influence the well-being of

human and nonhuman populations (Griswold, 2017). The combination of environmental instruction and social critique has become a hallmark of ecojustice education.

One of the principal ways that educators promote ecojustice is to situate environmental learning in a particular locale. The goal of place-based environmental education "is to change the way students feel about and act in the places of their everyday lives in order to promote a more just and sustainable world" (Israel, 2012, p. 76). Some observers (e.g., Clover, 2003) have argued that neoliberalism and industrial capitalism have diminished people's sense of connectedness with their social and biological surroundings. In effect, many of us in industrialized nations have intellectually and emotionally vacated the land. An appropriate response, according to advocates of place-based learning (e.g., Ontong & Le Grange, 2014), is for educators to promote "reinhabitation" of place, inviting learners to reclaim their relationships with people and living systems where they live. A place-based curriculum has the potential to advance ecojustice in multiple ways. In focusing on the local, learners might be motivated to take action to improve living conditions for people in their communities. Additionally, the microanalysis of social and environmental dynamics within a familiar region might help learners to understand larger-scale phenomena elsewhere in the world. It is worth noting, here, that the pedagogical focus of place-based eco-learning tends to be external to the learner. The assumption is that people need to become more aware of their surroundings.

Sometimes overlooked in discussions of place-based learning is the need for internal work, which, in many cases, is a prerequisite for ecojustice and intellectual decolonization. Consider, for example, how place-based principles might be applied with fishing groups of lower British Columbia. We could imagine we are organizing a workshop on sustainable salmon fishing in the region. It would be safe to assume that such a geographically specific topic would be of interest to local fishing groups. Moreover, we could make a reasonable guess that lifelong anglers would already feel connected to the places that they fish. The case studies discussed in this chapter imply that salmon fishers are strongly motivated to take action to improve the fishery to benefit future generations. These indicators might suggest that anglers would be primed for a place-based workshop devoted to salmon fishing. There is a risk, however, that their preexisting ideas about fishing could hinder critical learning. Strongly opinionated individuals may be less open to considering perspectives that do not align with their own. In Case One and Case Two, for example, some sport fishers were convinced that Aboriginal gillnetting should be abolished. Any instruction that supports ecojustice would need to include some means for participants to evaluate the origins and validity of their beliefs. This sort of critical self-reflection is essential for decolonizing dominant understandings of the environment.

Sumner (2008) described a means to incorporate critical self-reflection into a place-based curriculum. A crucial component of Sumner's place-based approach is a close analysis of how community members view their environment and social relations. She uses the term "indigenous knowledge" to describe perspectives that people develop over extended periods of time as they transact within their immediate environment (p. 9). Here, the word "indigenous" is used generically in reference to knowledge generated by any individual or group, regardless of racial/ethnic background. Sumner suggested that adult educators should make the examination of indigenous knowledge central to any discussion of sustainability in a given locale. If learners are long-time residents of a given locale, their knowledge becomes content for discussion and scrutiny. Sumner's intention is to make the concept of indigenous knowledge useful for all adult educators, whether they work with Aboriginal groups or not. I would suggest that any instructional effort to incorporate indigenous knowledge in environmental learning must include perspectives of those who first populated the land. This is especially important where Aboriginal populations have been removed from a given region and/or Aboriginal perspectives have been erased from public discourse (Tuck et al., 2014). Adult educators who promote just sustainability have a moral obligation to honor these voices.

The argument for including Aboriginal perspectives underlies land education, a historically contextualized approach to place-based education and environmental justice. Land education rests on the assertion that all lands were once Aboriginal territories and that any discussion of land use should acknowledge the displacement of Aboriginal peoples (Calderon, 2014). This methodology challenges us to rethink dominant Western conceptions that define land by its economic usefulness, to consider cultural and spiritual understandings of place (Tuck et al., 2014). Obviously, land education is relevant where decisions about environmental sustainability have an impact on Aboriginal communities. Additionally, I would argue, this approach is needed where Aboriginal peoples are not visibly present.

If we accept the premise that sustainability education must acknowledge Aboriginal perspectives, we (at least, those of us who teach in North America) must confront the stereotype of the Environmental Indian. As Krech (1999) has pointed out, association between Aboriginal peoples and environmental stewardship is deeply engrained in dominant mythologies of North America. How many have uncritically accepted portrayals of Natives in Disney's *Pocahontas* or in the "Crying Indian" advertisement (Anderson, 2013) from the 1970s? While these images may seem benign on the surface, they serve on a deeper level to perpetuate an oppressive stereotype of Aboriginal peoples as primitive innocents (Marker, 2006). If we intend to incorporate indigenous knowledge into our curricula, we need to look closely at how our students' perceptions have been influenced by such caricatures of indigeneity.

This requires us to distinguish between etic and emic knowledge. Etic knowledge is generated from the perspective of outsiders, whereas emic knowledge is created by insiders (Sumner, 2008). In Case One, for example, critics claimed that the use of modern nets is not consistent with Aboriginal culture. If we were to address this claim in an educational setting, we might ask students to scrutinize the source. To what extent is this criticism based on emic sources (e.g., personal experience living in an Aboriginal community) versus etic sources (e.g., seeing Native characters on television)? It would be important to counter any inaccurate etic claims with authentic emic perspectives.

There is a more fundamental challenge in decolonizing education: If we are to help learners understand Aboriginal perspectives, we must scrutinize our own assumptions about indigeneity. Those of us living in North America should ask ourselves how, if at all, our perceptions have been influenced by the Environmental Indian stereotype. As educators, we are well aware of the need to check our biases to make sure we are not misrepresenting or misunderstanding people. What may not be so familiar is the importance of checking the directionality of our biases. We are used to spotting negative stereotypes of marginalized groups. But do we apply the same level of scrutiny to seemingly benign stereotypes, such as the imagined Environmental Indian? Marker (2006) recommended that educators take what might be called a binocular approach to critical reflection. While we seek to understand Aboriginal perspectives, we must simultaneously interrogate and disclose the foundations of our own understandings.

This point hit home for me some years ago. I had an appointment to meet with a Tribal Council to propose a fisheries conservation project. This was my first meeting with this leadership group. As the Council Chair met me at the door, I anticipated we would have a quick round of introductions, perhaps with some pleasantries. Instead, he asked me a question: "Who are you?" I gave my name and institutional affiliation. There was an uncomfortable silence as I started to sweat. Apparently, that was not the right answer. The meeting went on but, honestly, I do not recall much. I was too discombobulated. I drove home that evening, wondering what just happened. Then it occurred to me that the Chair was trying to teach me something. The lesson was this: If I want to be an ally to Aboriginal peoples in addressing a controversial challenge, I would need to start with deep self-reflection. Who am I? What does salmon fishing mean to me? Why do I want to work with Aboriginal partners? If do not have honest answers to such questions, I am not prepared to enter into a meaningful partnership. Wow, humbling.

REFERENCES

Agyeman, J., Bullard, R. D., & Evans, B. (2002). Exploring the nexus: Bringing together sustainability, environmental justice and equity. *Space & Polity*, *6*(1), 77–90.

Anderson, R. (2013). The "crying Indian," corporations, and environmentalism: A half-century of struggle over environmental messaging. In M. P. McAllister & E. West (Eds.), *The Routledge companion to advertising and promotional culture* (pp. 403–419). Routledge.

Bhabha, H. (2004). *The location of culture*. Routledge

Bowers, C. A. (2017). An ecojustice approach to educational reform in adult education. *New Directions for Adult and Continuing Education*. No. 153. Wiley.

Boxburger, D. (1989). *To fish in common: The ethnohistory of Lummi Indian salmon fishing*. University of Nebraska Press.

Calderon, D. (2014). Speaking back to manifest destinies: A land education-based approach to critical curriculum inquiry. *Environmental Education Research*, *20*(1), 24–36.

Clover, D. E. (2003). Environmental adult education: Critique and creativity in a globalizing world. *New Directions for Adult and Continuing Education*, *99*, 5-15.

Gates, C. M. (1955). The Indian treaty of Point No Point. *Pacific Northwest Quarterly*, *46*(2), 52–58.

Glassman, M., & Erdem, G. (2014). Participatory action research and its meanings: Vivencia, praxis, conscientization. *Adult Education Quarterly*, *64*(3), 206–221.

Griswold, W. (2017). Sustainability, ecojustice, and adult education. *New Directions for Adult and Continuing Education*, *153*, 7–15.

Harkin, M. E., & Lewis, D. R. (2007) Introduction. In M. E. Harkin & D. R. Lewis (Eds.), *Native Americans and the environment: Perspectives on the ecological Indian* (pp. xix–xxxiv). University of Nebraska Press.

Heffernan, T. (2013). *Where the salmon run: The life and legacy of Billy Frank Jr.* State Heritage Center.

Hill, R. J. (2003). Environmental justice: Environmental adult education at the confluence of oppressions. *New Directions for Adult and Continuing Education*, *153*, 27–38.

Israel, A. L. (2012). Putting geography education into place: What geography educators can learn from place-based education, and vice versa. *Journal of Geography*, *111*(2), 76–81.

Knutson, P. (1987). The unintended consequences of the Boldt decision. *Cultural Survival Quarterly*, *11*(2), 1–6.

Krech, S. (1999). *The ecological Indian: Myth and history*. W. W. Norton & Co.

Lawson, H. A. (2015). *Participatory action research*. Oxford University Press.

Malick, M. J., & Cox, S. P. (2016). Regional-scale declines in productivity of pink and chum salmon stocks in western North America. *PLoS ONE*, *11*(1), 1–23.

Marker, M. (2006). After the Makah whale hunt: Indigenous knowledge and limits to multicultural discourse. *Urban Education*, *42*(5), 1–24.

McIntyre, A. (2008). *Participatory action research*. Sage.

Museum of the American Indian. (2020, April 8). *Back to Boldt*. https://americanindian.si.edu/nk360/pnw-fish-wars/backlash

Ontong, K., & Le Grange, L. (2014). The role of place-based education in developing sustainability as a frame of mind. *South African Journal of Environmental Education*, *30*, 27–38.

Reyes, L. L. (2016). *The last fish war: Survival on the rivers*. Chin Music Press.

Roberts, C. (2010). Treaty rights ignored: Neocolonialism and the Makah whale hunt. *Kenyon Review*, *32*(1), 78–90.

Ranco, D. (2007). The ecological indian and the politics of representation. Native Americans and the environment. *Perspectives on the Ecological Indian*, 32–51.

Sumner, J. (2008). Protecting and promoting indigenous knowledge: Environmental adult education and organic agriculture. *Studies in the Education of Adults*, *40*(2), 207–223.

Sun, D., & Hallin, L. (2018). *British Columbia's fisheries and aquaculture sector*, 2016 Ed. Report to British Columbia Ministry of Agriculture.

Tuck, E., McKenzie, M., & McCoy, K. (2014). Land education: Indigenous, post-colonial, and decolonizing perspectives on place and environmental education research. *Environmental Education Research*, *20*(1), 1–23.

Thurlow, C., & Mroczek, K. R. (2011). *Digital discourse: Language in new media*. Oxford University Press.

Verhovek, S. (1999, May 18). Reviving tradition, tribe kills a whale. *New York Times*, A18. https://www.nytimes.com/1999/05/18/us/reviving-tradition-tribe-kills-a-whale.html

Wadewitz, L. K. (2012). *The nature of borders: Salmon, boundaries, and bandits of the Salish Sea*. University of British Columbia Press.

CHAPTER 20

MAN-ENVIRONMENT INTERACTION IN THE RAINFORESTS AND SUSTAINABLE DEVELOPMENT

Practical Implications for Adult Education

Kofo A. Aderogba
Tai Solarin University of Education, Nigeria

Environmental changes and man's role in bringing the changes about are circularly causal (Abler et al., 1976). The interaction of people and their environments are necessitated by their needs. From cradle, people were known to need one item or the other to meet their needs. The needs may be simple or complex; they may be expensive or cheap. At times, they may be readily available or scarce. Sometimes, people source for resources within their community to be able to satisfy their needs. But often, the needs must be met. Invariably, therefore, someone must act (process) and then get (a structure). Incidentally, the needs, processes, and structures are continual. It is the same concept that results in an estate, the longest expressway, the most complex manufacturing plant, a farmland, and others. People dwell in the environment and continually interact with it

Advancing the Global Agenda for Human Rights, Vulnerable Populations, and Environmental Sustainability: Adult Education as Strategic Partner, pp. 323–337

to meet their needs. In the process, people change the face of the earth in micro and/or macro scales.

The Earth's climate seems to be warming, probably in response to human activities (Strahler, 2002). Moreover, because the rainforests can provide agricultural land, minerals, and timber, for example, the pressure to allow deforestation continues (Strahler, 2002). The interaction does not leave out any state of matter—solid, liquid, or gas. An example that may quickly come to mind is the *Human Impact on the Carbon Cycle* (Archer, 2010, and as described by Falkowski et al., 2000). Despite the usefulness and impact of the cycle, an effective global commitment to the reduction of carbon dioxide (CO_2) release and control of global warming still awaits human beings (Riebeek, 2011).

This chapter addresses the human-environment interaction using the rainforests of Southwestern Nigeria for generic discussion, identifies consequences of the interactions, and offers educational interventions for sustainable forest management (SFM). It is organized into eight parts: this introduction, the conceptual clarification, a brief discussion of the Southwestern Nigeria, foremost feature of the forests, human impacts on the forest and consequences, past and contemporary efforts towards sustainability of the rainforest, practical implications for teaching and learning in adult education, and conclusion.

Conceptual Clarification

The concepts of *man-environment interaction* can be further accentuated by that of *environmental sustainability* that seems to adequately explain the structure this author believes can best elucidate the natural progression of the phenomenon under discussion (Camp, 2001). It links with the empirical concepts and important systems used in promoting and systematizing the knowledge espoused by the authors of such works (Adom et al., 2018; Peshkin, 1993).

Environmental sustainability allows for the needs of human beings to be met in the present without jeopardizing the ability of future generations to meet their needs. It is responsible behavior to interact with the environment to avoid depletion or degradation of natural resources, for long-term environmental quality. The natural environment has a rather remarkable ability to rejuvenate itself and sustains its viability: When nature is left alone, it has a tremendous ability to care for itself. But when people enter the picture (human-environment interaction) and use many of the natural resources provided by the environment, things change. Human actions can deplete natural resources, and without the application of environmental sustainability methods, long-term viability is compromised. Thus, there is the need for care for the environment and enforcement of environmental education.

One of the ways environmental sustainability is being applied is through sustainable agriculture—the use of farming techniques that protect the environment. Sustainable agriculture has grown out of concerns over the industrialization of agriculture that began in the 20th century (Food and Agricultural Organization [FAO], 2010; Nigerian Environmental Study and Action Team, 2003). Although industrial agriculture could produce abundant amounts of food at affordable prices, this method of farming can be detrimental to the environment. Industrial agricultural methods are heavily reliant on chemical fertilizers and pesticides as well as high demands on soil and water resources. Also, industrial crops are often mono-crops, which involves growing a single crop year after year. These methods can lead to water pollution when chemicals run off into waterways, deplete the water resources due to overuse, and cause soil erosion and poor soil quality due to aggressive planting (FAO, 2010). With sustainable agriculture, however, farmers minimize water use and lower the dependence on chemical pesticides and fertilizers. They also minimize tillage of the soil and rotate crop planting each year to ensure better soil quality.

Similarly, sustainable forestry is another application of environmental sustainability approach. This is the practice of regulating the forest resources to meet the needs of society and industry while preserving the healthy and natural state of the forests (FAO, 2007; World Wildlife Fund, 2019). The forests are important to local and national economies. Wood can be used as a source of fuel, timber can be used in the construction industry, wood pulp can be used in the manufacture of paper, and so on. But beyond what forests can do for an economy, they also have environmental benefits: trees capture and store carbon dioxide, keeping it out of the atmosphere. The forests also play key roles in the water cycle. Tree roots gather water from the ground and release it into the air as water vapor. If forests are cleared without environmental sustainability methods in place, these benefits are certainly lost, with probably much greater cost over space and time.

Environmental sustainability is, in summary, a consideration of whether the rates of renewable resource harvest, pollution creation, and nonrenewable resource depletion can be continued indefinitely (Myers, 1994; Orimogunje, 2014). If they cannot be continued indefinitely, they are not sustainable (Omosanya & Ajibade, 2011; Onefeli & Adesoye, 2014; Orimogunje, 2014). The following describe the Southwestern Nigeria, the rainforest, and how it has been impacted over the years despite measures towards sustainable forest.

The Southwestern Nigeria

The tropical monsoon climate, designated by the Köppen climate classification as "Am," is the predominant climate in the Southwestern region of Nigeria. The climate is influenced by the monsoon wind originating from the South Atlantic Ocean, which is brought into the country by the maritime tropical (MT) air mass, a warm moist sea-to-land seasonal wind. Its warmth and high humidity give it a strong tendency to ascend and produce copious rainfall, because of the condensation of water vapor in the air (Odjugo, 2010).

The climate has very small temperature range, with the region experiencing heavy and abundant rainfall. The storms are usually convectional because of proximity to the equatorial belt. The annual rainfall is very high, usually above the 2,000 mm rainfall totals given for tropical rainforest climates worldwide. The region experiences a double rainfall maximum, characterized by two high rainfall peaks, with a short dry season and a longer dry season falling between and after each peak respectively. However, the tropical wet and dry climate exerts enormous influence on the vegetal cover.

The most expansive topography of the region is the rugged highland, comprised of Kukuruku (Yoruba) ranges, Asawo and Asamuni. The rivers (Ogun, Oshun, Ogunpa, Owena, Osse) and their tributaries flow in two general directions within the region: southwards into the lagoons and creeks which empty into the Atlantic Ocean and northwards into the Niger River.

Waste management including sewage treatment, the linked processes of deforestation, soil degradation and climate change or global warming are the major environmental problems directly and indirectly impacting on the forests (Aderogba & Bankole, 2016; Aikhionbare, 2015). More recently, cases of kidnapping and mayhem between farmers and Fulani herdsmen are becoming serious issues (Aderogba, 2018). Haphazard industrial planning, increased urbanization, poverty, attitudinal behavior, and lack of competence or political will (or technical know-how) of the municipal governments are the major reasons for high levels of waste pollution in major cities and towns (Aderogba & Bankole, 2016; Onefeli & Adesoye, 2014). Some of the so-called "solutions" have been disastrous to the environment, resulting in untreated waste being dumped in places where it pollutes the entire environment, including air, soil, waterways, and groundwater.

As it is for the entire nation (Central Intelligence Agency, 2013, 2019; Council of African Security & Development, 2015), the economic development had been hindered by years of military rule, corruption, and mismanagement. The restoration of democracy and subsequent economic reforms have not successfully put the country back on track toward achieving its full economic potential; the same goes for the region. As of 2014,

Southwestern Nigeria was the largest economy of the country (Nigeria National Bureau of Statistics [NBS], 2014). The region is at the forefront of the country in attempting to achieve the first of the Sustainable Development Goals, which is to end poverty in all its forms by 2030.

The region is defined by six of the states to the southwest of the Niger River in Nigeria, namely, Lagos, Ogun, Oyo, Osun, Ekiti and Ondo States whose state capitals are Ikeja, Abeokuta, Ibadan, Osogbo, Ado Ekiti, and Akure respectively. The Gulf of Guinea is the southern boundary, and the Republic of Benin is to the west. Kwara and Kogi States (of Nigeria) are in the northern boundary. Edo State (also of Nigeria) is the eastern boundary. The population of the entire region is 27,581,992, which is about 19.70% of the population of Nigeria. The population is growing fast, and it is the most populous and most densely populated region of Nigeria (Nigeria National Population Commission, 2006).

Apart from the high population concentration, western educational advancement (from primary to tertiary level) had attained a "highest level of development" too. But measuring by the Millennium Development Goal, social, economic, and infrastructural developments have been hampered through history. There remains a lot to do to eradicate extreme poverty, attain universal primary education, promote gender equality and empower women, reduce children mortality, improve maternal health, combat HIV/AIDs, malaria and other diseases, ensure environmental sustainability and develop global partnership for development (World Bank, 2016). The governments at the three levels (federal, state, and local) have not been able to achieve sustainability in these respects due to neglect from the vicious cycle of regional and national development over the years (Aderogba, 2018; Trager, 2001).

Agriculture is the main stake of the economy engaging over 65% of the population; more than 85% is dependent on it, at least for income and foods. The sector is being transformed by commercialization at the small, medium, and large-scale enterprise levels. Suffice to say that mechanized agriculture is not popular nor are any modern forms of agriculture. The practices are still largely peasant. Whereas the International Institute of Tropical Agriculture (IITA) is situated at Ibadan, the Oyo State capital, the impacts have not been astonishing.

Also, the sector used to be the principal foreign exchange earner for the nation at large. Apart from the food crops (yam, coco yam, cassava, maize, banana and plantain, vegetables, fruits, and others), cocoa, kola nut, rubber, and palm produce were major cash crops and the largest non-oil revenue spinners. Prior to the Nigeria civil war, the region was self-sufficient in food. However, the sector has failed to keep pace with the rapid population growth, and there is now huge reliance on food imports for sustenance (NBS, 2014). Also, since 1970s, the use of inorganic fertilizers has been promoted by the local, state, and federal governments. Compared to expectation, industrialization has been in its lowest ebb though it is the most industrialized part of the country with the largest concentration at Lagos-Abeokuta-Shagamu-Ibadan complex.

Foremost Features of the Forests

The natural forest vegetation has four main layers: emergent, canopy, understory and forest floor. Each has different plants and animals that have adapted for life in the area. The *Emergent Layer* has trees that are the tallest, towering as high as 60 meters above the forest floor with trunks that measure up to 3.5 meters. The trees are broad-based, hardwood evergreen. Since it towers to the topmost layer, it abundantly benefits from sunlight. Eagles, monkeys, bats, and butterflies are more plentiful.

The *Canopy Layer* is the primary layer. The trees here form a sort of roof over the two lower layers. Most of the trees have smooth, oval leaves that come together as maze of branches. There are many animals living here because of availability of abundant food to eat. The animals include snakes, toucans, and tree frogs.

The cool *Understory Layer* benefits only a little from rays of sunlight, thus plants must grow large leaves to reach the sunlight. The plants hardly ever grow to reach 8 meters. Many animals and a large concentration of insects live here. *The Forest Floor* is often very dark since it is the lowest layer. Almost no plant grows in this area; since hardly any sun reaches the floor of the forest, things begin to decay quickly. A leaf that might take one year to decompose in the regular climate will disappear in 6–7 weeks. It is often teeming with animal life, especially insects. The largest animals of the rainforest generally live here—the likes of anteater families.

The second and third layers are especially densely strewn with epiphytes, intertwined with lianas that rush towards the sun. The epiphytic plants attach to trunks and branches and obtain water and minerals from rain and debris that collects on the supporting plants. The undergrowth in some areas is restricted by poor penetration of sunlight to ground level. Only about 2% of the sun gets to the floor of the forests. Where the leaf canopy is destroyed or thinned, the ground beneath is colonized by dense, tangled growth of vines, shrubs, and smaller trees, called jungle.

There are many species of plants, insects, and microorganisms still undiscovered (Taylor, 2005). According to her, rainforests are "the jewels of the Earth and the largest pharmacy, simply because scores of natural medicines have been discovered there. The forest provides timber, firewood, leaves, fruits, and others,, as well as animal products such as meat. It is home to several birds, butterflies and beetles, bats and certain monkeys, chimpanzee, chameleons, turtles, snakes, and lizards, as well as some predators (FAO, 2010; Faleyimu et al. 2013). Fungi are also common. They feed on decomposing remains of plants and animals.

Incidentally, the forests, as well as the endemic forest species, are rapidly disappearing due to deforestation, the resulting habitat loss and pollution of the atmosphere. The forests have been subjected to heavy legal and illegal logging for valuable hardwoods and agricultural clearance (slash-and-burn, clear cutting); expanding urban areas, industrial and transportation land use; plantations, and others. Thus, many species of the forest animals are endangered, and many others have gone extinct as the number of hectares of forest decreases. Less than 75% of the natural vegetation can be observed, and the remaining 25% is certainly currently being threatened. In other words, there are more secondary vegetation and cultigens (FAO, 2010).

The region has therefore lost most of its forests because of development, slash-and-burn cultivation, and harvesting by the increasing population. It is rapidly being replaced by grassland at some localities particularly at the fringes and at the repeatedly long-cultivated areas. What is commonly found now is mostly secondary vegetation and cultigens (Faleyimu et al., 2013; FAO, 2010; Nigerian Environmental Study and Action Team, 2003).

The Human Impacts on the Forest and Consequences

As earlier noted, the dwellers depend on the forests for a lot of things, including food, herbal medicine, building materials, leaves and fruits for consumption, agricultural practices, and production. Moreover, industries and human settlements must be built; roads and aviation land use, railways and others must pass through the forests. These have been severally grouped under bush burning, unregulated logging, rapid urbanization, and urban processes, use of wood as cooking fuel, soil erosion, agricultural practices, oil spillage and others (Aderogba & Bankole, 2016; Aikhionbare, 2015).

The consequences of all of these on the forests are devastating. An Ijesha man (Oshun State origin), alarmed at the different dimensions and approaches of deforestation, described it this way:

> When next you come, you will see fresh land grabbing, slash-and-burn, ...
> The shrine of our gods and goddesses are expanding too ... we built new
> shrines.... People collect firewood for domestic use; the means of liveli-
> hood of many. Then, not now, if you come here and you shout, your voice
> will echo down the slope. Everywhere is opened now..... Most of our herbal
> materials—barks of stems and stems, leaves and branches of plants, roots,
> and so on, are derived from here, and we exploit them now than ever

before ... and others come here to pick leaves for their trades ... pick fruits at their seasons ... set traps for animals and birds, pick snails and hunt for animals like squirrel, antelope, python, and others. People come almost on daily basis for research ... years away, no road was here, there was only one-foot path and when you are passing through, it is under shade of trees all through. You will hear birds crying [chirping and buzzing]; late in the evening, insects will be crying [chirping and buzz-saw whine, droning chorus and a faint whirring sound]. Even snakes, squirrels....They have all been killed/driven away. (Chief Joseph Adelowo Fayemi, September 10, 2019)

The consequences are largely the reasons why the United Nations Food and Agricultural Organization (UNFAO) (2010) described deforestation in the entire nation (Nigeria) this way:

In 2005, Nigeria had the highest rate of deforestation in the world, ... In 2005 12.2%, the equivalent of 11,089,000 hectares had been deforested.... Between 1990 and 2000, Nigeria lost an average of 409,700 hectares of forests every year equal to an average annual deforestation rate of 2.38%. Between 1990 and 2005, in total, Nigeria lost 35.7% of its forest cover, or around 6,145,000 hectares. (United Nations Food and Agriculture Organization, 2010, Paper 163)

The United Nations Environmental Program (2008) observed similar deforestation processes and activities in Eastern Bolivia; the peat forests in Indragiri Hulu, Indonesia; Maranhaao State of Brazil; Madagascar deforestation for pastoral land/agriculture; Southeast Asian Islands of Borneo and Sumatra; Brazilian city of Rio de Janeiro, around Pakke; Tiger Reserve in India; and Blue Mountains of Australia, to name a few. The results and effects have been exceedingly grievous (Aderoba & Bankole, 2016; Omosanya & Ajibade, 2011; Vanguard News, 2019). Again, Aikhionbare (2015) grouped and listed some of the consequences that include loss of species and biodiversity; massive erosion; conflicts between farmers and herdsmen; disruption of water cycle, weather patterns and the ecosystems; and release of greenhouse gasses when the trees are felled. However, it is likely that, at the current rate and by the turn of the century, there will not be forests any more. But publicly and culturally, there have been some attempts to curb deforestation.

Past and Contemporary Efforts Toward Sustainability of the Rainforests

There have been efforts toward attaining sustainable forest management (SFM) in the region (and in the country). Managing forests sustainably means optimizing their benefits. This includes timber and contributions to food security to meet the needs of the society in a way that conserves and maintains forest ecosystems for the benefit of present and future generations (Environmental Education, 2008; Haugen, 2006; World Commission on Environment and Development, 1987). Despite the significant progress made towards SFM at the global level, the implementation is highly variable where the capacity to utilize or enforce SFM policies, laws, and regulations remains uneven. Moreover, other land uses such as agriculture can be financially more attractive in the short-term compared to forest management, motivating deforestation, and land-use changes.

As it is for the entire nation, there have been Forest Reserves created, and to some extent, preserved by the Central Government. Foremost among them is Olokemeji Forest Reserve, created in 1915, the first in the country. It is about 71.24 km² of which about 10.88 km² is now savanna (Akinsoji, 2013; Ogunleye et al., 2004). Other reserves include Akure (Ondo State) 66 km², Idanre (Ondo State) 561 km², Oba Hill (Osun State) 52 km², Oluwa (Ondo State) 829 km², Ise (Ekiti State) 142 km², Omo (Ogun State) 1,320 km², Idanre (Ondo State) 561 km², Ofosa (Ondo State) 394 km², IITA (Oyo State) 10 km² and Osho (Oyo Stat) 24 km². Many of them are located in Ondo State. Omo Forest Reserve is the most extensive. They are habitats to various endangered species of birds, insects, animals, and plants.

The UNFAO has been of help to overcome the challenges of the reserves in several ways. They have provided policy advice as well as supporting capacity building through field projects, workshops, seminars, and hands-on-training and assessed of forest resources, definition of the elements of sustainable forest management and monitoring the progress towards it. In addition, they have identified, tested, and promoted innovative, multipurpose forest management approaches and techniques that respond to the need for mitigating and adapting to a changing climate, increased demand for wood and non-wood forest products and services, and threats from fires, pests and natural disasters. The UNFAO has also promoted sustainable forest management by working at the national and international levels and through collaborative partnerships to address and help solve regional and global forest-related issues. It also manages the SFM Toolbox (SFMT), a comprehensive online technical package of tools and examples to facilitate and guide the implementation of sustainable forest management in various contexts.

In addition to the Federal Universities, two of which are exclusively for teaching and research into agriculture, forestry, and related fields of study, each of the six states has at least one university where Agricultural Sciences and Forestry are taught and researched (except University of Lagos and Lagos State University (in Lagos State). There are also more than 20 private universities. Apart from the IITA and the teaching and researching in the universities, there are eight institutes and a Cooperative College where the science and arts of agricultural sciences and forestry are directly and or indirectly absolutely taught. They have all been in the businesses of teaching, research, and development for decades. It may not be unexpected, therefore, that much must have been done in research and development in agriculture and forestry (Akinsoji, 2013; Orimogunje, 2014).

Furthermore, all the six states have a college of education each and agricultural science is being taught to the potential teachers. Suffice to say that all the states have a government ministry saddled with the responsibility of regulating agricultural and forest research and extension services throughout their respective states. In all, adults are the administrators, researchers, teachers/lecturers, and learners. Thus, agriculture and forestry are accorded "high priority" in the region. But these notwithstanding, forest degradations are humongous (Aderogba & Bankole, 2016).

Aderogba and Bankole (2016) like Aikhionbare (2015) assert that Nigeria can end deforestation if the results and recommendations of available research in the region (and in Nigeria) could be implemented. Sustainable forest management (SFM), as it addresses forest degradation and deforestation, is copiously desirable. Forests and trees, when sustainably managed, make vital contributions both to people and the planet, boosting livelihoods, providing clean air and water, conserving biodiversity, and responding to climate change (Myers, 1994; Oduro-Mensah, 1992).

Aderogba and Bankole (2016) and Aikhionbare (2015) have differently suggested the following, in straightforward approaches as panacea to deforestation and SFM in the region: reforestation, protection of existing forests, focus on alternative forms of cooking fuel, going paperless, eating less meat (bush meat), and orientation and reorientations of the general public. Alamu and Agbeja (2011), Ogunleye et al. (2004) and Ogundele et al. (2011) were indifferent to these too.

Despite these, environmental education (EE) as prescribed by Aderogba and Bankole (2016), Belanger (1999), Egunyomi, (2008), Haugen (2006), and Sumner (2003), was not given the priority that would have been adopted and practiced by all. United Nations Educational, Scientific and Cultural Organization (2014), Walker (2015), and Wals et al. (2014) are more suggestive, explicit, and emphatic about these.

Practical Implications for Teaching and Learning in Adult Education

Following from above, it is imperative to advance environmental education in adult education either towards entering the industry, advancing the careers, earning credentials, or learning for personal enrichment in natural environment functions, and particularly, how human beings can manage behavior and ecosystems to live sustainably. It should be perceived as a multidisciplinary field integrating disciplines such as biology, chemistry, physics, ecology, earth science, atmospheric science, mathematics, and geography. The United Nations Educational, Scientific and Cultural Organization (UNESCO, 2014) states that the EE will be vital in imparting inherent respect for nature amongst society, and in enriching public environmental awareness. The organization emphasizes the role of EE in safeguarding future global developments of societal quality of life (QOL) through the protection of the environment, eradication of poverty, minimization of inequalities and insurance of sustainable development (UNESCO, 2014).

The term *environmental education* (EE) here implies education within the school system, from primary to postsecondary and up to tertiary levels of education. However, it sometimes includes all efforts to educate the public and other audiences, using print materials, websites, media campaigns, and others. There are also ways that environmental education could be taught outside the traditional classroom: Aquariums, zoos, parks, and nature centers all have ways of teaching the public about the environment. Therefore, the components of the EE should include but not limited to: (a) creating awareness and sensitivity to the environment and environmental challenges by change agents; (b) knowledge and understanding of the environment and environmental challenges; (c) attitude of concern and love for the environment and motivation to improve or maintain environmental quality; (d) skills to identify and help resolve environmental challenges through mitigation; and (e) participation and collaboration in activities that lead to the resolution of environmental challenges. It should not advocate a viewpoint or course of action. Rather, it should teach individuals and groups how to weigh various sides of an issue through critical thinking and enhance their problem-solving and decision-making skills. These will certainly engender sustainable forest management, combat desertification, halt and reverse land degradation and halt biodiversity lost as targeted by one of the eight agendas of the Millennium Development Goals of the United Nations (which is binding on the nation). It is required that there will be a formidable regional and national leadership to advance environmental literacy; and the establishment of an EE center that will be responsible for coordination and or implementation of all concerned programs and activities.

CONCLUSION

The foregoing has demonstrated that the rainforests of Southwestern Nigeria are the free gifts of nature to the region. They are important to the region for: food and medicine; natural and original beauty; conservation of water and soil; home of birds, animals, and insects; human livelihood; storage and absorption of carbon; wood for fire, lumber and other products; shelter for people; regulation of climate within the region and beyond; controlling/mitigating flood; shrines of gods and goddesses; tourism and education; and others. However, they require proper care and maintenance for sustainability.

EE for sustainable forest management with sustainable curricular is required. Apparently, the existing EE curriculum needs to be reviewed and revised to enable it to become capable of addressing the contemporary challenges. Specialized aspects of forest management should be directed to all levels of education. The forests generally and the forest reserves need to be properly protected and fully funded so that the endangered species will continue to increase in population and spread, thereby increasing growth of the economy of the region.

There should be massive reforestation whenever any tree is cut down for economic or social reasons, (there should be simultaneous multiple replanting); aggressive protection of existing forests; identification, encouragement and development of alternative forms of cooking fuel; going paperless at homes, offices, schools and colleges, and others; discouragement in animal hunting and eating forest meat; orientations of members of the general public; and according greatest priority to Environmental Education with governments' political wills, policies and programs.

The International Union for the Conservation of Nature (IUCN) Species Survival Commission (SSC) is a science-based network of more than 8,000 volunteer experts from almost all countries of the world, all working towards achieving the vision of a just world that values and conserves nature through positive action to reduce the loss of diversity of life on earth. This commission is in the best position to give technical assistance. The commission may use the resources of the Institutes and Colleges of Agriculture and Forestry and those of the over 20 tertiary institutions in the region. Specifically, the Conservation Translocation Specialist Group (CTSG) of the International Union for the Conservation of Nature (IUCN) Species Survival Commission (SSC) should be challenged to face emerging threats, battle against extinction, restore species, and thereby yield wide-ranging benefits for nature and people.

As it is in India, Healthy Forest Reserve Program (HFRP) should be introduced as it will help private landowners restore, enhance, and protect forestland resources on private lands through easements and financial assistance. HRFP will aid the recovery of endangered and threatened species under the Endangered Species Act (that should be enacted), improve plant and animal biodiversity and enhance carbon sequestration.

REFERENCES

Abler, R., Adams, J. S., & Guold, P. (1976). *Spatial organization: Geographers' views of the world.* Prentice Hall Inco.

Aderogba, K. A. (2018, June). *Climate change and Fulani Herdsmen: Contemporary problems of sustainable agriculture and food security in Southwestern Nigeria; a clarion call for public enlightenment* [Paper presented]. The 2018 International conference of Faculty of Education, University of Ibadan on Building Safer World through Education.

Aderogba, K. A., & Bankole, M. O. (2016). Unsustainable exploitation of the Guinea Savannah, South of Sahara: Issues, policies and programs for sustainability, *Environment and Sustainable Development in the 21St Century, Ife Soc. Sci. Rev. Jr.* (Special Issue) 78–95.

Adom, D., Hussein, E. K., & Joe, A. (2018). Theoretical and conceptual framework: Mandatory ingredient of quality research. *Int. Journal of Sci. Research, 7*(1), 438–441.

Aikhionbare, I. (2015, November 7). Deforestation in Nigeria. InfoGuideNigeria. com. *InfoGuide Nigeria.* https://infoguidenigeria.com/deforestation-nigeria-7-causes-5-effects-6-ways-stop/

Akinsoji, A. (2013). Quantitative analysis of a forest fragment in Olokemeji Forest Reserve, Nigeria. *Journal of Natural Sciences Research, 3*(13), 111–114.

Alamu, L. O., &Agbeja, B. O. (2011). Deforestation and endangered indigenous tree species in South-West Nigeria. *International Journal of Biodiversity and Conservation, 3*(7), 291–297.

Archer, D. (2010). *The global carbon cycles.* Princeton University Press.

Belanger, P. (1999). *Adult environmental education: Awareness and environmental action.* A series of 29 booklets documenting workshops held at the Fifth International Conference on Adult Education (1997). UNESCO Institute for Education.

Camp, W. G. (2001). Formulating and evaluating theoretical framework for career and technical education research. *AVERA, 26*(1), 4.

Central Intelligence Agency. (2013). *The CIA world fact book 2014.* Skyhorse.

Central Intelligence Agency. (2019, February). *Nigeria—CIA World Factbook.* National Intelligence Agency of the United States of America.

Council of African Security and Development. (2015, January 20). The economic development of Nigeria from 1914–2014. *CASADE.* https://www.casade.org/economic-development-nigeria-1914-2014/

Egunyomi, D. A. (2008). Continuing education for environmental sustainability in the 21st century Nigeria: Issues and perspective. *Pakistan Journal. of Social. Sciences, 3*(3), 240–244.

Environmental Education. (2008). *The Modern Impetus for EE: The Tibilisi Declaration (1977).* http://www.gdrc.org/uem/ee/1-4.html

Faleyimu, O. I., Agbeja, B. O. & Akinyemi, O. (2013). State of forest regeneration in Southwest Nigeria. *African Journal of Agricultural Research, 8*(26), 3381–3383.

Falkowski, P., Schole, R. J., Boyle, E., Canadell, J., Canfield, D., Elser, J., Gruber, N., Hibbard, K., Hogberg, P., Linder, S., MacKenzie, F. T., Moore, B., Pedersen, T., Rosenthal, Y., Seitzinger, S., Smetacek, V., & Steffen, W. (2000). The global carbon cycle: A test of our knowledge of earth as a system. *Science, 290*(5490), 291–196.

Fayemi, J. A. (2019, September 10). An in-depth interview conducted with a community chieftain at Ila, Oshun State (Nigeria), on: *The history and status of Rainforest in Southwestern Nigeria.*

Food and Agriculture Organization. (2007). *Manual on deforestation, degradation and fragmentation using remote sensing and GIS* (MAR-SFM Working Paper 5 / 2007).

Food and Agriculture Organization. (2010). *Global forest resources assessment 2010, Country Report.* Food and Agricultural Organization Paper 163.

Food and Agricultural Organization. (2017). *The charcoal transition: Greening the charcoal value chain to mitigate climate change and improve local livelihoods.* Food and Agriculture Organization of the United Nations.

Haugen, C. S. (2006). *Environmental adult education theory and adult learning principles: Implications for training.* [Master's thesis, American University]. ProQuest Digital Dissertations.

Myers, N. I. (1994). Tropical deforestation: Rates and patterns in the causes of tropical deforestation. In K. Brown & D. Pearce (Eds.), *The economic and statistical analysis of factors giving rise to the loss of tropical forests* (pp. 27–40). UCL Press.

National Bureau of Statistics. (2014). *Nigeria's NBS forecast: Real GDP.* National Bureau of Statistics.

Nigeria National Population Commission. (2006). *The 2006 Census Results.* National Population Commission.

Nigerian Environmental Study and Action Team. (2003) *Nigeria's threatened environment: A national profile.* Nigeria Environmental Study and Action Team.

Odjugo, P. A. (2010). General overview of climate change impacts in Nigeria. *Journal of Human Ecology, 29*(1), 47–55.

Oduro-Mensah, D. (1992). Environmental education and awareness creation through adult education: Suggestions from Ghana. *Adult Education and Development*, (39), 251–264.

Ogundele, A. T., Eludoyin, O. S., & Oladapo, O. S. (2011). Assessment of impact of charcoal production on soil properties in the derived Savanna. Oyo State, Nigeria, *Journal of Soil Science and Environmental Management, 2*(5), 142–146.

Ogunleye, A. J., Adeola, A. O., Ojo, L. O., & Aduradola, A. M. (2004). Impact of arming activities on vegetation in Olokemeji Forest Reserve, Nigeria. *Global Nest: The International Journal, 6*(2), 131–140.

Omosanya, K. O., & Ajibade, O. M. (2011). Environmental impacts of quarrying on Otere Village, Odeda, Southwestern Nigeria. Ozean Journal of Applied Sciences, 4(1), 75–84.

Onefeli, A., & Adesoye, P. (2014). Early growth assessment of selected exotic and indigenous tree species in Nigeria. *South-east European Forestry: SEEFOR, 5*(1), 45–51.

Orimogunje, O. O. A. (2014). Forest cover change and land use dynamics in Oluwa Forest, Southwestern Nigeria. *Journal of Landscape Ecology, 7*(2), 25–44.

Peshkin, A. (1993). The goodness of qualitative research. *Educational Researcher, 22*(2), 23–29.

Riebeek, H. (2011). The Carbon Cycle. Earth Observatory. *NASA*. https://www. earthobservatory.nasa.gov/features/CarbonCycle

Strahler, A. H. (2002). *Geography: Science and systems of the human environment*. Wiley.

Sumner, J. (2003). Environmental adult education and community sustainability. *New Directions for Adult and Continuing Education, Fall* (99), 39–45.

Taylor, L. (2005). *The healing power of rainforest herbs: A guide to understanding and using herbal medicinal*. Raintree Group of Companies.

Trager, L. (2001). *Yoruba hometowns: Community, identity and development in Nigeria*. Lynne Rienner.

United Nations Educational, Scientific and Cultural Organization. (2014). *Ecological sciences for sustainable development*. http://www.unesco.org/new/en/ natural-sciences/environment/ecological-sciences/capacity-building-and-partnerships/educational-materials/>

United Nations Environmental Program. (2008). *The Belgrade charter adopted at the international workshop on environmental education in 1975*. http://portal.unesco. org/ education/en/ev.php-URL_ID=33037&URL_DO=DO_TOPIC&URL_ SECTION=201.html

United Nations Food and Agriculture Organization. (2010). *Global forest resources assessment 2010, Country Report*. Food and Agricultural Organization Paper 163.

Vanguard News (2019, October 26). High population eats up Nigeria's forest. *Vanguard News*. https://www.vanguardngr.com/2019/10/high-population-eats-up-nigerias-forests-2/

Walker, M. D. (2015). *Teaching inquiry-based science*. Sicklebrook.

Wals, A. E. J., Brody, M., Dillion, J., & Stevenson, R. B. (2014). Convergence between science and environmental education. *Science, 344*(6184), 583–584.

World Bank. (2016). *Working for a world free of poverty: How eight cities succeeded in rejuvenating their urban land*. World Bank.

World Commission on Environment and Development. (1987). *Our common future, report of the world commission on environment and development,* United Nations. [General Assembly document A/42/427. 3] United Nations.

World Wildlife Fund. (2019). Global forest wildlife populations in significant decline, new WWF report shows. *WWF Newsletter.* WWF.

CONCLUSION

ADULT EDUCATION FOR HUMAN RIGHTS AND SUSTAINABLE DEVELOPMENT

The Path Forward

Petra A. Robinson, Mary V. Alfred, and Elizabeth Roumell

In this book, *Advancing the Global Agenda for Human Rights, Vulnerable Populations, and Environmental Sustainability: Adult Education as Strategic Partner,* we contemplate the current condition of our global society, characterized by rapid technological innovation and advancements, neoliberalism, globalization, and the proliferation of mass media. In addition, we examine commodification, individualism, and other markers that highlight how power and privilege are operationalized across contexts that intersect with education, work, and the environment. Throughout the book, we focus on the role adult education plays in preparing global citizens to address social issues.

This book was inspired by the United Nations' work to advance human conditions globally through its historic agenda for a more peaceful, prosperous, and just world. In this regard, we ponder adult education's role in advancing the global agenda for human rights, vulnerable populations, and environmental sustainability. The compilation of chapters is an

Advancing the Global Agenda for Human Rights, Vulnerable Populations, and Environmental Sustainability: Adult Education as Strategic Partner, pp. 339–342
Copyright © 2021 by Information Age Publishing

indication of substantial intellectual and scholarly inquiry. The book makes a significant contribution to furthering our practical understanding of the myriad ways in which adult education can function as a strategic partner to disrupt and dismantle systemic inequities. Specifically, we focus on those social issues which infringe upon people's human rights, prohibit economic justice and social mobility, as well as harm environmental sustainability.

Advancing the Global Agenda for Human Rights, Vulnerable Populations, and Environmental Sustainability: Adult Education as Strategic Partner showcases how multiple threads that critique social injustice are intricately interwoven. In our critique, we create a symbolic representation of cultures, populations, and subgroups which are often marginalized and faced with circumstances that challenge their dignity, well-being, livelihoods, and even threaten their survival. Like supportive bands in a tapestry, critical frameworks, models, and practices regarding learning and leadership are described in the context of strategies for promoting social justice, equity, and human rights among those who are disenfranchised and find themselves victim of bullying, abuse, and other forms of prejudice and alienation. These strategies foreground a clear agenda to help move our society's often stagnant human rights and social justice needle towards the arc of justice and peace.

The need to engage and support our most vulnerable populations, as evidenced all over the world, has never been greater. This is especially true in light of the COVID-19 global pandemic. The chapters in this book echo a holistic vision for diversity, inclusion, and equity that corresponds to the United Nations' agenda of promoting world peace and economic justice, and addressing the needs of the world's most vulnerable populations, in addition to protecting the environment. This vision is at the crux of our hope for the future, directly aligned with the UNESCO (United Nations Educational, Scientific and Cultural Organization) Futures Literacy approach (Miller, 2011, 2017). This approach, according to Smyre and Richardson (2016), positions us to consider hope for adult learners and communities. A global futures literacy approach helps us to anticipate and shift our thoughts and activities to drive the agenda laid out by the United Nations. On the other hand, in order to design a future with anticipatory assumptions for justice, peace, and sustainability, it is important to think broadly and critically about our world.

By focusing on global perspectives and contexts, considering adult education broadly, and providing a wealth of information including different frameworks and models about learning and leadership, this book has laid the groundwork for us to think critically about important global issues. Nonetheless, it has left some issues unresolved. In doing so, it urges us to engage in critical reflection at an individual (micro) level as well as at an institutional or community (macro) level and to further contemplate important questions that can inform our work as educators in shaping a hopeful future for a more just world. As Mezirow (1998) explained, critical reflection and critical reflection of assumptions (CRA) is central to the work we do in the field of adult education. Becoming cognizant of how we, as adults, learn and think for ourselves, as opposed to acting on concepts, values, and thoughts of others, is central to critical reflection on our assumptions.

To guide our reflection, some of the unanswered questions we are encouraged to consider include:

1. What are the societal barriers to opportunity, social mobility, and justice for all?
2. How can we, as scholars, practitioners, policy makers and other key stakeholders, help to dismantle systems that disenfranchise vulnerable and underserved populations?
3. In what ways are we promoting or supporting the voices of victims of inequity?
4. How are we working towards preparing adult learners to develop skills and nontraditional literacies that are required in our complex, dynamic society?
5. What kinds of professional development opportunities are we providing to support our learners' livelihoods and success?
6. How are our scholarly and pedagogical practices informing, framing, and maintaining an agenda that resists hegemonic, xenophobic, racist, classist, and gendered systems that exist in our learning contexts?
7. What specific steps are we making to ensure the continued viability of our planet?
8. What messages are we communicating to others about our value for the life and well-being of others who are different from us?
9. In what ways can we, as adult educators, continue to forge ahead as partners and strategic allies in building partnerships to tackle challenges such as health disparities, bullying, and gender-bias?

By posing these questions, the authors encourage us to be critically reflective and to consider our actions, especially in terms of their social importance, not just for our individual sakes, but on a more global and transformative level as global citizens. To achieve this, we are asked to consider the contexts within which we live, and especially how we learn, work, and navigate our world and daily lives in diverse, globalized settings. Global citizenship, according to Sorrells (2016), requires a certain set of capacities that "reimagine citizenship based on human needs" (p. 232). To become a global citizen, we should consider which abilities are key to global citizenship. McIntosh (2005) proposes the following:

1. The ability to observe one's self and the world around one
2. The ability to make comparisons and contrasts between these worlds
3. The ability to see "plurally" as a result
4. The ability to understand that both "reality" and language come in many versions
5. The ability to see power relations and understand them systemically
6. The ability to balance awareness of one's own realities with the realities of others.

These abilities should serve as lampposts that help us frame our hope for the future as well as our critical reflection.

We recognize and acknowledge that there is a nexus between the decisions and actions we take, and the ones we do not, and so this book is a call to action. It sets the course for us to traverse a path that leads to a more hopeful, sustainable future in which we can celebrate our uniqueness, diversity, and humanity, living in harmony with each other and our environment, making our way on a critically-reflective path that leads towards social justice and peace in the world.

REFERENCES

McIntosh, P. (2005). Gender perspectives on educating for global citizenship. In N. Nodding (Ed.), *Educating citizens for global awareness* (pp. 22–39). Columbia Teachers College.

Mezirow, J. (1998). On critical reflection. *Adult Education Quarterly, 48*(3), 185–198.

Miller, R. (2011). Futures literacy: Embracing complexity and using the future. *Ethos, 10*(10), 23–28.

Miller, R. (Ed.) (2017). *Transforming the future: Anticipation in the 21st century.* Routledge.

Sorrells, K. (2016). *Intercultural Communication.* SAGE.

Symre, R., & Richardson, N. (2016). *Preparing for a world that doesn't exist, yet: Creating communities of the future.* Changemakers Books.

ABOUT THE AUTHORS

THE EDITORS

Mary V. Alfred, PhD, is Professor of Adult Education at Texas A&M University. Dr. Alfred's research interests include international adult education, learning and development among women of the African Diaspora, sociocultural contexts of adult learning, social welfare and economic disparities among low-income and low-literate adults, and issues of diversity, equity, and inclusion in education and the workplace. She joined the faculty of Texas A&M University in 2006, and from 2009 to 2017, she served as Associate Dean and later Executive Associate Dean in the College of Education and Human Development. She was inducted into the Adult and Continuing Education International Hall of Fame in 2017. Dr. Alfred served as President Elect, President, and Immediate Past President of the American Association for Adult and Continuing Education (2019–2021), an organization that is home to the diverse population of adult educators and learners in the United States and beyond. Dr. Alfred received her doctoral degree from the University of Texas at Austin.

Petra A. Robinson, PhD, is Associate Professor of Adult Education and Human Resource Development in the School of Leadership and Human Resource Development at Louisiana State University (LSU). Dr. Robinson is also Director, Faculty Affairs & Professional Development in the College of Human Sciences & Education. As Faculty Fellow with the Office of Academic Affairs and the Learning and Teaching Collaborative, she is interested in global lifelong learning and professional development in the academy, and her research focuses on issues related to colorism, critical literacies, equity, global citizenship, and social justice. Dr. Robinson received her doctoral degree from Texas A&M University and completed a postdoctoral appointment at Rutgers University prior to joining the faculty at LSU.

Elizabeth A. Roumell, PhD, is Associate Professor and program leader of the Adult Education specialization at Texas A&M University. She recently was awarded the Imogene Oakes award for outstanding research in the field of adult education and is a research fellow with the Barbara Bush Foundation for Family Literacy. Dr. Roumell's research interests include adult and workforce education policy analysis, distance learning and instructional technology, and comparative international education. Dr. Roumell is the Chair of the American Association for Adult and Continuing Education's Public Affairs Committee, past-Chair of the AERA Workplace Learning SIG, and she serves on the advisory board for the Texas Center for the Advancement of Literacy and Learning. Dr. Roumell earned her PhD in Postsecondary and Higher Education from the University of Wyoming in 2009.

THE AUTHORS

Kofo A. Aderogba, PhD, is an associate professor of Adult Education in the Department of Adult Education, College of Specialized and Professional Education and an adjunct faculty in the Department of Geography and Environmental Management, Tai Solarin University of Education, Ijebu-Ode, Nigeria. Her research focuses on Environmental Management, Community and Sustainable Development.

Geleana D. Alston, PhD, is a tenured associate professor in the Department of Leadership Studies and Adult Education in the College of Education at North Carolina A&T State University. Her scholarly engagement focuses on the sociocultural intricacies of women, minorities, and disenfranchised groups as adult learners.

Marcie Boucouvalas, PhD, is a Professor Emerita of Human Development (Adult Learning/Development/ Education). She has been immersed in the study and practice of International Adult Education since the early 1980s. She has traveled globally as researcher/author, Fulbright scholar, consultant, exchange professor, keynote speaker, delegate to international assemblies. She has also served in leadership roles such as VP/North America,

International Council for Adult Education; Director, International Adult Education Commission, AAACE; and inductee and Board Member of the International Adult & Continuing Education Hall of Fame.

Isaac Kofi Biney, PhD, is a senior lecturer and head of Accra Learning Center, University of Ghana. He is an adult education and lifelong learning researcher, writing extensively in adult education and learning, distance education, community development and entrepreneurship. He builds capacities of employees of statutory/private organizations in development-oriented programs.

Linda Caples, PhD, is the Director of Continuing Professional Development at the Medical College of Wisconsin. She has worked globally in continuing medical education since 2007, and her current research focus is clinical knowledge translation in sub-Saharan Africa.

Aynur Charkasova is a doctoral candidate in Workforce Education and Development at Southern Illinois University (Carbondale). Her research interests include immigration, STEM workforce, and the wage gap. Aside from her study, she teaches military and nontraditional students.

Jinhee Choi, PhD, is a postdoctoral researcher at Seoul National University and an Editorial Assistant for Asian Pacific Educational Review. Jinhee has published on issues related to (inter-)national lifelong learning policies, popular culture and public pedagogy, Universal Design for Learning (UDL), culturally responsive pedagogy, and social enterprises.

Saffet Fatma Dayıoğlu is an educator in Izmir, Turkey, who has a degree in Art and produces paintings, ceramics, and jewelry. She was the province coordinator for the Mother Child Education Foundation and an adult literacy educator. She continues her community involvement as a member/founding member of multiple nonprofit organizations.

Chris Dodgion, MD, is a trauma surgeon and associate professor at the Medical College of Wisconsin where he actively engages in global health. He earned his medical degree and MSPH at the University of Utah School of Medicine, completed residency at UW-Madison and his fellowship in Surgical Critical Care at OHSU.

Aydın Yücesan Durgunoğlu, PhD, is a retired Distinguished Global Professor at the University of Minnesota Duluth. Her research interests are cognitive and affective aspects of language and literacy development, bilingualism. Since 1994, she and her colleagues at the Mother Child Edu-

cation Foundation have developed award-winning literacy and empowerment programs for women.

Debora Adetunbi Egunyomi, PhD, is a professor of Adult Education
and former Head, Department of Adult Education, University of Ibadan,
Nigeria. Her research efforts focus on Community Development, Social
Welfare, Continuing and Nonformal Education. She was a member of the
Visitation Panel set up to reposition the College of Health Science and
Technology, Ijero-Ekiti.

J. Roy Gillis, is Associate Professor in the Department of Applied Psychology and Human Development at the University of Toronto. He is a recognized international expert in the areas of hate crime, violence, stigma,
prejudice, HIV prevention and sexual risk assessments, and classroom bullying involving LGBTIAI2S+ and other marginalized communities.

Stanford T. Goto, PhD, is an associate professor of adult and higher education at Western Washington University. He has worked with community
groups in British Columbia and Washington State to support fisheries
conservation and conflict resolution on local rivers. He is an avid salmon
fisherman.

Wendy Griswold, PhD, is an assistant professor in the Department of
Leadership at the University of Memphis. She teaches graduate courses in
the Higher and Adult Education Program. Her research interests include
community education/participatory action research, education for sustainability, and contemplative education.

Chad Hoggan, EdD, is an associate professor of Adult, Workforce and
Continuing Professional Education at North Carolina State University and
coeditor of the *Journal of Transformative Education*. His research interests re-
volve around transformative learning during times of transition, especially
with migrants, veterans, and historically underserved students.

Yvonne Hunter-Johnson, PhD, is an associate professor at Southern
Illinois University (Carbondale). Her research interest includes career
transition of veterans and international as adult learners.

Bora Jin, PhD, is an instructor in the Department of Educational
Administration & Human Resource Development at Texas A&M University.
Her research interests include older adult learning and development,
particularly in areas of physical activity, and health in later life, and mobile
learning.

Tetyana Kloubert, EdD, is an associate professor (Akademische Rätin) and the Chair of Adult and Continuing Education at University of Augsburg, Germany. Her research interests are migration and civic education (and indoctrination) in Eastern Europe, Western Europe, and the United States.

Wanda Krause, PhD, is the program head of Global Leadership Program, School of Leadership Studies, at Royal Roads University, Canada. She has worked globally in political studies and leadership, and her research focus is civil society development, women's participation, Middle East politics, integral theory, and global leadership.

Roula Kteily-Hawa, is Assistant Professor in Family Studies and Human Development at Brescia University College at Western in Ontario, Canada. She is a seasoned teacher educator, with experience leading community-engaged research in areas of resilience, mental health, stigma, and HIV prevention involving vulnerable populations and racialized groups, including South Asian women.

Hilary Landorf, PhD, is founding Executive Director of Global Learning Initiatives and associate professor of International and Intercultural Education at Florida International University. Her recent book is *Making Global Learning Universal: Promoting Inclusion and Success for all Students.*

Shuo Li, MD, is a master at Ningbo University. She studies lifelong education and adult education.

Ashley Stepanek Lockhart is a research consultant in areas of international education and development mainly for UNESCO and the University of Cambridge. Her content focus includes equity and inclusion in learning opportunities for people outside of school and throughout life, and she supports the monitoring of GRALE reports.

Yenisleidy Simon Mengana is the program manager of Global Learning Initiatives at Florida International University (FIU). Her work focuses on championing initiatives that promote global citizenship and challenge educational inequity.

Mitsunori Misawa, PhD, is an associate professor and Associate Department Head of the Department of Educational Psychology and Counseling at the University of Tennessee. He researches and writes about adult bullying, social justice, positionality, continuing professional education, Queer

Critical Race Theory, policy research, qualitative research methodologies, and professionalism in academia.

Birgitta Rausch-Montoto is Director of FIU Global at Florida International University. Her primary focus is on aligning the university's global strategy with institutional priorities and supporting the faculty's international work. She serves as Fulbright Campus Liaison and Chair of FIU's Travel Committee that is tasked with mitigating risks associated with global engagement.

Ricardo Sabates, PhD, is professor of Education and International Development at the Faculty of Education, University of Cambridge. He is a member of the Cambridge Network for Disability and Education Research (CaNDER). His research interests include equity in education over the lifecourse and has supported the monitoring of UNESCO GRALE reports.

Nidhi Singal, PhD, is professor of Disability and Inclusive Education, University of Cambridge. Her research addresses issues of educational inequity and social justice. She has worked extensively with persons with disabilities in South Asia and sub-Saharan Africa. She convenes the Cambridge Network for Disability and Education Research (CaNDER).

Sharlene Smith, PhD, is a behavior specialist at Rutgers University Center for Adult Autism Services for the Supporting Community Access, Leisure and Employment program. Her research focuses on adult education of general and special needs population.

Yuxin Song is a graduate student at Ningbo University. She studies lifelong education and English education.

Maja Stojanovic is a doctoral student and graduate assistant at Louisiana State University. Her research focuses on critical, multilingual literacy, diversity, equity, and globalization in adult education and human resource development.

Lixin Sun, PhD, is a professor at Ningbo University. Lixin has published on issues related to lifelong education policies, old-aged education, community education, the academic history of adult education, and comparative education.

Lauren Vilen is a doctoral student in the School of Education at Colorado State University. Her research interests include adult teaching and learning, environmental adult education, community-based education, and the professional identity and development of nonformal educators working on issues related to the environment and sustainability.

Thilanka Wijesinghe is a PhD candidate at the Faculty of Education, University of Cambridge and associated with University of Kelaniya, Sri Lanka. She is a member of the Cambridge Network for Disability and Education Research (CaNDER). Her research interests include disability related educational and employment inequity in the global South.

Kyung-Hwa K. Yang, PhD, is an adult educator and independent researcher based in the United States. Her research focuses on adult learning and visual methodology. She is the author of a book on participatory video and adult education and recently edited a journal volume on participatory visual approaches to adult education.

Jill Zarestky, PhD, is an assistant professor in the Adult Education and Training program in the School of Education at Colorado State University. Her research interests include STEM education and informal, nonformal, and community-based education, particularly in international nongovernmental and nonprofit organizations, as well as issues of sustainability and globalization.

CPSIA information can be obtained
at www.ICGtesting.com
Printed in the USA
LVHW081123130522
718141LV00001B/2

9 781648 026959